Nature, Grace, and Secular Culture

Nature, Grace, and Secular Culture

A Comparative Study of John Milbank and Joseph Ratzinger

CHRISTIAN C. IRDI

Foreword by John P. Cush

☙PICKWICK *Publications* · Eugene, Oregon

NATURE, GRACE, AND SECULAR CULTURE
A Comparative Study of John Milbank and Joseph Ratzinger

Copyright © 2024 Christian C. Irdi. All rights reserved. Except for brief quotations in critical publications or reviews, no part of this book may be reproduced in any manner without prior written permission from the publisher. Write: Permissions, Wipf and Stock Publishers, 199 W. 8th Ave., Suite 3, Eugene, OR 97401.

Pickwick Publications
An Imprint of Wipf and Stock Publishers
199 W. 8th Ave., Suite 3
Eugene, OR 97401

www.wipfandstock.com

PAPERBACK ISBN: 978-1-6667-6046-0
HARDCOVER ISBN: 978-1-6667-6047-7
EBOOK ISBN: 978-1-6667-6048-4

Cataloguing-in-Publication data:

Names: Irdi, Christian C., author. | Cush, John P., foreword.

Title: Nature, grace, and secular culture : a comparative study of John Milbank and Joseph Ratzinger / Christian C. Irdi ; foreword by John P. Cush.

Description: Eugene, OR : Pickwick Publications, 2024 | Includes bibliographical references and index.

Identifiers: ISBN 978-1-6667-6046-0 (paperback) | ISBN 978-1-6667-6047-7 (hardcover) | ISBN 978-1-6667-6048-4 (ebook)

Subjects: LCSH: Milbank, John. | Benedict XVI, Pope, 1927–2022.

Classification: BR115.S57 I73 2024 (paperback) | BR115.S57 I73 (ebook)

08/16/24

Scripture quotations are from the Revised Standard Version of the Bible, copyright © 1946, 1952, and 1971 National Council of the Churches of Christ in the United States of America. Used by permission. All rights reserved worldwide.

To Mary, Mother of the Church

Contents

Acknowledgments		ix
Foreword by John P. Cush		xi
Introduction		xvii
1	The Life and Works of Joseph Ratzinger and of John Milbank	1
2	The Nature and Grace Debate: A Historical and Theological Overview	48
3	Nature and Grace in the Thought of John Milbank	102
4	Nature and Grace in the Thought of Joseph Ratzinger	156
5	Milbank and Ratzinger Compared: Nature and Grace, Church and World	224
Conclusion		312
Bibliography		321
Author Index		337

Acknowledgments

I would like to express my sincere gratitude to Fr. Joseph Carola, SJ, STD, my dissertation director, for his constructive and thoughtful guidance during the planning and development of this research. His willingness to give of his time so generously is very much appreciated. I would also like to offer my special thanks to Prof. Tracey Rowland, PhD, STD, for her invaluable and insightful feedback on my research as it developed. Thanks also must go to Fr. Jonathan Vala, STL, for his assistance with the German translations, as well as to Fr. Joseph Laracy, STD, and Fr. John Cush, STD, for their advice and guidance along the way. I also wish to acknowledge the encouragement and fraternal support of Fr. Peter Harman, STD, of the Pontifical North American College, and of Fr. James Conn, SJ, JCD, superior of Casa Santa Maria. I also wish to express my gratitude to my family, especially my parents, Agostino and Anelia, for their unfailing support over the course of the years of my studies. I must also acknowledge, in a particular way, His Grace, Timothy Costelloe, SDB, DTheol, Archbishop of Perth, for appointing me to undertake doctoral studies in theology and for his continuing support of my priestly service in the archdiocese.

Most of all, *Deo gratias*!

Foreword

IT GIVES ME GREAT joy to write the foreword for Fr. Christian Irdi's text, *Nature, Grace, and Secular Culture: A Comparative Study of John Milbank and Joseph Ratzinger*. I have been blessed to know Fr. Irdi since he was a graduate student at the licentiate level, and I was a graduate student at the doctoral level, at the Pontifical Gregorian University in Rome, Italy. He and I both specialized in the field of fundamental theology at the Gregorian and I am pleased to state that his text is truly an important addition to the field of Roman Catholic fundamental theology.

One might be asking why I am emphasizing that this text is a work of fundamental theology in the Roman Catholic tradition. Perhaps it might be self-justification, but I emphasize the classification of Fr. Irdi's text as fundamental theology because fundamental theology is indeed its own discipline in theology.

Fundamental theology is not natural theology nor is it a form of philosophical theology. Natural theology is a topic in the study of philosophy and is an essential preparation for the study of theology, because it examines the nature of God, his existence, and his attributes.

Fundamental theology is not simply the first question of the *Summa Theologiae* (I, q. 1, a. 1), which states, "It is therefore necessary that besides philosophical science there should be a sacred science learned through revelation." In stating this, Aquinas is saying that this sacred science—what the Church also refers to as *sacra doctrina* or "sacred doctrine"—is distinct from the philosophical disciplines, as important as they are (and it is necessary for us to recall that, for St. Thomas, the term "philosophy" as used here encompasses all of human learning).

FOREWORD

Fundamental theology is not dogmatic theology. Nor is it just an "introduction to theology," as, sadly, it has been reduced to in many seminaries, universities, and schools of theology around the world. Dogmatic theology is the field that is, in many ways, the *what* of theology. It deals with the doctrine of the faith. It studies God, both as One and as the Most Blessed Trinity. It discusses Christology (who Jesus is) as well as soteriology (how Jesus is Savior). It studies pneumatology (which is the study of the Holy Spirit). It studies the Church and who we are as members of the Church (for which Vatican II's Dogmatic Constitution on the Church, *Lumen Gentium*, is a great aid to our understanding), as well as the manner in which the Church relates to and engages with the world (for which Vatican II's Pastoral Constitution on the Church in the Modern World, *Gaudium et Spes*, offers a great explanation). Dogma covers Mariology (the study of the Blessed Mother) and grace (God's life within us). In addition, theological anthropology (the study of who man is in light of Christ) is part of dogmatic theology, as well as protology (the study of creation) and eschatology (the study of the four last things: death, judgment, heaven, and hell). Finally, dogmatic theology studies the sacraments of the Church. In the *Catechism of the Catholic Church*, part 1, section 2, chapters 1 to 3, and part 2, sections 1 and 2, describe much of the content of dogmatic theology.

No, fundamental theology is, simply put, "its own thing," to use a colloquialism. So, with this in mind, what then is fundamental theology? This is a branch that studies the transmission of Divine Revelation through Sacred Scripture and Sacred Tradition, as well as how the Magisterium of the Church interprets them. It also speaks about the credibility of Divine Revelation, which is the field of apologetics. Fundamental theology is the area where theology is in dialogue with culture, science, and philosophy. As one can imagine, it is an essential field for the promotion of the New Evangelization. Faith, belief and unbelief, atheism, agnosticism, and secular humanism are all considered in the area of fundamental theology. One might say that fundamental theology is the *why* of theology. An important Vatican II document that can help us understand fundamental theology is *Dei Verbum* (the Dogmatic Constitution on Divine Revelation). In the *Catechism of the Catholic Church*, part 1, section 1, chapters 1 to 3, covers many of the areas studied in fundamental theology.

Fundamental theology involves bringing theological topics and issues of belief to the greater culture in order to dialogue with the cultural reality in which humankind finds itself. Fr. Irdi takes two of the most important thinkers of our contemporary age and puts them into dialogue with each other. Neither of these thinkers is used as a "straw man" for the other—that is, to present his thought simply to knock him down to demonstrate the superiority of the other.

Fr. Irdi treats the late Joseph Ratzinger/Pope Benedict XVI (d. 2022) with the utmost respect, as one would certainly expect from a Roman Catholic priest and theologian. He offers a thoughtful synthesis and explicates well Ratzinger's concepts of nature and grace, Church and world. Benedict published a social encyclical in 2009 titled *Caritas in Veritate*, in which he declares that love and truth must be intrinsically linked in the Christian life for the good of the world. He writes: "at the heart of the Church's social doctrine, it [love] must be linked to truth if it is to remain a force for good. Without truth, love can become an 'empty shell' to be filled with emotional influences which in the worst case can result in love turning into its opposite. Similarly, social action without truth can end up 'serving private interests and the logic of power.'"[1] Ratzinger is a perfect dialogue partner for Professor John Milbank.

Milbank (b. 1952) is a theologian whom I came to know and appreciate in my studies in Rome at the Angelicum under Pater Dr. Carsten Barwasser, OP. As a licentiate student, I found myself intrigued and fascinated by Milbank's project of Radical Orthodoxy and its proposals. Fr. Irdi offers insights into Milbank's complex theology and carefully, respectfully synthesizes and critiques it, while at the same time acknowledging its value and contribution. The prime phrase—the mantra, if you will—of Radical Orthodoxy can be found in the first chapter of Milbank's *Theology and Social Theory* (1991). Milbank writes: "Once, there was no 'secular.'"[2]

Everything for Milbank has a history. Everything has grown and developed within a particular culture and time period. The secular, "which in the Western European tradition is the world interpreted as separated from the stories and practices of the Christian faith—is not a given."[3] There is no reason objectively why secular reasoning is the norm. Milbank looks back to the notion of Christendom and speaks of its dual aspects, the *sacerdotium* and the *regnum*.[4] He contrasts the secular with the

---

1. Benedict XVI, *Caritas in Veritate*, §3.
2. Milbank, *Theology and Social Theory*, 9.
3. Shakespeare, *Radical Orthodoxy*, 7.
4. Milbank, *Theology and Social Theory*, 9.

saeculum and states: "The *saeculum*, in the medieval era, was not a space, a domain, but a time—the interval between fall and *eschaton* where coercive justice, private property and impaired natural reason must make shift to cope with the unredeemed effects of sinful humanity."[5]

In our contemporary moment, in Western Europe, Canada, and Australia (with the United States of America quickly following along), we see the results of the end of Christendom, both good and bad. Christians have the call to embrace the true end of Christendom and to engage in an apostolic mission to the world, but it must have a theological foundation; otherwise, it will descend in a plethora of "options," be it from Rod Dreher or from so many other commentators. Fr. Irdi's thoughtful text will offer the reader an insight into the "postmodern critical Augustinianism"[6] of Professor Milbank as well as the man whom Professor Tracey Rowland describes as "an Augustinian at Heart,"[7] Joseph Ratzinger/Pope Benedict XVI.

In a speech given in Subiaco at the convent of St. Scholastica in Subiaco, Italy, on April 1, 2005—that is, the day before Pope John Paul II died—Joseph Ratzinger said:

> Above all, that of which we are in need at this moment in history are men who, through an enlightened and lived faith, render God credible in this world. The negative testimony of Christians who speak about God and live against him, has darkened God's image and opened the door to disbelief. We need men who have their gaze directed to God, to understand true humanity. We need men whose intellects are enlightened by the light of God, and whose hearts God opens, so that their intellects can speak to the intellects of others, and so that their hearts are able to open up to the hearts of others.
>
> Only through men who have been touched by God, can God come near to men. We need men like Benedict of Norcia, who at a time of dissipation and decadence, plunged into the most profound solitude, succeeding, after all the purifications he had to suffer, to ascend again to the light, to return and to found Montecasino, the city on the mountain that, with so many ruins, gathered together the forces from which a new world was formed.

---

5. Milbank, *Theology and Social Theory*, 9.

6. Milbank credits Dr. Richard Roberts for the description. See Milbank, "Postmodern Critical Augustinianism," 278.

7. Rowland, "Pope Benedict's Theological Legacy."

Fr. Irdi's work in the field of fundamental theology can help us grasp the necessity of restoring the *saecula* while respecting the *saeculum*.

Rev. John P. Cush, STD
Professor of Dogmatic and Fundamental Theology
St. Joseph's Seminary, Yonkers, New York
Archdiocese of New York

Introduction

Go, therefore and make disciples of all nations, baptizing them in the name of the Father and of the Son and of the Holy Spirit, teaching them to observe all that I have commanded you; and lo, I am with you always, to the close of the age.[1]

CHRISTIANS ARE CALLED BY Christ to be witnesses to the world in which they live. Faithful to this missionary mandate, they are called to be the "salt of the earth" and the "light of the world" by means of their words and deeds, bringing all to the knowledge and love of God. This fundamental part of the Christian vocation, however, does not always prove to be an easy task. The Second Vatican Council in its pastoral constitution, *Gaudium et Spes*, acknowledged as much in noting just how difficult it can be to seek to harmonize the prevailing culture with Christian teaching.[2] Bearing these same difficulties in mind, Pope Paul VI, in his apostolic letter, *Evangelii Nuntiandi*, pointed out that, in our own epoch, "the split between the Gospel and culture is without a doubt the drama of our time, just as it was of other times."[3] This separation obviously presents numerous challenges to the church's missionary vocation, which nevertheless must continue to make "every effort . . . to ensure a full evangelization of

---

1. Matt 28:19–20.
2. Vatican II Council, *Gaudium et Spes*, §62.
3. Paul VI, *Evangelii Nuntiandi*, §20.

INTRODUCTION

culture, or more correctly, of cultures. They have to be regenerated by an encounter with the Gospel."[4]

Pope Francis, in his 2015 meeting with delegates from the Conference of European Rabbis, echoed Paul VI's concerns and spoke about the increasing secularity of contemporary society:

> Today ... it is more important than ever to emphasize the spiritual and religious dimension of human life. In a society increasingly marked by secularism and threatened by atheism, we run the risk of living as if God did not exist. People are often tempted to take the place of God, to consider themselves the criterion of all things, to control them, to use everything according to their own will. It is so important to remember, however, that our life is a gift from God, and that we must depend on him, confide in him, and turn towards him always.[5]

Francis also made similar remarks in his message for World Mission Day 2019, noting that "today's rampant secularism, when it becomes an aggressive cultural rejection of God's active fatherhood in our history, is an obstacle to authentic human fraternity."[6]

The Second Vatican Council recognized that man comes to a true and full humanity only through culture, that is to say, through the cultivation of the goods and values of human nature. Therefore, wherever human life is concerned, nature and culture are intimately connected. The council also noted that the word "culture" denotes everything whereby man develops and perfects his many bodily and spiritual qualities, and thus renders social life more human, both in the family and in the civic community.[7] It follows, therefore, that a culture that is deprived of the light of the gospel and that does not know the One who reveals "man to man himself"[8] cannot assist man in becoming truly and fully human: a concern that has vexed all the recent popes. It is, accordingly, the competence of fundamental theology to assist the church in its task of the evangelization of cultures, bearing in mind especially the classic "two hearings" characteristic of the discipline: the *auditus fidei* and the *auditus temporis*.[9] That is, of first importance is the question of correctly

---

4. Paul VI, *Evangelii Nuntiandi*, §20.
5. Francis, *Address to Conference of European Rabbis*.
6. Francis, *Message for World Mission Day 2019*.
7. Vatican II Council, *Gaudium et Spes*, §53.
8. Vatican II Council, *Gaudium et Spes*, §53.
9. McDonald, "Imagining a People," 16. This reflects the Second Vatican Council's

hearing and understanding God's Revelation, and of attending to the form of social life through which he mediates and expresses his gift. Secondly, just as divine Revelation is given in history, transmitted through the community of the church, and received through the inward gift of faith, so too do those who ask for an account of our hope (1 Pet 3:15) have a historical, cultural, and anthropological heritage that demands to be understood if we are to be successful in responding to them.[10] This, therefore, is the task of the *auditus temporis*, whereby the church strains to grasp the terms of her questioners.

It is clear that in our present time the church finds herself in the midst of a culture that has moved ever more profoundly away from the gospel. She finds herself, most notably in the West, before an aggressive form of secularism that concedes increasingly less and less room for the sacred, and that seeks to banish it from public life into the form of a "subculture," all in the name of human prosperity and flourishing, supposedly.[11] As Cardinal Walter Kasper puts it, the church in our own time is "dealing primarily with a crisis of relevance."[12] Kasper notes that among the key questions that the church should be asking herself are: "how does the central concept of the Christian faith relate to our modern and frightfully secular culture? How does it relate to our everyday experiences and issues that confront us on a daily basis? What is the meaning of the message of grace for the Church and our culture on our way into the third millennium?"[13] All of these concrete issues, when translated into the language of theology, touch immediately upon the notion of the relationship between nature and grace, and how in turn these two elements relate to and shape culture.[14] Henri de Lubac contends that the question of how nature and grace relate to each other "is at the very bottom of discussions with modern unbelief, and forms the crux of Christian humanism."[15] Indeed it can be said that the secularization of the European heart was

---

call to "scrutinize the signs of the times and to interpret them in the light of the Gospel"; cf. Vatican II Council, *Gaudium et Spes*, §4.

10. McDonald, "Imagining a People," 17.
11. Francis and Wolton, *Path to Change*, 319.
12. Kasper, "Nature, Grace, and Culture," 32.
13. Kasper, "Nature, Grace, and Culture," 32.
14. Kasper, "Nature, Grace, and Culture," 31. See also Francis, *Evangelii Gaudium*, §115. Here Francis, recalling *Gaudium et Spes*, §53, states that the human person is always situated in a culture, such that grace supposes culture, and "God's gift becomes flesh in the culture of those who receive it."
15. Lubac, *At the Service*, 35.

one of the main factors that motivated de Lubac's thinking on nature and grace and his vision for an unrelenting Christian humanism.[16]

In light of the importance of the discussion of nature and grace to the understanding and evangelization of Western secular culture, and given the scope of fundamental theology, this work will compare two relatively recent theologians who have both drawn from the insights of de Lubac and treated extensively the matter of secular culture—namely, Joseph Ratzinger and John Milbank.

The question guiding this investigation is: Can a theological comparison of John Milbank and Joseph Ratzinger on the question of nature and grace assist the church in understanding and evangelizing secular culture? In attempting to answer this question, this work will analyze the thought of Ratzinger and Milbank on the relationship between nature and grace, and then, in comparing each approach, it will attempt to draw out the possibilities and implications for the understanding and engagement of the church with secular culture. Given that both theologians have written extensively on a great many topics, I intend to use the nature-grace couplet as a lens to "limit" or focus the scope of the present work. It must be acknowledged too that the discussion concerning nature and grace, and that of secular culture and the church, is very broad indeed, encompassing theologians from a wide range of theological sympathies and approaches, each of whom ultimately adopts positions of varying degrees of similarity or difference. I am aware that in choosing Milbank and Ratzinger I choose two theologians who may be considered by some to be "on the same side" of the extremities of possible approaches to the question in that they both generally take the view that secularism presents a challenge to the church and her mission of the evangelization of culture. Nevertheless, as will become apparent, Milbank and Ratzinger differ greatly not only in terms of their respective methodologies, but, most importantly, in their ultimate conclusions. It is interesting to consider how these two theologians, who, while departing from more or less the same theological foundations (that is, both appropriate the thought of Augustine, as well as de Lubac), arrive at very different final positions.

Joseph Ratzinger, throughout his life, and most particularly during his pontificate as Benedict XVI, wrote and taught a great deal on the matter of the secularization of the West and the crisis of cultures. Ratzinger's mind was particularly exercised with the "soul of Europe" born from the

---

16. Swafford and Oakes, *Nature and Grace*, 25.

INTRODUCTION

weakening presence of Christianity in European culture and society, a reality that he thought would threaten the very identity of the same.[17] Given his lifetime of writings on the subject, Ratzinger firmly established himself as an incisive and subtle theologico-political thinker.[18]

John Milbank is a former reader in the Faculty of Divinity at Cambridge University. His seminal text, *Theology and Social Theory*, is generally considered to be the first text in the Radical Orthodoxy movement. This relatively recent movement has attracted much attention in the academic theological world.[19] At the heart of Radical Orthodoxy, and indeed of Milbank's writings, lies the notion that there should not be an autonomous secular sphere (or rather that there is no such thing as a theologically neutral social theory) and that there should be an alternative theology to simply correlationist theology.[20] The central thrust of Milbank's writings (and indeed of Radical Orthodoxy) is best summed up as follows:

> For several centuries now, secularism has been defining and constructing the world. It is a world in which the theological is either discredited or turned into a harmless leisure-time activity of private commitment. What emerges [from the writings of Radical Orthodoxy] is a contemporary theological project made possible by the self-conscious superficiality of today's secularism. For this new project regards the nihilistic drift of postmodernism (which, nonetheless, has roots in the outset of modernity) as a supreme opportunity. It does not—like liberal theology, transcendentalist theology and even certain styles of neo-orthodoxy—seek, in the face of this drift, to shore up universal accounts of immanent human value (humanism), nor defenses of supposedly objective reason. But nor does it indulge, like so many, in the pretense of a baptism of nihilism in the name of a misconstrued "negative theology." Instead, in the face of the secular demise of truth, it seeks to reconfigure theological truth.[21]

Following this introduction, chapter 1 sets out the life and works of both Joseph Ratzinger and John Milbank and gives a brief precis of the Radical Orthodoxy movement in order to better understand and situate Milbank's thought. I propose to highlight each author's major works

17. Ratzinger, *Reader*, 119.
18. Guerra, *Benedict XVI and Politics*, 1.
19. Cush, "Radical Orthodoxy: Overview."
20. Cush, "Radical Orthodoxy: Overview."
21. Milbank, Pickstock, and Ward, *Radical Orthodoxy*, 1.

and characteristics of their respective theological approaches including main influences.

In chapter 2, I examine the nature-grace debate as it has unfolded since the time of the Reformation. I have sought to limit the consideration of the nature-grace debate to the period from the Reformation onwards as this period saw the greatest and most rapid developments in the debate than any previous period. Accordingly, chapter 2 sets out the major historical stages in the development of the approach to the question of how nature and grace relate, taking into account the Reformation, the post-Reformation and Baroque periods, as well as the impact of the *Duplex Ordo* thesis, Leonine Thomism, and finally the *nouvelle théologie*. While I recognize that the *nouvelle théologie* can properly be said to encompass a wide range of authors (I will point to the most important of these in the first part of chapter 2), it is beyond the scope of this work to consider each of these in any great detail. Therefore, after tracing a broad outline and the distinguishing features of the *nouvelle théologie*, I will limit my considerations principally, and more closely, to the thought of de Lubac. It was de Lubac's insights on nature and grace, as we shall see, that were largely adopted by both Ratzinger and Milbank and that shape their respective approaches to the question of the relationship between nature and grace. The chapter will also present the theological particulars of the nature and grace debate in detail, such as the notion of the *debitum naturae*, and the natural desire for the supernatural, and it will offer a broad comparison and consideration of the intrinsicist versus the extrinsicist approaches to the question. I am aware that even limiting the debate in this way, an entire doctoral thesis could still be written on this topic. Given the scope and limits of the present work, my intention is, therefore, merely to provide a brief overview of the history and particulars of the nature and grace debate so as to provide an appropriately complete understanding, and historical context, for Milbank's and Ratzinger's own respective approaches to the question.

In chapter 3 I consider John Milbank's approach to nature and grace. The chapter begins by setting out Milbank's adoption of the ontological notion of participation as the foundation to his theological project, and his evaluation of the contribution of Duns Scotus and the univocity of being, and his consideration of Plato and Augustine. Once I have examined these foundations, I will turn to consider Milbank's methodology, and his appropriation (and admiration) of de Lubac and the *nouvelle théologie*. I then present Milbank's view of the notion of paradox, gift, and pure nature, as well as points of departure from de Lubac, including Milbank's criticisms of the same. The chapter then considers Milbank's approach to Aquinas's various contributions to the nature-grace question, and Milbank's assessment of Balthasar's thought relating to the same. Finally, the chapter presents Milbank's view of Rahner's integralism and approach to political theology.

Chapter 4 comprises a presentation of Ratzinger's approach to nature and grace. This chapter attempts to situate Ratzinger's thought within the context of the developments in twentieth-century theology, particularly as it stands with respect to neo-scholasticism and the *nouvelle théologie*. I then seek to extract Ratzinger's view of nature and grace by examining his adoption of theological personalism and Christocentrism, his idea of Christian humanism and the Incarnation, and also how he conceives of the church-world relation. In the final part of the chapter, I present a thorough examination of his work entitled "Gratia Praesupponit Naturam," which is his most explicit treatment of the topic of nature and grace in his corpus.

In chapter 5, the final chapter, drawing upon the research and insights of the preceding chapters, I present a comparison of Milbank and Ratzinger on their respective approaches to the relationship of nature to grace, highlighting the main points of contact and those of divergence. In particular, the chapter compares each author's approach to the foundational notions of participation and *analogia entis*, as well as their adherence to the *nouvelle théologie*, including de Lubac's paradox. In the second part of the chapter, I compare Milbank and Ratzinger on the church and secular culture. In my exposition of each author's position on this question, I demonstrate each one's approach to the link between nature and grace, the church and the world. Part of this consideration involves an examination of the notion of the secular, in particular by looking at Milbank's and Ratzinger's ideas of how this reality came to be. The comparison of each author's approach to secular culture will involve an examination of the question of Christian humanism, followed by an in-depth comparison of Milbank's political theology versus Ratzinger's theology of politics. In the final part of the chapter, I propose some conclusions by way of summations of the positive and negative aspects of each theologian's approach to nature and grace and to secular culture, considered in light of the church's duty, as elucidated by the Second Vatican Council, to bring Christ to all people by the evangelization of culture.

1

The Life and Works of Joseph Ratzinger and of John Milbank

JOSEPH RATZINGER

Biography

JOSEPH RATZINGER WAS BORN on April 16, 1927 (Holy Saturday), at Marktl am Inn (on the Inn River), a town forming part of the diocese of Passau. His father was a policeman from a family of farmers in Lower Bavaria, of modest economic means. His mother was the daughter of artisans from Rimsting and, before marrying, she worked as a cook in a number of hotels. His father was frequently transferred, given the nature of his work, and in 1929 Ratzinger's family moved to Tittmoning, a small locale on the Salzach River, near the Austrian border.[1]

In 1932, his father's outspoken criticism of the Nazis required that his family relocate again to Auschau am Inn, near the Alps. After his father's retirement in 1937, his family moved again to Hufschlag, outside of Traunstein, thirty kilometers from Salzburg. It was in this place, which he described as "Mozartian," that he received his Christian, cultural, and

---

1. For detailed biographical information on Ratzinger, see particularly Seewald, *Benedict XVI: Intimate Portrait*; Seewald, *Benedict XVI: Life*; and Ratzinger, *Milestones*.

human formation. He began studying classical languages at the local high school.

In 1939 he entered the seminary in Traunstein, his first formal step towards the priesthood. However, with the onset of World War II, his studies were forced into postponement, and he was enrolled in an auxiliary anti-aircraft corps until September 1944. At the end of the war, he reentered the seminary with his brother Georg. In 1947 he entered the Herzogliches Georgianum, a theological institute associated with the University of Munich. In 1951, both Ratzinger and his brother were ordained to the priesthood by Cardinal Faulhaber, in the cathedral at Freising, on the feast of Saints Peter and Paul.

The following year, Ratzinger began teaching at the Hochschule at Freising and in 1953 obtained his doctorate in theology with a thesis entitled "The People and House of God in Augustine's Doctrine of the Church."[2] Four years later, under the direction of the well-known professor in fundamental theology Gottlieb Söhngen, he fulfilled the requirements for teaching at the university level by completing a book-length treatise on Bonaventure's theology of history and Revelation.[3] On April 15, 1959, Ratzinger began lecturing as full professor of fundamental theology at the University of Bonn, which he continued until 1963. From 1962 to 1965 he was present during all four sessions of the Second Vatican Council as a *peritus* to Cardinal Joseph Frings of Köln.[4]

In 1963, Ratzinger began teaching at the University of Münster, while at the same time taking a second chair in dogmatic theology at the University of Tübingen. In 1968, with the wave of student uprisings in Europe, Marxism became the dominant intellectual system at Tübingen. Ratzinger was not in favor of the new theology proposed by Marxism and so in 1969 moved back to Bavaria to take up a teaching position at the University of Regensburg. He eventually there became dean and vice president. He also served as a member of the International Theological Commission of the Holy See from 1969 until 1980.

In 1972, together with Hans Urs von Balthasar, Henri de Lubac, and other important theologians, he initiated the theological journal *Communio*, a quarterly review of Catholic theology and culture.[5] Some claim

---

2. Ratzinger, *Volk und Haus Gottes*.
3. Ratzinger, *Offenbarungsverständnis*.
4. For an insight into Ratzinger's view of what a Catholic academy should be, see Ratzinger, "Interpretation, Contemplation, Action."
5. Ratzinger, "*Communio*: A Program," 436–49.

that this was done in response to the misinterpretation of the Second Vatican Council by Karl Rahner, Hans Küng and others, as epitomized by the theological journal *Concilium*.

On March 25, 1977, Pope Paul VI named Joseph Ratzinger as archbishop of Munich and Freising. He was ordained as bishop on May 28, 1977, and was the first diocesan priest in eighty years to have taken on the role as archbishop of Munich and Freising. He chose as his episcopal motto a phrase from 3 John 1:8, "Co-operators in the Truth," because he saw the connection between his previous task as professor and his new mission as archbishop. He always held that what was involved in both roles was following the truth and remaining in its service. He also held that the motto had particular significance in the world today.[6]

On June 27 that same year, he was elevated to cardinal (cardinal priest) by Pope Paul VI, with the titular church of Santa Maria Consolatrice al Tiburtino. In 1978 he took part in the conclave that elected Pope John Paul I, who named him his special envoy to the third International Mariological Congress, celebrated in Ecuador. In October that year, he took part in the conclave that elected Pope John Paul II.

In 1980, Pope John Paul II appointed him relator of the fifth Ordinary General Assembly of the Synod of Bishops, on the theme "Mission of the Christian Family in the World of Today," and was the delegate president of the sixth Ordinary General Assembly of 1983, on "Reconciliation and Penance in the Mission of the Church."

Pope John Paul II named him prefect of the Congregation for Catholic Education but Ratzinger declined as he felt that it was imprudent to leave the archdiocese too soon. In November 1981, he did become the prefect for the Congregation for the Doctrine of the Faith, and at the same time the *ex officio* president of the Pontifical Biblical Commission, and of the International Theological Commission. Cardinal Ratzinger was also president of the commission for the preparation of the *Catechism of the Catholic Church*.

In 1993, he was transferred to the order of cardinal bishops, with the suburbicarian see of Velletri-Signi. In November 1998, he was elected as vice-dean of the College of Cardinals, and subsequently as dean of the same college in November 2002, with the suburbicarian see of Ostia added to that of Velletri-Signi.

---

6. See Ratzinger and Seybold, "Interview," 11.

Besides his prefecture at the Congregation for the Doctrine of the Faith, his involvement in the Roman Curia was extensive. Cardinal Ratzinger was a member of the Council of the Secretariat of State for Relations with States, of the Congregations for the Oriental Churches, for Divine Worship and the Discipline of the Sacraments, for Bishops, for the Evangelization of Peoples, for Catholic Education, for Clergy, and for the Causes of the Saints, of the Pontifical Councils for Promoting Christian Unity, and for Culture; of the Supreme Tribunal of the Apostolic Signatura, and of the Pontifical Commissions for Latin America, "Ecclesia Dei," for the Authentic Interpretation of the Code of Canon Law, and for the Revision of the Code of Canon Law of the Oriental Churches.

Cardinal Ratzinger was also well known for his many publications, which spanned many years and constitute a point of reference for many people. He wrote a great deal on many different theological subjects, and particular mention should be made of his *Introduction to Christianity*, a compilation of university lectures on the Creed, published in 1968; *Dogma and Preaching*, an anthology of essays dedicated to pastoral arguments; and *Jesus of Nazareth*, a three-volume meditation on the life and teachings of Jesus Christ, the first volume of which was published in 2007.

He received numerous "Honoris Causa" doctorates: in 1984 from the College of St. Thomas in St. Paul, Minnesota; in 1986 from the Catholic University of Lima; in 1987 from the Catholic University of Eichstätt; in 1988 from the Catholic University of Lublin; in 1998 from the University of Navarre; in 1999 from the Libera Università Maria Santissima Assunta of Rome; in 2000 from the University of Wrocław in Poland; and in 2005 from the Universatea Babes-Bolyai in Cluj-Napoca.

After the death of Pope John Paul II, as dean of the College of Cardinals, Cardinal Ratzinger presided over the deliberations of the General Congregation during the vacancy of the Holy See and also at the funeral Mass of Pope John Paul II. He also presided at the Mass for the election of the Supreme Pontiff, concelebrated by the College of Cardinals on April 18, 2005. That same day, the conclave was solemnly inaugurated under the presidency of Cardinal Ratzinger.

On April 19, 2005, on the fourth ballot of the conclave, Cardinal Ratzinger was elected Bishop of Rome and the Supreme Pontiff of the Catholic Church. On Sunday, April 24, 2005, he celebrated the Mass for the inauguration of his pontificate, receiving the pallium and the Fisherman's ring.

At his first General Audience on April 27, 2005, Pope Benedict XVI later reflected on why he had chosen the name "Benedict":

> I chose to call myself Benedict XVI ideally as a link to the venerated Pontiff, Benedict XV, who guided the church through the turbulent times of the First World War. He was a true and courageous prophet of peace who struggled strenuously and bravely, first to avoid the drama of war and then to limit its terrible consequences. In his footsteps I place my ministry, in the service of reconciliation and harmony between peoples, profoundly convinced that the great good of peace is above all a gift of God, a fragile and precious gift to be invoked, safeguarded and constructed, day after day and with everyone's contribution. The name Benedict also evokes the extraordinary figure of the great "patriarch of western monasticism," St. Benedict of Norcia, co-patron of Europe with Cyril and Methodius. The progressive expansion of the Benedictine Order which he founded exercised an enormous influence on the spread of Christianity throughout the European continent. For this reason, St. Benedict is much venerated in Germany, and especially in Bavaria, my own land of origin; he constitutes a fundamental point of reference for the unity of Europe and a powerful call to the irrefutable Christian roots of European culture and civilization.[7]

In his time as pope, Benedict XVI published three encyclicals: *Deus Caritas Est*, *Spe Salvi*, and *Caritas in Veritate*. In *Deus Caritas Est*, the pope spoke of the unity of love in creation and salvation history, and that charity is the responsibility of the church because it is the manifestation of trinitarian love. In *Spe Salvi*, Benedict wrote on the theological virtue of hope, tracing specifically the relationship between Christian hope and redemption. In *Caritas in Veritate*, he spoke of the problems concerning global development and progress towards the common good, including detailed reflection on economic and social issues.

At the time of his resignation, Pope Benedict had also completed a draft of what would have been his fourth encyclical, *Lumen Fidei*, intended to accompany his first two encyclicals, thereby completing a trilogy of reflections on the theological virtues, faith, hope, and love. Pope Francis, his successor, completed and published *Lumen Fidei* four months after Pope Benedict's retirement. Although the encyclical is technically the

---

7. Benedict XVI, *General Audience, 27 April 2005*.

work of the reigning pontiff, Francis did however acknowledge Pope Benedict's substantial contribution.[8]

Pope Benedict released the post-synodal apostolic exhortation *Sacramentum Caritatis* in 2007, which concerns the Eucharist. The exhortation is divided into three parts regarding the Eucharist as a mystery firstly to be believed, secondly to be celebrated, and thirdly to be lived. He also released two other post-synodal exhortations, namely, *Verbum Domini*, dealing with the Word of God in the life and mission of the church, and *Africae Munus*, which deals with reconciliation, justice, and peace as fundamental to the mission of the church in Africa.

On the morning of February 11, 2013, Pope Benedict met in consistory with the College of Cardinals at the Vatican and announced his resignation from the papacy. In doing so, he noted that he had repeatedly examined his conscience before God and thereby come to the certainty that his strengths, due to his age, were no longer suited to the adequate exercise of the Petrine ministry. He declared that as of February 28, 2013, his resignation from the Petrine ministry would be effected, and that as of that date the see of Rome would be vacant. On his final day as pope, Benedict held an audience with the College of Cardinals, and later that same day he flew by helicopter to Castel Gandolfo, where he remained for the final hours of his papacy, and from where he addressed the faithful for the last time. Pope Benedict XVI was the first pope to have resigned the papacy of his own initiative since Pope Celestine V in 1294.[9] Benedict spent the years of his retirement residing at the Mater Ecclesiae Monastery in Vatican City, until his death on December 31, 2022.

Key Influences

Gottlieb Söhngen

It was Gottlieb Söhngen (1892–1971) who arguably exerted the greatest influence on the young Ratzinger and taught him to critically question neo-scholastic ideas and also insisted on developing theology from primary texts.[10] Söhngen was a professor of fundamental theology at

---

8 See Francis, *Lumen Fidei*, §7.

9. Pope Gregory XII was the last pope to resign before Benedict XVI and did so in 1415 in order to end the Western Schism.

10. Ratzinger, *Milestones*, 55. Ratzinger notes here that Söhngen "always developed his thought on the basis of the sources themselves, beginning with Aristotle and Plato,

the University of Munich; he supervised both of Ratzinger's theses, his doctoral dissertation on Augustine's ecclesiology and his *Habilitationsschrift* on St. Bonaventure's theology of history. It was under Söhngen that Ratzinger studied Newman's *Grammar of Assent*.[11] Söhngen also exposed Ratzinger to the Tübingen School of Theology and stressed the notion that the mystery of God was not reducible to any system. It was for this reason that, for Söhngen, Augustine and Bonaventure appeared congenial in overcoming the problematic rationalism that was prevalent at the time, and inspired the same in his most promising young protégé, Ratzinger.[12] For Söhngen, historic human nature was never an autonomous entity (as the notion of *pure-nature* would have it), but one that is, ever since its very beginning, open toward the supernatural. Söhngen demonstrated that for its ultimate deciphering, human nature requires the language of parables and signs. This is the modus operandi of the *analogia entis* (analogy of being). Natural knowledge of God, according to Söhngen, is different from faith's knowledge, but nevertheless cannot be divorced from it. The indivisibility of the two is grounded in the circumstance that natural knowledge of God is not abstract or metaphysical but indeed part of the divine economy. Ratzinger's approach is largely in continuity with that of Söhngen; however, with a slightly nuanced difference. Ratzinger would emphasize that an analogy-of-being approach may not be irresponsibly unrealistic. This thinking implies a difference between subject and object, which does not actually exist, as every human being is created in the image of God. Thus, for Ratzinger, there can be no measure outside the relationship of God and man.[13] Söhngen was at great pains to demonstrate that there does not exist an unbridgeable chasm between the *analogia entis* and the *analogia fidei* (against the Protestant view). For him, the *analogia entis* is the natural constituent of the parable between God and mankind grounded in creation. As Emery de Gaál puts it, "the creator God is identical to the savior God."[14] In contrast, the *analogia fidei* is the supernatural constituent of the parable between God and mankind grounded in the divine Incarnate Word. There can be no contradiction

---

then . . . Augustine, Anselm, Bonaventure, and Thomas." What impressed Ratzinger about him was that he was "never satisfied in theology with the sort of positivism that could usually be detected in other subjects."

11. Rowland, "Benedict's Intellectual Mentors."
12. Gaál, *Theology of Pope Benedict XVI*, 33.
13. Gaál, *Theology of Pope Benedict XVI*, 35.
14. Gaál, *Theology of Pope Benedict XVI*, 35.

between the two as both are part of the one act of faith. Neither faith, nor theology, could come to be if the two were not in collaboration. In this way, Söhngen overcame the regnant extrinsicist understanding of Revelation. In particular, his *Die Einheit der Theologie* greatly impressed the young Ratzinger and also significantly impacted modern theological thought's shift toward a salvation-historic perspective.[15]

Söhngen admired de Lubac's work and, when the young Ratzinger ran up against opposition by the eminent professor Michael Schmaus to his *Habilitationsschrift* on the grounds that it was anti-Suárezian, Söhngen defended him. Ratzinger recalls the experience of submitting his *Habilitationsschrift* at the University of Munich in 1955 as a particularly challenging time.[16] His *Habilitationsschrift*, entitled "Das Offenbarungsverständnis und die Geschichtstheologie Bonaventuras," was at first rejected by Schmaus (his second reader) on the grounds of containing a "dangerous modernism."[17] Ratzinger had supposedly merited such an accusation simply because he had dared, as mere beginner, to sharply criticize the positions of Schmaus, who was, after all, a famous professor. Effectively, Ratzinger had ascertained that in Bonaventure, there was nothing corresponding to the concept of Revelation as it had later come to be understood, particularly in Suárezian Thomism. He found that Revelation precedes Scripture and becomes deposited in Scripture but is not simply identical with it. This means that "Revelation is always something greater than what is merely written down."[18] For Schmaus, this proposition seemed to subjectivize Revelation and meant that Ratzinger was required to correct the problematic parts of his thesis (a process, Schmaus smugly remarked, that would probably take years).[19] In

---

15. Gaál, *Theology of Pope Benedict XVI*, 35.

16. Ratzinger, *Milestones*, 106; and Seewald, *Benedict XVI: Intimate Portrait*, 192. He describes the experience as though it were "a stab in the heart" and says that the "whole world was threatening to collapse around me."

17. Ratzinger, *Milestones*, 106. See also Ratzinger, *Offenbarungsverständnis*; and Ratzinger, *Theology of History*. This English translation, however, contains only the redacted form of Ratzinger's *Habilitationsschrift*, that is, the version that was finally accepted after Ratzinger had edited it, by simply submitting the last section of his work, which appeared to have very few objections from Schmaus. The full, unredacted, 1955 version is yet to be translated into English (although, at the time of writing, I am told by Dr. Christian Schaller of the Pope Benedict XVI Institute in Regensburg that it is a work in progress).

18. Ratzinger, *Milestones*, 108.

19. Seewald, *Benedict XVI: Intimate Portrait*, 192. See also Seewald, *Benedict XVI: Life*, 287. Söhngen managed to ensure that the work was not entirely rejected, but returned for corrections.

8

response, Ratzinger decided to make an independent work out of the final section of his research, which appeared to have only a few objections. Amazingly, only two weeks later, Ratzinger, having made the necessary changes, resubmitted the work, which was then accepted. This achievement is surely a testament to his academic brilliance. It is said that at the oral examination of the thesis, Ratzinger said very little and strategically allowed Söhngen to take on Schmaus in defense of Ratzinger's new ideas. Perhaps this is why, at Söhngen's funeral, Ratzinger described his former teacher as "a radical and critical thinker . . . but at the same time he was a radical believer."[20]

Romano Guardini

Romano Guardini was a figure of such importance that it can be said without exaggeration that he had influenced an entire generation of German theologians, thanks to his time as chaplain to the German youth movement. Guardini was also one of Ratzinger's professors at the University of Munich. Although Ratzinger only makes a brief mention of him in his autobiography, his prominence in 1970s Catholicism is undisputed.[21] A number of themes that permeate Guardini's writings reappear in Ratzinger's own works. These include the challenge of modernity, the affirmation of the truly real, love, freedom, the creative dimension of God, liturgical renewal as renewal of mankind more generally, and human life's becoming meaningful in the encounter with the mystery and person of Jesus Christ.[22] Guardini was not a Thomist and found neo-scholastic textbooks to be insufferable. He greatly impressed Ratzinger, during his Munich years, by the lectures he gave at Munich University (which were sometimes attended by more than a thousand students).[23] Ratzinger spoke of his flair for illustrating key theological concepts with literary examples and events drawn from the lives of the saints. In fact, Guardini's *The Essence of Christianity* (1938) can be read as a precursor to Ratzinger's *Introduction to Christianity* (1968), and Guardini's *Spirit*

---

20. Graulich, *Unterwegs*, 22. My translation. Original as follows: "Söhngen war ein radikal und kritisch Fragender . . . Aber zugleich war er ein radikal Glaubende."

21. Ratzinger, *Milestones*, 43.

22. Gaál, *Theology of Pope Benedict XVI*, 38.

23. Gaál, *Theology of Pope Benedict XVI*, 38.

of the Liturgy was the model for Ratzinger's own work of the same title.[24] Both Ratzinger and Guardini shared a preoccupation with the destiny of Europe and feared it was in the process of repudiating its Christian heritage.[25] It should therefore come as no surprise that Ratzinger wrote an introduction to the English reprint of Guardini's *The Lord*. For Guardini, the experience of conversion allows a transcendence of the modern mind that overcomes the subjectivist post-Kantian mindset. It is Christ who restores the relationship between thought and being. This conformity of thought to being brings about an alignment with truth and reveals the primacy of Logos over ethos (Ratzinger himself adopts this position).[26] The main connection between Ratzinger and Guardini is that Christianity is not an abstract idea but a concrete person. The essence of Christianity is beheld in the person of Christ. For Guardini (and Ratzinger likewise), the depersonalization of the individual expressed itself in the phenomenon of the anonymous, depersonalized masses. It is an age that grants existence to impersonal norms and abstract reality, with the attendant result that the modern world is complete in itself and self-isolated from its Creator. Guardini was able to demonstrate that while Jesus Christ transcends all human categories, he can nonetheless only be encountered in historic concretions whereby he is able to form and transform human existence. Likewise, Ratzinger states that truth, to which human beings are oriented by their very nature, is not found somewhere at random or by chance, but in the living-concrete, in the *Gestalt* (form) of Christ.[27] Following Guardini, Ratzinger himself could have stated that "we must confront all men, doctrines, epochs with Christ himself."[28]

Henri de Lubac

Henri de Lubac was another crucial figure in Ratzinger's theological formation. He studied de Lubac's works when he was a seminarian in the late 1940s, and notes that reading de Lubac had a major impact on him. He writes:

---

24. Seewald, *Benedict XVI: Life*, 226.
25. Gaál, *Theology of Pope Benedict XVI*, 38.
26. Gaál, *Theology of Pope Benedict XVI*, 40.
27. Gaál, *Theology of Pope Benedict XVI*, 41.
28. Guardini, *Lord*, 319.

Another circumstance came to my aid. In the fall of 1949, Alfred Läpple had given me *Catholicism*, perhaps Henri de Lubac's most significant work, in the masterful translation by Hans Urs von Balthasar. This book was for me a key reading event. It gave me not only a new and deeper connection with the thought of the Fathers but also a new way of looking at theology and faith as such. Faith had here become an interior contemplation and, precisely by thinking with the Fathers, a present reality.[29]

Ratzinger points out that de Lubac was leading his readers out of a narrowly individualistic and moralistic way of living the faith and into:

the freedom of an essentially social faith conceived and lived as a *we*—a faith that, precisely as such and according to its nature, was also hope, affecting history as a whole, and not only the promise of a private blissfulness to individuals.[30]

It is difficult to overstate the importance of de Lubac for Ratzinger's generation of theologians. According to Kerr (speaking of de Lubac's *Catholicism*), "many, including Congar, Balthasar, Wojtyla, and Ratzinger, regarded it as the key book of twentieth-century Catholic theology, the one indispensable text."[31]

After having read de Lubac's *Catholicism*, Ratzinger then read his *Corpus Mysticum*, in which he found a new understanding of the unity of church and Eucharist beyond the insights he had already gained from Pascher, Schmaus, and Söhngen. These new perspectives, he says, helped him to enter into the required dialogue with Augustine, which was something that he had attempted to do for a long time in various different ways.[32]

Ratzinger discovered in de Lubac a "selflessly heroic theologian" who was willing to be marginalized without becoming embittered or losing his love for the church. Through the lens of de Lubac, Ratzinger began to comprehend the profound unity of faith, the Eucharist, and the church in a "new sacramental-mystical perspective."[33] As Hemming

---

29. Ratzinger, *Milestones*, 98.
30. Ratzinger, *Milestones*, 98. See also Imbelli, "Christocentric Mystagogy," 122.
31. Kerr, *Twentieth-Century Catholic Theologians*, 71.
32. Kerr, *Twentieth-Century Catholic Theologians*, 71.
33. Gaál, *Theology of Pope Benedict XVI*, 37.

observes: "it was de Lubac's invigorating influence that fed Benedict's emerging theological mind."[34]

Ratzinger and de Lubac both found themselves serving as *periti* at the Second Vatican Council, and then in 1972, together with Balthasar, they founded the journal *Communio: International Catholic Review*. Ratzinger had formerly been involved in the foundation of the theological journal *Concilium* (in 1965) with figures such as Hans Küng, Karl Rahner, and Edward Schillebeeckx; however, this association did not last. Ratzinger later referred to the approach of such theologians towards the Second Vatican Council as promoting a "hermeneutic of rupture," whereas he favored instead a "hermeneutic of continuity."[35]

Hans Urs von Balthasar

Another great mind that Ratzinger found to be inspiring was Hans Urs von Balthasar. Balthasar, like Ratzinger himself, was disappointed at the dreary neo-scholasticism that was prevalent in the mid-twentieth century. He could not reconcile the staleness of the neo-scholastic approach with the new personalist approach to theology that de Lubac and other leading figures of the *nouvelle théologie* had shown him. Ratzinger and Balthasar are thus of a congenial mindset. They were both influenced in central ways by the *ressourcement* (one as a student of de Lubac, and the other as a reader of him) and both expressed their sympathy with the *anawim*. Both also were founding members of *Communio*.[36] Ratzinger subsequently observed that it was impossible for him to say how much he owed to de Lubac and Balthasar as intellectual mentors. In fact, Ratzinger hosted Balthasar's eightieth birthday party and delivered the homily at his funeral.[37]

---

34. Hemming, *Benedict XVI: Fellow Worker*, 47.

35. Rowland, *Benedict XVI: Guide*, 4.

36. Gaál, *Theology of Pope Benedict XVI*, 38. See also D. L. Schindler, *Hans Urs von Balthasar*.

37. Ratzinger, "Homily at Funeral for von Balthasar," 512–16. During the homily, Ratzinger made the following remarks: "What Balthasar wanted may well be encapsulated in a single phrase of St. Augustine: 'Our entire task in this life, dear brothers, consists in healing the eyes of the heart so they may be able to see God.' That is what mattered to him, healing the eyes of the heart so they would be able to see the essential, the reason and goal of the world and of our lives: God, the living God."

Predominant Features of His Thought

Ratzinger's contribution to Catholic theology is immense. In more than fifty years of writing, there is barely a theological theme that he has not treated. Ecclesiological themes are common, including liturgy, Eucharist, Petrine primacy, the nature of the church, episcopal collegiality, the Second Vatican Council, the church-world relationship, and ecumenism.[38] Eschatology is a major theme for him, as is the theology of history and the relationship between salvation history and metaphysics, as well as faith and love.

Ratzinger in various interviews described himself as a "decided Augustinian" and "to a certain extent a Platonist."[39] He was never particularly enchanted by preconciliar Thomism, acknowledging that while Scholasticism had its greatness, he had found it to be too dry and impersonal. In contrast, he found that in the works of Augustine "the passionate, suffering, questioning man is always right there, and one can identify with him."[40]

While at Tübingen University (1966–69) he was shocked by the student riots that took place in 1968 and the anti-authoritarian feelings of the time (initiated by a generation of students that was reading the works of Marcuse, Adorno, and other neo-Marxists). According to Lieven Boeve, this meant that his initial openness to the achievements of modernity and his willingness to enter into dialogue with the world seemed to evaporate at this point and his writings increasingly began to display polemical features. In particular, Ratzinger opposed the tendency, which seemed to be prevalent at the time, to understand human salvation in terms of what is merely internal and subjective.[41] In later chapters we will return to the topic of Ratzinger's openness or otherwise to the world in greater detail.

Given the immensity of Ratzinger's corpus, James Corkery proposes the metaphor of predominant "facial features" as a practical way of understanding the broad features of Ratzinger's theology. Ratzinger's works exhibit a great consistency over the five decades of his writing; this is the one characteristic that marks his work above all else.[42] As Michael Fahey writes:

38. Corkery, *Ratzinger's Theological Ideas*, 28.
39. Ratzinger and Seewald, *Salt of the Earth*, 33.
40. Ratzinger and Seewald, *Salt of the Earth*, 61.
41. Ratzinger, *Reader*, 3.
42. Ratzinger, *Reader*, 29.

His thought shows amazing consistency. The emergence of cautious writings in recent years is not based on some new dramatic conversion but is the logical conclusion of years of reflection. Prior to Vatican II he expressed impatience with the lack of vitality in Catholic theology and wrote critically about procedures in the Roman Curia. Shortly after the Council he grew more and more convinced that its real goals had been misunderstood or distorted by certain theologians.[43]

The "facial features" of Ratzinger's work flow from the consistency that marks his writings across the spectrum of thematic areas and, as proposed by Corkery, are set out in the subsections that follow.

The God of Philosophy and the God of Faith Are One

At his inaugural lecture as a professor of fundamental theology at the University of Bonn in 1959, Ratzinger chose as the subject the God of faith and the God of the philosophers—a contribution to the problem of natural theology.[44] In the course of the lecture he juxtaposed two positions: one from Thomas Aquinas, which presents the Christian understanding of God as elevating and completing but not destroying the philosophical idea of God; and the other from Reformed theologian Emil Brunner, in which the Christian God, as revealed in the Bible as a personal God with a name, runs counter to the philosophical tendency to see God in general, non-personal terms.[45] Ratzinger proposed that the dilemma that is raised in the juxtaposition of these two approaches could be solved by holding both together. That is, the One, the Absolute of Greek philosophy is also the one, personal, addressable, named God of biblical Revelation. Corkery sees here an Augustinian "facial feature" in that Augustine refused to eliminate the connecting line (the *Bindestrich*) between Neoplatonic ontology and Christian faith, because to do so would fail to give the radical monotheism of the Bible its most adequate expression. This is because Christianity would lose not only its ability to speak to us about who we are, but also more importantly its claim to be true. Robbed of its foundation in truth, Christianity would risk being relegated to the panoply of religions.[46]

43. Fahey, "Ratzinger as Ecclesiologist," 76.
44. Ratzinger, *Gott des Glaubens*.
45. Corkery, *Ratzinger's Theological Ideas*, 30.
46. Corkery, *Ratzinger's Theological Ideas*, 30.

Ratzinger does maintain that philosophy remains philosophy and that faith, while robustly standing with philosophy, must nevertheless set about purifying and transforming the very philosophy on which it draws. The notion of the "purification" of philosophy is, according to Corkery, another Augustinian feature of Ratzinger's thought and is expressed in his first papal encyclical as Benedict XVI: *Deus Caritas Est*.[47]

The juxtaposition of the God of faith and the God of philosophy is a central idea in Ratzinger's theology and relates to the notion of truth, that is, that Christianity is the true philosophy, as expressed by Justin Martyr. Christianity expresses the truth about who God is and who man is. The *Bindestrich* connecting the metaphysical God to the God of Judeo-Christian Revelation who speaks to us in love, as Love, exists to ensure the truth of Christianity, particularly in the face of relativistic secular philosophies.[48]

Logos before Ethos

The notion of the priority of *Logos* over *Ethos*, of receiving over making, of being over doing, is a central concept in Ratzinger's thought. This is the natural outcome of the juxtaposition of the God of faith and the God of philosophy (metaphysics). God is the "absolute and ultimate source of all being but this universal principle of creation—the *Logos*, primordial reason—is at the same time a lover with all the passion of true love."[49] Ratzinger, much like Balthasar, places great emphasis on the notion that we are not the products of blind chance but are instead willed specifically by God. This stands as the basis for our human worth and goodness, our originating from meaning and truth rather than from the blind confluence of the universe's forces. All this is to say that *Logos* precedes and shapes us, and we are therefore good. Corkery points out that this position is unmistakably Neoplatonic-Augustinian, that is, the idea "human being" precedes actual human beings, just as the universal precedes the particular. Given that essence precedes existence, it follows that we are first and foremost *receivers* and not *makers*; we are much more a gift received than a task achieved.[50] This reality gives meaning to the act of

---

47. Corkery, *Ratzinger's Theological Ideas*, 31.
48. Corkery, *Ratzinger's Theological Ideas*, 31.
49. Benedict XVI, *Deus Caritas Est*, §§5, 6, 27, 28.
50. Corkery, *Ratzinger's Theological Ideas*, 32.

faith, as faith is trusting in and relying on that which we cannot give ourselves; of being open so as to receive that which we need, namely, meaning, truth, and love.[51]

Ratzinger is not here seeking to delimit human freedom and the importance of the human will. He is however seeking to properly set out what human freedom truly means. Freedom is not blind choice, or rather choice among an infinite number of options, as if increasing the number of options increases our freedom. Instead, true human freedom means being guided by what we were created as from the start. Materialistic philosophies are wrong *ab initio* as they deny the primacy of *Logos*, putting in its place matter, hence adopting the erroneous notion that rationality can emerge from that which is originally non-rational (matter). This is the view of Pelagianism in that the rational has to be *made*, as that which is original (matter) is inherently non-rational. Ratzinger, however, would say that *making* cannot be prior, because if one observes those elements of human life that are of greatest importance, namely, love, salvation, affection, forgiveness, one finds that they are all predicated upon *receiving*. A love that is "made" is not love at all (it is manipulation).[52] Corkery points out that Augustine here again shines through Ratzinger's thought. Augustine himself was able to recognize that that which is truly important in life is ultimately received, not made. This notion also reveals a certain Neoplatonism that establishes the principle that what is invisible (spiritual) takes priority and precedence over that which is visible (material). Thus, we do not make who we are through what we do, but rather we receive who we are from prior creative love. This Neoplatonic-Augustinian notion is of fundamental importance to Ratzinger's thought and underlies much of his opposition to existentialism, idealism, materialism, and positivism.[53]

Ratzinger's theology presents a strong soteriological character. He is convinced of the importance of the notion of truth as essential to the salvation of man. Only the truth can set us free. In submitting to the truth, the preordained nature of things, the human person is already constituted in an original and fundamental relationship. Therefore, holiness consists in living from the truth that God revealed in Jesus Christ. Ratzinger proposes:

---

51. Ratzinger, *Introduction to Christianity*, 42.
52. Corkery, *Ratzinger's Theological Ideas*, 32.
53. Corkery, *Ratzinger's Theological Ideas*, 32.

> Christianity is not a philosophical speculation; it is not a construction of the intellect. Christianity is not "our" work, it is a Revelation, a message that has been given us, and we have no right to reconstruct it as we wish.[54]

In *Deus Caritas Est*, as Benedict XVI, he also argues that Christianity is not a moral system, but rather an encounter with the person of Jesus Christ.[55] Therefore, a Christian person is one who submits to the person of Christ in the loving encounter with him who is the sanctifying Truth, and in this way rejects the unjust prerogative of absolute self-determination and the pursuit of creating one's "own truth."[56] He sees a fundamental conflict between Christian faith and the foundations of modernity. In studying the issue, Ratzinger states that the problem of the relation between *being* and *time* was solved in favor of *being*, that is, after Hegel, *being* is *time*.[57] In *Principles of Catholic Theology* Ratzinger states that:

> the decisive turning point lies with Hegel, since which being and time have been more and more intertwined in philosophical thinking. Being itself is now regarded as time; the logos becomes itself in history. It cannot be assigned, therefore, to any particular point in history or be viewed as something existing in itself outside of history.... [In modernity] Truth becomes a function of time; the true is not that which simply *is* true, for truth is not simply that which *is*; it is true for a time because it is part of the becoming of truth, which *is* by becoming.[58]

In contrast to this Hegelian position, Ratzinger sets himself the task of demonstrating that the human person is given an original truth that, despite all cultural mediations, always remains true because he/she *is* true.[59] As prefect of the Congregation for the Doctrine of the Faith, Ratzinger spent a great deal of time clarifying the function of papal teaching authority and the limits of the competence of bishops and theologians. What underpins these efforts was Ratzinger's basic conviction that the salvific truth granted by God has not been given over to the free disposal of the human person. Revealed truth is that which we are called to live from,

---

54. Ratzinger, *Co-Workers of the Truth*, 265.
55. Benedict XVI, *Deus Caritas Est*, §1.
56. Ratzinger, *Reader*, 8.
57. Ratzinger, *Reader*, 8.
58. Ratzinger, *Principles of Catholic Theology*, 16.
59. Ratzinger, *Reader*, 9.

and, as such, the only appropriate response to this truth is an attitude of diffidence, because what is at stake is the salvation of the human person.[60]

During his papacy, Benedict spoke extensively against the "dictatorship of relativism," as he termed it. In his address to the participants in the Ecclesial Diocesan Convention of Rome in 2005, he referred to the destructive predominance in today's society of the notion of relativism and warned of the fact that under the semblance of freedom, relativism separates people from each other and locks each person in his or her own ego. At the root of this problem is Kant's self-limitation of reason, which leads to pathologies of religion such as extremism, and pathologies of science, such as ecological disasters. Benedict pointed out the danger that the absolutization of what is relative poses. Absolutizing what is not absolute produces totalitarianism.

A predominant part of Pope Benedict XVI's teaching was also to reinforce the notion that Christianity is a religion according to reason, and that the act of faith is not inherently contradictory to reason. In his Wednesday audience address on November 21, 2012, Benedict reflected on the reasonableness of faith:

> The Catholic Tradition, from the outset, rejected the so-called "fideism," which is the desire to believe against reason. Credo quia absurdum (I believe because it is absurd) is not a formula that interprets the Catholic faith. Indeed, God is not absurd, if anything he is a mystery. The mystery, in its turn, is not irrational but is a superabundance of sense, of meaning, of truth. God came close to man, he offered himself so that man might know him, stooping to the creatural limitations of human reason (cf. Second Vatican Ecumenical Council, Dogmatic Constitution, *Dei Verbum*, n. 13). At the same time, God, with his grace, illuminates reason, unfolds new horizons before it, boundless and infinite. For this reason, faith is an incentive to seek always, never to stop and never to be content in the inexhaustible search for truth and reality. The prejudice of certain modern thinkers, who hold that human reason would be, as it were, blocked by the dogmas of faith, is false. In the irresistible desire for truth, only a harmonious relationship between faith and reason is the right road that leads to God and to the person's complete fulfilment. It is reasonable to believe, and the whole of our existence is at stake.[61]

---

60. Ratzinger, *Reader*, 9.
61. Benedict XVI, *General Audience, 21 November 2012*.

The Paschal Pattern of Authentic Christian Existence

Corkery maintains that there is a pattern to the way that Ratzinger envisages the relationship between the divine and the human (which obviously includes the question of nature and grace). This relationship is seen through a distinctly theological lens that is firstly aware of humanity's fallenness, but also aware of the fact that God's dealings with us are always directed towards our healing, conversion, and transformation. In other words, the divine relates to nature in a distinctly paschal fashion, where grace purifies and perfects nature.[62] In his work *Introduction to Christianity*, Ratzinger presents not so much an "Incarnational theology" but rather a newly emphasized "theology of the Cross."[63] This emphasis places conversion (and specifically receiving a forgiveness that we can never bestow upon ourselves) at the center of the human person's relationship with God. This theology of the Cross that stands as one of the main pillars of Ratzinger's thought means that, for him, the Cross reveals who God is and who we ourselves are.[64] Along with Henri de Lubac, Ratzinger understood that there could be no grace without the Cross.[65] Corkery points out that this is one of the reasons that Ratzinger greatly approved of article 22 of *Gaudium et Spes*, because it managed to present a corrective to formulations of the earlier *Lumen Gentium* that he found to be too emphatic of the activity of human beings, as if we were able to be agents of our own salvation. Ratzinger instead saw the value in *Gaudium et Spes* emphasizing not only that Christ remains at the center of all things, but that it is our participation in the paschal mystery of the Cross that stands at the heart of human existence, history, and ultimately salvation. Nevertheless, Ratzinger was never fully at ease with the reception of *Gaudium et Spes*, seeing in its interpretive reception a license to an unlimited adaptation of the Christian faith in the world and that this fact could offer a key to understanding the malaise in the church at that time. We see here the influence of both Augustine and Bonaventure, who both knew the destructive capacity of sin and the lame inability of humanity to work its own salvation.[66] Ratzinger, therefore, was at pains to emphasize that:

---

62. Corkery, *Ratzinger's Theological Ideas*, 33.
63. Corkery, *Ratzinger's Theological Ideas*, 33.
64. Ratzinger, *Introduction to Christianity*, 205.
65. Ratzinger, *Theology of History*, 117.
66. Corkery, *Ratzinger's Theological Ideas*, 34. See Ratzinger's commentary on *Gaudium et Spes*, part 1, ch. 1, "Dignity of the Human Person," in Vorgrimler, *Commentary*,

evangelization is not simply adaptation to the culture . . . nor is it dressing up the gospel with elements of the culture, along the lines of a superficial notion of inculturation that supposes that with modified figures of speech and a few new elements in the liturgy, the job is done. No, the gospel is a slit, a purification that becomes maturation and healing. It is a cut that demands patient involvement and understanding, so that it occurs at the right time, in the right place, and in the right way . . . [it involves] an ongoing and patient encounter between the Logos and the culture . . . mediated by the service of the faithful.[67]

The Primacy of Love

In all of Ratzinger's texts the central importance of love shines through. It is a pivotal focus of his theological corpus and again belies the great influence of Augustine and Bonaventure on his thought.

Indeed, *Deus Caritas Est* makes the love of God its central theme. In that encyclical, as Pope Benedict, he spoke of the importance of friendship with Christ, such that we may love those whom God himself loves; that we may be friends of God's own friends.[68] The notion of loving friendship with Christ flows from this emphasis. At the conclusion of his first homily as pope, Benedict cited his predecessor Pope John Paul II's words, "do not be afraid! Open wide the doors for Christ!" He stressed that everything depends upon this friendship with Jesus Christ and our willingness to speak to him as a friend, the only One who can make the world good. Benedict's three-volume work *Jesus of Nazareth* was written with a view to fostering this friendship with Jesus Christ.

In 1964, as a young professor at the Second Vatican Council, during one of his Advent sermons at the cathedral of Münster, Ratzinger spoke of the fact that love is so important as to form the very essence of Christianity:

> God himself lives and works according to the rule of superabundance, of that love which can give nothing less than itself. That is the simple answer to the question about the essence of Christianity, which confronts us again at the end and which, properly understood, includes everything.[69]

---

vol. 5.
   67. Ratzinger, *On the Way*, 48.
   68. Benedict XVI, *Deus Caritas Est*, §18.
   69. Ratzinger, *What It Means*, 83.

The Question of the Theological "Volta-Faccia"

According to Boeve, there is no question that in the second half of the 1960s, Ratzinger's theological position was somewhat different from that which preceded it, and similarly, that he took theological positions during the Second Vatican Council that he would no longer hold. This has given rise to the notion that within Ratzinger's theological corpus there could be said to be a Ratzinger I and a Ratzinger II. Nevertheless, Boeve maintains that despite the "adjustments" in his theology over the years, his works still maintain a fundamental continuity. Instead, it is the tone and "polemical" writing style that distinguishes a number of his later works from his earlier writings.[70]

Ratzinger's earlier works display a willingness to contemplate church reform and even a *rapprochement* with the world, in which he states that the theology of the Incarnation can never be regarded without the theology of the Cross. Nevertheless, after the council, Ratzinger grew suspicious of his fellow theologians and the postconciliar developments in theology and he became more pessimistic and concerned. A sign of this concern was his persistent and ever more severe assessment of the content and reception of *Gaudium et Spes*. For Ratzinger, the Second Vatican Council has been used as a license for far too extensive reforms. According to Boeve, Ratzinger eventually abandoned his attitude as a moderate reformist and began a defense of Catholicism that in his view had sold out to modernity. This abandonment is what drove the marked change in the tone and emphasis of his later works.[71] Notwithstanding the change in the tone of his writings over the decades, as earlier stated, there still remains a consistency in his fundamental theological ideas, which display a firm internal consistency.

JOHN MILBANK

Biography

Alasdair John Milbank was born on October 23, 1952, in Kings Langley, Hertfordshire, England, to John Douglas and Jean Hislop (Maclagan) Milbank and baptized in the Anglican Church. He received a bachelor of arts degree with third-class honors in modern history from the University of

---

70. Ratzinger, *Reader*, 11.
71. Ratzinger, *Reader*, 11.

Oxford. He then was awarded a postgraduate certificate in theology from Westcott House in Cambridge, having studied under Rowan Williams.[72] He completed a doctorate at the University of Birmingham with philosopher Leon Pompa on the Italian humanist, rhetorician, and philosophical historian Giambattista Vico.[73] Milbank's doctoral studies overlapped with lecturing at Lancaster funded by the Christendom Trust, a charity founded by Anglo-Catholic socialist and philanthropist Maurice Reckitt. Milbank was eventually created an honorary doctor of divinity by the University of Cambridge, where he held a readership and then eventually moved to Virginia. Presently, Milbank is a professor emeritus of religion, politics, and ethics at the University of Nottingham.[74] In 1990 Milbank published his seminal text, *Theology and Social Theory*. This text is generally considered to be the first text in the Radical Orthodoxy movement. In considering, therefore, the predominant features of Milbank's thought, it is advantageous to have an understanding of the Radical Orthodoxy movement and its salient features. Milbank's work has contributed very much to the establishment and ongoing features of this movement.

Radical Orthodoxy

Radical Orthodoxy is best considered to be a theological movement that arose in the 1990s out of Cambridge University. In addition to Milbank, the other foundational authors of this movement include Catherine Pickstock and Graham Ward. It is not a school of theology in the traditional sense of the term, but rather a collection of authors that, while differing in some of their notions of how Radical Orthodoxy should operate, all share a common conviction that dominates their theology, namely, that there should not be an autonomous secular sphere and that there should be an alternative theology to the correlationist theology that seems to dominate in most theological schools.[75] Perhaps the following may illustrate best the common notions that run through the diversity of writers in the Radical Orthodoxy movement:

> The present collection of essays attempts to reclaim the world by situating its concerns and activities within a theological

---

72. Grumett, "Radical Orthodoxy."
73. Grumett, "Radical Orthodoxy."
74. Grumett, "Radical Orthodoxy."
75. Cush, "Radical Orthodoxy: Overview."

framework. Not simply returning in nostalgia to the premodern, it visits sites in which secularism has invested heavily—aesthetics, politics, sex, the body, personhood, visibility, space—and resituates them from a Christian standpoint; that is, in terms of the Trinity, Christology, the church and the Eucharist. What emerges is a contemporary theological project made possible by the self-conscious superficiality of today's secularism. For this new project regards the nihilistic drift of postmodernism (which, nonetheless, has roots in the outset of modernity) as a supreme opportunity. It does not—like liberal theology, transcendentalist theology and even certain styles of neo-orthodoxy—seek, in the face of this drift, to shore up universal accounts of immanent human value (humanism), nor defenses of supposedly objective reason. But nor does it indulge, like so many, in the pretense of a baptism of nihilism in the name of a misconstrued "negative theology." Instead, in the face of the secular demise of truth, it seeks to reconfigure theological truth.[76]

Seven of the twelve contributors to *Radical Orthodoxy: A New Theology* (1999) are Anglicans of the High Church persuasion.[77] However, as Fergus Kerr points out: "this is not simply a High Anglican project. As we shall see, the project is easy enough to locate, historically and textually, in terms of a controversy internal to Roman Catholic theology throughout most of the twentieth century."[78] In terms of a strict affiliation to either (or any) denomination of Christianity, Gavin D'Costa writes: "neither of these ecclesial communities ever make their real presence felt . . . it is a church theology, with no accountability to any real church."[79]

In his work on Radical Orthodoxy, R. R. Reno proposes that Radical Orthodoxy ecclesiology is where:

> predominant Anglican practice could not provide an adequately rich, catholic tradition, and the Roman church, as currently constituted, could not provide an adequate institutional basis for faithfulness to the catholic tradition. Therefore, a tradition had to be invented. Of course, the invention was denied. The three leading figures of Radical Orthodoxy—Milbank, Pickstock, and Ward—are Anglican, deeply influenced by the piety

---

76. Milbank, Pickstock, and Ward, *Radical Orthodoxy*, 1.
77. Kerr, "Catholic Response," 47.
78. Kerr, "Catholic Response," 47.
79. D'Costa, "Seeking after Theological Vision."

and practice of Anglo-Catholicism, and this encourages them to replace particularity with theory, identity with ideality.[80]

As should be clear, Radical Orthodoxy is firmly rooted in a British, Cambridge, Anglo-Catholic mentality, but holds a bond of loose affiliation with all who wish to reject the terms imposed on theology, and the church, by secular postmodernity; and with those who wish to reclaim an archaeology, and application, of patristic and medieval texts to the postmodern context.[81]

Catherine Pickstock sums up Radical Orthodoxy, saying: "Radical Orthodoxy has never seen itself as an exclusive movement, but rather as a loose tendency."[82] John Milbank holds to the catholicity of Radical Orthodoxy, despite its non-ecclesiastical affiliations:

> Radical Orthodoxy, if Catholic, is not a specifically Roman Catholic theology; although it can be espoused by Roman Catholics, it can equally be espoused by those who are formally protestant, yet whose theory and practice essentially accords with the Catholic vision of the patristic period to the High Middle Ages.[83]

Radical Orthodoxy certainly makes use of the language of postmodernism; however, it rests on a different foundational assumption, which Reno calls "the glue that holds the world together."[84] According to him:

> It is Augustine's vision of heavenly peace, made effective in the dynamic and binding power of divine purpose, that shapes Radical Orthodoxy's reflections, not Nietzsche's violence wrought by an omnipotent will-to-power. This difference allows Radical Orthodoxy to interpret postmodern thought without being drawn into its orbit, giving Milbank & Co. the perspective from which to expose the nakedness of postmodern nihilism.[85]

Radical Orthodoxy takes the view that the situation that the world finds itself in is one of great difficulty. The aims of Radical Orthodoxy can be set out in relation to four crucial claims: (1) secular modernity is the creation of a perverse theology; (2) the opposition of reason to Revelation

80. Reno, "Radical Orthodoxy Project."
81. Cush, "Radical Orthodoxy: Overview."
82. Smith, *Introducing Radical Orthodoxy*, 66.
83. Milbank, "Programme," 33.
84. Reno, "Radical Orthodoxy Project."
85. Reno, "Radical Orthodoxy Project."

is a modern corruption; (3) all thought that brackets out God is ultimately nihilistic; (4) the material and temporal realms of bodies, sex, art, and sociality, which modernity claims to value, can truly be upheld only by acknowledgment of their participation in the transcendent.[86]

In the first chapter of Milbank's *Theology and Social Theory* he writes: "Once, there was no secular . . . . The secular as a domain had to be instituted or imagined, both in theory and in practice. The institution is not correctly grasped in merely negative terms as a desacralization."[87]

For Milbank, there is no reason to accept assertions that secular culture is "neutral" territory and therefore should be accepted as normative for all public life. In his view, all ideas, including those that shape secular culture, have a history. They do not just appear ready-made from a timeless world above. They are formed by historical, social, and economic forces. As such, just because an idea seems natural or obvious to proponents of postmodern secular culture, this does not mean that it would seem so to a person in another culture. Part of Milbank's project is to tell the story of why certain ideas have taken hold and become dominant in today's world. The point is that by showing that ideas have a beginning, they can also have an end. Thus, in positioning the idea of the secular in the form of a story, that is, "once [upon a time] there was no secular," shows how limited and questionable it is. Stories, for Milbank, are invented.[88]

These words in turn reveal one of Radical Orthodoxy's core convictions, namely, that the secular (conceived as the world as separate from the stories and practices of the Christian faith) is not a given. The secular is not an objective fact, waiting to be discovered, proper to the nature of reality. It is a human creation. Given this, Milbank spends much time arguing that it has been created to serve human interests, interests that have more to do with conquest and domination than with reason and tolerance.[89]

In What Sense "Radical"? In What Sense "Orthodox"?

According to Milbank, Pickstock, and Ward, the term "orthodox" is used in the most straightforward sense of commitment to creedal Christianity

---

86. Cush, "Radical Orthodoxy: Overview."
87. Milbank, *Theology and Social Theory*, 9.
88. Shakespeare, *Radical Orthodoxy: Critical Introduction*, 7.
89. Shakespeare, *Radical Orthodoxy: Critical Introduction*, 7.

and the exemplarity of its patristic matrix. It also denotes the more specific sense of reaffirming a "richer and more coherent Christianity," which, according to them, was gradually lost sight of after the late Middle Ages.[90] The notion of "orthodoxy" transcends confessional boundaries as both Protestant biblicism and post-Tridentine Catholic positivist authoritarianism are seen as aberrations arising from theological distortions already present before the early modern period. This perspective is in continuity with the *nouvelle théologie*; however, Radical Orthodoxy wishes to reach further by recovering and extending a fully Christianized ontology and practical philosophy consonant with authentic Christian doctrine.[91] Milbank contends that the consequences of modern theological decadence for philosophy and modern culture more generally were never considered by the *nouvelle théologie* (which itself sometimes uncritically accepts various modes of secular knowledge). While this decadence was considered by Thomistic currents in the wake of Gilson and Maritain, the exclusively Thomist perspective is not seen by Radical Orthodoxy as necessarily decisive.[92] In contrast to Barthian neo-orthodoxy, which tends to assume a positive autonomy for theology, rendering philosophical concerns a matter of indifference, Radical Orthodoxy is "more mediating, but less accommodating," since while it assumes that theology must speak also of something else, it seeks always to cognize a theological difference in such speaking. Radical Orthodoxy thus tends to mingle exegesis, cultural reflection, and philosophy in a complex but coherent collage.[93]

This theological approach is also "radical" in the sense of a return to patristic and medieval roots, especially to the Augustinian vision of all knowledge as divine illumination. This notion, it is claimed, transcends all modern dualisms of faith and reason, grace and nature. The term "radical" is also intended to mean a seeking to deploy this recovered vision systematically in order to criticize modern society, culture, politics, art, science, and philosophy with an unprecedented boldness. The term also means that, given such critiques, Radical Orthodoxy encourages a reassessment of Christian tradition. Milbank claims that the fact of its late medieval collapse, and indeed even that the tradition was possible at all, can sometimes point to even earlier weaknesses. Furthermore, given that the Enlightenment was in effect a critique of decadent early

---

90. Milbank, Pickstock, and Ward, *Radical Orthodoxy*, 2.
91. Milbank, Pickstock, and Ward, *Radical Orthodoxy*, 2.
92. Milbank, Pickstock, and Ward, *Radical Orthodoxy*, 2.
93. Milbank, Pickstock, and Ward, *Radical Orthodoxy*, 2.

modern Christianity, it remains possible to learn from it, even though the Enlightenment itself eventually repeated the decadence. Finally, the critics of the Enlightenment, such as Hamann, Jacobi, Kierkegaard, Péguy, and Chesterton, in different ways saw that what secularity had most ruined and actually denied were the very things it apparently celebrated, namely, embodied life, self-expression, sexuality, aesthetic experience, and the human political community. These authors contend that only transcendence, which "suspends" them in the sense of interrupting them, also suspends them in the sense of upholding their relative worth over against the void.[94]

All this considered, according to John Montag, both words—"radical" and "orthodox"—have different receptions among different audiences, and their juxtaposition elicits all sorts of reactions. Montag claims that some who champion "orthodoxy" may bristle at the connotations of "radical"; others may run away from "orthodoxy." Catholics hear a range of tonalities in both words to which even High Church Anglicans often remain deaf; Americans often embrace what the British eschew; and none of these groups cut cleanly on anything.[95] If Radical Orthodoxy is to find its place, it must avoid becoming a hostage to a variety of political, ecclesial, and academic fortunes in an increasingly polarized, postmodern world.[96]

Five Hallmarks of Radical Orthodoxy

Given that Radical Orthodoxy is not a clearly defined school or movement but rather a "loose tendency," as Pickstock puts it, James K. A. Smith proposes a heuristic approach to understanding it. Smith uses the metaphor of a symphony made up of different movements as a way of understanding the program of Radical Orthodoxy and its sensibilities, which are set out as follows.

A Critique of Modernity and Liberalism

In many ways, Milbank's seminal text *Theology and Social Theory* expresses the spirit of what would come to be known as Radical Orthodoxy.

---

94. Milbank, Pickstock, and Ward, *Radical Orthodoxy*, 3.
95. Montag, "Radical Orthodoxy and Christian Philosophy," 96.
96. Cush, "Radical Orthodoxy: Overview."

Given this, Radical Orthodoxy presents a sharp critique of modernity as a flawed, imploding project.[97] Milbank, along with the other contributors to Radical Orthodoxy, sees in modernity the institution of dualisms that form the grounds for the exclusion of the divine and transcendent; hence the notion of "implosion" related to the end of metaphysics. According to Milbank, these modern dualisms became the rules of the game according to which modern theology had to play. Radical Orthodoxy, on the other hand, sets out to challenge these rules and calls into question the assumptions of modernity itself.[98] Milbank asserts:

> With this ending [of modernity], there ends also the modern predicament of theology. It no longer has to measure up to accepted secular standards of scientific truth or normative rationality. Nor, concomitantly, to a fixed notion of the knowing subject, which was unusually the modern, as opposed to the premodern, way of securing universal reason. This caused problems for theology, because an approach grounded in subjective aspiration can only precariously affirm objective values and divine transcendence.[99]

Radical Orthodoxy is critical of theological liberalism, because it views it as accommodating theology to modernity rather than grounding it in Revelation. Radical Orthodoxy is also a critic of classical political liberalism because of its assumptions (taken from Hobbes, etc.) about human nature, and its atomistic account of the social sphere.[100] Nevertheless, James K. A. Smith asserts that notwithstanding Radical Orthodoxy's critique of modernity, it is not itself anti-modern. To be anti-modern would mean the simple negation of modernity (such as in the case of Protestant fundamentalism), and, in this way, it would still operate within a modern paradigm. Radical Orthodoxy on the other hand seeks to circumvent modernity's assumptions, rather than to simply negate them. Thus, it can be said that Radical Orthodoxy is truly *postmodern*, that is, *other than* modern.[101] Milbank claims that "Radical Orthodoxy, although it opposes the modern, also seeks to save it. It espouses, not the pre-modern, but an alternative version of modernity."[102]

97. Smith, *Introducing Radical Orthodoxy*, 70.
98. Smith, *Introducing Radical Orthodoxy*, 71.
99. Milbank, "Postmodern Critical Augustinianism," 225.
100. Smith, *Introducing Radical Orthodoxy*, 71.
101. Smith, *Introducing Radical Orthodoxy*, 71.
102. Milbank, "Programme," 45.

Milbank claims that Radical Orthodoxy, therefore, seeks to empower theologians to call into question the foundational metaphysical, epistemological, and anthropological assumptions that undergird modernity. In Milbank, this means calling into question the "ontology of violence," as he terms it, which construes human intersubjective relationships as being governed by power and war. His text *Theology and Social Theory*, particularly in the latter chapters, sets out this critique and seeks to demonstrate the internal inconsistencies of construing the world in this way. Milbank then proposes in place of this ontology of violence an "ontology of peace," which construes human intersubjective relationships as grounded in a fundamental harmony, and which is unapologetically grounded in Christian (specifically Augustinian) metaphysics.[103] Obviously in so doing Milbank runs the risk of having this position rejected *ab initio* because it bases itself on the Christian faith. To this, Milbank demonstrates that even the modern, purportedly secular accounts of intersubjectivity are founded themselves on particular faith perspectives. The fundamental shifts that characterize modern, secular social theory, which Milbank argues are in fact simply modifications or rejections of Christian orthodoxy, are no more rationally justifiable than the Christian perspectives themselves.[104] Milbank also argues for not only just the right of Christian accounts to compete as just another perspective but that in fact Christian accounts are better or more viable than all others. Milbank states that:

> Christianity, therefore, is not just in the same position as all other discourses vis-à-vis postmodernity; it can, I want to claim, think difference, yet it perhaps uniquely tries to deny that this necessarily (rather than contingently, in a fallen world) entails conflict.[105]

Milbank seeks not only to create the space for radically Christian accounts to be admitted into the marketplace of ideas as yet another option for consumers of ideas, but also to show that such accounts have an internal consistency and ability to account for reality that non-Christian perspectives do not have.[106]

---

103. Smith, *Introducing Radical Orthodoxy*, 72.
104. Milbank, *Theology and Social Theory*, 1.
105. Milbank, "Postmodern Critical Augustinianism," 228.
106. Smith, *Introducing Radical Orthodoxy*, 72.

Post-secularity

A major part of Radical Orthodoxy's project is calling into question the dualisms of modernity, most particularly the notion of the separation of the sacred and the secular. In so doing, it seeks to undo the very notion of secular reason. As a result, the false opposition between faith and reason is also questioned. Radical Orthodoxy therefore:

> protests equally against assertions of pure reason and of pure faith; equally against denominational claims for a monopoly of salvation and against indifference to church order; equally against theology as an internal autistic idiolect, and against theology as an adaptation to unquestioned secular assumptions . . . . However, it further asserts that the apparently opposite poles refused are in secret collusion: more specifically it contends that the pursuit of pure faith is as much a *modern* quest as the pursuit of pure reason; that the investing of salvific security entirely in institutions and formulae is as modern as the individualistic neglect of such matters, while the eschewing of all apologetics is likewise as modern as regarding apologetics as the essential foundation for a truthful theology.[107]

Radical Orthodoxy attempts to walk a *via media*, without at the same time being middle of the road. It seeks to articulate a Christian account of human experience in all its elements. Radical Orthodoxy also seeks to challenge the orthodoxy of the academy, specifically the secularity that is prevalent therein, which sets out purportedly objective accounts of human life untainted by faith perspectives. It considers the very notion of "the secular" to be a myth, and a late one at that.[108] According to Smith, the rejection by Radical Orthodoxy of modern dualisms and the myth of secularity allows theology in mainstream discourse to be "unapologetically confessional" and for Christian research across the disciplines to be "unapologetically theological." The goal is that once the theoretical foundations of secularity are dismantled, Christianity will be given new opportunities in public discourse for the expression of a properly theological or Christian account of reality.[109]

---

107. Milbank, "Programme," 33.
108. Smith, *Introducing Radical Orthodoxy*, 74.
109. Smith, *Introducing Radical Orthodoxy*, 74.

Participation and Materiality

The first two movements, just described, are more epistemological in their focus and are grounded in and grow out of an ontological commitment to participation (*methexis*) as the only proper metaphysical model for understanding creation and particularly the relation between creature and Creator.[110] The emphasis on participation shows that Radical Orthodoxy is not primarily targeting Christian theology per se, but rather the contemporary theological currents that traffic under the banner of postmodernism. Postmodern ontology is characterized by flatness and materialism, which ultimately and inexorably lead to nihilism. By means of this flatness, all that remains to the world is the immanent, which only eventually implodes in upon itself. In contrast, Radical Orthodoxy proposes participatory ontology (in which the immanent and material is suspended from the transcendent and immaterial), which alone can give the world true meaning. According to Pickstock:

> the theological point here is that Christianity is as equally removed from nihilism as it is from finite positivism, because, following Augustine, every created reality is absolutely nothing in itself. This point is fundamental to Radical Orthodoxy's pitting of participation against postmodern tendencies to nihilism.[111]

Participation is of fundamental importance for the first two themes because, according to Radical Orthodoxy, nothing *is* autonomously or in itself but *is* only insofar as it participates in the gift of existence granted by God (following Augustine). As Milbank sets out:

> The central theological framework of radical orthodoxy is participation as developed by Plato and reworked by Christianity, because any alternative configuration perforce reserves a territory independent of God. The latter can lead only to nihilism (though in different guises). Participation, however, refuses any reserve of created territory, while allowing finite things their own integrity. Underpinning the present essays, therefore, is the idea that every discipline must be framed by a theological perspective; otherwise these disciplines will define a zone apart from God, grounded literally in nothing.[112]

---

110. Smith, *Introducing Radical Orthodoxy*, 74.
111. Pickstock, "Reply," 424.
112. Milbank, Pickstock, and Ward, *Radical Orthodoxy*, 3.

Consequently, every sphere of creation, and one's inhabitation of it, participates in the primal gift of the Creator. Milbank emphasizes that this notion of participation extends also to language, history, and culture, indeed the whole realm of human making. Not only do being and knowledge participate in a God who is and who comprehends, also human making participates in a God who is infinite poetic utterance, namely, the Second Person of the Trinity. Given that the world is created, it must be investigated as such, which must also mean *in the light of the Cross*.[113] According to Milbank, the postmodern valorization of appearances only ends up dissipating the reality of the immanent world:

> In contrast, the theological perspective of participation actually saves the appearances by exceeding them. It recognizes that materialism and spiritualism are false alternatives, since if there is only finite matter there is not even that, and that for phenomena really to be there they must be more than there. Hence by appealing to an eternal source for bodies, their art, language, sexual and political union, one is not ethereally taking leave of their density. On the contrary, one is insisting that behind this density resides an even greater density—beyond all contrasts of density and lightness. This is to say that all there is *only* is because it is more than it is.[114]

Radical Orthodoxy is therefore marked by a theological materialism because it affirms what is beyond the material. By affirming transcendence, it supports a proper valuation of immanence. Pickstock asserts that "one of the most central aims of a radically orthodox perspective is to restore time and embodiment to our understanding of reality."[115] This forms part of the goal of revaluing materiality as part of a broader incarnational ontology, whereby Radical Orthodoxy emphasizes the material and the bodily as a site of both Revelation and redemption. Only such a suspension of the material in relation to a transcendence that exceeds it can do justice to the material as such without lapsing into simple materialism.[116] Only transcendence that "suspends" human existence and activity, in the sense of interrupting them, also "suspends" them also in the other sense of upholding their relative worth over against the void.[117]

---

113. Smith, *Introducing Radical Orthodoxy*, 75.
114. Milbank, Pickstock, and Ward, *Radical Orthodoxy*, 4.
115. Pickstock, "Radical Orthodoxy and Mediations of Time," 64.
116. Smith, *Introducing Radical Orthodoxy*, 76.
117. Milbank, Pickstock, and Ward, *Radical Orthodoxy*, 3.

Sacramentality, Liturgy, and Aesthetics

It follows as a consequence of Radical Orthodoxy's incarnational account of the revelation of transcendence, along with an ontology of participation, that in Radical Orthodoxy a high value is placed upon the liturgy and its ability to lead us to the divine. Milbank states:

> Since God is not an item in the world to which we might turn, he is only first there for us in our turning to him. And yet we only turn to him when he reaches us; herein lies the mystery of liturgy—liturgy that for theology is more fundamental than *either* language *or* experience, and yet is both linguistic and experiential.[118]

The incarnational focus in Radical Orthodoxy also means an emphasis on aesthetics and the arts as a medium of Revelation and worship. This points to the experiential aspect in postmodernity, which is treated at length by Ward. He observes that the experiential aspect is fundamental in Christianity as one element in the mechanism of repentance and conversion.[119]

Jean-Luc Marion sums up Radical Orthodoxy's emphasis on liturgy as follows:

> Where, then, is the paradigmatic kenosis of the image for the benefit of the holiness of God accomplished? In the liturgy. The liturgy proposes to demonstrate a visible spectacle, which summons and possibly fills vision, but also the senses of hearing, smell, touch, and even taste. It accomplishes an entire possible aesthetic and perhaps thus appears to be a complete spectacle, more than opera, which moreover is its mimic and, by the *oratio*, results from it.... The attitude of my gaze before the liturgy determines my general attitude before the crossing of the visible by invisible.[120]

Cultural Critique and Transformation

Given that Radical Orthodoxy is grounded in participatory ontology that revalues time and embodiment, it follows that it also articulates a

---

118. Milbank, "Programme," 43.
119. Ward, *Theology and Contemporary Critical Theory*, 121.
120. Marion, *Crossing of the Visible*, 64.

distinctive Christian approach to being-in-the-world. One of the important contributions of Radical Orthodoxy is to call into question the tendency of some strains of Christianity to write off the world as entirely "in the power of the evil one" (1 John 5:19). Given its incarnational account of God's Revelation in the world, and building on the participatory account of the relationship between Creator and creation, Radical Orthodoxy emphasizes both God's Revelation of himself in the material world (e.g., in art) and God's concern for the redemption and transformation of this world (socially, politically, and economically). Radical Orthodoxy also emphasizes the fact that participation spills over into the sphere of human culture and making, that is, the sphere of *poiesis*.[121] Milbank states:

> I have always tried to suggest that participation can be extended also to language, history, and culture: the whole realm of human making. Not only do being and knowledge participate in a God who is and who comprehends; also human making participates in a God who is infinite poetic utterance: the second person of the Trinity.[122]

Ward describes Radical Orthodoxy as "cultural politics" or "constructive cultural criticism."[123] He suggests that:

> Radical Orthodoxy is involved in reading the signs of the times . . . . It looks at "sites" that we have invested much cultural capital in—the body, sexuality, relationships, desire, painting, music, the city, the natural, the political—and it reads them in terms of the grammar of the Christian faith; a grammar that might be summed up in the various creeds. In this way Radical Orthodoxy must view its own task as not only doing theology but being itself theological—participating in the redemption of Creation.[124]

Radical Orthodoxy's project therefore is de(con)structive in that it sets out by "unmasking the cultural idols, providing genealogical accounts of the assumptions, politics, and hidden metaphysics of specific varieties of knowledge—with respect to the constructive, therapeutic project of disseminating the Gospel."[125] Therefore, for Ward at least,

---

121. Smith, *Introducing Radical Orthodoxy*, 79.
122. Milbank, *Being Reconciled*, 9.
123. Ward, *Cities of God*, 47.
124. Ward, "Radical Orthodoxy and/as Cultural Politics," 103.
125. Ward, "Radical Orthodoxy and/as Cultural Politics," 104.

what makes Radical Orthodoxy radical is that it carries left-wing political connotations: "In the collapse of socialism as a secular political force I see Radical Orthodoxy as offering one means whereby socialism can be returned to its Christian roots."[126] Radical Orthodoxy understands itself to be a Christian *Kulturkritik* in the vein of Benjamin, Marcuse, and Habermas—a Christian baptism of social theory, or indeed even a rededication of the same, given that Milbank too argues that such a social critique requires a Christian foundation.[127] The church does not so much *have* a cultural critique; she *is* a cultural critique. According to Radical Orthodoxy, the church's politics is an ecclesiology. Therefore, a centerpiece of Radical Orthodoxy is the radical consideration of politics—and the political nature of the church and gospel—in a way that does not simply concede political expertise to the secular, but rather attempts to unfold a distinctively Christian politics, such that even this "socialism by grace" is not confused with its secular parodies.[128]

"Postmodern Critical Augustinianism"

In considering the historical notion of Christendom, particularly of the Middle Ages, Milbank draws attention to its dual aspects, namely, the *sacerdotium* and the *regnum*. He contrasts the secular with the saeculum, and states:

> The saeculum, in the medieval era, was not a space, a domain, but a time—the interval between fall and eschaton where coercive justice, private property, and impaired natural reason must make shift to cope with the unredeemed effects of sinful humanity.[129]

One can see the influence of Augustine on Milbank in these assertions. These Augustinian thoughts are one reason why Milbank originally envisioned Radical Orthodoxy as "postmodern critical Augustinianism."[130] Milbank writes:

> Explication of Christian practice, the task of theology, tries to pinpoint the peculiarity, the difference, of this practice by

126. Ward, "Radical Orthodoxy and/as Cultural Politics," 105.
127. Smith, *Introducing Radical Orthodoxy*, 80.
128. Smith, *Introducing Radical Orthodoxy*, 80.
129. Milbank, *Theology and Social Theory*, 9.
130. Cush, "Radical Orthodoxy: Overview."

"making it strange," finding a new language for this difference, less tainted by the overfamiliarity of too many Christian words, which tend to obscure Christian singularity.[131]

Smith tends to concur with the Augustinian tendency in Radical Orthodoxy, claiming that the world lends itself to the application of the same. The situation of the contemporary world also lends itself to an application of an Augustinian worldview, according to Smith.[132] Ward maintains:

> We stand, culturally, in a certain relation to Augustine's thinking. Poised as he was on the threshold between radical pluralism (which he called paganism) and the rise of Christendom, we stand on the other side of that history: at the end of Christendom, and the re-emergence of radical (as distinct from liberal) pluralism.[133]

Reno claims:

> This ambition to see all creation as matter for redemption explains Radical Orthodoxy's self-designation as "Augustinian." The proponents of Radical Orthodoxy do not simply use the heavenly city as a gesture by which to escape from the dead-ends of postmodernism. They want to substitute a Christian and participatory account of the glue that holds the world together for the postmodern and violent one. Only then can theology escape the gravitational pull of the postmodern commitment to power and violence. Once Radical Orthodoxy escapes, under the guidance of a metaphysic of participation, its proponents can show how the diverse features of human life find fulfillment in God's consummating purposes. The way is open to recover and reconstitute a comprehensive Christian vision.[134]

Narrative, Non-Foundational, and Non-Apologetic Theology

At its essence, Radical Orthodoxy treats of the decline of modern Western culture, and searches for a remedy for the problems of modernity. The overall approach taken by Radical Orthodoxy can be described as

---

131. Milbank, "Postmodern Critical Augustinianism," 228.
132. Smith, *Introducing Radical Orthodoxy*, 46.
133. Ward, "Questioning God."
134. Reno, "Radical Orthodoxy Project."

"narrative," "non-foundational," and "non-apologetic."[135] Radical Orthodoxy is "narrative" in the sense that it is trying to tell the Christian story freed from the shackles of postmodern skeptical relativism.

If, according to Milbank, modern secular social theory's prime assumption is the modification or the rejection of orthodox Christian positions, and the view that traditional Christian orthodoxy is not justifiable by reason, we can conclude that "there simply are no universally recognized foundations for truth."[136] Thus, Radical Orthodoxy is "non-apologetic." This "non-foundational" freedom to posit the Christian story is described by Stephen Shakespeare:

> Once we accept this, however, we start to understand that the way is opened for particular world-views to tell their story of reality without embarrassment. If secularism is just one more story, it can't have the last word. So, the Christian story can once more be told and heard. Postmodern skepticism clears away the prejudices of the Enlightenment against anything which is not a self-evident, almost mathematical, truth.[137]

Radical Orthodoxy is not a theology of compromise. Milbank is not interested in acknowledging the bias promulgated by secularity, which states that the cultural and intellectual heritage of the West has nothing to do with Christianity. Milbank states that "the secular *episteme* is a post-Christian paganism, something that, in the last analysis, [is] only to be defined negatively, as a refusal of Christianity and the invention of an anti-Christianity."[138]

According to Milbank, secular liberalism is not value-neutral; it is not a purely scientifically based and supposedly objective view of reality and has, in fact, established itself as an alternate religion, opposed to Christianity. Radical Orthodoxy attempts to call out this secular alternate religion, masquerading as pure objectivity, as just one more story striving not for tolerance and reason, but for domination, authoritarianism, and conquest. It seeks to reclaim the place of the Christian Church as a viable alternate reality.[139]

---

135. Cush, "Radical Orthodoxy: Overview."
136. Shakespeare, *Radical Orthodoxy: Critical Introduction*, 55.
137. Shakespeare, *Radical Orthodoxy: Critical Introduction*, 55.
138. Milbank, *Theology and Social Theory*, 280.
139. Cush, "Radical Orthodoxy: Overview."

The Christian story, by its very nature, according to Milbank, simply has to recommend itself to the world *as a story*.[140] No amount of apologetic can succeed in persuading people to convert and to join the flock. Instead, Christianity should stand by itself as something that is an attractive, compelling worldview. Christianity is a story, but it is one that "encompasses all others" and is "a metadiscourse."[141]

However, Milbank is not content with the *general* idea of narrative as an alternative to secular reason. Radical Orthodoxy requires and indeed demands a specific commitment to the Christian story alone as the way to combat nihilism.[142] Merely returning to story, myth, or tradition is not enough, as a plurality of stories cannot stand in the way of the secular. Capitalism is perfectly happy for many religions to exist and to compete with each other in the marketplace of ideas.[143] Milbank rejects this notion on the basis that variety can be meaningless and empty, as though extending our choices would extend our freedom. In the face of the arbitrariness of an abundance of choices, Radical Orthodoxy, accepting that there are no universal rational foundations, and that Christianity will be seen as merely one story among others, still insists on taking a stand on the "plain unfounded narrative of Christianity which is the only universal for those who situate themselves within it."[144]

Milbank claims that Christianity is not just another story, but the only one that can give ultimate meaning to our lives. Therefore, Christianity must seek to master and defeat all other stories, because it is the only story that is able to renounce mastery and domination. In the end, only Christianity can tell a story about everything that is at the same time a story of peace. It is able to do this because those who tell the Christian story participate in the mind of God.[145] Milbank states that:

> theology purports to give an ultimate narrative, to provide some ultimate depth of description, because the situation of oneself within such a narrative is what it means to belong to the church, to be a Christian. However, the claim is made by faith, not a reason which seeks foundations.[146]

---

140. Smith, *Introducing Radical Orthodoxy*, 71.
141. Smith, *Introducing Radical Orthodoxy*, 71.
142. Shakespeare, *Radical Orthodoxy: Critical Introduction*, 56.
143. Shakespeare, *Radical Orthodoxy: Critical Introduction*, 56.
144. Milbank, *Theology and Social Theory*, 57.
145. Shakespeare, *Radical Orthodoxy: Critical Introduction*, 57.
146. Milbank, *Theology and Social Theory*, 249.

This ultimately is what Milbank means when he speaks about going "beyond secular reason" (which is the subtitle of his seminal text, *Theology and Social Theory*).

A Non-Correlative Theology

One of the criticisms of Radical Orthodoxy has been that it is unwilling to entertain correlative theology. Radical Orthodoxy maintains the exclusive ability of the Christian narrative to master reality. This unwillingness is an essentially premodern position that uncritically asserts one narrative as supreme above all others, and that, in turn, leads Radical Orthodoxy to characterize all non-Christian discourse as "nihilistic, pagan perversion."[147] Shakespeare, for example, wonders why Radical Orthodoxy consistently refuses to acknowledge any idea derived from the secular sciences as anything less than evil. He writes: "Radical orthodoxy runs the risk of positing an idealized creation accessible only to the elect (those who can see) its own Gnostic fantasy of perfection."[148] On the other hand, David Burrell notes that the correlationist mode of theology is always "catching-up" with the vanguard of contemporary thought; whereas Radical Orthodoxy puts theologizing ahead of the pack with its uncompromising critique of postmodern idioms.[149]

The Importance of Tradition

One of the main features of Radical Orthodoxy is that it is generally scathing about the modern world's abandonment of tradition. Thus it is no surprise that much of its work is carried out through an engagement with thinkers and texts of the past, most notably Plato, Augustine, Aquinas, and Duns Scotus.[150] Nevertheless, according to Shakespeare, the grand nature of Radical Orthodoxy's vision has led it to "play fast and loose with careful readings of its forebears."[151]

Critics of Radical Orthodoxy claim that it gives Plato too prominent a role in its thought. Shakespeare also notes that critics "worry that his

---

147. Shakespeare, "New Romantics," 166.
148. Shakespeare, "New Romantics," 166.
149. Burrell, "Radical Orthodoxy: Appreciation," 76.
150. Shakespeare, *Radical Orthodoxy: Critical Introduction*, 32.
151. Shakespeare, *Radical Orthodoxy: Critical Introduction*, 32.

[Plato's] philosophy is too world-denying, too hostile to time and the body."[152] Smith notes that, from Radical Orthodoxy's earliest intimations, it has been allied with a (certain) retrieval of (a certain) Platonism, such that Milbank could speak of a "Platonism/Christianity" and the "Neo-Platonic/Christian infantilization of the absolute" as crucial for the theological ontology that marks the radical distinction between Christianity and nihilism.[153] Smith also points out that this retrieval of Neoplatonism is not the retrieval of more Gnostic strains of "henological" Neoplatonism that one would find in Plotinus and the Valentinian tradition. Rather, Radical Orthodoxy counters the nihilism and flattened materialism of post/modernity with the *theurgical* Neoplatonism in the tradition of Iamblichus. The invocation of Platonic philosophy is meant to counter the reductionisms of both nihilism and naturalism, pointing instead to a material world being "suspended" from the Good that transcends it.[154]

As earlier stated, Augustine also holds an important place for Radical Orthodoxy. Indeed, Milbank himself characterizes Radical Orthodoxy as a form of "postmodern critical Augustinianism."[155] Smith notes that:

> the substance of Augustine's thought—in particular his epistemology, his cultural analysis, and his theological vision—resonates with the post-foundationalist project that rejects the autonomy of reason and, hence, also the autonomy of the sociopolitical sphere. In short, for Augustine there is no secular, non-religious sphere as construed by modernity; there is only paganism or true worship.[156]

Thomas Aquinas

Thomas Aquinas is a seminal figure for Radical Orthodoxy, especially for Milbank and Pickstock. As we shall see, many disagree with their interpretation of Aquinas, especially in their understanding of the doctrine of participation, and claim that "Radical Orthodoxy imposes the idea of participation on the texts for its own purposes (prime among them which

---

152. Shakespeare, *Radical Orthodoxy: Critical Introduction*, 32.
153. Smith, *Introducing Radical Orthodoxy*, 48.
154. Smith, *Introducing Radical Orthodoxy*, 49.
155. Milbank, "Postmodern Critical Augustinianism."
156. Smith, *Introducing Radical Orthodoxy*, 47.

is to deny any role for philosophy independent of theology)."[157] Smith contends that, in Radical Orthodoxy, Aquinas is mediated through the lens of the *nouvelle théologie*, which in turn presents a very Augustinian Aquinas who rejects the notion of an autonomous nature and also of a "universal, natural, unaided human reason."[158] This means that Aquinas is presented as one who rejects any rationalist account of the human person as well as an overly confident notion of natural law that would play out under the banner of a universal human reason. Furthermore, because the Eucharist is a central idea in the ontology of Radical Orthodoxy, Aquinas must be retrieved in the postmodern context.[159]

Olivier-Thomas Vénard asserts that Radical Orthodoxy takes from Aquinas the notion that theology must be seen as *sacra doctrina*:

> It could sound redundant to present Christian theology as sacra doctrina, were the situation not as I have just described it from the American scene. Certain key factors constitute this description, redolent of the Summa Theologiae of Aquinas: creation and participation, faith as a mode of knowing, and reliance on the resources of the Christian faith-tradition for guidance in assessing current preoccupations. The inclusion of creation, with participation, signals a deconstruction of the neo-Thomist separation of philosophy from theology, presaged by Josef Pieper's prescient remark that creation is the "hidden element" in the philosophy of Aquinas (Pieper 1957). For if Aquinas's own appropriation of Hellenic philosophies turned on the axial asseveration of free creation, then we ought at least be wary of appropriating enlightenment philosophies predicated on removing that obstacle to autonomous human reason.[160]

Milbank and Pickstock's text *Truth in Aquinas* serves as a prime example of a Radical Orthodoxy Thomism.[161] According to Burrell, this text presents a "trenchant argument relating faith to reason intrinsically, thereby elevating faith to an operative presupposition of knowing, so articulating the manner in which theology is understood as sacra doctrina."[162] According to Burrell, in Radical Orthodoxy:

---

157. Shakespeare, *Radical Orthodoxy: Critical Introduction*, 32.
158. Smith, *Introducing Radical Orthodoxy*, 48.
159. Smith, *Introducing Radical Orthodoxy*, 48.
160. Burrell, "Radical Orthodoxy: Appreciation," 74.
161. Cush, "Radical Orthodoxy: Overview."
162. Burrell, "Radical Orthodoxy: Appreciation," 75.

it is a decidedly "neo-Platonic" Aquinas, beholden to Augustine's proposal of divine illumination to secure our knowing as a quest for truth, and so incorporating a dialectic between *reason* and *faith* redolent of John Paul II's *Fides et Ratio*.[163]

Radical Orthodoxy's position on Aquinas, according to Paul DeHart, and the scale and aggressive originality of the text *Truth in Aquinas*, certainly provoked many responses (not all of them favorable, it must be said), especially given the widespread and deep investments made by so many theologians in the enterprise of interpreting Aquinas.[164] Much by way of response was given at the summer symposium in 1999 at Heythrop College, now published in the text *Radical Orthodoxy? A Catholic Enquiry*.

Duns Scotus

According to Shakespeare, Radical Orthodoxy looks upon Duns Scotus as "the key villain of the piece."[165] Scotus is accused of playing a major part in the breakdown of the analogical worldview associated with Aquinas. The effects of Scotus's denial of the analogy and promotion of univocity and nominalism lead to the Enlightenment, which in turn leads to modernity, which in turn leads to the secular state of postmodernity.[166] This negative account of Duns Scotus is highly controversial. Whether or not it is an accurate interpretation of his work, however, its role in Radical Orthodoxy's story of how we got where we are today is undeniable.[167]

Critique of Social Theory

The conclusion that flows from Radical Orthodoxy's position on Duns Scotus is that the postmodern criticism of Christianity that gathers pace from the Enlightenment into the nineteenth century is actually a development of Christian theology gone wrong. On the one hand, the notion of God is criticized by secularists for supporting arbitrary, oppressive power, the assumption being that the same is merely a projection of our

---

163. Burrell, "Radical Orthodoxy: Appreciation," 75.
164. DeHart, *Aquinas and Radical Orthodoxy*, 23.
165. Shakespeare, *Radical Orthodoxy: Critical Introduction*, 10.
166. Cush, "Radical Orthodoxy: Overview."
167. Shakespeare, *Radical Orthodoxy: Critical Introduction*, 11. See also Kizewski, "God-Talk."

own desire for power (or our irrational fear of a Father figure). On the other hand, the banishment of God from public life creates an opportunity for the secular to assert its independence. The assumption is that we know what being is apart from God. Thus, God becomes irrelevant, and the vacuum left by his absence is filled by other forces, which unfortunately, according to Shakespeare, are formed in the image of the Power-God. Thus, a new "cultural winter" of militarism, imperialism, and dictatorship is the result, all under the cover of increased "enlightenment," "civilization," or socialism.[168] Milbank's text *Theology and Social Theory* uses this reading of history as its starting point to critique the modern discipline of social science, which claims to give objective facts about how society functions. According to Milbank:

> Secular "scientific" understanding of society was, from the outset, only the self-knowledge of the self-construction of the secular as power. What theology has forgotten is that it cannot either contest or learn from this understanding as such, but has either to accept or deny its object.[169]

Milbank argues that secular social science is anything but scientific, if we mean by that term "based on empirical evidence alone and free from all ideological bias."[170] According to Milbank, social science only exists as an expression of a deeply questionable set of prejudices and ideas about value and truth. By bracketing out ideas of the transcendent, divine, or supernatural, it presents us with a world that makes sense only in reference to the truth claims of theology or the reality of God's creative grace.[171] But, according to Shakespeare, it cannot do without some overriding order or principle in its view of the world. Something must take the place of God—such as Darwinism, or capitalist theory, or Marxist theory, self-interest, the market, or the notion of the inevitable march of history towards civilization and revolution—to ensure that the secular has foundations. Irrespective of which of these is chosen, what are presented as being neutral "facts" accessible to any reasonable observer are instead merely value judgments, asserted with all the dogmatism that might be associated with religious fundamentalism.[172] For Milbank,

---

168. Shakespeare, *Radical Orthodoxy: Critical Introduction*, 12.
169. Milbank, *Theology and Social Theory*, 10.
170. Shakespeare, *Radical Orthodoxy: Critical Introduction*, 12.
171. Shakespeare, *Radical Orthodoxy: Critical Introduction*, 12.
172. Shakespeare, *Radical Orthodoxy: Critical Introduction*, 12.

these dogmatic assertions, passing themselves off as objective facts, in the end, serve only to conceal that they are founded on nothing other than the force of power and domination itself. As Ward points out, "there is no view from nowhere, no objective knowledge; the view from nowhere is itself a cultural ideology."[173] Thus, for Radical Orthodoxy, the Enlightenment project of unbiased reason and universal values ends up concealing a horrible violence at its core. Milbank observes that the age of "progress" coexists with European imperialism and racism, with concentration camps, and acts of genocide.[174]

The Nouvelle Théologie

Radical Orthodoxy has found natural allies among theologians and philosophers who have sought to challenge the priorities and assumptions that are characteristic of modern and postmodern thought. In particular, one may point to Charles Péguy, Maurice Blondel, Karl Barth, Hans Urs von Balthasar, Louis Bouyer, Alasdair MacIntyre, and Charles Taylor. Above all, however, is the fact that Radical Orthodoxy finds itself in profound continuity with the *nouvelle théologie*, especially with the thought of Henri de Lubac.[175] As we shall see, de Lubac is most relevant for Milbank on the question of nature and grace. Milbank has treated extensively of his thought in his work *The Suspended Middle: Henri de Lubac and the Debate concerning the Supernatural*.

Tradition Rethought

Lawrence Hemming in giving his assessment of Radical Orthodoxy writes that "Radical orthodoxy does not lead us into how to 're-think the tradition'; rather it presents us with a vision of what the tradition looks like as rethought."[176] According to him, it is precisely reading a "tradition within the tradition" that makes Radical Orthodoxy such a fascinating aspect of contemporary Anglo-American theology.[177]

---

173. Ward, *Cities of God*, 237.
174. Milbank, Ward, Pickstock, "Introduction," 1.
175. Oliver, "Henri de Lubac," 395.
176. Hemming, "Radical Orthodoxy's Appeal," 13.
177. Cush, "Radical Orthodoxy: Overview."

Three Primary Philosophical Themes of Radical Orthodoxy

Participation

Chief among the philosophical themes that form the basis of Radical Orthodoxy is the notion of participation (*methexis*).[178] Milbank, Pickstock, and Ward state that "any alternative configuration [instead of participation] perforce reserves a territory independent of God" that will, ultimately, lead to nihilism.[179] Participation permits the finite its own natural integrity without encroaching on the territory of the divine. Participation extends to all aspects of life, including each academic discipline.[180] It means that the world only has being because it shares in the being of God. This sharing has to be understood in a specific way. Steven Shakespeare proposes two rules that govern Radical Orthodoxy's use of this idea:

> Rule One: Participation is not identity. The being of the world (or our own human being) is not the same as God's. Only by keeping to this rule do we stop ourselves taking a part of the world and turning it into an object of unlimited worship. This is our protection against idolatry, and all the domination and cruelty which flows from it.

> Rule Two: Participation does not assume a genuine relationship. We can only understand the being of the world in relation to God. It is God's creative act which gives being to the world. It is the same creative act which makes it possible for us to become like God. The infinite is revealed in and through the finite, limited, worldly, time-bound, material world.[181]

Analogy

Analogy, likewise, is a key philosophical notion for Radical Orthodoxy. A major reason for Radical Orthodoxy's criticism of Duns Scotus is his distortion of the Christian understanding of God and truth, because he maintained that being is a univocal concept. According to Radical

---

178. Cush, "Radical Orthodoxy: Overview."
179. Milbank, Ward, Pickstock, "Introduction," 3.
180. Cush, "Radical Orthodoxy: Overview."
181. Both block quotes are from Shakespeare, *Radical Orthodoxy: Critical Introduction*, 22.

Orthodoxy, Scotus's univocity, which he proposed in an attempt to preserve the uniqueness of God, actually distances the divine from us.[182] Shakespeare notes:

> A further consequence is that, as God is no longer related to us by a living chain of analogy, God becomes ever more hidden and dark to us. God retreats into the heavens, exercising his will from afar. And God's will becomes the arbitrary exercise of power. It has no inner relationship to human worth and fulfilment. God becomes the Law, imposed upon an essentially godless world.[183]

Analogy for Radical Orthodoxy is something dynamic, and not just a dry theory about how words work. It is about a living way of relating to God, ultimately and most excellently expressed in Christian life and worship.[184]

Gift

Another major philosophical theme in Radical Orthodoxy is that of the notion of gift. Milbank asks:

> Why "gift" exactly? The primary reason is that gift is a kind of transcendental category in relation to all the topoi of theology, in a similar fashion to "word." Creation and grace are gifts; Incarnation is the supreme gift; the Fall, evil and violence are the refusal of gift; atonement is the renewed and hyperbolic gift that is for-giveness; the supreme name of the Holy Spirit is *donum* (according to Augustine); the church is the community that is given to humanity and is constituted through the harmonious blending of diverse gifts (according to the apostle Paul).[185]

In Radical Orthodoxy, all is seen within the relational aspect of gift. Tradition, church, Eucharist, reconciliation, indeed, life itself is gift.[186] In contrast to Derrida, Radical Orthodoxy argues for the possibility of "pure gift": one of reciprocity and mutuality. This theme of gift is an essential basis for Radical Orthodoxy's theology and, in particular, in establishing Pickstock's eucharistic theology of presence. All three prime

---

182. Cush, "Radical Orthodoxy: Overview."
183. Shakespeare, *Radical Orthodoxy: Critical Introduction*, 11.
184. Shakespeare, *Radical Orthodoxy: Critical Introduction*, 23.
185. Milbank, *Being Reconciled*, ix.
186. Cush, "Radical Orthodoxy: Overview."

philosophical themes emphasized by Radical Orthodoxy are closely connected. Participation, *analogia entis*, and gift are all tied together within the thought of Radical Orthodoxy.[187] Milbank states:

> So long as Christian theology retained a somewhat Neo-Platonic approach to causality, in which every higher level until that of Godhead not only caused, but also "gave to be," the lower level, it was possible to combine the idea that God is "the total cause" of everything, including the free decisions of spiritual beings, with the equal stress that finite causes are also "total" at their own level. Within this outlook, the higher cause is not "one factor" at the lower level; rather, it "gives" in its integrity the entire lower level with its own self-sufficient (in one sense) modes of operation. This Proclean understanding of cause reaches its apogee within Aquinas's Christian translation, for which what is participated, is being as such. Hence, that which belongs to a thing—its very existence—is yet that which is most received as a gift. All the same, this giftedness of created being by no means cancels the integrity and the autonomy proper to existence as such. Rather, the point is that even this is a gift.[188]

---

187. Cush, "Radical Orthodoxy: Overview."
188. Smith, *Introducing Radical Orthodoxy*, 14.

2

The Nature and Grace Debate
A Historical and Theological Overview

THE NOTION OF HOW nature and grace relate to one another is not merely an arcane matter proper to in-house debate between theologians. Rather, it is an issue that goes to the very heart of what it means to be a Christian. The relation between nature and grace is also one of the most consistently debated issues among twentieth-century Catholic theologians. In fact, it can be said that the topic of nature and grace touches almost any and every theological and human question because it underlies the very notion of the encounter between man and God.[1] Henri de Lubac contended that this issue is "at the heart of all great Christian thought . . . at the bottom of discussions with modern unbelief, and forms the crux of Christian humanism."[2] Therefore, the question of how Christianity relates to modern secular culture, to our every experience of social, economic, and political issues, is a question that is fundamentally theological because it treats of the notions of nature, grace, and culture.

The manner in which theories of how nature and grace relate came about over the centuries is multifaceted and complex. Although Thomas Aquinas had a great deal to say on the matter, arguably the most significant developments on the question of how nature and grace relate to one another, however, occurred in the period following the Reformation. We will therefore take this period as the starting point in our historical

---

1. Swafford and Oakes, *Nature and Grace*, 1.
2. Lubac, *At the Service*, 35.

survey (even as we refer to Aquinas along the way) as we turn now briefly to consider the question.

A SHORT HISTORY OF THE NATURE-GRACE DEBATE

The Reformation

During the time of the Reformation, Catholic theologians were attempting to find a middle ground between two claims that were radically in opposition, namely, Calvinist anthropology, which tended to denigrate human nature, and the Baianist heresy, which tended to make extravagant claims for it. Ratzinger summarized Karl Barth's Calvinist position as follows:

> [For the Calvinist] man as he really lives in history, man in his autonomy vis-à-vis God and in his reflection of himself, does not live in his true nature; instead, an unnatural state has become his nature. To continue and perfect that state would mean to accomplish the self-destructive conclusion of man, to canonize his misery instead of leading him into salvation. For this sort of man, grace cannot be continuation or perfection but only disruption, paradox, thwarting.[3]

Michael De Bay (Baius) (1513–89), a professor of the Catholic University of Leuven, responded to the Calvinist position by stating that humanity, in its state of innocence, had no need of grace. Grace was not viewed as divine assistance that flowed from the goodness of God, and freely given, but was simply humanity's right. In Baius's view, human beings in the state of innocence could attain their end in God by means of purely natural merit. In this way, Baius practically collapsed the supernatural into the natural, as grace was seen as simply a part of the human constitution and not a gift at all. Henri de Lubac, quoting Du Chesne, author of *Histoire du Baianisme*, notes that Baius "attributes everything to nature in the state of innocence, and nothing to grace: that is his crime."[4] In this way, the thesis of Baius approaches that of Pelagius. De Lubac notes that:

> the difference [of Baius] from Pelagius lies only in manner . . . Pelagius's man is prouder, more demanding, but neither

---

3. Ratzinger, *Dogma and Preaching*, 147.
4. Lubac, *Augustinianism and Modern Theology*, 3.

displays the attitude of a son towards his father: "God made me man, I make myself just"—the essence of Pelagianism is to be found in this proud formula. According to Baianism, the rational creature cannot by itself attain to its end, and hence there is discontinuity and obligatory recourse to divine intervention.... What God bestows on it is not received as a gift; it is still something belonging to its nature, not a constituent of its nature, as Pelagius would have it, but a natural requirement. Strictly speaking, it is not an integral part of this nature, but it is something indispensable to the integrity of this nature and therefore essentially required by it.[5]

Baius's failure to maintain the notion of the gratuity of grace, holding instead that man was owed it, merited a response from Pope Pius V, who condemned him in 1567 by means of his papal bull *Ex omnibus afflictionibus*.[6]

The Post-Reformation and Baroque Period

By the time of the late sixteenth and early seventeenth centuries, theologians continued to steer a path through the opposing extremes of Calvinism and Baianism. Part of the solution that they devised was the *Duplex Ordo* and the notion of "pure-nature" (we will consider these concepts in more detail in the second part of the chapter). The origin of the pure-nature thesis rests principally in the work of Cardinal Thomas Cajetan (1469–1534; commonly known as Tommaso de Vio, or Gaetanus), a sixteenth-century Thomist who had defended Catholic doctrine against Lutheranism.[7] Cajetan was of the view that the *Duplex Ordo* theory found strong support in Aquinas's works with antecedents in Aristotelian philosophy. Cajetan addressed the question of whether it was possible for human beings to have a *natural* desire for God. He concluded that a purely natural desire for God was not possible for man. His answer rested on Aristotle's *Physics*, which maintained that human nature was a reality closed in on itself having its own intrinsic powers, desires, and proper ends. The implication of Cajetan's position was the notion that human

---

5. Lubac, *Augustinianism and Modern Theology*, 4.
6. Denzinger and Hünermann, *Enchiridion Symbolorum*, 1901–80.
7. There is, nevertheless, an ongoing debate about the extent to which Cajetan can be said to be the source of the pure-nature concept. See J. Wood, *To Stir a Restless Heart*.

nature was not in and of itself made for union with God. Incremental developments of this idea can be traced through the works of Ruard Tapper (1487–1559) to Luis de Molina (1535–1600), who proposed another key concept of the *Duplex Ordo*, that is, the idea of a *finis naturalis*, which denotes a natural end corresponding to man's natural order.[8]

The Jesuit philosopher Francisco Suárez (1548–1617) developed Molina's notion of the *finis naturalis* and proposed the theory of "pure-nature" by drawing on a text from Aquinas:

> Man is perfected by virtue, for those actions whereby he is directed to happiness, as was stated above (I–II, q. 5, a. 7). Now man's beatitude or happiness is twofold (*duplex hominis beatitudo*), as was also stated above (I–II, q. 5, a. 5). One is proportionate to human nature, a happiness, to wit, which man can obtain by means of his natural principles. The other is a happiness surpassing man's nature, and which man can obtain by the power of God alone, by a kind of participation of the Godhead.[9]

Suárez invoked this text in order to authorize, supposedly in the name of Aquinas, the new doctrine of a purely natural order. It did seem to Suárez, after all, that Aquinas was sanctioning two possible ends for humanity: one natural and due as a matter of justice, and the other supernatural, given as a gift.[10] The theory of pure-nature rests upon the notion that human nature is completely devoid of any natural orientation to the grace of God.[11] In this way, Suárez, via Molina, brought Cajetan's ideas into the mainstream of theology. His account of "extrinsic grace" was developed into a systematic account in two books: *De ultimo fine hominis* (1592), and *De Gratia* (published posthumously in 1619). The final shape given by Suárez to the *Duplex Ordo* thesis would remain more or less consistent for centuries after his death. His influence is particularly evident in the works of John of Thomas, the Salamanca Carmelites, Peter of Godoy, Lessius, Vasques, and more recently, Charles Boyer, and Reginald Garrigou-Lagrange. It is difficult to overstate the extent of Suárez's influence on theology both during his own time and subsequently. Nevertheless, there are some aspects concerning the fact of the widespread

---

8. Denzinger and Hünermann, *Enchiridion Symbolorum*, 1901–80.

9. Aquinas, *Summa Theologica*, I–II, q. 62, a. 1.

10. Aquinas, *Summa Theologica*, I–II, q. 62, a. 1. is often cited in rebuttal of de Lubac's rejection of the pure-nature framework. For his treatment of this question, see Lubac, "Duplex Hominis Beatitudo."

11. For a more detailed discussion of this point, see Riches, "Christology," 44–69.

adoption of the *Duplex Ordo* thesis that remain puzzling, namely, that the adoption of the notion of Suárezian "pure-nature" tends to contradict the traditional way in which the relationship of nature and grace had been conceived in the past. St. Augustine's *cor inquietum*, for example, reveals just such a position that tends against the *Duplex Ordo*.[12] It also seems that Augustine stands within the consensus of the church fathers on this point. This consensus generally points to three conclusions: firstly, that man was created in the image of God, and continues to bear this divine image, which, despite the Fall, has not been corrupted beyond redemption; secondly, that man is called to a divine destiny, for example, the words of Irenaeus: "He became what we are to empower us to become what He is";[13] thirdly, that man's "divinization" was brought about by adoption into the family of God through identification with Christ. Given this, it is difficult to reconcile this patristic tradition with the notion of *Duplex Ordo*. This, at least, is the argument of Henri de Lubac and of other *ressourcement* theologians, as we shall see.

Nonetheless, Augustine's own historical circumstances provided some difficulties for the way in which he explained the relation between nature and grace. Much of his own work was in answer to Pelagianism, against which Augustine insisted that eternal life remained entirely beyond man's efforts alone. While Augustine's approach certainly was an effective rebuttal against the threat of Pelagianism, O'Shea maintains that it had unintended and long-term negative consequences. According to him, Augustine's insistence upon the inadequacy of human nature to reach eternal life on its own fed into the eventual denigration of the same.[14] G. K. Chesterton makes the case in his biography of Francis of Assisi that there were good reasons in the time subsequent to Augustine that would have caused devout Christians to try to avoid emphasizing the goodness of creation. Nevertheless, it took centuries for the European imagination to be cleansed of the associations that nature, or the "flesh," held for them:

> It is no metaphor to say that these people needed a new heaven and a new earth; for they had really defiled their own earth and even their own heaven. How could their case be met by looking at the sky, when erotic legends were scrawled in the stars across it? . . . Nothing could purge this obsession but a religion that was

12. Augustine, *Confessions*, I, 1.
13. Irenaeus, *Against Heresies*, III, 19.
14. O'Shea, "Nature or Grace," 5.

literally unearthly. It was no good telling such people to have a natural religion full of stars and flowers; there was not a flower or even a star that had not been stained. They had to go into the desert where they could find no flowers or even into the caverns where they could see no stars. Into that desert and that cavern the highest human intellect entered for four centuries; and it was the very wisest thing it could do.[15]

Chesterton claims that it was only after the purge of the pagan religious imagination was complete that we could speak again, in the person of St. Francis of Assisi, about fire and water, sun, moon, and stars, although this time they were considered as being one's brothers and sisters under one Creator-God:

> Now the historic importance of St. Francis and the transition from the twelfth to the thirteenth centuries lies in the fact that they marked the end of this expiation. Men at the close of the Dark Ages may have been rude and unlettered and unlearned in everything but wars with heathen tribes, more barbarous than themselves, but they were clean. They were like children; the first beginnings of their rude arts have all the clean pleasure of children . . . . The flowers and stars have recovered their first innocence. Fire and water are felt to be worthy to be the brother and sister of a saint. The purge of paganism is complete at last.[16]

It was against the background of the reemergence of the notion of nature in the twelfth and thirteenth centuries as something not to be rejected that the Scholastics began their enquiry. In dealing with the legacy of Augustine, theologians of the Scholastic period attempted to reconcile the view that human nature bore the continuing image of God with a widespread popular denigration of nature considered to be "sinful flesh." It was Philip the Chancellor (1160–1236) who began using the terms "natural" and "supernatural" to make this distinction. The use of these terms advantageously brought an end to the confusion between sinfulness and finitude and allowed theologians to differentiate conceptually between the natural and supernatural dimensions of human beings, which in fact were united in the same human person.[17] Thomas Aquinas clarified the point further by arguing that supernatural grace humanizes by divinizing:

15. Chesterton, *St. Francis of Assisi*, 22.
16. Chesterton, *St. Francis of Assisi*, 23, 27.
17. O'Shea, "Nature or Grace," 6.

> It is necessary that some supernatural disposition should be added to the intellect in order that it may be raised up to such a great and sublime height. Now since the natural power of the created intellect does not enable it to see the essence of God . . . it is necessary that the power of understanding should be added by divine grace.[18]

At first inspection it may seem that Aquinas is here arguing for separated orders of nature and grace, that is, the conceptual distinction between the natural and the supernatural appears to be an actual separation of two realties in support of the *Duplex Ordo* thesis. On the other hand, it is also arguable that this was not Aquinas's position and that while he acknowledged that there were aspects of human happiness that were attainable through the powers of human nature, these could never truly satisfy man, as this example illustrates:

> Imperfect happiness that can be had in this life, can be acquired by man by his natural powers . . . . But every knowledge that is according to the mode of created substance, falls short of the vision of the Divine Essence . . . . Consequently, neither man nor any creature, can attain final happiness by his natural powers.[19]

Baroque Scholasticism would reify and classify natural and supernatural activities into a two-story world of nature and grace. Yet, as we shall see, later theologians sought to challenge this interpretation of Aquinas's work on nature and grace. In fact, much of the subsequent theological debate on the issue of nature and grace, particularly after Pope Leo XIII's *Aeterni Patris* (1879), centers around the exegesis of Aquinas's treatment of the question of nature and grace. This is because one can cite passages in Aquinas's writings that appear to lend support to the *Duplex Ordo* thesis, and yet other passages that reject this thesis in support of a more intrinsicist position. What broadly differentiates the present-day opposing theological approaches to the question of nature and grace is the interpretation one gives to Aquinas's approach to nature and grace, that is, that his work supports either an intrinsicist or an extrinsicist position. We will subsequently return to this theme to treat of it in greater detail.

---

18. Aquinas, *Summa Theologica*, I, q. 12, a. 5.
19. Aquinas, *Summa Theologica*, I–II, q. 5, a. 5.

The Impact of the *Duplex Ordo* Thesis

The *Duplex Ordo* thesis, which had become predominant in Catholic theology after Suárez, inevitably continued to exert a powerful hold among Catholic scholars. It seemed that Aquinas's synthesis of science, philosophy, and theology was being challenged by the new tendency to separate reality into the natural and the supernatural, which in turn led to the compartmentalization of the Catholic message.[20] Louis Dupré refers to this tendency as the "disintegration of the Thomistic synthesis into an order of pure-nature separate from one of grace."[21] Furthermore, Dupré notes that this same tendency became most evident in the middle of the Baroque period:

> Around 1660, the last comprehensive integration of our culture began to break down into the fragmentary syntheses of a mechanist world picture, a classicist aesthetics and a theological scholasticism. Soon a flat utilitarianism would be ready to serve as midwife to the birth of what Nietzsche called modern man's small soul.[22]

Dupré identifies this moment of history as a turning point because it was at this time that the elite intellectual movement, which had its origins in Renaissance humanism, was separating itself from Christianity and preparing the way for the Enlightenment. What added impetus to this movement was the unsettling of Europe by means of the Thirty Years War (1618–48), which resulted in the unfortunate settlement of *cuius regio, eius religio*, which meant that one's religion would be determined by the local ruler. The conflict between Catholics and Calvinists in France, which resulted in the revocation of the Edict of Tolerance in 1685, also contributed to the difficulties. The unfortunate spectacle of religion, whose intellectual and spiritual teachings could be subverted by politics and judicially sanctioned violence, undermined the credibility of Christianity at that time, and so many of the intellectual class looked upon Christianity with a degree of bitterness. It was in such circumstances that secular humanism was presented as not only a viable, but indeed an attractive, alternative to the bickering and warring of religious groups. It was the former union between "throne and altar" that until then had

---

20. O'Shea, "Nature or Grace," 7.
21. Dupré, *Passage to Modernity*, 174.
22. Dupré, *Passage to Modernity*, 248.

been thought of as essentially unbreakable that ironically only served to expedite the demise of religious sentiment because Christianity had been portrayed as the major contributing cause of the Wars of Religion and had effectively goaded state rulers to acts of barbarity in the pursuit of political goals.[23] The proponents of the emerging secular humanism, however, were able to retain what was thought best about Christianity, namely, the notions of justice, mercy, compassion etc., while at the same time detaching themselves from the demands of an obscurantist faith whose doctrines resisted testing by the principles of human reason. It was in this context that the *Duplex Ordo* was found to be very useful in serving the ends of the rising secular humanism, because secular affairs were now conceptually more easily cut off from those of religious faith. What also added speed to this movement was the rise of technical science. Apologists for the new humanism were able to posit that science had now developed to the point that what had previously defied explanation could now be explained; hence the invocation of a mysterious Creator God had become less necessary. Philosophy likewise kept pace with the demand for new explanations, and philosophers such as Thomas Hobbes (1588–1679) and David Hume (1711–76) were able to offer ways in which it could be undergirded. As in the field of science, so now also in the field of philosophy, the *Duplex Ordo* gave the advantage of creating the possibility of bracketing out God from the equation, and then reintroducing God for the edification of believers only. This possibility would allow Catholic intellectuals to sidestep the charge of obscurantism and make their mark on intellectual debate.[24]

Leonine Thomism and Neo-Scholasticism

By the mid-nineteenth century, philosophical study within the Catholic community was in need of renewal. The French Revolution, the Napoleonic Wars, and the newly formulated modern philosophies had presented significant challenges to the church. A serious attempt at restoration was made in 1879 with the publication of Pope Leo XIII's *Aeterni Patris*. By means of this encyclical, the pope declared that the philosophy of Thomas

---

23. O'Shea, "Nature or Grace," 7.
24. O'Shea, "Nature or Grace," 8.

Aquinas is and would be the "perennial philosophy" of the church. This declaration was the stimulus for the neo-scholastic project.[25]

The term "neo-scholasticism" refers to the recovery and development of the Scholasticism of the Middle Ages during the latter part of the nineteenth century, following *Aeterni Patris*. The Scholasticism of the Middle Ages had been gradually in decline with the advent of humanism in the fifteenth and sixteenth centuries, although it did not entirely disappear.[26] The term "neo-scholasticism" is also often equated with "neo-Thomism," partly because of the notion that it was Aquinas who gave Scholasticism its final form in the thirteenth century; and with "Leonine Thomism," because of Pope Leo XIII's promotion of the same in *Aeterni Patris*. Key scholars associated with this (neo) Scholastic revival were Tommaso Zigliara, OP, Alberto Lepidi, OP, Carlo Maria Curci, SJ, Luigi Taparelli d'Azeglio, SJ, Matteo Liberatore, SJ, and Joseph Kleutgen, SJ. The motivating factor for these contributors, who were responding to Leo XIII's call, was to find in the medieval thinkers, above all in Aquinas, the tools to respond to the challenges of post-Cartesian and post-Kantian philosophy. The basic strategy was to cull philosophical ideas from the Thomist corpus that could be presented as a perennial philosophy impervious to historical influence and marketable to intellectuals of any species anywhere, untouched by historical factors and absolutely rational. Aquinas's theology could then be added to this philosophical base

---

25. O'Shea, "Nature or Grace," 8. The most prominent schools of the twentieth century and contemporary Catholic theology can be typically traced back to one or other of two orientations. Firstly, an orientation that is focused on eighteenth-century issues about rationality and universal human nature, or secondly, an orientation that is focused on nineteenth-century issues about history, tradition, and human particularity. It may be argued that the preconciliar theological establishment was focused on responding to the intellectual criticism of Catholicism that arose in the eighteenth century, whereas Vatican II scholars, influenced by existentialism in philosophy and the salvation history debates in Protestant theology, were more interested in nineteenth-century issues concerning the role of history in the development of dogma and the formation of the human person. The interest of the Vatican II generation in the theological significance of history (Ratzinger among them) led to a confrontation with the Scholastic approaches to doctrinal development and other foundational theological concepts that came to dominate the theological academies after the promulgation of *Aeterni Patris*, often meriting these scholars the accusation of "modernism," such as occurred with Ratzinger's *Habilitationsschrift*. See also Rowland, "Neo-Scholasticism," 29.

26. Scholasticism did experience somewhat of a revival in the sixteenth century (although some would argue that it always persevered within the Dominican Order) by contributors such as Thomas de Vio Cajetan (1469–1534), Gabriel Vásquez (1551–1604), Toletus (1532–96), Fonseca (1528–99), and especially Francisco Suárez (1548–1617).

for those to whom it was relevant. It was typical of Thomism of this period to be presented to seminarians and theological students in the form of handbooks or manuals.[27]

Various schools of interpretation of Aquinas had existed since the sixteenth century and one could make the case that every generation read Aquinas with the intention of finding answers for the questions of their own age. This dynamic necessarily resulted in different theological approaches to different questions. At the time of Pope Leo XIII, however, many theologians were convinced that medieval philosophy and theology were homogenous enough in their essential parts so as to produce a "scholastic synthesis" of timeless value.[28] The idea was that philosophy does not have to vary with each passing phase of history and that the truth of many hundreds of years ago is still true today. Therefore, if the great medieval thinkers (Aquinas, Bonaventure, and Scotus) succeeded in constructing a sound philosophical system on the data supplied by the Greeks, especially by Aristotle, it must be possible to gather, from the speculation of the Middle Ages, the soul of truth that it contains. In this way, neo-scholasticism sought to respond to the challenge of modernism and relativism by adopting a theological system that would give direction to the universal church, by presenting a form of the faith that was distilled, perennial, and above history.[29] Despite these attempts, it soon became apparent that the claimed homogeneity in medieval Thomism was no homogeneity at all, and that there existed considerable differences in the schools of the Middle Ages that resulted consequently in different schools of neo-scholasticism. The situation became so challenging to the desired synthesis that in 1914 Pope Pius X issued the *motu proprio*,

---

27. Rowland, *Catholic Theology*, 50. Balthasar, for example, dismissively spoke of his seminary training in "sawdust Thomism." See Ruddy, "*Ressourcement*," 185. Also, Kenny speaks of an experience at the Gregorian University in Rome, where he recalls Paolo Dezza, a professor of metaphysics, "sitting totally motionless, he enunciated rheumily, in a barely audible voice, theses about the analogy of being and the varieties of potentiality and actuality." See Kenny, *Path from Rome*, 47.

28. Rossi, "Neo-Scholastic to Vatican II," 2.

29. Mettepenningen describes this method as beginning with Roman texts, which constituted the background and determined the degree of openness to history. This meant that theologies took these texts as their point of departure, arriving by way of deduction at new faith insights that were completely compatible with existing tenets of the magisterium's articulation of the faith (i.e., a combination of both so-called "Denzinger theology" and "conclusion theology"). Theology therefore centered around its method of reaching Denzinger-compatible conclusions via a logically correct reasoning built on Catholic and non-disputable premises. See Mettepenningen, "*Nouvelle Théologie*," 173–74.

Doctoris Angelici, and a month later the Congregation for Studies published a statement of twenty-four theses on the fundamental points of Thomistic philosophy. This was a concerted attempt to expel Suárezianism and Scotism from the church. Despite this attempt, neo-scholasticism became the undisputed pillar of Catholic thought at the time.[30]

In his *Three Rival Versions of Moral Enquiry*, Alasdair MacIntyre criticizes the Thomism of this era for its alleged misreading of the integration of Aristotelian and Augustinian thought in Aquinas. Specifically, he accused the Leonine scholars of anachronistically reading Aquinas as if he were answering questions to epistemological problems only raised by or after Descartes. The most well-known proponent of this approach was Kleutgen. MacIntyre further points out that while these scholars may have been correct to notice that there had been a rupture in the discipline of philosophy, a *modern* and *premodern* philosophy as it were, Kleutgen was wrong to see Descartes as the moment of rupture. According to MacIntyre, the moment of rupture actually began with the late Scholastics and is particularly evident in the works of Suárez, who is "more authentically than Descartes the founder of modern philosophy."[31] MacIntyre concludes that the effect of this Thomism was to foster a variety of different Thomisms in the twentieth century depending on the preferred epistemological starting points of individual scholars. For example, another form of Thomism, named neo-Thomism (and probably the most nebulous of all the labels) came to prominence in the years between the death of Leo XIII and the beginning of the pontificate of Paul VI. One of the main streams of neo-Thomism was to continue along Kleutgen's trajectory, giving priority to epistemological issues and the recovering of Baroque commentators in order to have the material to be able to respond to modern-day opponents. Theologians of this school included Ambroise Gardeil (1859–1931), founder of *Le Saulchoir*, and Réginald Garrigou-Lagrange (1877–1964). The outcome for the nature-grace relationship among these thinkers was the revival of the Suárezian notion of the *Duplex Ordo*, which continued to form part of priestly theological studies until the mid 1960s.[32] The other main stream of neo-Thomism stood along the lines of the historical school of interpretation of Étienne Gilson (1884–1978) and

---

30. Rossi, "Neo-Scholastic to Vatican II," 3. See also Rowland, "Neo-Scholasticism"; Ruddy, "*Ressourcement*."

31. MacIntyre, *Three Rival Versions*, 73.

32. O'Shea, "Nature or Grace," 9.

Marie-Dominique Chenu (1895–1990), who thought that Aquinas had to be read in the context of the historical circumstances and influences of his time.[33] Chenu accused the Leonine Thomists and those of the Kleutgen school of thought of relying too heavily on Baroque commentaries and of failing to pay sufficient attention to primary sources and historical contexts.[34] Consequently, in order to distinguish themselves from the followers of Kleutgen, these neo-Thomists went on to form what became known as the *nouvelle théologie*.

The Nouvelle Théologie

The crisis in French society in the latter part of the nineteenth century finally came to a head between World Wars I and II. It was in the context of these turbulent times that a new theological project named the *nouvelle théologie* emerged. It was composed mainly of Jesuits based at the Fourvière theologate in Lyon and of Dominicans at *Le Saulchoir*, first located in Tournai, Belgium, then Paris. These theologians sought greater theological appropriation of modern categories of history, concrete philosophy, and political engagement. They drew from the philosophy of Maurice Blondel (1861–1949) and embarked on a method called *ressourcement*, which was an attempt to return to the sources and recover various Neoplatonic patristic writings that offered a counter-theology to the dominant neo-scholasticism of Leonine Thomism. It is difficult to overstate the influence that Blondel's method had on these young scholars, particularly Henri de Lubac. For the students of his generation, Blondel's text *L'Action* was like an order of release. It liberated men's spirits and reconciled intellectual ambitions with apostolic energies under the aegis of the concept of "action."[35] In fact de Lubac credited to Blondel the "main impulse" for Latin theology's "return to a more authentic tradition."[36]

The main proponents of the *nouvelle théologie* were Henri de Lubac (1896–1991), Jean Daniélou (1905–74), Henri Bouillard (1908–81), Gaston Fessard (1897–1978), Yves de Montcheuil (1900–44), and Dominicans Marie-Dominique Chenu (1895–1990), Yves Congar (1904–95),

---

33. Rossi, "Neo-Scholastic to Vatican II," 4.
34. Rowland, *Catholic Theology*, 53.
35. Tilliette, "Henri de Lubac," 335.
36. Lubac, *Brief Catechesis*, 37. See also Conway, "Maurice Blondel," 65.

Louis Charlier (1898–1981), Henri-Marie Féret (1904–92), and René Draguet (1896–1980).[37]

The name *nouvelle théologie* was first applied to this movement in a critical article published in *L'Osservatore Romano* in 1942, and gained widespread currency after a controversial piece published in 1946 by the neo-scholastic Dominican Réginald Garrigou-Lagrange that was titled "La nouvelle théologie où va-t-elle?"[38] While the term remains somewhat elusive, not least because some of the major figures with which it was associated denied the existence of such a movement, it nonetheless denotes a movement composed primarily of Jesuits and Dominicans that flourished from the mid 1930s until its condemnation by Pius XII's encyclical *Humani Generis* in 1950.[39]

Although there may be some debate concerning the inclusion of some peripheral theologians in the *nouvelle théologie*, it seems settled that the core group was comprised of de Lubac, Daniélou, Chenu, and Congar. Notwithstanding the evident personal and intellectual diversity of even these core members of the group, certain broad parallels, aims, and endeavors clearly mark the bounds of the movement. Jürgen Mettepenningen provides a useful analysis that traces four central characteristics. The *nouvelle théologie* was firstly, and fundamentally, a French movement; secondly, it was eager to appropriate the historical method; thirdly, it was strongly in favor of positive theology; and finally, it was hostile to neo-scholasticism.[40] This final point is critical as it was neo-scholasticism that vehemently opposed the *nouvelle théologie's* particular embrace of history and positive theology.[41] The *nouvelle théologie* effectively sought to foment a revolt from its speculative strictures and implement a *ressourcement* methodology that would facilitate a retrieval of medieval sources as well as various church fathers more readily compatible with certain modern philosophical, theological, and political concerns.[42] Far from being an ancillary problem, this was the central

37. Kirwan, *Avant-Garde Theological Generation*, 4. See also Flynn and Murray, *Ressourcement*, 2.

38. Garrigou-Lagrange, "Nouvelle théologie," 126–45.

39. Kirwan, *Avant-Garde Theological Generation*, 5.

40. Mettepenningen, "*Nouvelle Théologie*," 7–13.

41. The opposition between the *nouvelle théologie* and neo-scholasticism, typified by the battle between de Lubac and Garrigou-Lagrange, has been described by Kerr as the "most bitter theological controversy of the twentieth century." See Kerr, *After Aquinas*, 134.

42. Mettepenningen, "*Nouvelle Théologie*," 7–13. See also Komonchak, "Vatican

issue confronting modern Catholic theology in the twentieth century: the relation between the historical character of human existence and human knowledge and the supposedly absolute, unchanging truth claims of Christian Revelation.

The importance of the theological inheritance of the *nouvelle théologie* is evident in the four significant theological schools that continue to draw inspiration from its work: firstly, those gathered around the Catholic journal *Communio*, such as Ratzinger; secondly, the more liberal-minded coalition of transcendental Thomists and other theologians gathered around the journal *Concilium*; thirdly, the largely Anglican Radical Orthodoxy movement, to which Milbank belongs; and finally, certain evangelicals who find in the *nouvelle théologie* a deeper sense of tradition.[43]

Of the core founders of the *nouvelle théologie*, the most important in considering Ratzinger's and Milbank's approach to nature and grace is undoubtedly de Lubac, as it was he who provided the most profound challenge to the regnant *Duplex Ordo* in his seminal work, *Surnaturel*. He developed his thesis further in three later works: *Augustinianism and Modern Theology* (1967), *The Mystery of the Supernatural* (1967), and *A Brief Catechesis on Nature and Grace* (1981).

Many consider de Lubac to be one of the most influential theologians of the twentieth century. Born in Cambrai, France, on February 20, 1896, he undertook his formation in the aftermath of the First World War, a time of great social and theological ferment for French Jesuits such as de Lubac. At the age of seventeen, he joined the Society of Jesus; however, due to the expulsion in 1902 from France of religious teaching communities, de Lubac pursued most of his studies abroad in England, though his studies were cut short the following year, 1914, when he was drafted into the French army with the outbreak of the First World War. He served until his demobilization in 1919. During the war he received numerous injuries, including a head wound that would plague him with headaches and dizzy spells for the rest of his life.[44]

De Lubac resumed his studies, first at Canterbury and then in the Jesuit philosophate on the island of Jersey. In 1926 he moved to Lyon to complete his remaining studies and was ordained a priest the following

---

II," 76–99; Fédou, "*Sources Chrétiennes*," 781–96; and Grégoire de Nysse, *Vie de Moïse*, specifically Jean Daniélou's preface.

43. Mettepenningen, "*Nouvelle Théologie*," 7–13.
44. Voderholzer, *Meet Henri de Lubac*, 11.

year. In 1929 de Lubac was appointed the professor of fundamental theology at the Catholic Theological Faculty at Lyon, on the central Presqu'île peninsula on the western side of the Rhône. He continued to teach there until, with the outbreak of the Second World War, he was forced to go underground as he assisted in the publication of a journal of Nazi resistance. In 1942 he co-founded, with Daniélou, *Sources Chrétiennes*, a series of patristic texts with translations.[45]

In contrast to the neo-scholasticism at the time, particularly following Pope Leo XIII's encyclical *Aeterni Patris*, de Lubac's embrace of the controversial *ressourcement* (which was an attempt to reread the fathers in the light of contemporary concerns) meant that in 1950 Pope Pius XII in *Humani Generis* disapproved of de Lubac's ideas (even though he didn't specifically mention de Lubac), and consequently, he was removed from his position as professor. He was not allowed to return to his post at the college until 1958. In 1960 Pope John XXIII appointed de Lubac as a consultant to the Preparatory Theological Commission for the Second Vatican Council. De Lubac was later made a member of the Theological Commission by Pope Paul VI. Following the council, de Lubac continued to write, and together with Ratzinger and several others, he founded the journal *Communio*. In 1983 at the age of eighty-seven, Pope John Paul II raised de Lubac to the College of Cardinals, and he received the red biretta and the deaconry of S. Maria in Dominica on February 2, 1983. He died on September 4, 1991, in Paris, and is buried in a tomb of the Society of Jesus at the Vaugirard cemetery in Paris.

One of the main motivating factors for de Lubac's thinking on nature and grace was the growing secularization of the European heart and mind. De Lubac wished to set out a Christian humanism for postwar Europe, one that could link man's beatitude to the supernatural order of grace. One of de Lubac's main influences was the Jesuit Pierre Rousselot (1878–1915), who made an important contribution to the study of the relation between nature and grace in Aquinas. Rousselot drew on the insights of Cajetan and Suárez and also nineteenth-century neo-scholasticism; however, in contrast to these, Rousselot saw human nature in Aquinas's doctrine as having a natural capacity for God. De Lubac was clearly influenced by this idea, and in his *Surnaturel* he actually went further. While Rousselot maintained the Suárezian notion of pure-nature, de Lubac proposed that such a notion should not be considered since,

---

45. Grumett, *De Lubac*, 5.

in his view, it was a late and wrong interpretation of Aquinas, and was undermining the evangelical mission of the church. He made the observation that it also had never received universal acceptance:

> These theories, unknown to both the Greek and the Latin Fathers . . . were never universally accepted in the West, and were unknown or denied both by the majority of Orthodox theologians and the Christian philosophers of modern Russia.[46]

De Lubac, for his part, was also greatly interested in the history of Baianism, and subsequently Jansenism, so much so that two-fifths of his *Mystery of the Supernatural*, and one third of his *Augustinianism and Modern Theology* treat of it. In both books, de Lubac develops an argument he first articulated in a two-part article that appeared in the Jesuit *Recherches de sciences religieuses* in 1931. That article was entitled "Deux Augustiniens fourvoyés: Baius et Jansenius," and argued, as its title announces, that Baius and Jansen were two "Augustinians astray." His point is that, although they strayed into heresy, they had nevertheless started from the sound Catholic tradition represented by Augustine, who, according to de Lubac, never even considered the concept of pure-nature or the *Duplex Ordo*. The reason this history interested de Lubac was that it explains how a chasm opened up between France (or, more broadly, the West) and Christianity, which in a sense was the main motivating factor for de Lubac's work.[47] Specifically, de Lubac differed from the neo-scholastics in his approach to the discipline of theology, the notion of Revelation, the understanding of tradition, his theological anthropology (including his understanding of nature and grace), his analysis of the causes of secularism, his ecclesiology, and more particularly in relation to Garrigou-Lagrange, his opposition to the Vichy government and support for the French resistance.[48]

Louis Dupré points out that the rediscovery of the works of Aristotle in the twelfth and thirteenth centuries loosened the link between philosophy and theology such that philosophy attempted to establish its own idea of God by means of arguments attained by independent reason.[49] The rigid separation attending the study of philosophy and theology and the secularization of politics and empirical sciences all reflected the notion

---

46. Lubac, *Brief Catechesis*, 24.
47. Mulcahy, *Aquinas's Notion*, 244.
48. Kerr, *After Aquinas*, 134.
49. Dupré, "Natural Desire," 82.

of separation between nature and grace. This separation also meant that theology, formerly considered to be queen of the sciences, was relegated to the sidelines, isolated. According to de Lubac, this meant that religion was separated from the mainstream of human and cultural life, and in its place arose a secular humanism that was and still is convinced of its own self-sufficiency apart from any notion of God. De Lubac did not dispute the fact that the sacred and the profane play different roles but made the point that this distinction is a necessary mental abstraction, an acknowledgment that human thought is incapable of God-like apprehension of everything simultaneously and must proceed by putting together different aspects of reality by analysis and synthesis. De Lubac's thesis was not meant to be a description of that actual state of human affairs, but rather an attempt to explain how the gifts of nature and grace could be intrinsically related if they were two separate gifts, otherwise he would be accused of Baianism. For de Lubac, to say that grace is *merely* given to complete an already existing pure-nature means to give the impression that grace is an added optional extra. He stressed that human nature exists to receive grace—grace does not exist for the sake of human nature; the purpose of nature is to receive grace, even though nature can still function in some attenuated form without it.[50] This thesis was, not unexpectedly, met with a degree of controversy especially by neo-scholastic thinkers who were themselves proponents of the *Duplex Ordo*, the prevalent thesis of the time. According to Balthasar:

> With *Surnaturel*, a young David comes onto the field against the Goliath of the modern rationalization and reduction to logic of the Christian mystery. The sling deals a death blow, but the acolytes of the giant seize upon the champion and reduce him to silence for a long time [a reference to the rejection of his thesis by Pius XII].[51]

The desire for a more intrinsic alignment of nature and grace served as the foundation of his Christian humanism (in his view the only true humanism), the motivation for which was a renewed attempt at establishing contact between Catholic theology and contemporary thought. For de Lubac, the church's inability to engage with the increasingly secular culture of post-Enlightenment France was a direct result of the predominant conception of the nature-grace framework.

50. O'Shea, "Nature or Grace," 10.
51. Balthasar, *Theology of Henri de Lubac*, 63.

De Lubac utilizes the theological category of "paradox" as a hermeneutical lens that enables a theologian to hold two essential truths together. It allows him to embrace the fullness of the ontological mystery of faith in its integral unity. On the other hand, de Lubac maintains that without the use of paradox, human reason tends naturally to emphasize one aspect of a given mystery over another, attempting to alleviate the tension between various dimensions of a particular mystery of faith. De Lubac thus contends that paradox is the only way to retain the ontological unity and integrity of any given mystery of faith, especially that of nature and grace.[52]

De Lubac stresses that the theologian must be cognizant of one's "ontological humility" (*humilité ontologique*) as he states: "the I who aspires is not the I who requires."[53] This is why de Lubac tends to eschew the categories of "need" and "debt" in engaging the question of nature and grace, as is common in the *Duplex Ordo* tradition, opting instead to frame the response in terms of "love" and "gift."[54] It was this recasting of the debate that significantly changed the discussion, and decisively in de Lubac's favor.

Notwithstanding the initial opposition he received, the fact remains that much of de Lubac's teaching would be adopted by the Second Vatican Council, some of it even appearing almost verbatim. An example of this is the statement in *Gaudium et Spes*, §22: "Christ, the final Adam, by the Revelation of the mystery of the Father and his love, fully reveals man to man himself," which mirrors de Lubac's comments in his work *Catholicism*: "By revealing the Father and by being revealed by him, Christ completes the revelation of man to himself."[55] Another notable example is from the *Compendium of the Social Doctrine of the Church*:

> The likeness with God shows that the essence and existence of man are constitutively related to God in the most profound manner. This is a relationship that exists in itself, *it is therefore not something that comes afterwards and is not added from the outside. The whole of man's life is a quest and a search for God.* This relationship with God can be ignored or even forgotten or dismissed, but it can never be eliminated. Indeed, among all

---

52. Swafford and Oakes, *Nature and Grace*, 51.

53. Lubac, *Surnaturel*, 484. My translation. Original as follows: "Le moi qui aspire n'est pas un moi qui réclame."

54. Lubac, *Mystery of the Supernatural*, 207.

55. Lubac, *Catholicism*, 339.

the world's visible creatures, only man has a "capacity for God" (*homo est Dei capax*). The human being is a personal being created by God to be in relationship with him; man finds life and self-expression only in relationship, and *tends naturally to God*.[56]

In recent years, however, there has been a significant resurgence in the pure-nature tradition.[57] Andrew Swafford notes that perhaps what had led to this phenomenon is the vigor of the shift at the Second Vatican Council towards intrinsicism that has given rise to the perception that the pendulum perhaps has moved *too* far in that direction. It is in the postconciliar context where we tend to find the perception that the transcendent and supernatural character of grace has been lost. It is this perception that has given rise to the resurgence of the pure-nature tradition.[58]

THE THEOLOGICAL PARTICULARS OF THE NATURE-GRACE DEBATE

From the foregoing discussion, one can summarize the diversity of views on the nature-grace question by grouping them into two broad schools of thought: (1) the *Duplex Ordo*, pure-nature framework, which tends to relate nature and grace more extrinsically, that is, the necessity of distinguishing between nature and grace for the purpose of preserving the supernatural transcendence and gratuity of grace; (2) a *Christocentric* framework that emphasizes that Christ is at the center and end of all things, and that tends to correlate nature and grace more intrinsically. This second position is maintained predominantly by theologians of the *nouvelle théologie*. This chapter will now proceed to a more detailed examination of the main features of each of these approaches as well as of other relevant concepts concerning the same.

Extrinsicism vs. Intrinsicism

As already stated, the two positions of the *Duplex Ordo* and *Christocentrism* broadly form two approaches to the nature-grace question. In a more general sense, they correspond respectively to perhaps the better-known titles of "extrinsicism" and "intrinsicism." These terms denote the

---

56. Pontifical Council for Justice and Peace, *Compendium*, §109. My emphasis.
57. See Feingold, *Natural Desire*; and Long, *Natura Pura*.
58. Swafford and Oakes, *Nature and Grace*, 84. See also Lubac, *Brief Catechesis*, 177–90.

degree of proximity, or otherwise, to which they conceive of the relation of the orders of nature and grace. Put another way, intrinsicism and extrinsicism indicate the closeness or lack of closeness with which they correlate human nature with the gift of grace. Extrinsicism emphasizes the distinction of nature and grace for the purpose of preserving the supernatural and transcendent gratuity of grace over and against human nature. Intrinsicism, on the other hand, holds that human nature is inherently open and oriented to the supernatural order of grace. This means that man's fulfilment lies only in and through Christ, and likewise, that to speak of a purely "natural" beatitude is simply not possible.[59]

Extrinsicism

Extrinsicists make the case that their approach to the question of nature and grace finds its origin in Scripture. An example of this is St. Paul's exclamation about salvation far exceeding the created natural order: "What no eye has seen, nor ear heard, nor the heart of man conceived, what God has prepared for those who love him." (1 Cor 2:9; cf. Isa 64:4).

In order for grace to "surpass" the natural order, or to be considered "supernatural," one must presuppose some notion of the "natural."[60] According to St. Paul: "if anyone is in Christ, he is a new creation; the old has passed away, behold, the new has come" (2 Cor 5:17); thus, man's new creation in Christ through supernatural participation by divine grace surpasses his original creation in *imago Dei*, since he now shares in the very filiation of the Son of God. Hence St. John's words: "See what love the Father has given us, that we should be called children of God; and so we are" (1 John 3:1). While man's original *imago Dei* is restored in Christ, the New Testament goes beyond this primordial restoration, stating that man is now "conformed to the image of his Son" (Rom 8:29), whereby man has now become a "son in the Son."[61] Man's salvation in Christ is a supernatural work of divine grace as it is a gift that goes above and beyond the parameters of human nature. According to extrinsicists, the distinction therefore between the first creation and the new creation (between nature and grace, in other words) is necessary for the purpose of preserving the supernatural transcendence of grace. This distinction

---

59. Swafford and Oakes, *Nature and Grace*, 6.
60. Swafford and Oakes, *Nature and Grace*, 4.
61. John Paul II, *Veritatis Splendor*, §17.

also presupposes the independent coherence of the natural order, or else it would not be possible for it to be distinguished from grace.[62]

The English writer and apologist C. S. Lewis also adopts this line of reasoning when he describes Christianity as a religion in which God encounters man from the "outside," that is, in terms of God's pursuit of man and not contrarywise. That is, supernatural grace comes to man from without, as something over and above his nature:

> To be frank, we do not at all like the idea of a "chosen people." Democrats by birth and education, we should prefer to think that all nations and individuals start level in the search for God, or even that all religions are equally true. It must be admitted at once that Christianity makes no concessions to this point of view. It does not tell of a human search for God at all, but of something done by God for, to, and about, Man.[63]

The point that Lewis makes is that Christianity is able to present itself as a supernatural religion precisely because it is founded upon the divine initiative, an initiative that enters into the created order, from the top down, as a matter of divine descent, rather than one of man's purported ascent. As stated, in order to have an understanding of grace as something that is over and above nature, one must have an understanding of what constitutes human nature in the first place. Without a sense of the coherence of nature *as* nature, grace loses its specificity. In other words, if one cannot speak about nature, then the term *supernatural* becomes unclear. The question of how precisely the integrity and coherence of nature *as* nature can be reconciled with Christocentrism (intrinsicism) is certainly part of the nature and grace debate as it has unfolded in theology over the course of the last centuries.

Extrinsicist thinkers point to many passages in Aquinas that purport to support this position. One example is Aquinas's notion of "limbo" as a possible final state. The interpretation of this idea by extrinsicists infers a lack of suffering in limbo that amounts to a purely natural beatitude, which in turn supports the thesis of pure-nature:

> Man endowed with only natural powers would be without the divine vision if he were to die in this state, but nevertheless the debt of not having it would not be applicable to him. For it is one thing not to be bound to have, which does not have the nature

---

62. Swafford and Oakes, *Nature and Grace*, 5.
63. Lewis, *Miracles*, 187.

of punishment but of defect only, and it is another thing to be bound not to have, which does have the nature of punishment.[64]

Despite this position, Swafford makes the point that the speculative question regarding man's natural end (in contradistinction to the historical and exegetical one) is probably not best adjudicated by recourse to the final state of limbo because such a concept is less universally available in the present context than it used to be in the era of Aquinas. It is likely that Aquinas considered limbo to have been established church teaching, so one might suppose that (had this not been the case) he would not have come so close to affirming the possibility of man's purely natural end in the present economy.[65] On the other hand, there is much support in Aquinas for at least the *intelligible* distinction between man's proportionate natural end and his disproportionate supernatural end. For example:

> Man by his nature is proportioned to a certain end for which he has a natural appetite, and which he can work to achieve by his natural powers. This end is a certain contemplation of the divine attributes, in the measure in which this is possible for man through his natural powers; and in this end even the philosophers placed the final happiness of man. But God has prepared man for another end, one that exceeds the proportionality of human nature. This end is eternal life, which consists in the vision of God in his essence, an end which exceeds the proportionality of any created nature, being connatural to God alone.[66]

Such statements as this one seem to have provided the pure-nature tradition with enough impetus to move on in its development, the key moment of which seems to have come when Cajetan expounded the rudiments of the pure-nature tradition in his commentary on Aquinas's *Summa Theologiae*. Cajetan's work gave the impression that he was merely expounding Aquinas's teaching, and, in so doing, bolstering the authority of the growing pure-nature tradition.[67] By the time of Suárez, the pure-nature tradition had taken a massive leap forward.[68] By the seventeenth century, the codification of the extrinsicist system was said to have been largely complete such that from Cajetan to Garrigou-Lagrange

---

64. Aquinas, *On Evil*, q. 5, a. 15.
65. Swafford and Oakes, *Nature and Grace*, 40.
66. Aquinas, *Questiones Disputatae de Veritate*, q. 27, a. 2.
67. Lubac, *Augustinianism and Modern Theology*, 113.
68. Lubac, *Augustinianism and Modern Theology*, 157.

there seems to be a virtually unbroken lineage. In fact, the dominance of the extrinsicist tradition appears to have been so strong that even the Jesuits and the Dominicans were of the same mind on the matter:

> Suárez completed the work of forming a classical synthesis concerning the interpretation of the natural desire to see God that remained basically unchanged for over three hundred years .... Later writers develop various points but add little that is substantively new.[69]

Pope Pius V's condemnation of Baius above all else ensured the rigid use and enduring hegemony of the pure-nature tradition.[70] The notion of "pure-nature," considered as a conceptual understanding of human nature apart from grace, was a useful tool in responding to Baius as well as Jansenius, who held a similar anthropology. As we have seen, both Baius and Jansenius attempted to revive what they held to be the teaching of St. Augustine, and, in so doing, they exaggerated humanity's postlapsarian state to the point that the integrity of man's nature, *qua* nature, seemed to dissipate. Henri Rondet describes Baius's teaching as follows:

> His thought can be characterized quite simply. For the *primitive state* of man, Baius admits neo-Pelagianism which was seeking to take hold along with Renaissance ideas. But in regard to *fallen* man, he adopts a somewhat mitigated form of the Protestant theses.[71]

This means that, after sin, man appears to have a certain exigency for grace in order to do any good at all; in other words, grace is necessary. On Baius's account, the pristine state of man before sin is one in which man could quite literally have earned salvation as if by right. Given man's postlapsarian state, however, his free will is so corrupted that without the grace of Christ he cannot do any good.[72]

The theological problem that then emerges is that if man's nature stood in strict need of grace, then it seems that grace must be necessary in order for man to do anything good, given the extent of his depravity. If grace were utterly necessary, then it would no longer seem to be gratuitous, that is, a personal gift of God to man to which man is not entitled. If grace, on the other hand, is taken to be more or less necessary for the

---

69. Feingold, *Natural Desire*, 276.
70. Denzinger and Hünermann, *Enchiridion Symbolorum*, 1901–80.
71. Rondet, *Grace of Christ*, 314.
72. Denzinger and Hünermann, *Enchiridion Symbolorum*, 1901–80.

operation of postlapsarian human nature, then it could be construed as a necessary aspect of human nature. Though this is not strictly the position of Baius or Jansenius, it is nevertheless how matters would have appeared to the pure-nature tradition. The pure-nature tradition holds that human nature is self-contained and integral in its own right and for that reason has no strict exigency for anything beyond what is contained within the definition of its nature. This means that it cannot be said that grace is necessary for the functioning of human nature as this would negate the gratuity of grace. According to Stephen Long, pure-nature involves a twofold claim:

> (1) that even here and now, in the concrete order, there is impressed upon each human person a natural order to the proximate, proportionate, natural end from which the species of man is derived, an end that is in principle naturally knowable and distinct from the final and supernatural end; and (2) that the human person could *without injustice* have been created with this natural ordering alone, outside of sanctifying grace, *in puris naturalibus*, and without the further ordering of man to supernatural beatific vision (for the call to grace is an unmerited gift).[73]

The concept of "pure" nature represents the coherent and hypothetical possibility that God could have ordained a purely natural order, an order that may not include the possibility of any offer of grace or of the beatific vision. For the purely natural order, man would have a purely natural end, one that would suffice for his natural beatitude but would fall far short of the beatific vision. For pure-nature thinkers, natural beatitude would be "perfect" *secundum quid*, according to the proportionate good of human nature. The beatific vision, on the other hand, constitutes a perfect beatitude *absolutely speaking* that is radically disproportionate to human nature and proportionate only to God.[74]

According to the pure-nature tradition, the hypothetical possibility of a purely natural order is necessary for the purpose of preserving the gratuity of supernatural grace. Aaron Riches notes that:

> the distinction [between nature and grace] serves, among other things, to safeguard the gratuity of the beatific end achieved in Christ: becoming a "partaker of the divine nature" surpasses

---

73. Long, *Natura Pura*, 8. Emphasis in original.
74. Swafford and Oakes, *Nature and Grace*, 43.

every capacity of human nature and therefore entails "being receptive" to the divine gift upon gift of union in Jesus Christ.[75]

That is, grace must be extrinsic to man's nature as such, meaning that man's nature must be capable of existing without it (at least hypothetically), otherwise one cannot maintain the gratuity of grace. This is what led Balthasar (certainly not an extrinsicist) to acknowledge the utility of the pure-nature tradition in the context of formulating a response to Baius:

> To pose such a hypothesis, to maintain that a graceless order of nature or creation is at least *possible*, only became urgent for theology when a heretic wanted to make the fluid bond between nature and the supernatural a forced and juridical one. This happened when Baius chose to derive a *de jure* compulsory right to grace understood as a strict requirement (*debitum*) from nature based on the *de facto* configuration of both orders, which were linked because of grace, not necessity. The "No" that the church had to pronounce against this sclerosis of the mystery of grace and of its laws and necessities must be understood within the confines of this intent.[76]

Balthasar however notes that this late-medieval/early-modern functional utility later took on a life of its own:

> In other words, the concept was functional, intended to preserve God's freedom *vis-à-vis* nature and the underivability of the Covenant from creation. But this conceptual hypothesis, which was not even necessary before Baius, soon managed to develop into a full system detached from its *theological* presuppositions, and on that basis took on a life of its own.[77]

Given these considerations, and this historical context, when Pope Pius V condemned the teaching of Baius, it seemed to many as though the pure-nature tradition was receiving *ipso facto* papal approval.[78] According to Pelikan:

---

75. Riches, "Christology," 46.
76. Balthasar, *Theology of Karl Barth*, 269.
77. Balthasar, *Theology of Karl Barth*, 269.
78. Denzinger and Hünermann, *Enchiridion Symbolorum*, 1901–80.

> These official proscriptions of extreme Augustinianism appeared to some to be putting the public doctrine of the church on the side of those whom Baius and Jansen had been attacking.[79]

It is also true that many of Baius's propositions directly contradict Aquinas, which would also have given the impression that the pure-nature tradition was itself of high-theological pedigree.[80] Of these propositions, what is most relevant for present purposes concerns his inability to consider man's nature in abstraction from his existential conditions, either before or after the Fall. As Rondet states, it seems that Baius had too high of a view of human nature *before* the Fall, only to be followed by too low of one *after* the Fall:

> Baius grants innocent man the power of accomplishing his destiny all by himself, but he thinks that fallen man is incapable of any good whatsoever without Christ's grace.[81]

This observation relates to Baius's notion that the role of grace serves medicinal purposes as ordered towards the healing of man's nature wounded by sin; that is, Baius does not have a robust notion of the elevating nature of grace, which runs contrary to Aquinas. This theme forms part of the historical context of the Council of Trent, which itself was careful to describe man's original state as "constituted" in a state of grace rather than as one of being "created" in a state of grace.[82] This subtle difference aims to preserve the fact that man's original state was not one of pure-nature, but one that included the gift of grace, as something over and above human nature. Rondet points out that:

> when Aquinas recalls that man could have been created *in naturalibus*, he means that Adam, who was in fact created with habitual grace and its accompanying virtues, could have been brought into being without these supernatural gifts.[83]

For Baius, however, man's prelapsarian gifts are in fact simply those of human nature, implying that "the sublimation and its elevation to participation with the divine nature was due to the integrity of the

---

79. Pelikan, *Reformation*, 376.
80. Swafford and Oakes, *Nature and Grace*, 44.
81. Rondet, *Grace of Christ*, 319.
82. Denzinger and Hünermann, *Enchiridion Symbolorum*, 1511.
83. Rondet, *Grace of Christ*, 218.

human being in its first state and is therefore to be called *natural* and not *supernatural*."[84]

Baius also thought that it was absurd to hold that from the beginning man was raised above the natural human condition through a certain supernatural and gratuitous gift. He was specifically condemned however for holding that prelapsarian man could have attained eternal life in virtue of his natural powers alone, apart from grace. This is because, according to him, prelapsarian man's immortality was not a gift of grace but a natural condition. Likewise he states that "the merits of pre-lapsarian man were the gifts of the first creation, but according to manner of speech in Sacred Scripture they are not rightly called grace; for this reason they should be called merits only, not grace."[85]

These statements would seem to imply that man's original state was basically that of "pure-nature." Baius thus was ultimately condemned for denying that God could have created and constituted the human being without natural justice.[86] The pure-nature tradition would take Baius's statement regarding natural justice as implying that God could not have created man without the original grace with which he was originally constituted, that is, that this prelapsarian grace was merely *natural*, rather than supernatural, and hence not gratuitous. Accordingly, for the pure-nature tradition, Baius's account undermines the gratuity of grace. Aquinas, on the other hand, states that man's original state was constituted by grace and was not merely one of nature: "The primitive subjection, by virtue of which reason was subject to God, was not a merely natural gift, but a supernatural endowment of grace."[87]

For Aquinas, as for the pure-nature tradition, neither man's prelapsarian state nor his postlapsarian state is the equivalent of pure-nature. Both instead are *states* in which human nature either has existed or does exist, which—while necessarily modifying the existential condition of human nature—do not eradicate the objective intelligibility of human nature as such.[88] Baius's choice to view human nature's original state as his natural state leads him to view grace as primarily medicinal (as previously said) and serves only to give man back the natural powers that sin had destroyed. This point serves to further distinguish Baius

84. Neuner and Dupuis, *Christian Faith*, 1984.
85. Swafford and Oakes, *Nature and Grace*, 45.
86. Neuner and Dupuis, *Christian Faith*, 1984.
87. Aquinas, *Summa Theologica*, I, q. 95, a. 1.
88. Swafford and Oakes, *Nature and Grace*, 47.

from Aquinas as the latter emphasizes both the medicinal and elevating nature of grace, where the second pertains even to prelapsarian man: "In innocent man, grace was only elevating. But in fallen man, and in general for man wounded by sin, grace is both elevating and medicinal."[89] The reason for the distinction here between Baius and Aquinas is the lack in Baius's account of the difference between man's nature and the conditions or states in which that nature exists. To speak of "pre-lapsarian" or "postlapsarian" is to refer to states or conditions in which human nature existed or does exist. It is important to remember however that man's nature remains the same despite the condition, as Aquinas reiterates: "Man's nature is the same before and after sin, but the state of his nature is not the same."[90]

This distinction presupposes the integral coherence of human nature, which then lends itself to the distinction between man's natural and proportionate end, as distinct from his supernatural and disproportionate end. In other words, this distinction between nature and condition quickly gives rise to the whole logical edifice of the pure-nature tradition. This same tradition presupposes the coherence of nature as distinct from any given existential condition, which in the mind of pure-nature advocates preserves the sublime transcendence and gratuity of grace.[91] Aquinas states:

> Now no act of anything whatsoever is divinely ordained to anything exceeding the proportion of the powers which are the principles of its act; for it is the law of Divine providence that nothing shall act beyond its [proportionate natural] powers. Now everlasting life is a good exceeding the proportion of created nature.... And hence it is that no created nature is a sufficient principle of an act meritorious of eternal life, unless there is added a supernatural gift which we call grace.[92]

Recalling that Aristotle held that nature is a principle *in* things rather than a thing itself, Aquinas and the pure-nature tradition are able to hold that man's nature remains specifically one and the same throughout each and every condition, despite the obvious fact that some conditions presuppose important modifying factors (e.g., sin, grace). This means

---

89. Rondet, *Grace of Christ*, 314.
90. Aquinas, *Summa Theologica*, III, q. 61, a. 2, ad 2.
91. Swafford and Oakes, *Nature and Grace*, 47.
92. Aquinas, *Summa Theologica*, I–IIae, q. 114, a. 2.

that the claim that nature is intelligibly distinct from its existential conditions need not be taken to mean that the intelligibility of nature implies the natural order's independent existence as if man could concretely exist in such a way so as to be devoid of any influence whatsoever. It is this method of abstracting human nature in precision from its existential conditions that enabled the pure-nature tradition to respond to Baius. De Lubac maintains that it was this controversy with Baius that provided the *raison d'être* for the pure-nature tradition:

> The principal motive that has pushed modern theology to forge its hypothesis of "pure nature" and to place it at the base of all its speculation on the final end . . . was the concern to assure, against the modern deviations of Augustinianism, the full gratuity of the supernatural gift.[93]

On de Lubac's account, while the pure-nature tradition may have offered solutions to Baius's problems, it did so at its own peril as it played right into the hands of a much more formidable foe, namely, modern secularism, a point that we shall revisit in later chapters.

The Divine Economy

To speak of the divine "economy" is to speak of God's providential ordering and governance over all things. In referring to the concrete divine economy, what is meant is the present order of God's providence as opposed to a hypothetical ordering of things that, while possible, does not actually exist. This concept speaks directly to the notion of man's ultimate end, since in the concrete, actual divine economy, man's last end is the beatific vision. Since this vision of God is necessarily a supernatural end, it raises the question of whether or not the beatific vision is man's *only* possible end, or whether man might obtain to a purely *natural* end in a hypothetical economy. If one holds that the beatific vision is man's only possible end, then further questions can be raised as to God's justice as well as the gratuity of grace and the beatific vision. Put another way, one is left questioning whether God could have *refused* the offer of the beatific vision if this were man's *only* possible end. If one says that God could *not* have refused the beatific vision to man (since it is man's only possible end), then it would seem that the beatific vision is no longer a free gift, since it would become necessary on account of man's nature. On

93. Lubac, *Mystery of the Supernatural*, 80.

the other hand, if we maintain that God could have refused the beatific vision to man, we retain the essential gratuity of man's supernatural end, but we would have to entertain the possibility of a purely natural end for man, otherwise we are committed to the possibility that God could have created man with only the possibility of the beatific vision as a final end—an end which he could refuse man—in which case man could have been created with only the prospect of suffering and frustration as his final end. The question to be asked at this point is how this might square with God's justice, or if in fact it tends towards a form of voluntarism, which is, after all, incompatible with Christian tradition.[94]

Given these considerations, theologians that fall within the extrinsicist tradition assert that man has *two* final ends: one natural, accessible by way of his natural powers, and the other, supernatural, accessible only by way of supernatural grace. This would mean, strictly speaking, that only the latter is gratuitous (and therefore not necessary), which implies that God could have refused the beatific vision without any injustice on his part; all that is necessary on God's part as a matter of justice is that he supply for man's *natural* end, which, after all, flows from his nature.[95] This speaks to what theologians call the "*debitum naturae*," which we will now briefly consider.

The *Debitum Naturae*

The term *debitum naturae* denotes the "debt of nature" that is owed to the creature by God by virtue of the creature's nature or essence. It means, as a matter of God's justice to the creature, that God provide whatever is necessary to reach its natural end, that is, the end given to it on account of its nature, and that is accessible by way of its own natural principles. The principle of the *debitum naturae* implies that God is not free in his offer of man's natural end, that is, God could not have withheld this natural end from man without injustice on his part. De Lubac famously objected to the concept of the *debitum naturae* by pointing out that creation itself is a gratuitous gift and therefore God cannot be said to owe anything to any creature whatsoever. The response to this objection by extrinsicists is to concede that the act of creation is indeed gratuitous; however, once

---

94. Swafford and Oakes, *Nature and Grace*, 10. See also Benedict XVI, *Meeting Representatives of Science*.

95. Swafford and Oakes, *Nature and Grace*, 10.

God chooses to create, there is a natural order that is intelligible in its own right and that should, therefore, be taken as an expression of divine wisdom and providence. For this reason, God is not so much indebted to the creature as God is to himself, so that it is actually God—not the creature—who is the source of the *debitum naturae*. Thus, the *debitum naturae* is nothing other than a recognition of the natural order as, firstly, independently intelligible, and secondly, a manifestation of divine wisdom and providence.[96]

Since man's elevation in Christ actually surpasses the order of nature, one can speak of two levels of gratuity, namely, one of creation, and another surpassing the natural order of creation. It is the *debitum naturae* that preserves this twofold gratuity, because gratuity can refer both to that which is not owed (in which case creation itself is gratuitous) and to a divine gift that is over and above the natural order. If this analysis is accepted, then supernatural grace is "doubly" gratuitous because it elevates man over and above the endowment of his specific nature. If, however, gratuity is reduced simply to that which is not owed, this twofold link fails. Therefore, while extrinsicist theologians concede that the natural order is gratuitous in the first sense above, it is not gratuitous in the second sense; hence only the gifts of grace and glory are gratuitous in both senses.[97] This means that the notions of *dependence* and *gratuity* are not the same thing, and according to Swafford, it is generally the blurring of these two concepts that constitutes the basis for objections against the *debitum naturae*. While it is certainly true that all of creation is dependent upon God and his providence, the gratuity of creation and that of supernatural grace are not on the same level. This means that the dependence of creation on God can be conceived of in two ways (corresponding to the aforementioned levels of gratuity), namely, creaturely dependence on God according to his *natural* providence in the natural order, and creaturely dependence on God according to his supernatural providence and supernatural elevation by divine grace.[98]

Aquinas sets out the importance of the *debitum naturae* in addressing the following objection: "The act of justice is to pay what is due. But God is no man's debtor."[99] Aquinas responds as follows:

---

96. Swafford and Oakes, *Nature and Grace*, 11.
97. Swafford and Oakes, *Nature and Grace*, 11.
98. Swafford and Oakes, *Nature and Grace*, 12.
99. Aquinas, *Summa Theologica*, I, q. 21, a. 1, obj. 3.

> In the divine operations debt may be regarded in two ways, as due either to God, or to creatures, and in either way God pays what is due. It is due to God that there should be fulfilled in creatures what his will and wisdom require, and what manifests his goodness. In this respect God's justice regards what befits Him, inasmuch as He renders to himself what is due to himself. It is also due to a created thing that it should possess what is ordered to it.... Thus also God exercises justice when He gives to each thing what is due to it by its nature and condition.[100]

Aquinas emphasizes that what is due to a creature according to its "nature and condition" refers to the natural order, in contrast to the transcendent and supernatural gift of grace. Aquinas continues this line of thinking in addressing the question regarding the need for predestination, which arises because God's providence has supernaturally ordered man to an end beyond the parameters of his own nature:

> The end towards which created things are directed by God is twofold, one which exceeds all proportion and faculty of created nature; and this end is life eternal, that consists in seeing God which is above every creature .... The other end, however, is proportionate to created nature, to which end created being can attain according to the power of its nature .... Hence the type of the aforesaid direction of a rational creature towards the end of life eternal is called predestination.[101]

Natural Desire

For extrinsicist thinkers, man's natural desire is contained entirely within the natural order, the possible fulfilment of which is included in the *debitum naturae*. This means that man's natural desire is necessarily due to the creature as a matter of justice. Accordingly, for extrinsicists, man cannot be said to have a *natural* desire for the beatific vision since that would nullify the gratuity of this supernatural end. The reasoning behind this extrinsicist position is based on a principle found in Aristotle, namely, that *nature does nothing in vain*.[102] The appropriation of this principle and its application to man's natural desire solidified what eventually became

---

100. Aquinas, *Summa Theologica*, I, q. 21, a. 1, ad 3.
101. Aquinas, *Summa Theologica*, I, q. 23, a. 1.
102. Swafford and Oakes, *Nature and Grace*, 13.

the principal opposition against de Lubac in the twentieth century. De Lubac argued that man has a *natural* desire for the beatific vision, yet he *also* maintained that this supernatural end retained its gratuity. For the extrinsicist, these two positions are incompatible: since a merely natural desire cannot be in vain, the fulfilment of natural desire is therefore *not* gratuitous. Louis Dupré, in his introduction to de Lubac's *Augustinianism and Modern Theology* writes:

> To a theology that had accepted the existence of two relatively independent orders of reality, the idea of a natural desire for a supernatural end was *a priori* excluded. The principal objection against it the new theologians strangely derived from Aristotle's static cosmology. In *De Caelo II*, the philosopher had written that heavenly bodies stay their course, because no being desires what its nature has no means to attain. If the stars had the power to move beyond their course, nature would have given them the means to do so. In the same way, Cajetan and Suárez [extrinsicists], and their followers, argued a human being can feel no desire for what its nature cannot attain.[103]

By way of contrast, for de Lubac, who can be rightly considered an intrinsicist, the beatific vision is man's *only* final end; any other end would result in man's frustration and suffering. As he writes:

> In me, a real and personal human being, in my concrete nature—that nature I have in common with all real men, to judge by what my faith teaches me, and regardless of what is or is not revealed to me either by reflective analysis or by reasoning—the "desire to see God" cannot be permanently frustrated without an essential suffering. To deny this is to undermine my entire Credo.[104]

Notwithstanding de Lubac's position, Pope Pius XII's encyclical *Humani Generis* (1950) appears at first inspection to teach along the lines of an extrinsicist tradition, and as we have already seen, it appears to condemn de Lubac's teaching on the matter. Pius XII writes:

> Others destroy the gratuity of the supernatural order, since God, they say, cannot create intellectual beings without ordering and calling them to the beatific vision.[105]

---

103. Lubac, *Augustinianism and Modern Theology*, xiv.
104. Lubac, *Mystery of the Supernatural*, 54.
105. Pius XII, *Humani Generis*, §26.

Irrespective of whether Pius XII had specifically named de Lubac or not, what remains clear is that there was apparent tension between de Lubac and *Humani Generis* on this point. After all, de Lubac had stated in his *Surnaturel* that "the spirit is the desire for God," a position that clearly precludes any possibility of a purely natural end.[106] To add to matters, the Second Vatican Council also appears to weigh in on this issue; however, it comes down in favor of de Lubac. As *Gaudium et Spes* states at §22:

> All this holds true not only for Christians, but for all men of good will in whose hearts grace works in an unseen way. For, since Christ died for all men, and *since the ultimate vocation of man is in fact one, and divine*, we ought to believe that the Holy Spirit in a manner known only to God offers to every man the possibility of being associated with this paschal mystery.[107]

Hence it seemed that de Lubac had been rehabilitated, and his thinking on the question of nature and grace became one of the leading influences of the Second Vatican Council.[108]

Obediential Potency

According to extrinsicists, man's capacity for the beatific vision cannot be described as a natural potency or inclination, because, according to the Aristotelian principle, a natural potency inclines a thing to its natural end, the fulfilment of which relates to the *debitum naturae* and is therefore owed to the creature by means of divine justice. It is for this reason that the extrinsicist tradition employs the concept of *obediential potency* in order to account for the relationship between human nature and the beatific vision. In general terms, what this concept refers to is man's *capacity* to obey God, because, as a finite creature, man is always susceptible to being transformed or elevated by divine omnipotence.[109] This concept on the one hand can be used to explain God's working of miracles in the transforming of finite creatures in such a way that would have been impossible for the same by means of their natural powers alone. On the other hand, the concept of *obediential potency* also can

---

106. Lubac, *Surnaturel*, 483. My translation. Original as follows: "L'esprit est donc désir de Dieu."
107. My emphasis.
108. See Lubac, *Brief Catechesis*, 177.
109. Swafford and Oakes, *Nature and Grace*, 15.

explain man's capacity for the beatific vision; however, unlike in the case of miracles, man remains *man* throughout this divine elevation. This means that while in the case of miracles there appears to be no specific relation to the creature as such (God could after all transform anything into any other thing whatever), the capacity for the beatific vision does have some relation to human nature since not every creature can be elevated in such a manner.[110]

Obediential potency can therefore be said to have two distinct meanings: firstly, a *generic* obediential potency that corresponds to the case of a miracle and that indicates no real relation between the specific nature of the creature and its transformation; and secondly, a *specific* obediential potency that corresponds to man's specific capacity for the beatific vision, and that requires that the capacity for this elevation be rooted in the nature of the creature and that is perfective of that nature, albeit in a way that transcends the powers of its nature.[111]

An example of the first of these meanings is seen in Matt 3:9: "do not presume to say to yourselves, 'We have Abraham as our father'; for I tell you, God is able from these stones to raise up children to Abraham." This illustrates a *general* obediential potency because, after all, the stones would no longer be stones after such a miraculous transformation. Furthermore, should these stones-now-turned-human receive the beatific vision, they would not do so *as* stones. Hence stones have no *specific* obediential potency for the beatific vision. On the other hand, the capacity for human nature to be elevated to the beatific vision is a specific obediential potency precisely because it is based in man's specific nature; not every nature can be elevated to any end whatsoever as only spiritual and intellectual nature possesses this capacity. Accordingly, the reason that extrinsicist thinkers insist upon the classification of man's potency for the beatific vision as *obediential* (and not natural) is because of the fact that human nature cannot actualize this potency itself. Furthermore, because this obediential potency means a going beyond what is possible in the natural order, its actualization is not contained within the *debitum naturae*. The extrinsicist tradition thus judges the concept of obediential potency as successfully being able to balance rooting the capacity for the beatific vision in human nature, on the one hand, while simultaneously

---

110. Swafford and Oakes, *Nature and Grace*, 15.
111. Swafford and Oakes, *Nature and Grace*, 15.

preserving the sublime gratuity of this elevation as supernaturally transcending the powers of human nature, on the other.[112]

Intrinsicism

An example of the intrinsicist (Christocentric) approach to the question of nature and grace appears in Pope John Paul II's first encyclical *Redemptor Hominis* where he writes that "Jesus Christ is the centre of the universe and of history."[113] This theme finds its origin in Scripture: "For in him all things were created . . . all things were created through him and for him . . . [and] in him all things hold together" (Col 1:16–17). Likewise, the letter to the Ephesians states:

> For he has made known to us in all wisdom and insight the mystery of his will, according to his purpose which he set forth in Christ as a plan for the fulness of time, to unite all things in him, things in heaven and things on earth. (Eph 1:9–10)

Also, in the prologue to the Gospel of John:

> In the beginning was the Word, and the Word was with God, and the Word was God. He was in the beginning with God; all things were made through him, and without him was not anything made that was made. (John 1:1–3)

Furthermore, Irenaeus echoes the Christocentric Pauline theme:

> So the Lord now manifestly came to his own, and, born by his own created order which he himself bears, he by his obedience on the tree renewed what was done by disobedience in connection with a tree; and the power of that seduction by which the virgin Eve, already betrothed to a man, had been wickedly seduced was broken when the angel in truth brought good tidings to the Virgin Mary, who already by her betrothal belonged to a man . . . . Therefore he renews these things in himself, uniting man to the Spirit . . . . He therefore completely renewed all things.[114]

According to the patristic scholar Robert Wilken, Irenaeus uses Eph 1:10 to draw attention to Christ's bringing to completion what was

---

112. Swafford and Oakes, *Nature and Grace*, 17.
113. John Paul II, *Redemptor Hominis*, §1.
114. Irenaeus, *Against Heresies*, V, 19–20.

originally begun in creation. This suggests that Christ is not only the beginning but also the end of all creation—the one in whom creation reaches its final goal:

> [Irenaeus] favors terms like *renew* and *restore* . . . . Drawing on the language of Saint Paul in Ephesians, he says that Christ "summed up" or "united" all things in himself (Eph 1:10) . . . Christ does not simply reverse what had been lost in the fall: he brings to *completion* what had been partial and imperfect.[115]

As we have seen, de Lubac is considered to be the preeminent proponent of the intrinsicist approach, having challenged the erstwhile regnant extrinsicism. De Lubac read the writings of Aquinas on the matter in a manner somewhat contrary to the received neo-scholastic orthodoxy and so subsequently became the center of a long-standing controversy, which has resurfaced in more recent times.[116]

In his inaugural lecture on apologetics and fundamental theology in 1929, which was subsequently published as an article entitled "Apologétique et théologie," de Lubac marks the general shift in the church's thinking on apologetics, that is, a shift away from neo-scholastic apologetics and towards fundamental theology.[117] De Lubac argues that the church's mode of apologetics should seek to show the inherent connections between the human condition and the mysteries of the faith. In other words, de Lubac advocates a more *intrinsic* alignment between reason's assessment of the human condition and the perspective afforded by the Christian faith.[118] The divide between neo-scholastic (extrinsicist) apologetics and de Lubac's teaching on fundamental theology is nothing other than the epistemological expression of their respective orientations towards either extrinsicism or intrinsicism.[119] De Lubac notes the same here:

> The error [of neo-scholasticism] consists in conceiving of dogma as a kind of "thing in itself," as a block of revealed truth with no relationship whatsoever to natural man, as a transcendent object whose demonstration (as well as the greater part of

---

115. Wilken, *Spirit of Early Christian Thought*, 66.
116. Gourlay, "Nature, Grace," 108.
117. Körner, "Henri de Lubac," 714.
118. Swafford and Oakes, *Nature and Grace*, 68.
119. Swafford and Oakes, *Nature and Grace*, 68.

its content) has been determined by the arbitrary nature of a "divine decree."[120]

Traditional apologetics aimed to demonstrate the *preambula fidei* (e.g., that God exists) and to establish motives of credibility for accepting the divine foundations of Christianity and the church. As typically understood, it did so with very little emphasis upon the actual content of dogma; instead, the main aim was to demonstrate the absence of contradiction in the same, and thereby, its credibility. In the neo-scholastic approach, faith is correlated with grace such that there can be no direct or inherent link between human nature and the supernatural mysteries of the faith. The two *ab initio* cannot be related intrinsically to one another (only extrinsically) such that the faith, and supernatural grace, only come to man from without.

De Lubac was critical of this form of apologetics, particularly in light of his attempt to establish a true Christian humanism (in rebuttal of the secular variety), because the manner in which the church seeks to engage the culture is directly affected by her adoption of either an extrinsicist or intrinsicist nature-grace framework. Broadly speaking, an extrinsicist approach corresponds to neo-scholastic apologetics, whereas an intrinsicist approach corresponds to fundamental theology. For de Lubac, an overly extrinsicist framework will have great difficulty engaging secularism.[121] According to Komonchak, in the neo-scholastic approach:

> all encounter between faith and the world outside the church was assigned to apologetics, while theology itself was considered "the science of revealed truths," for which an understanding of faith was a matter of drawing ever more numerous and ever more remote conclusions, but was no longer an understanding of all reality through the faith. To suggest that theology and apologetics were integrally related, that theology must seek to display its inner intelligibility and beauty of Christian doctrine and its ability to interpret all of reality, was to risk being accused of naturalism and of confusing the natural and the supernatural.[122]

At his inaugural lecture, de Lubac stated:

---

120. Lubac, *Theological Fragments*, 93.
121. Swafford and Oakes, *Nature and Grace*, 69.
122. Komonchak, "Theology and Culture," 582.

> A theology that does not constantly maintain apologetical considerations becomes deficient and distorted, while on the other hand, all apologetics that wishes to be fully effective must end up in theology.[123]

Natural Desire

For de Lubac, created spirits naturally desire the beatific vision as their final end, without exception. In 1932, de Lubac wrote to Blondel to express the same:

> This concept of a pure nature runs into great difficulties, the principal one of which seems to me to be the following: How can a conscious spirit be anything other than an absolute desire of God?[124]

This is a central thesis in the thought of de Lubac, that man finds within himself a natural desire for supernatural union with God, a desire that precludes the possibility of purely natural beatitude as proposed by extrinsicists. This natural desire is so fundamentally constitutive of the nature of man that to fall short of the object of this desire (ultimate union with God) leaves man frustrated and unhappy. De Lubac remarks:

> For is not this, in effect, the definition of the "pain of the damned"? And consequently—at least in appearance—a good and just God could hardly frustrate me, unless I, through my own fault, turn away from Him by choice. The infinite importance of the desire implanted in me by my Creator is what constitutes the infinite importance of the drama of human existence.[125]

As stated, this *natural* desire for God is constitutive of man's very being as a created spirit. In other words, it is what makes man *man*:

> For this desire is not some "accident" in me. It does not result from some peculiarity, possibly alterable, of my individual being, or from some historical contingency whose effects are more or less transitory. A fortiori it does not in any sense depend upon my deliberate will. It is in me as a result of my

---

123. Lubac, *Theological Fragments*, 96.
124. Lubac, *At the Service*, 184.
125. Lubac, *Mystery of the Supernatural*, 54.

belonging to humanity, as it is, that humanity which is, as we say, "called." For God's call is constitutive. My finality, which is expressed by this desire, is inscribed upon my very being as it has been put into this universe by God. And, by God's will, I now have no other genuine end, no end really assigned to my nature or presented for my free acceptance under any guise, except that of "seeing God."[126]

De Lubac is at pains to emphasize that man is naturally oriented to the beatific vision, and that this orientation is not something that is extraneous or accidental to his nature but constitutes his "ontological fabric," such that his nature and his desire for the beatific vision cannot be separated from each other.[127] Thus, for de Lubac, man's nature cannot be considered coherently on the hypothesis of pure-nature or of a purely natural end, as in so doing would be to consider a different nature altogether.

The danger in maintaining the notion of a pure-nature with its proportionate natural end is that if nature can be fulfilled without grace, why should nature bother with grace at all, if it can get by using its own powers of self-fulfilment?[128] In the words of Karl Rahner:

> The orientation of "nature" to grace is conceived of in as negative a way as possible. Grace is, it is true, an unsurpassable perfectioning [sic] of nature; God as the Lord of this nature can command man to submit to his *de facto* will and to be receptive to his grace, which directs man to a supernatural life and end. But of itself nature has only a "*potentia oboedientialis*" to such an end, and this capacity is thought of as negatively as possible. It is no more than non-repugnance to such an elevation. Of itself, nature would find its perfection just as readily and harmoniously in its own proper realm, in a purely natural end, without an immediate intuition of God in the beatific vision. When it finds itself in immediate possession of itself—as part of the essence of the spirit, *reditio completa in seipsum*—it meets itself as though it were "pure nature."[129]

Some claim that Thomas Aquinas is better known for emphasizing the distinction between nature and grace; however, intrinsicists maintain that, correctly read, Aquinas's thought actually supports the

---

126. Lubac, *Mystery of the Supernatural*, 54.
127. Swafford and Oakes, *Nature and Grace*, 73.
128. Oakes, "*Surnaturel* Controversy," 626.
129. Rahner, *More Recent Writings*, 165.

Christocentric perspective. This is apparent, for example, in his correlation of the Eternal Law with the person of the Word, which is significant since for Aquinas the notion of nature and the natural order finds its ontological root in the Eternal Law, in which case the natural order itself is Christocentric in its foundation.[130]

As we have seen, according to de Lubac, Aquinas held that man has *one* final end rather than two (one being natural, the other supernatural).[131] Intrinsicist thinkers contend that Aquinas was no exponent of the pure-nature tradition pure and simple; even contemporary advocates of extrinsicism would concede as much; however, they do maintain that their *interpretative tradition* is that which develops organically from the principles readily found in Aquinas's thought on nature and grace.

What becomes evident from this fact is the exegetical question pertaining to the original texts of Aquinas, which unfortunately is largely insoluble because it depends on which texts in Aquinas are interpretively privileged over others. That is, one set of texts could be said to support the extrinsicist position, while another, the intrinsicist position. As Rossi points out:

> It may seem astonishing that serious scholars were so divided on the interpretation of Thomas, but the fact is that the Angelic Doctor's writings contain some ambiguities, especially when the early works are compared with the more mature ones.[132]

An example of texts that would tend to support the intrinsicist position would be: "Final and perfect happiness can consist in nothing else than the vision of the Divine Essence."[133] Also Aquinas states:

> There resides in every man a natural desire to know the cause of any effect which he sees . . . . But if the intellect of the rational creature could not reach so far as to the first cause of things, the natural desire would remain void.[134]

Furthermore, in his *Summa contra Gentiles* he states:

---

130. Swafford and Oakes, *Nature and Grace*, 3.
131. Swafford and Oakes, *Nature and Grace*, 36.
132. Rossi, "Neo-Scholastic to Vatican II," 6.
133. Aquinas, *Summa Theologica*, I–IIae, q. 3, a. 8.
134. Aquinas, *Summa Theologica*, I, q. 12, a. 1.

> Now, a person has not attained his ultimate end until natural desire comes to rest. Therefore, for human happiness which is the ultimate end it is not enough to have merely any kind of intelligible knowledge; there must be divine knowledge, as un ultimate end, to terminate the natural desire. So, the ultimate end of man is the knowledge of God.[135]

It is clear that for Aquinas, man's final end must consist in the vision of God:

> Natural desire does not come to rest as a result of this knowledge which separate substances have of God; rather, it further arouses the desire to see the divine substance.[136]

Man can be said to have a natural desire for this supernatural end—and yet such a natural desire cannot be in vain. This is a key point, which de Lubac emphasizes, and which is found clearly in Aquinas's own writings, namely, that man has a natural desire for his supernatural end—the only end in which his beatitude consists—yet this supernatural end is nonetheless gratuitous. Aquinas continues:

> Since it is impossible for a natural desire to be incapable of fulfilment, and since it would be so, if it were not possible to reach an understanding of divine substance such as all minds naturally desire, we must say that it is possible for the substance of God to be seen intellectually, both by separate intellectual substances and by our souls.[137]

The *Imago Dei*

A privileged starting point for intrinsicists, particularly for de Lubac, is the notion of the *imago Dei*, rather than the Aristotelian *physis*, as favored by extrinsicists. The notion of the *imago Dei* speaks to man's privileged place in creation, indeed, even as created in the image and likeness of God. As the book of Genesis tells us:

> Then God said, Let us make mankind in our image, in our likeness, so that they may rule over the fish in the sea and the birds in the sky, over the livestock and all the wild animals, and

---

135. Aquinas, *Summa contra Gentiles*, III, q. 25, c. 12.
136. Aquinas, *Summa contra Gentiles*, III, q. 50, c. 2.
137. Aquinas, *Summa contra Gentiles*, III, q. 51, c. 1.

over all the creatures that move along the ground. So God created mankind in his own image, in the image of God he created them; male and female he created them. (Gen 1:26–27)

The Incarnation further elevates the grandeur of this anthropological mystery, the fullness of which includes man's participation in the glory of Christ himself. Considering this fact, de Lubac criticizes what he calls Cajetan's "naturalization" of the soul.[138] Specifically, de Lubac objects to the tendency of extrinsicists to treat man merely as one of the many aspects of creation rather than as its capstone. De Lubac laments Cajetan's neglect of the grandeur of mankind and notes that extrinsicism is too beholden to Aristotelian anthropology:

> We shall not agree with him [Aristotle] in determining the laws of the spirit according to the laws of the stars. We shall reply that though Aristotle may have been right about the stars, the analogy could not in any circumstances apply to men. We shall not be misled by an apparent induction which is really begging the question. We shall take exception to any arguments based on so deceptive a method.[139]

Part of the reason why the *Duplex Ordo* thesis greatly advanced at the time of Suárez was the superimposition of Aristotelian philosophy onto Christian anthropology, particularly as it pertains to man's natural desire. As we have seen, one of the key concepts for the extrinsicist thesis is the notion of the *debitum naturae*, which is drawn from the Aristotelian principle that *nature does nothing in vain*, which is then applied to man and his natural desire. This superimposition effectively codified the notion of man's *Duplex Ordo*, which in turn created the necessity of positing the notion of pure-nature.[140]

De Lubac sets out the methodological difference that distinguishes him from an extrinsicist framework:

> The end of natural being is always in strict proportion to its means. For Suárez, this is an absolute principle and its application to the case of man is no less absolute, no less undeniable. By virtue of his creation man is therefore made for an essentially natural beatitude. If we suppose that in fact he is called to some higher end, strictly speaking this could only be superadded. The

---

138. Lubac, *Mystery of the Supernatural*, 140.
139. Lubac, *Mystery of the Supernatural*, 156.
140. Swafford and Oakes, *Nature and Grace*, 75.

first, by right, was sufficient; alone therefore it remains naturally knowable and alone it can come to a definition of man. If it is objected that there is a desire for this higher beatitude, Suárez, before even examining the objection, answers that it is impossible, because, still according to Aristotle, the natural appetite follows the natural power.[141]

De Lubac points out that even Aquinas himself failed to avoid this problem, that is, by giving due credence to Aristotle, he conceded far too much and actually created the space for which later distortions could emerge. Specifically, de Lubac is of the view that Aquinas allowed the Aristotelian philosophical framework and the patristic inheritance of faith to stand side by side without making it clear which was ultimately architectonic over the other. This juxtaposition exists in an uneasy synthesis and resulted in the tensions that later devolved into the problems that de Lubac saw in the extrinsicist, pure-nature approach.[142] Aquinas represents, therefore, a crucial stage in this anthropological deviation, one that is certainly related to the problems that de Lubac sees in Cajetan:

> Now everywhere in Saint Thomas, these two conceptions of Aristotelian nature and of the Patristic image are mingled without it being possible to say whether they really combine, or collide, or which of the two finally succeeds in taming the other. However vigorous his spirit of synthesis may be, he does not always succeed in merging the elements received from two different traditions into a perfect unity.[143]

De Lubac maintains that the presence of the spirit in creation requires a revision in the terms under which the debate of nature and grace takes place. In other words, spirit is a different kind of nature from the natural forms found in the rest of creation and thus requires a different kind of ontology. Therefore, it is difficult to bring objections to de Lubac's methodological framework if one is starting from the Aristotelian

---

141. Lubac, *Augustinianism and Modern Theology*, 158.

142. Swafford and Oakes, *Nature and Grace*, 77.

143. Lubac, *Surnaturel*, 435. My translation. Original as follows: "Or, partout, chez saint Thomas, ces deux conceptions de la *nature* Aristotélicienne et de l'*image* patristique se mêlent, sans qu'on puisse dire si elles s'y combinent vraiment ou si elles s'y heurtent, ni laquelle des deux finalement réussit à dompter l'autre. Si vigoureux que soit son esprit de synthèse, il ne réussit pas toujours à fondre les éléments reçus de deux traditions diverses en une parfaite unité."

physis.¹⁴⁴ As Edward Oakes points out, "Spirit . . . demands its own logic."¹⁴⁵ On this basis Swafford contends that de Lubac's position is virtually impregnable. Indeed, the debate between him and extrinsicists stands or falls on this very issue.¹⁴⁶

Paradox and the Gratuity of Grace

De Lubac attempts to avoid two extremes in his theology of grace: immanentism and secularism. In the first, grace is equated with nature; in the second, nature is independent of grace. To avoid either, he must guard the gratuity and distinctiveness of grace and yet keep it from being extrinsic to nature and thus to some degree superfluous to the needs of nature.¹⁴⁷ For extrinsicists, the way of achieving this is to posit the notion of obediential potency. For de Lubac, this notion is wholly inadequate because, as we have seen, it fails to lay sufficient stress upon the absolutely special case of spirit. Human nature, according to de Lubac, is not like other natures, and cannot be analyzed as such.¹⁴⁸ De Lubac points out that if human nature is conceived of as having a purely natural finality and yet is in obediential potency to a second and quite different finality, this destroys the whole notion of nature or finality or both. All natures possess finalities and these finalities are intrinsic to that nature and help define that nature. If finality can be changed, this implies that finality is extrinsic to nature, which is a contradiction.¹⁴⁹

Christianity presents us with two unimpeachable truths, both of which must be taken as non-negotiable, namely, that man cannot live except by the vision of God; and that the vision of God depends totally on God's good pleasure.¹⁵⁰ According to de Lubac, the Christian theologian must strive to maintain the unified integrity of a mystery of faith

144. For a detailed treatment of the issue of supernatural finality and nature desire, particularly in light of Feingold and Long and other more recent contributors to the debate, see Healy, "Henri de Lubac," 543–64; Malloy, "De Lubac"; J. Wood, "Henri de Lubac," 1209–41; Bushlack, "Return of Neo-Scholasticism?," 83–100; Sánchez and Watson, "Revival," 171–250; Feingold, *Natural Desire*; Long, *Natura Pura*; and Oakes, "*Surnaturel* Controversy."

145. Oakes, "Paradox," 674.

146. Swafford and Oakes, *Nature and Grace*, 79.

147. S. Wood, "Nature-Grace Problematic," 389.

148. Lubac, *Mystery of the Supernatural*, 6.

149. S. Wood, "Nature-Grace Problematic," 392.

150. Lubac, *Mystery of the Supernatural*, 179.

rather than seek at all costs to alleviate whatever tension may arise from the juxtaposition of various aspects of a given mystery. De Lubac writes:

> All too often there remains the same timidity, the same impatient anxiety to eliminate every paradox from the human situation and arrive at a positive and clearly understandable result; so much so that this "natural desire" to see God which they [extrinsicists] have been trying to re-establish is twisted almost at once into a vague "wish," a wholly Platonic "prayer" quite inadequate for the work it should be doing [that is, establishing a bridge between man's nature and the gift of union with God].[151]

For this reason, where others accuse him of contradiction, de Lubac posits the notion of "paradox," and this is most clearly demonstrated on the issue of man's natural desire and its relation to the gratuity of grace:

> The desire to see him [God] is in us, it constitutes us, and yet it comes to us as a completely free gift. Such paradoxes should not surprise us, for they arise in every mystery; they are the hallmark of a truth that is beyond our depth. "Faith embraces several truths which appear to contradict one another." It "is always a harmony of two opposing truths."[152]

The category of the "paradox" allows de Lubac to preserve both orthodoxy and the mystery of the faith. Without this, one ends up in a rationalistic reduction of mystery, which while preserving orthodoxy, ultimately compromises the integrity of the faith. De Lubac uses the notion of "circumincession"[153] to describe the relationship between the creature and the Creator, nature and the supernatural. This is his way of maintaining the distinctiveness of the two orders of nature and grace, while yet maintaining their close interaction. As Susan Wood comments:

> The paradox is not explained or resolved philosophically on the basis of an analysis of nature and its capabilities, but by faith. The paradox of the human condition being called to a supernatural finality is wholly shaped and developed in direct dependence on the Christian revelation. The analogue is the hypostatic union of the divine and human natures in Jesus Christ which are neither mingled nor confused.[154]

---

151. Lubac, *Mystery of the Supernatural*, 180.

152. Lubac, *Mystery of the Supernatural*, 167.

153. Lubac, *Brief Catechesis*, 43. De Lubac here uses the term in reference to the Persons of the Trinity, a perfect model of "reciprocity in unity."

154. S. Wood, "Nature-Grace Problematic," 396. See also Lubac, *Mystery of the Supernatural*, 167.

The notion of the paradox is fundamentally phenomenological, founded on the existential experience of being fallen, and inspired by the Augustinian tradition. Interestingly, de Lubac also tries at this point to draw upon the Thomistic and Aristotelian categories of accident and substance, which are not phenomenological or experiential but deal with natures and structures. This mixture of two levels of discourse leads to ambiguities in de Lubac's thought, which he himself would not acknowledge. The fundamental problem will be whether grace can be considered as a structure of creation or whether transcendence, grace, and redemption are only present within creation in the event of Christ, who represents divine immanence within history. As a free historical event, Christ (and thus grace) can never be considered a necessary structure of creation.[155]

For de Lubac, paradox becomes a hermeneutical lens by which a theologian is able to hold two essential truths together, especially when they may not appear to cohere easily together. This, in turn, allows the theologian to embrace the fullness of the ontological mystery of faith in all its integral unity. Without the possibility of paradox, human reason tends to emphasize one or other aspect of a given mystery, attempting to alleviate tension between various dimensions of a particular mystery of faith, which may ultimately lead to a truncating of the same. The problem is not with theological distinctions per se, but that the separateness of various aspects of a given mystery is something that pertains only to our "side of the veil" and not to the ontological mystery itself.[156] Therefore, the notion of paradox allows us to move beyond the conceptual frailty of man's finite intellectual faculties in order to behold the mystery as it truly is in itself, in its integrity. He writes:

> Where it is between two truths of faith that positive conciliation is not visible, the choice of one of the two to the exclusion of the other constitutes, properly speaking, heresy . . . . Without leaving the bounds of orthodoxy, a theology overly concerned about tangible conciliations and definitive explanations always risks compromising the balance of the synthesis by taking away something.[157]

---

155. S. Wood, "Nature-Grace Problematic," 397.
156. Swafford and Oakes, *Nature and Grace*, 51.
157. Lubac, *Theology in History*, 311.

To this point, the question that continues to be disputed between de Lubac and extrinsicist thinkers is the status of what Aquinas called the "natural desire for the vision of God."[158] As already stated, de Lubac maintains that man has a *natural* desire for beatitude that as a matter of fact can only be attained through the second gift of grace. The desire for beatitude that God has inscribed in nature is a sign that the first gift is made for the second gift.[159] At the same time, the natural desire for the vision of God ensures that the grace bestowed in and through Jesus Christ represents a surpassing but genuine fulfilment of human nature. For de Lubac, the paradox lies precisely in the nobility of man who is created for an ultimate end that is radically beyond his own nature, that is, that one can *naturally* desire what is supernatural. As Aquinas notes: "even though by his nature man is inclined to his ultimate end, he cannot reach it by nature but only by grace, and this owing to the loftiness of that end."[160] Created in the *imago Dei*, man is thereby *capax Dei*; this capacity however is not yet grace, but defines our nature itself as a non-anticipating readiness for God's gracious and unmerited self-communication in Christ.[161]

In defending his notion of the paradox, de Lubac notes his grave reservations about the development of doctrine that takes place in the midst of the heat of polemic since such an approach tends to lead to fragmented and truncated theological solutions. Polemic usually results in the reaffirmation of some disputed point, often with the neglect of other aspects of the integral mystery. De Lubac, for this reason, laments the neo-scholastic tendency to learn the catechism *against* someone.[162] The necessary refinement in the heat of polemic tends to produce a certain theological impatience on the part of the theologian and so it is inevitable the heretic frames the question and defines the issue, setting forth the terms of the debate. This means that both interlocutors end up sharing common assumptions in their approach to the question despite the fact that they may well come to opposite conclusions, and worse still, this deeper commonality between them usually goes unnoticed by the

---

158. Aquinas, *Summa Theologica*, I, q. 12, a. 1; I–II, q. 3, a. 8; Aquinas, *Summa contra Gentiles*, III, cc. 25, 48–54.

159. Healy, "Henri de Lubac," 541.

160. Aquinas, *Super Boethium De Trinitate*, q. 6, a. 4, ad 5.

161. Healy, "Henri de Lubac," 542.

162. Lubac, *Catholicism*, 309.

orthodox protagonist.[163] De Lubac notes that this is precisely what had happened in the development of the nature-grace framework as it first attempted to counter Baius, and then the Enlightenment:

> The very conflict between two doctrines nearly always implies certain presuppositions common to both . . . . Thus there arises another danger for the theologian who makes too many concessions to the demands of the controversy. In its struggle against heresy he always sees the question, more or less, willingly or unwillingly, from the heretic's point of view. He often accepts questions in the form in which the heretic propounds them, so that without sharing the error he may make implicit concessions to his opponent . . . . For about three centuries, faced by the naturalist trends of modern thought on the one hand, and the confusions of bastard Augustinianism on the other, many could see salvation only in a complete severance between the natural and the supernatural. Such a policy ran doubly counter to the end which they had in view . . . . Such dualism [the *Duplex Ordo*], just when it imagined that it was most successfully opposing the negotiations of naturalism, was most strongly influenced by it, and the transcendence in which it hoped to preserve the supernatural with such jealous care was, in fact, a banishment. The most confirmed secularists found in it, in spite of itself, an ally.[164]

The limitation of this neo-scholastic rationalism is the loss of the integral unity of the mystery of the faith, a unity that, according to de Lubac, can only be preserved by means of recourse to the category of paradox. In fact de Lubac feared, perhaps even to excess, this rationalism in its many forms, characterized by its self-sufficiency and its compulsive appetite for appropriation (the model of which is the Hegelian system) and thought that its method was merely the theft of sacred things, to the detriment of the faith.[165] The overemphasizing of theological distinctions leads first to a separation of the mystery's integral unity, and subsequently to disregard for some other aspect of the integral mystery of faith.[166] For de Lubac, the category of paradox serves as an expression of the virtue of humility and as such it is the only proper response to God's Revelation:

---

163. Swafford and Oakes, *Nature and Grace*, 52.
164. Lubac, *Catholicism*, 312.
165. Tilliette, "Henri de Lubac," 338.
166. Swafford and Oakes, *Nature and Grace*, 54.

> Antinomies loom everywhere, and always, to be faithful, we must begin again to hold in the night "the two ends of the chain." No mystery is a simple truth, and if we become attached with too narrow an attention to one of its aspects in order to establish the main part of it, we risk ending in many an absurdity or many a heresy. A mystery can never be . . . handled in the way a natural truth can; we will never have the right to apply the laws of our human logic to it univocally, without precautions and correctives.[167]

For de Lubac, an example of this problematic rationalism is the tendency of extrinsicist theologians to want to preserve the notion of the gratuity of grace at all costs. That is, in their attempts to preserve the same, they neglect the basic fact that creation itself is already gratuitous, which for de Lubac implies the absolute gratuity of all else, a fortiori.[168] De Lubac is in complete agreement with the notion that God is in no way governed by our desire, and that there can be no question of anything being "due" to the creature. Thus, for de Lubac, the whole notion of the *debitum naturae* is completely inapplicable:

> God could have refused to give himself to creatures, just as he could have, and has, given himself. The gratuitousness of the supernatural order is true individually and totally. It is gratuitous in itself. It is gratuitous as far as each one of us is concerned, It is gratuitous in regard to what we see as preceding it, whether in time or in logic. Further—and this is what some of the explanations I have contested seem to me not to make clear—its gratuitousness remains always complete. It remains gratuitous in every hypothesis. It is forever new. It remains gratuitous at every stage of preparation for the gift, and at every stage of giving of it. No "disposition" in creatures can ever, in any way, bind the Creator.[169]

De Lubac makes plain that, for him, no exigency on the part of the creature can in any way make a claim on God or force his hand, no matter how much in need of grace the creature may be. The gift of grace remains gratuitous on any hypothesis, whether man's nature has an exigency for grace, and whether or not the beatific vision is man's only possible end. Thus for de Lubac, the importation of the Aristotelian axiom that *natural*

---

167. Lubac, *Theology in History*, 265.
168. Swafford and Oakes, *Nature and Grace*, 81.
169. Lubac, *Mystery of the Supernatural*, 236.

desires cannot be in vain actually created this purported theological problem of the *debitum naturae* and the concomitant attempts to preserve the gratuity of grace in the first place. De Lubac notes the dictum of Ockham that states that "God is debtor to no one in any way."[170] Interestingly, this dictum, which de Lubac proposes as the "first principle of the Christian faith," is precisely that which is denied by Aquinas. As we have seen, Aquinas employs the category of justice to demonstrate that God is indeed just towards his creatures in giving them their due in accordance with their "nature and condition."[171] This point of contact demonstrates that, at least on this limited issue, the extrinsicist thesis of pure-nature aligns with that of Aquinas, despite the claims of de Lubac.[172]

De Lubac stresses that everything that God does is gratuitous, and that therefore the theological problem of the gratuity of grace is really a false problem arising on account of the insistence of theologians to frame the issue in Aristotelian categories.[173] He writes:

> The monster of exigency was only a phantom. The attempt was made to resolve a false problem. In reality, the question of exigency does not arise. However pressing, in effect, the desire for the supernatural may be, however strict the spirit's need which the desire manifests, how can one speak of something in man which would weigh on God, putting Him in dependence on man, since such desire or such a need—if it is in man—is not from Him? It is first entirely willed by God.[174]

The basis for the hermeneutic of paradox is ultimately the Incarnation. De Lubac remarks:

> If the union of nature and the supernatural was brought about in principle by the mystery of the Incarnation, the union of

---

170. Lubac, *Augustinianism and Modern Theology*, 12.
171. Aquinas, *Summa Theologica*, I, q. 21, a. 3.
172. Swafford and Oakes, *Nature and Grace*, 82.
173. Swafford and Oakes, *Nature and Grace*, 82.

174. Lubac, *Surnaturel*, 487. My translation. Original as follows: "Le monstre de l'exigence n'était donc qu'un fantôme. On s'évertuait à résoudre un faux problème. En réalité, la question de l'exigence *ne se pose pas*. Si pressant, en effet, que soit le désir du surnaturel, si strict que soit dans l'esprit le besoin qu'il traduit, comment pourrait-on parler a son sujet de quelque chose de l'homme qui pèserait sur Dieu, mettant Dieu sous la dépendance de l'homme, puisqu'un tel désir ou qu'un tel besoin, s'il est dans l'homme, n'est pas de lui? Il est tout entier d'abord voulu par Dieu."

nature and grace can be fully accomplished only through the mystery of the redemption.[175]

This notion responds to the structural problem of the relation between nature and grace in terms of the historical event of the Redemption. Importantly, this means that an analysis of nature and grace, creation and redemption, and ultimately therefore church and world, is incomplete without a consideration of the role of the Cross. It is the Cross that brings about the "new creation" and represents the historical resolution of the polarities between the two orders of nature and grace. Accordingly, this resolution is none other than the new covenant since the Cross is the blood of the covenant. This historical resolution of the polarities lies not only in the events of the Incarnation and Redemption, but also in the Eucharist, where the covenant is actualized sacramentally.[176]

Put simply, the resolution of the paradox between nature and grace is ultimately Christological. Without the unity between nature and grace in Christ's Incarnation and redemptive death, the supernatural would remain extrinsic to the human person.[177]

CONCLUSION

The relationship between nature and grace forms the crux of the question of how the Christian faith relates to modern culture. The manner in which these two elements relate to each other has been the subject of theological debates for centuries, especially since the time of the Reformation. Catholic theologians attempted to steer a path through the opposing extremes of Calvinism, which tended to denigrate human nature, and Baianism, which elevated it such that in his state of innocence, man could obtain God merely by means of natural merit. In response to this challenge, Catholic theology, purporting to base itself on the work of Aquinas and Aristotle's *Physics*, proposed the notion of the *Duplex Ordo*, from which the notion of "pure-nature" derives. The effect of the *Duplex Ordo* was to regrettably separate reality into natural and supernatural realms, contrary to the Thomistic synthesis. As de Lubac has pointed

---

175. Lubac, *Brief Catechesis*, 121.

176. S. Wood, "Nature-Grace Problematic," 400.

177. For an approach to the nature-grace question by means of the application of a Chalcedonian Christological hermeneutic using the grammar of unified distinction, specifically, *inconfuse, immutabiliter, indivise, inseparabiliter*, see Riches, "Christology."

out, this effect played into the hands of secular humanists, who now had theological premises for the cutting off of religious affairs from the public life of the state. Along with the rise of modern science, theology had, in a sense, conspired in its own bracketing out of public life. The late-nineteenth-century revival of Thomism, in the form of neo-scholasticism, while seeking to respond to the challenges of the Enlightenment and responding to Leo XIII's *Aeterni Patris*, tended to anachronistically read Aquinas, and led to the formation of a variety of different Thomisms in the twentieth century. One of the streams of these newly formed Thomisms was the revival of the Suárezian notion of the *Duplex Ordo* and the extrinsicist separation of nature and grace. The *nouvelle théologie*, in contrast to this, sought greater theological appropriation of modern categories of history, concrete philosophy, and political engagement. Drawing from the insights of Blondel, and embarking upon a project of *ressourcement*, the *nouvelle théologie*, led by de Lubac and others, sought a counter-theology to that of Leonine neo-scholasticism. By turning to the fathers and to medieval sources, the *nouvelle théologie* sought to engage modern philosophical, theological, and political concerns in a manner that went beyond the rationalistic categories of neo-scholasticism by rereading these ancient sources in light of the present challenges, and accordingly, by renouncing traditional apologetics in favor of fundamental theology. Principal among these concerns was the problem of secularization, and so de Lubac and his confrères set out to devise a new Christian humanism to challenge the secular variety. Part of this project involved a new understanding of the relationship between nature and grace, eschewing the Suárezian extrinsicist conception in favor of the notion of the intrinsicist paradox. While at first viewed with suspicion, and indeed, opposition, de Lubac's synthesis of nature and grace came to be largely adopted by the church in the Second Vatican Council and has formed the basis of most of theology in the second half of the twentieth century and beyond. Ratzinger and Milbank most certainly are two such inheritors of de Lubac's intrinsicist insights, which provide the church's theologians with formidable tools in addressing the problem of secularization.

3

Nature and Grace in the Thought of John Milbank

IN *RADICAL ORTHODOXY: A New Theology*, considered to be the theological manifesto of the Radical Orthodoxy movement, John Milbank notes that, for several centuries, secularism has been defining and constructing the world.[1] The world that has come about is one in which the theological is either discredited entirely or else turned into a merely private, leisure-time activity. While it may seem to us that the regnant secular culture possesses an unvarying momentum, according to Milbank, fractures are beginning to appear. For him, the logic of secularism is beginning to implode, and the lack of ultimate values and meaning in secular culture has led to a materialism that is soulless, aggressive, nonchalant, and nihilistic. In direct challenge to this state of affairs, Radical Orthodoxy sees itself as an attempt to reclaim the world by resituating its same concerns and activities within a *theological* framework.[2] This theological framework is based upon the ontology of participation (as developed by Plato and reworked by Christianity), because, according to Milbank, "any other configuration perforce reserves a territory independent from God."[3] This

---

1. Milbank, Pickstock, and Ward, *Radical Orthodoxy*, 1.
2. Milbank, Pickstock, and Ward, *Radical Orthodoxy*, 1.
3. Milbank, Pickstock, and Ward, *Radical Orthodoxy*, 3.

in turn serves the central objective of Radical Orthodoxy, which is a critique of the possibility of an autonomous secular sphere.

As we have seen in chapter 1, the *nouvelle théologie*, and specifically the thought of Henri de Lubac, is also of critical importance to Milbank's theology, particularly his notion of nature and grace. Confronted with the ravaging atheism that developed out of the nineteenth century, de Lubac also sought to give a theological response to atheistic nihilism and its social, political, and psychological consequences by means of the recovery of the notion of the supernatural. Milbank's emphasis on participation and de Lubac's emphasis on the supernatural provide the strongest point of contact between each other's theological thought, given their shared aim of confronting modern secular atheistic nihilism.[4] De Lubac's choice of the supernatural as his central theological concept was intended to accentuate the presence of grace in creation in opposition to the immanentist view of nature typical of modern secular thought. The modern view supposes that nature can exist in its own right without reference to the supernatural. De Lubac attempts, in other words, to "supernaturalize nature."[5] Against modern secular thought, Milbank's approach puts the primary emphasis on the absolute dependency of creation on God against the assertion of human autonomy by means of the notion of participation. In the end, although the idea of participation does not come to the fore in de Lubac's theology, Milbank argues that the two notions are interchangeable because they express the same reality in two different ways. Common to both ideas is the shared notion that creation is not complete in itself but is paradoxically dependent on God.[6] This equivalence is not without its limitations, as we shall see.

In examining Milbank's contribution to the nature-grace debate, we will firstly consider in greater depth the purpose and place that participation occupies in his thought, given its critical importance to his entire theological project, especially the nature-grace question. We will then turn to consider Milbank's notion of "graced nature" in relation to de Lubac's thought, before finally turning to an analysis of his treatment of Aquinas, as well as of Balthasar and Karl Rahner.

---

4. Lim, "John Milbank," 47. See also Milbank, "Programme," 43–44. Milbank here notes that the theological turn against nihilism is common ground also between Radical Orthodoxy and the French Catholic phenomenologists like Jean-Luc Marion.

5. Lim, "John Milbank," 47.

6. Lim, "John Milbank," 47.

THE FOUNDATIONAL NOTION OF PARTICIPATION

Given Radical Orthodoxy's stated desire to situate itself within postmodernism, it is perhaps surprising that it would seek to affirm the value and importance of metaphysics, given postmodernity's rejection of it.[7] Even though Milbank is suspicious of what Heidegger described as the "totalizing project of onto-theo-logy," Milbank has resisted the abandonment of the project of ontology altogether.[8] According to Milbank's reading of Western philosophy, there has been a gradual forgetting of the idea of participation, which in turn has led to the loss of meaning and depth in the world. He proposes that it is only by the recovery of this notion that philosophy can be rescued from the dead-end of nihilism. This is because participation makes possible the link between God and all creation without undermining the integrity of the same. Following de Lubac, Milbank makes use of the notion of paradox to best describe the participation of the finite in the infinite. At the risk of oversimplification, his position can be summed up as "participation through paradox."[9] According to Milbank, paradox is a "mediating" concept that falls within the domain of the *metaxological*.[10] He describes paradox as follows:

> Whereas dialectics is concerned with impossible contradiction that must be overcome, paradox is concerned with a *coincidence of opposites* that can be persisted with. The logic of paradox can also be described as the constitutively relational or *metaxological*, because it is about that which is "shared" and lies "between" identity and difference, univocality and equivocality.[11]

The advantage Milbank sees in the notion of participation is that it "refuses any reserve of created territory [which the secular could inhabit], while allowing finite things their own integrity."[12] He notes that, unfortunately, the traditional understanding of participation has neglected the cultural and political significance of the concept. Therefore, he proposes,

---

7. Smith, *Introducing Radical Orthodoxy*, 187.

8. Milbank, *Word Made Strange*, 44–45. See also Hankey, "*Theoria*," 390; and Cross, "Duns Scotus," 64–80.

9. Vorster, "Critical Assessment," 279.

10. Vorster, "Critical Assessment," 279. The notion of the concept of paradox as "mediating" is an important part of the repudiation of the position of Scotus, who, according to Milbank, failed to relate God to creation through a hierarchical process of emanation.

11. Žižek and Milbank, *Monstrosity of Christ*, 163. Emphasis in original.

12. Milbank, Pickstock, and Ward, "Introduction," 3.

participation should be reenvisioned in a postmodern context because, for him, the postmodern concern with the problem of language, culture, time, and history, far from being inimical to the Christian faith, can and should be embraced by it by means of a participatory framework.[13] The goal of Milbank's theological vision is therefore to attempt to reclaim all the realms of human life by means of the tool of participation—realms that, he thinks, have been too long colonized by secularism.[14] In the section that follows, we will briefly examine Milbank's idea of how postmodern culture arrived at the rejection of participation and how Radical Orthodoxy proposes to recover it in a Christian context.

A Narratival, Meta-Historical Perspective

An aspect of great importance to Milbank's theology and indeed the entire Radical Orthodoxy project is the account of the history of philosophy and theology.[15] This is because the way that Radical Orthodoxy communicates its own identity is by way of *narrative* (in line with its embracing of postmodern categories).[16] In saying this, and according to Lucy Gardner, it is fundamental to Radical Orthodoxy's program and to its own sense of identity that the story it narrates be one of opposition. That is, the history narrated by Milbank involves a "genealogy of error," an archaeology of sorts, in answer to the question of what went wrong, and where.[17] There is a sense in which Radical Orthodoxy must be historically situated, and indeed calls into question the notion of systematic theology, articulating instead a theology *of* and *for* culture in response to the times without sacrificing on the altar of relevance.[18] Radical Orthodoxy's polemical histories are an effort to read the signs of the times genealogically, asking with a critical mind of postmodern secular

---

13. For a dissenting perspective concerning the value of the ontology of participation, particularly as it concerns the Christian affirmation of the intrinsic being and goodness of creatures, see Triffett, "*Processio*," 900–916.

14. Lim, "John Milbank," 48. For other approaches to the question of the postsecular turn and the attempt to reclaim secular space, see Bielik-Robson, "Post-Secular Turn," 57–82.

15. Smith, *Introducing Radical Orthodoxy*, 89.

16. For a detailed treatment of the relation between participatory ontology and narrative in Milbank's thought, and also the notion of the incarnational account of language, see Lim, "John Milbank," 115–18, 124–31.

17. Gardner, "Listening," 135.

18. Smith, *Introducing Radical Orthodoxy*, 90.

culture how we got here.[19] From a meta-historical perspective, Radical Orthodoxy's histories tend to be narratives that are qualified by rupture and discontinuity rather than by progress and continuity. For example, Milbank and other authors in the Radical Orthodoxy movement point to a paradigm shift in Western culture (modernity) that gave birth to a new, unparalleled account of the world and social relationships. These philosophical and theological shifts gave birth to new social arrangements, political ideals, and economic models as well as to new accounts of human nature, all of which were slowly globalized through the exportation of liberal democracy and capitalist economics.[20] In his text *Theology and Social Theory*, Milbank adopts an "archaeological approach that traces the genesis of the main forms of secular reason, in such a fashion as to unearth the arbitrary moments in the construction of their logic."[21] In other words, Milbank possesses a methodological hermeneutic of suspicion in his genealogy of postmodern thought, noting that contemporary ontologies are not what they claim to be.[22]

James K. A. Smith points out that postmodernism typically conceives of itself as a rupture with modernity, such that Western culture now lives an entirely different cultural configuration (hence the notion of *post*modernism). Milbank is especially keen to challenge the postmodern account of the supposed superiority of the present age. He judges that the postmodern tendency to see itself as having risen above modernity is nothing more than "ahistorical hubris which denies tradition."[23] It should be noted however that postmodernity's self-understanding as being in discontinuity with the modern ironically at the same time assumes a fundamental continuity of all that has gone before, namely, the history of metaphysics from Plato to Husserl. Smith notes that this is why the question of Augustine is so contested, because many accounts of him, particularly his notion of selfhood, construe him as simply the precursor to Descartes.[24] The "Augustine self" is taken to be a proto-Cartesian subject, indicating a fundamental continuity between ancient and modern. The story is then taken a step further by tracing the lineage of this modern subject back through Augustine, and ultimately to Plato.

19. Smith, *Introducing Radical Orthodoxy*, 90.
20. Smith, *Introducing Radical Orthodoxy*, 91.
21. Milbank, *Theology and Social Theory*, 3.
22. Smith, *Introducing Radical Orthodoxy*, 91.
23. Smith, *Introducing Radical Orthodoxy*, 91.
24. Smith, *Introducing Radical Orthodoxy*, 91.

As Charles Taylor points out, "on the way from Plato to Descartes stands Augustine."[25] The filiation of the modern self is narrated by positing a continuity between the Platonic, Augustinian, and Cartesian accounts of the subject, ultimately locating in Plato an anticipation of the modern self.[26] There is a reason, according to Michael Hanby, why postmodern authors want to tell such a story, that is, having linked Christianity to modernity, in rejecting modernity they can also reject Christianity.[27]

In contrast to postmodern authors, Milbank sees a deep continuity between modern and postmodern thought such that what goes under the banner of postmodernism is really just "hyper-modernism."[28] Milbank emphasizes the degree to which the supposedly postmodern thinkers such as Derrida and Foucault replay and play out the ontology of modernity. On the other hand, he contests the purported continuity between medieval and modern thought, perceiving there to be a definitive rupture in the Middle Ages. As stated, postmodern thinkers tend to posit a line of continuity from Augustine via Aquinas and Scotus to Descartes. Milbank instead argues that Scotus represents a paradigm shift in ontology that eventually results in modernity as well as, ultimately, nihilism.[29] For Milbank, it was Scotus's shift away from a metaphysics of participation towards an ontology predicated on the univocity of being that "rent the cords of suspension that hooked the immanent to the transcendent, the material to the more than material."[30] What issued was modernity's flattened ontology, and inevitable nihilism.

Duns Scotus and the Univocity of Being

According to Smith, one of the unique contributions of Radical Orthodoxy's reading of history is the claim that the supposed origins of modernity are not where most would think they are. In most postmodern accounts, to discover the origins of modernity, all one need do is to look to the Enlightenment, particularly to the figures of Descartes and Kant. It should be noted however that Radical Orthodoxy does not deny that

25. Taylor, *Sources of the Self*, 127.
26. Smith, *Introducing Radical Orthodoxy*, 92.
27. Hanby, *Augustine and Modernity*, 135.
28. Smith, *Introducing Radical Orthodoxy*, 92.
29. Smith, *Introducing Radical Orthodoxy*, 93.
30. Smith, *Introducing Radical Orthodoxy*, 93.

Descartes and Kant were fundamental to the project of the Enlightenment; however, it seeks what made a Descartes or a Kant possible.[31]

As stated, for Milbank, the answer to this question is found in the late medieval shift in ontology away from participation and towards the univocity of being, epitomized especially in the work of Scotus. Milbank's critique of Scotus (itself the subject of criticism for his purported fixation with him), is not however without precedent. Milbank took his lead from the insights of Étienne Gilson and Jean-Luc Marion, among others, on this score.[32] In contrast to Aquinas's participatory metaphysics and his *analogia entis*, Scotus proposed an ontology predicated upon the univocity of being. Put simply, for Aquinas, the notion that "God is" can only be understood by analogy with the sense in which a creature "is." For Aquinas, the mode of being of God is fundamentally different from the mode of being of creatures; God's essence is existence, whereas a creature exists only to the extent to which it participates in the being of God. Aquinas makes a distinction between existence that is *per essentiam* and existence that is *per participationem*, that is, by essence or by participation.[33] Aquinas writes:

> Every thing, furthermore, exists because it has being. Consequently, a thing whose essence is not its being is not through its essence, but by participation in something, namely, being itself. But that which is through participation in something cannot be the first being, because prior to it is the being in which it participates in order to be. But God is the first being, with nothing prior to Him. The essence of God, therefore, is his own being.[34]

Contrary to Scotus, the implication of Aquinas's notion is that creation does not stand *alongside* God or even *outside* God; creation is never completely autonomous because creation is, at every moment, *suspended over* the *nihil*, held in existence by *participating in* existence

---

31. Smith, *Introducing Radical Orthodoxy*, 95. See also Milbank, "Programme," 38–39. Here Milbank sets out why Radical Orthodoxy does not situate itself in a post-Kantian intellectual space. Milbank is not of the view (contra transcendental Thomism) that Kant can in any way be reconciled with the patristic and high medieval tradition, because his rejection of speculative metaphysics is a refusal of a late-Scholastic distortion of the tradition (falsely claiming that man enjoys a special intellectual intuition of the first cause of Being as such). Milbank maintains instead that Kant is the *fulfillment*, not the overturning, of late Scholasticism.

32. Smith, *Introducing Radical Orthodoxy*, 95.

33. Cf. Aquinas, *Summa Theologica*, I, q. 3, a. 4, ad 3.

34. Aquinas, *Summa contra Gentiles*, I, q. 22, c. 9.

itself. Radical Orthodoxy emphasizes that creation has no existence that is self-standing and properly its own, instead receiving its being at every moment from an infinite and gratuitous God.[35]

For Milbank, therefore, creation *is* only insofar as it participates in or *is suspended from* the Creator. Smith notes that Radical Orthodoxy employs the metaphor of "suspension" in a dual sense: on the one hand, it indicates the way in which the created, immanent order is linked to the transcendent divine order. On the other hand, the created order is "suspended by" the transcendent order in the sense that it is always interrupted by the transcendent, the site for the in-breaking of the transcendent.[36] Scotus's position, in contrast, is that being should be predicated *univocally*, meaning that both the Creator and the creature exist *in the same way* or in the same sense. Milbank points out that this idea has meant that the notion of *being* became a category that is unhooked from participation in God and became a neutral or abstract qualifier that is applied *to* God and to creatures in the same way.[37] Philip Blond notes that "Duns Scotus, when considering the universal science of metaphysics, elevated being (*ens*) to a higher station over God, so that being could be distributed to both God and his creatures."[38] In this way, the suspension of creation from the Creator was severed, and because being is thereby "flattened," the world is free to become autonomous from its Creator. Simon Oliver points out that:

> [For Radical Orthodoxy] it is the loss of the centrality and meaning of creation's participation in God in the late Middle Ages that inaugurated the rise of the secular and the notion of an autonomous sphere of existence standing alongside God that would eventually become the *natura pura*.[39]

Milbank points out that Scotus's univocity's producing an autonomous (effectively secular) metaphysics treats finite creatures as wholly available for comprehension, and that they univocally *are* as much as the infinite. This notion, for Milbank, is tantamount to an "idolatry toward

---

35. Oliver, "Henri de Lubac," 388.

36. Smith, *Introducing Radical Orthodoxy*, 97.

37. For another view on this issue, see D. C. Schindler, *Love*, 14–15. Schindler uses the term "bourgeois metaphysics" to explicate the implications of the univocity of being and its negative consequences.

38. Blond, *Post-Secular Philosophy*, 6.

39. Oliver, "Henri de Lubac," 397.

creatures."[40] In *The Word Made Strange*, he points out that, by way of contrast, Christian thought, which flowed from Gregory of Nyssa and Augustine, was able to concede the utter unknowability of creatures, which continually alter and have no ground within themselves.[41] This concept is what marks the difference between Aquinas and Scotus. For Aquinas, finite being is not on its own account subsistently anything but is only granted to be in various ways.[42] Milbank is concerned with the space for modernity that is opened up by Scotus's univocal ontology. The immanentization or "flattening" of the world, as opposed to the Platonic account of suspension (*methexis*), is a matter that is of fundamental importance. Univocity has meant the separation of the Creator from the creature, which in turn has made possible a discrete, secular order. Milbank seeks to call attention to the fact that behind modernity's politics (liberal, secular), is an epistemology (autonomous reason) that is in turn supported by an ontology (univocity and the denial of participation). The modern turn towards epistemology is predicated upon the shift to a univocal ontology.[43] Smith points out that Milbank's (and Radical Orthodoxy's) interpretation of Scotus remains the most contested aspect of its historical narrative. He notes that it is important to distinguish between the historical claim (that Scotus's development of a univocal ontology generated what would become secular philosophies of immanence) from the systematic or conceptual claim that adherence to the univocity of being engenders a secular metaphysics that is devoid of the transcendent. It could be possible perhaps to hold to the first without necessarily entailing the second.[44]

As we have seen, for Milbank, one of the greatest challenges of secular modernity is that it ends in nihilism. He sees the nihilist narrative as the only serious rival to the Christian narrative because all other ideologies (whether they be scientific truth, Enlightenment humanism, market economies, liberal polities, or secular reason) are but masked or disguised versions of nihilism.[45] This is so because, for Milbank, to deny

---

40. Milbank, "Only Theology," 334.
41. Milbank, *Word Made Strange*, 44.
42. Milbank and Pickstock, *Truth in Aquinas*, 34.
43. Smith, *Introducing Radical Orthodoxy*, 100.
44. Smith, *Introducing Radical Orthodoxy*, 100. For a further discussion on this point, including a challenge to Milbank's claim that secular ontologies are necessarily non-analogical, see Adsett, "Milbank and Heidegger."
45. Smith, *Introducing Radical Orthodoxy*, 101.

God is to invite nihilism, because it is a direct result of the flattening of the cosmos by means of univocity. A system of thought that is cut off from its suspension from the transcendent is effectively a closed system, autonomous in its supposed self-sufficiency. In this way, it is the antithesis of the Christian account of creation and shuts the cosmos up in a "suffocating immanence."[46] Thus only the suspension of the material from the ideal or transcendent is able to guard the material from nothingness (the *nihil*). For Milbank, if one really wants to value immanence, it must be suspended from the transcendent; if one wants to valorize appearances, it must be done by exceeding them.[47]

Platonism/Christianity

If the antithesis of the Christian narrative is secularist nihilism, then according to Milbank the antidote (as stated) is the recovery of a metaphysics of participation in which creation recognizes its suspension from the transcendent. In other words, what is required is an ontology that recharges *immanence* with *transcendence*. Radical Orthodoxy does this by turning to Plato.[48] Milbank has stressed the importance of a "Platonic theurgic Christian vision."[49] The recovery of Platonism for Radical Orthodoxy is arguably a recovery not of the dualistic Neoplatonism of Plotinus, but the theurgical Neoplatonism of Iamblichus (AD 250–325).[50] As Smith contends, it is in theurgical Platonism that one finds a much more robust valuation of the body, materiality, and sacramentality.[51] Milbank, however, goes beyond a merely Platonic notion of *methexis* and turns to a Christian theological framework to establish that the relationship of dependence of creation on the Creator could be described in terms of grace or giftedness: "one could interpret this to mean that, for Aquinas, all creatures subsist by grace in the sense that they only subsist in their

---

46. Milbank, Pickstock, and Ward, *Radical Orthodoxy*, 3.
47. Smith, *Introducing Radical Orthodoxy*, 193.
48. Smith, *Introducing Radical Orthodoxy*, 103.
49. Milbank, *Theology and Social Theory*, xx.
50 Smith, *Introducing Radical Orthodoxy*, 93. See also Hankey, "Philosophical Religion," 17–30; and Hedley, "Radical Orthodoxy and Apocalyptic Difference," 107. Hedley here notes that Milbank agrees with Hankey's diagnosis that the theology of Radical Orthodoxy is rooted in the "Dionysian legacy of theurgic Neoplatonism."
51. Smith, *Introducing Radical Orthodoxy*, 93.

constant 'return' to full divine self-presence."[52] Everything is therefore "engraced," and in this way a participatory ontology is at root an affirmation of the goodness of creation. It is on this point that Smith contends that Milbank actually goes beyond the *nouvelle théologie*, a fundamental point to which we will return later in the chapter.[53] It is *transcendence* that properly retains the depth of immanence, and also the value of embodiment. Therefore, despite postmodern philosophy's talk about the body, Milbank ultimately criticizes it for being Gnostic.[54]

According to Smith, the most radical way to articulate Milbank's notion of participation is in his persistent assertion that "in itself matter is nothing,"[55] which echoes Augustine's assertion that "matter participates in something belonging to the ideal world, otherwise it would not be matter."[56] Milbank argues that the immanentism of nihilistic modernity generates a dualism-within-a-monism, and that, as such, it is unable to value the material specifically *as* material. Rather, its flattening of materiality simply ends up evacuating materiality. In this respect, modern rationalism is but the inversion of Nietzschean nihilism, as both have much in common with the traditional dualisms and their account of the body.[57] Radical Orthodoxy's interest in Plato, as we have seen, has the specific goal of overcoming nihilistic ontologies of immanentism or of reductionistic materialism by means of the "suspension of the material." Only by means of suspension from the ideal or transcendent can the material be guarded against descent into the "nihil." Radical Orthodoxy therefore "retrieves" Plato, however, through an Augustinian filter.[58] This is why Milbank describes his project as "postmodern critical Augustinianism," as we saw in chapter 1.

Fundamentally, what stands at the core of Milbank's theological vision is the drive to reclaim the entire realm of human life from secularity by means of the Platonic/Augustinian notion of participation, a notion that, as we will see, directly impacts Milbank's idea of how nature and grace relate.[59]

52. Milbank and Pickstock, *Truth in Aquinas*, 37–38.
53. Smith, *Introducing Radical Orthodoxy*, 192.
54. Milbank, "Materialism and Transcendence," 11.
55. Milbank, "Materialism and Transcendence," 26.
56. Augustine, *Of True Religion*, 22.
57. Smith, *Introducing Radical Orthodoxy*, 105.
58. Smith, *Introducing Radical Orthodoxy*, 105.
59. Radical Orthodoxy considers the only radical critique of modernity (that

AN ENGRACED NATURE

In considering Milbank's approach to the question of nature and grace, it is opportune to recall his methodology, which will assist us in more fully understanding what will be presented. In returning to the riches of Christian thought prior to modernity, Milbank's method lies between the genealogical approach of late modern philosophy and the *ressourcement* theology of de Lubac and his confrères. According to Simon Oliver (a close collaborator of Milbank in the Radical Orthodoxy project), this approach refuses to accept the fixed disciplinary boundaries of modern academic discourse and reflects the traditional Thomist view that theology does not have a strictly defined subject matter but is about all things in relation to God.[60] De Lubac's *ressourcement* was similarly concerned with tracing the history of theological concepts in opposition to the "ossifying tendencies of Neo-Scholasticism."[61] Uncovering shifts in the understanding of nature and grace is an example of this genealogical methodology explored by Milbank, particularly in his *Theology and Social Theory*.

Henri de Lubac and the *Nouvelle Théologie*

As we have seen, Radical Orthodoxy considers itself to be in profound continuity with the *nouvelle théologie* and especially with the figure of Henri de Lubac. For instance, de Lubac is the only modern thinker who has been the subject of a book-length treatment in Milbank's *Suspended Middle: Henri de Lubac*. Milbank also devoted sympathetic pages of his *Theology and Social Theory* to de Lubac's efforts to recover an integral view of the human person, for which, as we have seen, the supernatural was the fulfilment of natural human desire. As Oliver points out, Radical Orthodoxy sees itself as an extension of the project of the *nouvelle théologie*.[62] According to Edward T. Oakes:

---

which denies the existence of the secular as a self-subsisting, immanent self-ordering of the world that has no need for God) to be the doctrines of the Incarnation and Creation, which stand opposed to closed, immanent systems. Thus to counter the politics and epistemology of secular modernity, Radical Orthodoxy attempts to unveil the status of the same as *mythos* and to articulate a counter-ontology that does justice to materiality and embodiment. For a detailed treatment of such counter-ontologies, see Smith, *Introducing Radical Orthodoxy*, 189–228.

60. Oliver, "Henri de Lubac," 396.
61. Oliver, "Henri de Lubac," 396.
62. Oliver, "Henri de Lubac," 396. See also Milbank, "Programme," 36. Milbank

> Milbank's admiration for de Lubac seems ultimately grounded, at least as I read his text, in his insistence that de Lubac was really the first advocate, *avant la lettre*, of Radical Orthodoxy: "In effect, the *Surnaturel* thesis *deconstructs* the possibility of dogmatical theology as previously understood in modern times, just as it equally deconstructs the possibility of philosophical theology or even of a clearly autonomous philosophy *tout court*."[63]

Radical Orthodoxy's alliance with Roman Catholic thought, particularly the *nouvelle théologie*, is stronger than with Barthian neo-orthodoxy. De Lubac is considered to be a greater theological revolutionary than Karl Barth because of his questioning of the hierarchical duality of grace and nature, which allowed him to transcend (unlike Barth) the shared background assumption of all modern theology.[64] In this way, according to Milbank, de Lubac inaugurated a properly *post*modern theology, as he notes in his *Truth in Aquinas*, describing de Lubac's work as:

> continuing and recommencing the real theological revolution of the twentieth century . . . [t]he overcoming of the grace/nature duality—with Blondel, de Lubac and, in a very flawed manner Karl Rahner—finally arrived at a theologically "postmodern" questioning of modern assumptions, whereas Karl Barth remained basically within those assumptions and so within modernity.[65]

Milbank draws upon the research of Jacob Schmutz, who traces the development of the nature-grace debate and who demonstrates how the "united movement of God" (grace) and "free creatures" (nature) had developed in the late-medieval and Baroque periods into the separation between the "creature's free action" and the extrinsic "concurrence or general influence of God."[66] In other words, Schmutz demonstrates

---

here addresses the question: If Radical Orthodoxy considers itself to be a continuation of the *nouvelle théologie*, why is there a need for a new name? Milbank, in many respects, thinks that de Lubac and the *nouvelle théologie* do not go far enough and that Radical Orthodoxy is not a specifically Roman Catholic movement (it can be espoused by Protestants as well). He also observes that the Roman Catholic tradition still finds it difficult to come to terms with the legacy of de Lubac (such as the accusation against it by traditionalists of having colluded with modernism).

63. Oakes, "Paradox," 682. Emphasis in original.
64. Milbank, "Programme," 34.
65. Milbank and Pickstock, *Truth in Aquinas*, 38.
66. Levering, "Note," 526. See also Schmutz, "Doctrine médiévale," 217–64.

how a more intrinsically correlated notion of nature and grace became separated into an extrinsic notion in the late-medieval and Baroque periods (a development we explored in chapter 2). Drawing upon Schmutz's contributions, Milbank argues for what he terms "gift without contrast" (essentially a rejection of the pure-nature notion). Given Milbank's adoption of much of de Lubac's insights in the nature-grace debate, it is no surprise that he too would be an intrinsicist. Thus, as we have seen, it is on the specific question of the relationship between nature and grace that Milbank has found the most consonance with de Lubac's work, such that the defense of de Lubac's position on nature and grace has proved central to the various debates in which Radical Orthodoxy is most invested.[67]

Paradox

With de Lubac, Milbank has diagnosed the inherent dangers of separating existence into dual realms that stand over and against each other on a univocal plane (that is, an extrinsicist view of nature and grace).[68] The central thesis of *The Suspended Middle* (fundamentally an exegesis of de Lubac's theology of grace) is as follows:

> If Creation implies both autonomous being and entirely heteronomous gift, while grace implies a raising of oneself as oneself to the beyond oneself, then the natural desire of the supernatural implies the dynamic link between the two orders that constitutes spirit, such that this link is at once entirely an aspect of the Creation and entirely also the work, in advance of itself, of grace which unites human creatures to the Creator.[69]

As if to anticipate objections to the intrinsicist position, Milbank acknowledges in *The Suspended Middle* that the turning of the Cajetanian Aquinas inside out threatens to compromise both the gratuity of God in offering grace and the whole capacity of the created order to act for its own intrinsic end, goals, and purposes. It would seem (to the objector) then that the philosophical basis of theology, the truth of revealed dogmas, and the ethics of the natural law all stand at risk of implosion.[70] This problem he defines as "the suspended middle" (a phrase he borrows

---

67. Oliver, "Henri de Lubac," 394.
68. Oakes, "Paradox," 682.
69. Milbank, *Suspended Middle*, 39.
70. Fields, Review of *Suspended Middle*, 747.

from Balthasar, who in turn derived it from Erich Przywara), hence the title of the book.

According to Milbank, de Lubac succeeds in returning Catholic theology and philosophy to the authentic standpoint of the fathers and the High Middle Ages, and successfully addresses the concerns raised more recently by postmodern philosophy. As we have seen in chapter 2, de Lubac's solution to the problem of the gratuity of grace was first to admit the paradox that arises in the juxtaposition of the concepts of nature and grace, a paradox that he sought to resolve in what Milbank terms a "revisionary" ontology:

> [De Lubac's] account of grace and the supernatural is *ontologically revisionary*. The natural desire cannot be frustrated, yet it cannot be of itself fulfilled. Human nature in its self-exceeding seems in justice to require a gift—yet the gift of grace remains beyond all justice and all requirement. This paradox is for de Lubac only to be entertained because one must remember that the just requirement for the gift in humanity is itself a created gift.[71]

Milbank rightly considers de Lubac's theology to be revisionary because de Lubac realized, more than any other theologian of the twentieth century, that the presence of spirit in the cosmos requires a revision in the standard terms under which debates on grace and nature take place. That is, he realized that spirit is a *different kind of nature* from the natural forms found in the rest of the natural world, thus requiring a different kind of ontology from that which Aristotle's more biologically determined ontology could provide.[72]

As Oliver notes, maintaining the paradox of grace and nature in this way is part of Radical Orthodoxy's commitment both to creation as the gift *ex nihilo* and also to the metaphysics of participation. The difference between God and creation is unlike the difference between creatures; God establishes creation as other than himself. For Milbank, the difference between God and creation is itself a gift. Importantly, creation's participation in God is not proper to creation; God grants to creation a participation in his own substantiality.[73] Oliver clarifies that creation's ability to receive the gifts of God is *itself* a gift. There is nothing

---

71. Levering, "Note," 30. Emphasis in original.
72. Oakes, "Paradox," 673. See also Lim, "John Milbank," 56.
73. Oliver, "Henri de Lubac," 402.

that stands outside this economy of divine gratuity. What creation has is genuinely its own, but what belongs to creation is always a gift.

For Milbank, man's natural desire for the beatific vision does not constitute an obligation that is external to God, lying outside the divine economy of creation, because that desire also finds its ultimate source in God. Oliver notes that the natural desire for the supernatural is still genuinely the rational creature's own, but its ultimate first cause is God. Man's "just requirement" for the "genuinely new second gift of grace which will bring humanity to the beatific vision must be understood as 'beyond all justice and requirement,'" because that just requirement arises from a natural desire for the supernatural, which is God's first gift in creation.[74] Put more simply, humanity renounces any claim upon God because its primary nature is receptivity to the divine gift, first of "being" and second of "beatitude."[75] Oliver is quick to point out, however, that the view that the natural desire for the supernatural is a gift of God carries with it an obvious danger, namely, that it seems to turn everything into a matter of grace and rids human nature of any integrity. As we have seen, this is one of the objections that extrinsicists maintain; however, Milbank adheres to the notion of the paradox notwithstanding.

As stated, Milbank holds that creation is the first gift of an existence that is other than God, while grace is the second and wholly new gift of deification, in which humanity is united to God without losing creaturely integrity. Oliver proposes that in Milbank's thought, "the natural desire for the supernatural is 'the gift of the bond' between the first and second gifts, 'negotiated by the spirit's freedom.'"[76] In this way, the natural desire for the supernatural is a "suspended middle" that indicates:

> the unity-in-distinction of the orders of grace and nature. It rests in a double paradox: creation is autonomous being and yet heteronomous gift, while grace is the raising of human spirit, as human spirit, to be beyond human spirit.[77]

For many modern theologians (particularly of the extrinsicist sort), paradox is a sign of incoherence and confusion and must therefore be resolved; a thing must belong either to the realm of nature or to the realm of grace. Oliver notes that for these theologians, as nature is relinquished,

---

74. Oliver, "Henri de Lubac," 402.
75. Oliver, "Henri de Lubac," 403.
76. Oliver, "Henri de Lubac," 403.
77. Oliver, "Henri de Lubac," 403.

it gives way to grace in a kind of "zero-sum game," in which we have either one or the other. He points out that for de Lubac, Christian theology is paradoxical in the sense that it is structured around both/and, not either/or. Oliver states:

> Creation is *both* other than God *and* nothing; Christ is *both* divine *and* human; spiritual creatures are *both* natural *and* intrinsically orientated to the supernatural; grace is *both* innately desired by nature *and* a wholly new gift. Paradox is not a logical contradiction to be overcome or a mystery that will be clarified on the far side of the *eschaton*. It is not a fog that will clear once further investigation has been undertaken or the concepts clarified.[78]

According to Oliver, paradox is not simply a function of language that could be resolved if only we sorted out our conceptual schemata, but is part of the highest reaches of metaphysics. The tension of paradox is itself (paradoxically) revealing. So it is only by holding together divine and human, grace and nature, faith and reason, sacred and secular, that the non-competitive and blended structure of these concepts becomes apparent and each reveals the other.[79] Oliver points out that Milbank sees the paradoxical nature of metaphysics and theology as contrasted with modern dialectics that is associated particularly with the philosophy of Georg Wilhelm Friedrich Hegel (1770–1831) (that is, the proposal of thesis and antithesis that is resolved into synthesis).[80] In short, dialectics overcomes all tension and resolves into a unity, whereas paradox requires the maintenance of tension as intrinsic to the depths of created being.[81]

Oliver rightly notes that the importance of paradox for Milbank (and Christian theology more generally) can be understood in relation to the paradox that stands at the heart of our faith, that is, the Incarnation. Christ is both fully divine and fully human yet remains only one person. Oliver points out that attempts to resolve this paradox, that is, to decide that Christ is really divine *or* human, were rejected by ecumenical

---

78. Oliver, "Henri de Lubac," 404–5.

79. Oliver, "Henri de Lubac," 406.

80. For a critique of Milbank's treatment of Hegel, see Peddle, "Theology, Social Theory," 117–32.

81. Oliver, "Henri de Lubac," 406. I am reminded of the image of a guitar string that must remain in tension between two poles in order for it to produce a sound when plucked.

councils of the church.⁸² Christ must stand in a "suspended middle" between divine and human, finite and infinite, by being *both* divine *and* human. Because these are not mutually exclusive univocal natures (they do not, as it were, compete for space in Christ), Christ is fully both.⁸³ Oliver goes on to say that, for Radical Orthodoxy, this paradoxical relationship between infinite and finite is mirrored in the paradoxical relationship between Christ's body, the church, and the world, and between the grace that Christ offers and the nature that always intrinsically desires that grace. The paradox of Christ, which seeks no synthesis or resolution, reveals implications beyond Christology in the paradoxical nature of metaphysics itself, in which tensions give rise to tensions and there cannot be any final and complete analysis outside God, in whom all opposites coincide.⁸⁴ According to Oliver, the insight of Radical Orthodoxy is that whereas modern thought seeks mastery and control in terms of resolution, the philosophy and theology of antiquity and the Middle Ages understood paradoxical mystery to lie at the heart of a symbolically created reality that points, paradoxically, to a Creator who lies beyond all image and symbol.

Gift

For Milbank, it would seem that it is conscious spirit that stands in a "suspended middle" that cannot be simply a part of nature or purely a matter of grace. Oliver proposes that "conscious spirit" is something natural and supernatural, something human and divine. Following de Lubac, Milbank answers this question through a category that has been central to Radical Orthodoxy's engagement with wider theology and philosophy, namely, the notion of "gift." Oliver explains that, for Milbank, spirit is conscious of continuously receiving itself as gift. This is more than a feeling of absolute dependence; it is the drive to know the source of what we are as recipient spirits who cannot fully command what is received because a gift must always "flow," continually giving itself anew.⁸⁵

---

82. Specifically, the Council of Nicaea (325), which condemned both Docetism and Arianism (representing the two extremes of an attempt to resolve the paradox of the Incarnation) as Christological heresies.

83. Oliver, "Henri de Lubac," 404.

84. Oliver, "Henri de Lubac," 407.

85. Oliver, "Henri de Lubac," 407.

The appropriate response to this gift is, of course, gratitude. According to Oliver, this establishes an important characteristic of the gift for Milbank, namely, reciprocity. Milbank insists that for a gift truly to be gift it must be acknowledged as such, hence the importance of gratitude. Thanksgiving is itself a reciprocal, return gift. This notion is in contrast to Derrida, who maintains that for a gift to be truly a gift it must be only one-way—from giver to recipient (and thereby totally selfless or purely altruistic); for Milbank the gift requires reciprocal exchange because the gift must be acknowledged as such. Therefore, for Milbank, gift establishes relationship through reciprocity.[86]

Given that Milbank grants the radical ontological difference between God and creatures (analogy rather than univocity), he critiques "the supposed discovery of fixed general *conditioning* circumstances within which the conditioned must operate."[87] Understanding the created order as "fixed general conditioning circumstances" in which grace must operate, in Milbank's view produces a separation between God and his creation, so that an "ontological contract" between God and creatures replaces the "ontological gift-exchange" (the position that Milbank favors).[88] For Milbank, this means that creatures would become autonomous agents whose properties are the "contractual" foundations of an extrinsic gift of grace (similar to the *debitum naturae*). In other words, the gift of grace would conform to creatures' autonomous structure, as though God's activity in creating and sustaining being was unrelated to his gift of grace, and as though God's grace could only impact the created order in an extrinsic fashion, according to which the created order is determinative.[89] With respect to the notion of the metaphysics of gift, Milbank describes de Lubac's insight:

> The divine gift descending exceeds conditioning/conditioned specularity, just as the aspiring *élan* to the supernatural exceeds the contractual reciprocity of immanent being and opens to view a "non-ontology," or what Claude Bruaire calls an "ontodology."[90]

Fundamentally, the key for Milbank is overcoming the "contrast" that pits the gift of creation against the gift of grace. That is, the "divine

---

86. Oliver, "Henri de Lubac," 407.
87. Milbank, *Suspended Middle*, 101. Emphasis in original.
88. Milbank, *Suspended Middle*, 100.
89. Levering, "Note," 527.
90. Milbank, *Suspended Middle*, 102.

gift descending" (grace) cannot be limited by the conditions imposed by the gift of creation, and neither can the gift of creation be understood in "contractual" terms as though it were not already caught up, as ascending spirit, in the gift-exchange accomplished in and through the "divine gift descending." In short, this means that the gift of creation and the gift of grace are already united in the one divine gifting.[91]

Pure-Nature and the Gratuity of Grace

Against the extrinsicist view of the created order, considered as a closed system, Milbank turns to de Lubac in order to "recover the unity of divine action in creatures and the priority of divine gifting over against the notion of autonomous creatures' structures."[92] Milbank points out that in concrete, historical humanity, there is no such thing as a state of "pure-nature"; rather, "every person has always already been worked upon by divine grace, with the consequence that one cannot analytically separate 'natural' and 'supernatural' contributions to this integral unity."[93] Following de Lubac, Milbank maintains that the notion of pure-nature, despite what it is intended to achieve, actually fails to guarantee the absolute gratuity of grace because it conceives of grace in a way that is univocal with gifts *within* the created order.[94] Donation within creation implies the gift of something to an already established recipient. Similarly, pure-nature "implies a recipient standing in purity outside the economy of gift prior to the receipt of any gift."[95] Oliver states:

> How, asks Milbank, does this "pure nature" receive this gift? Does it do so purely of its own volition, recognizing and thereby receiving the gift by virtue of its own willful power, a power kept in reserve beyond the gift? Indeed, if a pure nature is understood to stand outside the economy of gift in this way, it establishes an autonomy for the created order and a distance from God whereby humanity can willfully require of God the gift of beatitude on the basis of its self-standing "pure nature."[96]

---

91. Levering, "Note," 527.
92. Levering, "Note," 527.
93. Milbank, *Theology and Social Theory*, 206.
94. Oliver, "Henri de Lubac," 402.
95. Oliver, "Henri de Lubac," 403.
96. Oliver, "Henri de Lubac," 403.

This position would be essentially Pelagian, according to de Lubac. Crucially, for grace to be truly gratuitous it must presume nothing, "not even creation." This is why, according to Milbank, creation *ex nihilo* is not the establishment of a pure-nature to which grace is later added, but the expression of an eternal gratuity into which nature is always drawn, even from the moment of its being spoken into existence by God. This notion is what Milbank means when he speaks of "gift without contrast."[97] Oliver points out that there are modes or distinctions of gift and always the possibility of the genuinely new gift, but there is nothing lying outside the economy of divine gratuity against which it can be contrasted.

Milbank is aware that these reflections are of critical importance for the theology and pastoral outreach of the church, as opposed to what he considers the missteps that followed in the wake of Aquinas, particularly those of Scotus and Luther, who helped to contribute to the devastating divisions of the Western church.[98] As Milbank points out:

> [With the concept of "pure-nature"] one still faces the sort of problems which plagued all theologians after Scotus and especially those of the seventeenth century: namely, how does pure nature receive the gift—of its own volition or by the gift as standing over against its natural ungivenness? The first solution is Pelagian; the second, in Lutheran fashion, sees grace as overriding our freedom.[99]

According to Oliver, Milbank gives de Lubac's understanding of the gratuity of grace an even more radical reading. For Milbank, Aquinas's Neoplatonic understanding of causation involves the inflowing, or *influentia*, of divine causal power into secondary causes in such a way that God is not simply one cause among others. This notion has the crucial consequence that creation is not an object upon which God acts by means of the delivery of grace, but is "the very instantiation of causation or 'influence.'"[100] So rather than God acting *on* something through the delivery of grace, Milbank proposes that the correct Thomist view (as followed by de Lubac) is that the act of creation is at one and the same time "a gift of a gift to a gift."[101] God's creation establishes a threefold order of

---

97. Oliver, "Henri de Lubac," 404.
98. Oakes, "Paradox," 674.
99. Milbank, *Suspended Middle*, 45.
100. Oliver, "Henri de Lubac," 404.
101. Milbank, *Suspended Middle*, 96.

gratuity: the recipient of the gift, the gift itself, and the donation of one to the other. This proposition seems to establish, according to Oliver, a radically unilateral gift: God simply gives everything.[102] Oakes is of the view that one of the great contributions of *The Suspended Middle* is Milbank's ability to show how much was lost in the nature-grace debate when the term *influentia* was no longer interpreted according to the Neoplatonic schema of participation but instead was interpreted as a merely external influence.[103] To contrast the two different metaphysics of causality, Milbank employs the image of a teenager doing her evening's homework as against the influence of a mystic influencing a person's whole approach to their life duties:

> On the older, fundamentally Proclean model, the higher and especially secondary cause. [Aquinas, *Summa Theologiae*, I, q. 105, a. 5] . . . But on the newer view, a higher cause operating on a lower level is just "one other" causal factor—like homework set by a teacher for the evening which is only one factor, alongside the demands of boyfriends and girlfriends, what's on downtown, etc., determining how the evening will actually be spent. It is quite *unlike* the instructions of a mystical master which might "inform" the entire way one spent the evening.[104]

Oliver asks: Does this fatally compromise the gratuity of grace and the proper autonomy of the creature? The response that is proposed is that it is quite to the contrary; it is the only way of preserving the sovereignty of God and the gratuity of grace. To understand why this is the case, Oliver recalls that the difference between God and creation is not like the difference between creatures. He notes that whereas the difference between creatures (e.g., between two people) belongs properly to creatures because of their separate and autonomous substantial natures, as stated, the difference between a creature and God is itself a gift of God. In itself, the creature is nothing; it does not instantiate itself as other than God and thereby exert its own causal influence or claim. It is God who, in the act of creation, gives existence to that which is other, holding creation at a distance so that it can be creation. Having received itself as the unilateral and all-encompassing gift of God *ex nihilo*, creation's only response is to return itself in gratitude to the source of its being. A

---

102. Oliver, "Henri de Lubac," 404.
103. Oakes, "Paradox," 674.
104. Milbank, *Suspended Middle*, 92.

creature's expression of its nature in its very existence is its return to, or desire for, God. Yet God does not receive anything because whatever God receives, God has already donated.[105]

As we have seen, against the notion of pure-nature, Milbank proposes a profound paradox at the heart of the Christian doctrine of creation: a "unilateral exchange."[106] Oliver notes that while there can only be genuine reciprocity in the Trinity or between creatures, the apparently reciprocal exchange between God and creation is only ever a matter of God's *influentia*, by which creation is given the power of responding and returning to God. This notion guarantees the gratuity of grace because it refuses any purely natural autonomy that can be the basis of a claim by creation on God's gratuity. In short, there is nothing outside the gift and no position from which creation can assert itself over and against God. On this view, grace is the genuinely new (yet always inchoately anticipated) gift arising from within the primordial gift of creation by means of God's *influentia*.[107]

Contrary to Milbank's notion that the concept of pure-nature is inadmissible, Matthew Mulcahy maintains that by making room for the possibility of pure-nature, one creates vast possibilities for the communication between church and world, between faith and all human disciplines, to the benefit of all concerned.[108] Interestingly, he further seeks to connect the strength of Milbank's intrinsicism with his eschewing of correspondence theory, labeling it "methodological arrogance."[109] This position goes too far. The intrinsicist approach to the nature-grace debate does not *necessarily* imply that one must reject secular sources of truth, or mandate the adoption of a methodology such as Milbank's, even if it can be admitted that Milbank's judgments tend to be rather non-conciliatory. Mulcahy does however validly question Milbank's view that the entire ecclesial task falls to the theologian alone, "who must perpetuate the original making strange which was the divine assumption of human flesh."[110] He wonders whether it is a good thing for the theologian to be so alone; for theology to be so isolated. If a theologian feels that he bears

---

105. Oliver, "Henri de Lubac," 404.

106. Oliver, "Henri de Lubac," 405.

107. Oliver, "Henri de Lubac," 405.

108. Mulcahy, *Aquinas's Notion*, 326. Mulcahy's comments here are indicative of an extrinsicist position.

109. Mulcahy, *Aquinas's Notion*, 326.

110. Milbank, *Word Made Strange*, 1.

the whole ecclesial task, that he must redeem the world, and perpetuate the presence of the Word made flesh, "both theology and the theologian are living in unhealthy solitude."[111]

Points of Departure and Criticisms

Despite the fact of de Lubac's pervasive influence on so many writings in Radical Orthodoxy, it would be a misunderstanding, however, to think that it simply picks up what de Lubac says about nature and grace in isolation. The alignment with de Lubac is possible because of more fundamental and basic agreements, as we have seen, concerning the importance of *ressourcement* (particularly, for Radical Orthodoxy, the Neoplatonic legacy), the interpretation of Aquinas, the understanding of philosophy's relation to theology, and the basic structure of creation *ex nihilo* centered on the metaphysics of participation.[112] It is clear that Milbank and Radical Orthodoxy are not merely repeating de Lubac but regard his legacy as unfulfilled. According to Mulcahy, de Lubac has a twofold importance in Milbank's theology. Firstly, de Lubac offers an account of how modern theology went astray, and secondly, he suggests a corrective course through certain orientations in the theologies of Augustine and Aquinas. However, given the postmodern emphasis in Milbank's thought, and despite his genealogical methodology, Milbank does not share de Lubac's belief that his historical research (*ressourcement*) discloses objective truth.[113] This is because, as we have noted, Milbank holds to the notion of "narrative knowledge," which eschews both objectivity and subjectivity and insists that no discourse "tells us what reality is like. Rather, objects and subjects are [only] narrated in a story."[114]

ECCLESIAL STRUCTURES

As stated, as much as Milbank relies on the theology of de Lubac, it is not however a wholesale acceptance, devoid of any scrutiny. Milbank charges de Lubac (and Balthasar, for that matter) with having developed an ecclesiology that is tinged with dualism, given de Lubac's habit of

---

111. Mulcahy, *Aquinas's Notion*, 327.
112. Oliver, "Henri de Lubac," 416. See also Sánchez and Watson, "Revival," 243.
113. Mulcahy, *Aquinas's Notion*, 308.
114. Milbank, "Postmodern Critical Augustinianism," 225.

"distinguishing between a lay, receptive, mystical, cultural 'Marian' aspect [of the church] and a more legal, regulative, intellectual, abstract, 'Petrine' aspect."[115] Another of Milbank's criticisms of de Lubac is that de Lubac holds back when faced with the political implications of his denial of pure-nature.[116] Milbank notes that even though de Lubac's *Catholicism* affirms the "social and historical character of salvation," it refuses to address the political, trying instead "to insulate the church from wider social processes."[117] Milbank is of the view that de Lubac's affirmation of the traditional Catholic distinction between the church and the *saeculum* effectively "rediscovers the evasive spark of purely psychic [that is, purely natural] life" and so "actually implies—like Weberian sociology—that there *is* a realm which is merely 'social' [secular] and which the individual [the Christian] might stand outside."[118] He goes even further, stating that de Lubac (as well as Balthasar) have failed to face up to the radical demands of genuine "Christian aversion to the existing secular order," falling short in their understanding of the "humanly constructed character of cultural reality."[119] Milbank thinks that de Lubac remains too wedded to the existing social structures (the existing secular order) and to naïve ideals of objectivity. These shortcomings, as far as Milbank is concerned, undermine de Lubac's otherwise valuable repudiation of the pure-nature tradition.[120] Mulcahy rightly points out that even to those who are not postmodern radicals, de Lubac's rejection of the notion of pure-nature must seem at variance with his conviction that the church ought to stand aloof from politics. That is, if human beings can only be properly understood as creatures ordained to a supernatural end, and if salvation is inherently social, then surely it is not only remiss of Christians to abandon politics, but also to allow any political influence to those lacking faith.[121] Milbank would agree that, apart from theology, politics has no way of considering humanity's true good, namely, the supernatural *telos* to which we are all destined.

---

115. Milbank, "Postmodern Critical Augustinianism," 110.
116. Mulcahy, *Aquinas's Notion*, 312.
117. Milbank, *Theology and Social Theory*, 228.
118. Milbank, *Theology and Social Theory*, 228.
119. Milbank, *Theology and Social Theory*, 209.
120. Mulcahy, *Aquinas's Notion*, 312; See also Lim, "John Milbank," 303.
121. Mulcahy, *Aquinas's Notion*, 312.

The *Humani Generis* Controversy

Milbank is also extremely critical of de Lubac's "capitulation" to the papacy following *Humani Generis* and his subsequent republishing of his *Surnaturel*[122] (which became two volumes: *Augustinianism and Modern Theology* and *The Mystery of the Supernatural*), which, for Milbank, made too many concessions to the legitimacy of the concept of pure-nature, "such as to render his revisions incoherent to his genuine theory."[123] For Milbank, these concessions to the church hierarchy appear to move him towards a Scotist (and even latently Jansenist) exposition of his theory that makes the natural desire for the supernatural not any longer participatory, but only vaguely aspirational, and in consequence more voluntaristic. Milbank, however, concedes at this point that it is by no means clear from de Lubac's later writings that he really did abandon his earlier (pre–*Humani Generis*) position.[124] Milbank states:

> After *Humani generis*, outside his historical work, de Lubac comes across as a stuttering, somewhat traumatized theologian, only able to articulate his convictions in somewhat oblique fragments.[125]

According to Komonchak, however, Milbank goes too far in maintaining that de Lubac became a "traumatized" theologian after *Humani Generis*.[126] He notes that it is difficult to finds signs of "trauma" in de Lubac's later works, for example, *The Mystery of the Supernatural* and *A Brief Catechesis on Nature and Grace* (a book that, quite unbelievably, Milbank never mentions), both of which were written long after the original controversy surrounding de Lubac had passed. Komonchak suggests that the problem seems to be less de Lubac's psyche than Milbank's belief that, in his later writings, de Lubac departed (by means of concessions to the church hierarchy) from the position that he thinks had been set out in the final few pages of *Surnaturel*, a position he notes

---

122. De Lubac's *Surnaturel* is yet to be translated into English, perhaps because he meant *Augustinianism* and *Mystery of the Supernatural* to supersede it.

123. Milbank, *Suspended Middle*, 41. Milbank here cites as an example of a concession to de Lubac's *Mystery of the Supernatural* wherein he discards the idea that there is a positive advance manifestation of the supernatural that "gives the natural desire for the supernatural," even though, Milbank claims, it is affirmed by Aquinas.

124. Milbank, *Suspended Middle*, 43.

125. Milbank, *Suspended Middle*, 8.

126. The tendency to overstate his case seems to be typical of Milbank, as others have also observed. See Burrell, "Radical Orthodoxy: Appreciation," 76.

"not so coincidentally happens to coincide with Milbank's own view."[127] It seems that Milbank fails to provide a close comparison of de Lubac's early and later works in order to maintain his position, nor does he engage other works on de Lubac that make an effort to come to the opposite conclusion.[128]

Oakes is also of the view that Milbank's attempt to pit Pius XII against de Lubac is overblown and a number of objections should be registered. In the first place, he points out that Milbank appears to be using the 1958 translation of *The Mystery of the Supernatural* and not the more recent 1998 edition published by Crossroad. It is the new edition that carries an important introductory essay by Schindler on the significance of the book; he notes the following:

> When Pius XII learned through de Lubac's superiors and the mediation of Cardinal Bea of the continuing criticisms of de Lubac, he had Cardinal Bea send a letter to de Lubac "whose every word he dictated," in which he thanked de Lubac "for the work accomplished up until then" and encouraged him about continuing such work since it "promised much fruit for the church."[129]

Furthermore, de Lubac himself did not see *Humani Generis* as a flat-out condemnation of his central thesis in *Surnaturel*, as he stresses in a letter to a friend:

> It seems to me, like many other ecclesiastical documents, unilateral; that is almost the law of the genre; but I have read nothing in it, doctrinally, that affects me. The only passage where I recognize an implicit reference to me is a phrase bearing on the question of the supernatural; now it is rather curious to note that this phrase, intending to recall the true doctrine on this subject, reproduces exactly what I said about it two years earlier in an article in *Recherches de science religieuse*.[130]

Oakes maintains that the concept of pure-nature was introduced to provide a merely conceptual safeguard to the concept of the supernatural, which, by definition, must be gratuitous. De Lubac does not deny

---

127. Komonchak, Review of *Suspended Middle*, 467.
128. Komonchak, Review of *Suspended Middle*, 467.
129. Lubac, *Entretien*, 13. See also Lubac, *At the Service*, 88.
130. Lubac, *Mystery of the Supernatural*, 71.

the conceptual utility of the concept of pure-nature, despite Milbank's attempts to obscure this fact.[131]

Ontology

As we have seen, the ontological approach of participation is of critical importance to Milbank's theological project. Given that Milbank adopts much of de Lubac's theology, it is relevant to ask: What metaphysical or ontological approach does de Lubac himself adopt? In answer to the question, Milbank recognizes that de Lubac never explicitly presents a distinct metaphysic, and even suggests that de Lubac offers a "non-ontology" by way of a return to authentic Christian discourse.[132] According to Boersma, Milbank is right to claim that much of de Lubac's "non-ontology" represents an exploration of the field of the "suspended middle" between nature and the supernatural. Milbank however clarifies that by "non-ontology" he does not mean that de Lubac *refused* ontology, but that he articulated an ontology between "the field of pure immanent being proper to philosophy on the one hand and the field of the revelatory event proper to theology on the other."[133] Boersma is of the view that de Lubac's concern for sacramentality stands at the heart of his theology, which informs not only his ecclesiology but especially his idea of the nature-grace relation. De Lubac does therefore consciously operate with a particular ontology, one that is sacramental in character.[134]

Correspondence Theory

Considering that Milbank rejects "accepted secular standards of scientific truth or normative rationality," it is unsurprising that he also denies that truth is a correspondence between the intellect and extramental reality, insisting rather that "the point of theology is not to represent . . . externality, but just to join in its occurrence; not to know, but to intervene, originate."[135] We should recall that Milbank's theology is *poiesis*, meaning

---

131. Oakes, "Paradox," 681.
132. Milbank, *Suspended Middle*, 5.
133. Milbank, *Suspended Middle*, 5.
134. Boersma, "Sacramental Ontology," 243.
135. Milbank, "Postmodern Critical Augustinianism," 265. It is beyond the scope of this work to enter fully into a consideration of Milbank's epistemology, particularly

that it is an artistic "making" or "begetting." It is neither *praxis* (practical action) nor *theoria* (contemplative knowledge) and has its own validity as an act that constitutes or originates reality.[136] For Milbank, objects and subjects are as they are narrated in a story, and so, as far as its narrators are concerned, it remains impervious to "objective" or factual (non-narrative) critique.[137] This ostensibly postmodern approach to sources has unsurprisingly been the subject of intense criticism, as we have seen.

It is concerning the notion of objective knowledge that Milbank is most at odds with de Lubac. Unlike de Lubac, Milbank rejects the notion of objective knowledge, detached reasoning, and universally accessible evidence. Such evidence and sources are invoked mainly for their value as "actors" in the drama of the Radical Orthodoxy story. That story appeals to a truth that lies not in the correspondence of thought to reality but in the doctrine of the Incarnation of the eternal Word in a human discourse.[138] In this respect, Radical Orthodoxy is unwilling, and indeed unable, to admit a dialectic in relation to other approaches nor to invite dialogue with non-theological scholarly perspectives or points of view. Its core message, after all, is that the horizon of Christian theology can confidently include everything in its purview, as everything is numinous in a world made for God in Christ.[139]

Michael Mawson (one among many Thomists critical of Milbank), however, rejects such a notion, and maintains that Milbank has misread Aquinas in his stated attempt to overcome "the usual interpretations" within which "Aquinas is seen as espousing a sharp distinction between reason and faith and concomitantly between philosophy and theology."[140] It should be noted that Mawson himself is arguing from more of an extrinsicist position, and, as such, notes that Milbank's theology is "primarily characterized by a more persistent refusal of distinct 'natural' and

---

as it concerns his interpretation of Aquinas. This can be found, in major part, in his *Truth in Aquinas*, coauthored with Catherine Pickstock. A central idea is that there can be no neutral epistemic access to the structures of the world and thus no notion of an autonomous reason. Nevertheless, it should be noted here that some authors have found his interpretation of Aquinas regarding epistemology, and the notion of faith and reason, to be problematic. See, e.g., Mawson, "Understandings," 347–61; Marenbon, "Aquinas," 49–63; and DeHart, *Aquinas and Radical Orthodoxy*, 99–111.

136. Mulcahy, *Aquinas's Notion*, 314.
137. Milbank, "Postmodern Critical Augustinianism," 265.
138. Janz, "Radical Orthodoxy," 325.
139. Janz, "Radical Orthodoxy," 325.
140. Milbank and Pickstock, *Truth in Aquinas*, 19.

'supernatural' phases and a consequent assault upon an autonomous naturalism as 'nihilistic,'" as well as an inability to sustain this position by adhering to "a particular interpretation of Aquinas."[141] Mawson argues that Milbank's understanding of nature as thoroughly dependent on grace implies an understanding of nature as (on its own terms) nihilistic or irretrievably fallen. In this way, he says, Milbank's "dissolution of any qualitative distinction between nature and grace closes down any natural space for even a limited non-theological politics or ethics."[142] Further, he states that "Aquinas's clear distinction between grace and nature, by contrast, allows at least some space for natural political and moral knowledge and activity."[143]

Creation and Redemption

The influence of de Lubac and the *nouvelle théologie* upon Milbank lies predominantly in its "historical method and strategy."[144] This importance granted to history has two consequences. The first is substantive, namely, that it is *within* rather than outside or above history that Christian theology finds the substance of Christian truth. The second consequence is hermeneutical, namely, that Christian theology always carries an element of historical interpretation because Christian truth has been revealed, articulated and expressed within history and within particular sociohistorical contexts.[145] Both de Lubac and Milbank consider that God is constantly at work in creation and that all of history bears the mark of God's activity. Thus, both consider salvation as historical, not only because it is tied to a historical event, the Christ-event, but also because it unfolds throughout history. De Lubac and Milbank also both understand the Christ-event as an *interruption* of history, but they differ in their interpretation of the character of this interruption.[146] For Milbank, the Christ-event interrupted history by unveiling the violence upon which antique societies were founded, and by inaugurating a community in which a peaceful and harmonious way of life can be found.

141. Mawson, "Understandings," 347–48.
142. Mawson, "Understandings," 348.
143. Mawson, "Understandings," 348.
144. Smith, *Introducing Radical Orthodoxy*, 46.
145. Nguyen, "Legacy," 29.
146. Nguyen, "Legacy," 29.

De Lubac, however, sees the Christ-event as the turning point of the Christian dialectic. It is therefore at once in fundamental continuity and radical discontinuity with the order of creation, an introduction of a new principle that transfigured creation.[147] Therefore, while Milbank posits a discontinuity of states within the same order of creation, de Lubac posits an essential continuity within the order of creation, and the radical discontinuity of a *passage to a different order*.[148]

The difference is consistent with Milbank's and de Lubac's respective understandings of God's original intent in creating the cosmos. For Milbank, God's original intent was "Creation *as* Creation" and this intent was fulfilled within creation itself.[149] This is because Milbank considers creation to have originally already *participated* in the Immanent Trinity to the fullness of its capacity to do so. Thus, Milbank does not posit creation's supernatural destiny as *exceeding* the order of creation.[150]

De Lubac, however, insists on the distance between humanity's creation in the *imago Dei* and the supernatural *resemblance* to which it is called, and which *exceeds* the order of creation.[151] This difference has a profound impact on how Milbank and de Lubac respectively judge the present times and how each accounts for the violence and hatred that sadly seems to characterize much of the human social condition. For Milbank, the state of violence and disharmony we presently live in can only be explained by a failure of the Christian interruption of history. If Christian salvation has the shape of a community of peace, then it is only available if such a community does in fact exist. It would be apparent, however, that we do not live in a community of peace, causing Milbank to render a verdict of failure upon the Christian interruption of history. The present state of the world would therefore be the result of this failure and if Christian salvation is to be available again, the church must exist again as a community of peace within the violence of the world.[152] For de Lubac, however, although redemption was once and for all acquired in Christ, the battle he won will keep on being fought until the final manifestation of this victory. There is therefore an element of resignation in de Lubac with respect to the violence and evil in the world, for he thinks

---

147. Nguyen, "Legacy," 30.
148. Nguyen, "Legacy," 30.
149. Milbank, *Word Made Strange*, 229.
150. Milbank, *Word Made Strange*, 229.
151. Nguyen, "Legacy," 31.
152. Nguyen, "Legacy," 31.

of them to a certain extent as congenial to our human condition and as insurmountable for as long as the present state of the world will last. It also means that the presence of evil, even within the church, does not contradict the victory of Christ or the progress of salvation throughout the world. On the other hand, while Milbank tends to be more optimistic with regard to the possibility of peace within this world, this causes him to be more pessimistic with respect to the present state of the world.[153]

As we have seen, it is clear that both de Lubac and Milbank reject an extrinsicist notion of nature and grace and support the notion that human nature was created with a supernatural destiny inscribed in nature. Consistent with de Lubac, Milbank posits an essential continuity between human nature and its supernatural destiny; however—and this is where he exceeds de Lubac—the two consist in diverging degrees of participation in God. Human nature and even all of creation is always already intrinsically raised above itself, while grace always already reaches down to nature. According to Thuy-Linh Nguyen, this notion would mean that nature and the supernatural thus both belong to the order of creation, and the passage from one to the other does not require the introduction of any novelty that would be in discontinuity with the created order.[154] For Milbank, sin and evil are understood as distortions of creation's original harmony, and redemption in Christ is understood as the restoration of "Creation *as* Creation."[155]

Nguyen asserts that de Lubac, however, unequivocally maintained the distinction between nature, founded upon the distance between human nature's creation in the *imago Dei*, and the "supernatural resemblance it is called to attain."[156] This distance means that even in prelapsarian nature, the passage to the supernatural could not occur without some form of death as well as the introduction of a new principle within creation that could only be received as a gift. Because of original sin, the distance between human nature and its supernatural destiny became doubly insurmountable. Not only is there now a heterogeneity between the two orders, but also a rebellion and an enmity.[157] Although de Lubac does not make of evil a substance, he does consider it as an

---

153. Nguyen, "Legacy," 31.
154. Nguyen, "Legacy," 16.
155. Milbank, *Word Made Strange*, 229.
156. Nguyen, "Legacy," 17.
157. Nguyen, "Legacy," 17.

antagonistic force.¹⁵⁸ For de Lubac, even without original sin, however, the passage from nature to the supernatural would have required a second cycle of creation.¹⁵⁹ Although grace and redemption do remedy the consequences of sin, their goal is not ultimately to bring creation back to its original state, but to bring humanity to the fulfilment of its supernatural vocation. Indeed, divine economy is not caused by original sin, but is necessary in order to lead humanity to the fulfilment of its supernatural vocation, which is divine filiation.¹⁶⁰

It is of course inarguable that Milbank has taken his lead from de Lubac's desire to overcome the extrinsicist position in the nature-grace debate. However, Radical Orthodoxy should not necessarily be underwritten as simply a more coherent and unrepressed continuation of de Lubac's theology.¹⁶¹ At the same time, it may be acknowledged that de Lubac is difficult to understand. From the beginning of his career there was a great deal of disagreement as to the content and implications of his theology (e.g., the *Humani Generis* controversy). Adding to the difficulty of course is the fact that a lot of what is now known about de Lubac is not so much what he himself said as what is said *about* him. For example, de Lubac specifically rejected the notions of both *nouvelle théologie* and *ressourcement*. De Lubac himself maintained that his thoughts were not only misinterpreted but also polemically instrumentalized by his opponents as well as by his supporters.¹⁶²

The Supernatural

According to Nguyen, despite Milbank's claims to recover and follow through with de Lubac's theology, his misinterpretation of fundamental concepts in his theology, specifically his notion of the supernatural, in many ways means that Milbank is at odds with de Lubac.¹⁶³ Concerning de Lubac's writings on the supernatural, Nguyen notes that they contain for the most part an historical argumentation against the theory of purenature and against a reductive interpretation of the natural desire for

---

158. Nguyen, "Legacy," 17.
159. Lubac, *Mystery of the Supernatural*, 81–82.
160. Nguyen, "Legacy," 17.
161. Nguyen, "Legacy," 99.
162. Nguyen, "Legacy," 101.
163. Nguyen, "Legacy," 99.

the supernatural. It does not however constitute a fully articulated and systematic theology of the supernatural. De Lubac regrettably is often made to say (by Milbank) that which he did not say on the supernatural, but also that which he did say is mistakenly interpreted as belonging to a fully elaborated work of dogmatic theology.[164] The dominant interpretation (which has persisted to this day) is that de Lubac's theology points towards an elimination of the distinction between nature and grace.[165] For de Lubac, however, "unity is in no way confusion, no more than distinction is separation."[166] De Lubac's emphasis on the union between nature and grace was therefore not aimed at any limitation of the distinction between the two orders; on the contrary, a better understanding of the union meant also a better understanding of the distinction: "to distinguish in order to unite . . . union differentiates, solidarity consolidates."[167] Thus, Nguyen sees that there has been a trend, symptomatic of the most common interpretations of de Lubac, towards a conflation of nature and grace in de Lubac (as well as of faith and reason, and of sacred and secular), a trend to which, in her view, Milbank and Radical Orthodoxy ascribe. According to Nguyen, de Lubac meant to outline a theology of the relationship between nature and grace but never fully articulated it.[168] Even if it is conceded that Milbank simply picks up on what had been a common interpretation of de Lubac, this does not compromise the coherence of the Radical Orthodoxy project per se, but perhaps it may simply weaken Milbank's claim that his theology is a straightforward continuation of de Lubac's project.

According to Nguyen, Milbank must explain how his tendency towards a "supernaturalizing of nature" avoids also "naturalizing the supernatural."[169] One cannot arrive at the supernatural, according to Nguyen's understanding of de Lubac, without "passing to a different order," which must, by definition, exceed that of nature. Nguyen sets out:

> If there is no order but that of nature, then there is no supernatural, no matter how "super" nature is made out to be. No matter how full of the divine radical orthodoxy construes nature to be, therefore, as long as there is no passage to a different order, it

---

164. Nguyen, "Legacy," 102.
165. Nguyen, "Legacy," 102.
166. Lubac, *Catholicism*, 330.
167. Lubac, *Catholicism*, 330.
168. Nguyen, "Legacy," 103.
169. Nguyen, "Legacy," 105.

remains, from a Lubacian point of view, still nature and *not yet* the supernatural. By way of consequence, following de Lubac's categories, radical orthodoxy's understanding of Revelation is *not yet* Revelation and its theology *not yet* theology.[170]

Nguyen's criticisms of Milbank's tendency to supernaturalize nature as opposed to naturalizing the supernatural can also be levelled at many theological systems that took the *nouvelle théologie* and de Lubac's insights as a starting point. As Nguyen concedes herself, the (mis)interpretation of de Lubac on the specific issue of the supernatural seems to be symptomatic of strains within post-Lubacian Catholic theology more generally, rather than a particular issue with the reading of de Lubac by Milbank, who, after all, can be lumped in with many others who, on Nguyen's view, have misread de Lubac.[171]

Thomas Aquinas

As we have seen, Milbank builds his theology in large part upon de Lubac's account of Thomism, in particular, adopting de Lubac's diagnosis in *Surnaturel* of the pure-nature tradition as being a distortion in Catholic theology. Milbank is of course well aware of the challenges to the Lubacian position, dedicating a section of *The Suspended Middle* to the treatment of such dissenting voices, particularly Feingold, but in the end purports to side with de Lubac and the *nouvelle théologie*. Milbank has not yet written in any detailed way on the history of Thomism, nor has he undertaken a close reading of Thomistic texts, at least not on any notable scale. Aquinas, nevertheless, is often invoked by Milbank and Radical Orthodoxy more generally.[172]

---

170. Nguyen, "Legacy," 105–6.

171. This is perhaps why Nguyen calls upon not only Milbank but Catholic theology more generally to revisit their own assumptions about the theology of de Lubac. Nguyen also sets out concerns regarding the status of Radical Orthodoxy's ecclesiology, concerns that are beyond the scope of this work. It is Nguyen's view that Radical Orthodoxy is fundamentally a sociology that lacks an *ecclesia*. See Nguyen, "Legacy," 106–7.

172. I do not here intend to provide a complete presentation of Milbank's treatment of Aquinas in all its aspects (such would require another book), but only those that are pertinent in a more direct way to the nature-grace question.

Interpretation

An example of Milbank's engagement with Aquinas is his *Truth in Aquinas*, which he coauthored with Catherine Pickstock and which presents an interpretation of Aquinas's teaching on the relationship between theology and philosophy, and between faith and reason. Mulcahy notes that "interpretation" is the key word when it comes to Milbank's treatment of Aquinas. As we saw in chapter 1, according to Shakespeare, Radical Orthodoxy tends to impose the idea of participation on the texts of Aquinas, primarily to "deny any role for philosophy independent of theology."[173] It is clear that Aquinas is mediated through the lens of the *nouvelle théologie*, which, according to Smith, in turn presents a very Augustinian Aquinas who rejects the notion of an autonomous nature (pure-nature) and also of a "universal, natural, unaided human reason."[174] This means that Milbank's Aquinas is presented as one who rejects any rationalist account of the human person as well as an overly confident notion of natural law. The Aquinas that Milbank presents can, like his Plato, be thought of as a "new" creation. Hemming notes that Milbank has given the impression (along with Pickstock) that if modernity or the rationalism of the Enlightenment could be bracketed out, a certain return to something prior to it could be opened up. That "something prior" he says is best exemplified for Radical Orthodoxy by Aquinas.[175] Hemming is of the view that it is in Milbank's articulation of Aquinas that what is "most cavalier and hazardous about Radical Orthodoxy can be seen most clearly at work."[176] James Keating goes so far as to describe Milbank and Pickstock's treatment of Aquinas as "notorious"![177] Mulcahy suggests recognizing Milbank's treatment of Aquinas as akin to an "interpretive dance" (DeHart calls it an "interpretive lunge"), as for him it displays an inherently subjective approach, and in effect, purports to be nothing else than that. "Scholarship of an objective kind, must be sought

---

173. Shakespeare, *Radical Orthodoxy: Critical Introduction*, 32.

174. Smith, *Introducing Radical Orthodoxy*, 48. See also Gregory and Clair, "Augustinianisms," 176–95.

175. Hemming, "*Quod Impossibile Est!*," 77.

176. Hemming, "*Quod Impossibile Est!*," 77. Hemming is referring to Milbank's tendency to present his own version (often ahistorical) of the authors that he turns to, rather than a faithful rendering of their thought. This is specifically Hemming's criticism of Radical Orthodoxy's (particularly Pickstock's) treatment of Aquinas, a thesis that he develops in this work.

177. Keating, Review of *Aquinas and Radical Orthodoxy*, 155.

elsewhere," he says.[178] Thus, for Mulcahy, Milbank's recourse to Aquinas is not a work of exegesis, but a "project of creative expression" because, according to Milbank, "exegesis is easy; it is interpretation that is difficult, and Aquinas, more than most thinkers, requires interpretation."[179] DeHart goes even further and states that, in his view, almost everything that Milbank and Pickstock say about Aquinas is wrong. He asks how it could be that someone of Milbank's intellectual gifts could so badly misinterpret Aquinas. His answer is that, in his view, Milbank is not interested in Aquinas himself, but rather in using Aquinas as the linchpin for Radical Orthodoxy's genealogy of the rise of secularism.[180] DeHart cautions about using Aquinas in this way because of the propensity to distort Aquinas in so doing.[181] As Keating notes, when Aquinas is called upon to be the symbol of everything that modernity is not, his positions are already determined beforehand.[182] Milbank and Radical Orthodoxy's interpretations of Aquinas have also been labeled as "gnostic idealism," "blithely imprecise, ideologically driven historical revisionism," "free-floating, self-perpetuating insularity," and so on.[183] Despite this, it must be said however that Milbank, from the beginning, had disclaimed the canons of scholarly objectivity and verifiable accuracy, setting himself to challenge accepted theological opinion and eschewing any type of dialogical relationship with other views or types of rationality.

---

178. Mulcahy, *Aquinas's Notion*, 316.

179. Milbank, "Intensities," 447.

180. Keating, Review of *Aquinas and Radical Orthodoxy*, 155.

181. Keating, Review of *Aquinas and Radical Orthodoxy*, 155. Keating notes that DeHart does not comment on the viability of Milbank's genealogy, including his notion that it was thanks to Scotus that the decline started; this idea after all, has already been subjected to criticisms by others. See, e.g., Cross, "Duns Scotus."

182. Keating, Review of *Aquinas and Radical Orthodoxy*, 155. See also DeHart, *Aquinas and Radical Orthodoxy*, 49–63. DeHart here gives his critique of Milbank's notion of analogy in Aquinas, which DeHart claims is shaped by his dissatisfaction with the grammatical approaches to the question promoted by Lash, McCabe, and Burrell. DeHart is particularly critical of Milbank's claim that Aquinas's metaphysics of participation implies a proper, albeit remote, knowledge of God in this life: "an inchoate but nonetheless actual experience of God's mode of perfection."

183. Janz, "Radical Orthodoxy," 378.

Grace and Participation

Interestingly, many of the charges that Milbank levels against Scotus had been initially laid at the feet of Aquinas—for example, the notion that it was Aquinas not Scotus who first unhooked creation from the Creator by granting autonomy to nature, which could be properly understood (though not fully) apart from Revelation.[184] In another example, Milbank states that Aquinas "has moved too far" down the road that allows a sphere of secular autonomy, and that "by beginning to see social, economic, and administrative life as essentially *natural*, Aquinas opens the way to regarding the church as an organization specializing in what goes on inside men's souls."[185] These notions of autonomous nature, as we have seen, run contrary to the central thesis of Radical Orthodoxy, namely, that a participatory ontology "refuses any reserve of created territory" for fear that a notion of nature as autonomous may then become secular.[186] Milbank argues that it is not possible to have any kind of secular or neutral metaphysics because the world can be properly understood only in its dependence on and relation to God, nor can nature be considered in abstraction. In other words, to speak of nature is not to speak of a world devoid of grace. Having said this, however, Milbank then turns to Aquinas to support the contrary position. In "Only Theology Overcomes Metaphysics," Milbank contrasts Aquinas's "theological metaphysics" with Scotus's "autonomous metaphysics" and notes that as he reads Aquinas, metaphysics, insofar as it is an account of being, cannot be divorced from theological considerations.[187] There can be no metaphysics apart from Revelation. Milbank suggests that:

> [for Aquinas] the difference of *esse* from essence in the *ens commune* of creatures . . . is "read" in *entirely* theological terms as the site of the internal fracture of creatures between their own nothingness and their alien actuality which is received from God. This means that the domain of metaphysics is not simply to subordinate to, but completely *evacuated* by theology, for metaphysics refers its subject matter—"Being"—wholesale to a

---

184. Smith, *Introducing Radical Orthodoxy*, 120.
185. Milbank, *Theology and Social Theory*, 407.
186. Milbank, Pickstock, and Ward, *Radical Orthodoxy*, 3.
187. This is an example of Milbank's tendency to impose his own interpretation on Aquinas.

first principle, God, which is the subject of another, higher science, namely God's own, only accessible to us via revelation.[188]

As stated, for Milbank's Aquinas, there can be no possibility of secular metaphysics that operates irrespective of the created nature of being.[189] For Milbank (in the place of Scotist ontology), Aquinas offers a theo-ontology (that is, a fully Christianized ontology) because "it did not need first to be situated in a general discourse about being, essence and substance, indifferent to finite and infinite, as later articulated by Scotus."[190] As Milbank and Pickstock set out in *Truth in Aquinas*:

> It is surely clear that this new theological ontology of constitutive supernatural supplementation and ecstatic relationality reveals a cosmos already in a sense graced, and in such a fashion that the supplement of grace will not seem in discontinuity with existing principles of ontological constitution.[191]

This does not mean that nature or creation is inherently deficient and always already in need of redemption, but that its "creaturehood" is being emphasized.[192] For Milbank, creation cannot be understood as autonomous in any way, and thus "grace goes all the way down" and the leading characteristic of Aquinas's theological ontology is "a grasp of creation in the light of grace, as itself graced or supplemented."[193] Critically, Milbank attempts to link his fundamental notion of participation to the notion of engraced nature. For him, nature "is" only insofar as it participates in God. It is thus suffused with the divine, *and hence with grace*. Everything, therefore, for Milbank is "engraced" (in this way he presses even beyond the *nouvelle théologie*).[194]

---

188. Milbank, *Word Made Strange*, 44.

189. See DeHart, *Aquinas and Radical Orthodoxy*, 67–70. Here, DeHart criticizes Milbank's view that Aquinas requires *sacra doctrina* for metaphysics's own rational coherence, despite what Thomistic scholars say (Milbank opines that they have erroneously taken support for this view from Aquinas's texts when there is none). DeHart shows that all Milbank has to offer is his own belief that Aquinas's philosophical arguments need theological support, and not proof that Aquinas thought so.

190. Milbank and Pickstock, *Truth in Aquinas*, 35. For another critique of this position, see Kerr, "Catholic Response," 56. Kerr (a Thomist) notes that a "fully Christianized ontology" of the sort that Milbank is here proposing would be "an illegitimate obliteration of metaphysics by Scripture, an obliteration of reason and nature by faith and grace."

191. Milbank and Pickstock, *Truth in Aquinas*, 44.

192. Smith, *Introducing Radical Orthodoxy*, 121.

193. Milbank and Pickstock, *Truth in Aquinas*, 51.

194. Milbank, *Being Reconciled*, 115.

While it is true that, for Aquinas, nature does not have a *sui generis* autonomy, Aquinas does not describe this gifted nature as grace. Milbank's argument for an "engraced nature" seems to collapse the orders of creation and redemption such that the Fall is either ignored, or undone in such a way that it has no enduring impact on the postlapsarian world.[195] Milbank refers to the "lost and renewed gift of grace" and to "the aporetic loss of divine glory in the world through the Fall which God immediately corrects, although our own realization of this correcting must be gradual."[196] It seems that Milbank is so concerned to keep the graciousness of creation at center stage that he is at risk of eschewing further distinctions between creation and election, and between creation and Incarnation, without which Christian narratives crumble into incoherence.[197] According to Smith, however, even these criticisms (valid as they are) do not mitigate Milbank's more constructive account. That is, while the notion of a "graced nature" is not found in Aquinas, Milbank's constructive theological vision is an important account, even if there is a tendency to merge creation and redemption.[198]

What is evident is that the goal of Milbank's formulations is to recover the unity of God's governance as his gifting in the creature, and to deny that this gifting occurs in an extrinsic fashion (as though God merely works alongside the creature rather than exercise a profoundly interior operation).[199] Milbank is afraid of the attempt to view created powers outside their entire teleological framework because this results in an extrinsicism that fails to understand what "created" means. In creating rational creatures, God does not build an edifice that then proves a constraint to him as he seeks to add grace to it. Instead, God's gifting exhibits a profound unity, that is, the rational creature is made in and for graced union with the triune God.[200]

Matthew Levering however points out that there are issues with some of Milbank's stronger formulations about "gift without contrast," in which the "determining would only be posited along with the determined," such that "there is no spiritual existence without grace" and so that grace gives the rational creature "something of what is proper to

195. Smith, *Introducing Radical Orthodoxy*, 122.
196. Milbank, *Being Reconciled*, 42.
197. Smith, *Introducing Radical Orthodoxy*, 122.
198. Smith, *Introducing Radical Orthodoxy*, 122.
199. Smith, *Introducing Radical Orthodoxy*, 122.
200. Smith, *Introducing Radical Orthodoxy*, 122.

it."[201] Milbank appears to equate man's spiritual power (that is, his freedom and "the gift of our power to shape ourselves with true artistry") with "the gift of supernatural destiny."[202] For Levering, the value of distinguishing between created and graced participations in God's goodness needs reasserting, despite the fact that both have the gifting God as their source.[203] That is, if "spiritual existence" requires grace, then what happens after, in Aquinas's words, "the loss of grace dissolved the obedience of the flesh to the soul"?[204] Levering rightly asks (if we equate the notions of participation and grace): Does this imply that our spiritual existence entirely dissolves when we fall from a state of grace by means of mortal sin? Put another way, if "the determining would only be posited along with the determined," what would happen when "the determined" (nature) experiences the loss of "the determining" (grace)? Does the fallen human person thereby fall into radical indetermination, and if so, how would they remain meaningfully human?[205]

According to Levering, it could be that Milbank simply means to underscore the teleological finality of deification, a finality that cannot be lost. If this is the case, then the value of the distinction (not separation) between capacities as created and as graced would be all the more evident. This distinction serves to make clear that the loss of grace does not destroy the graced teleology of the rational creature (this is the paradox of the nature-grace relation). Similarly, if the loss of grace deprives the rational creature of "something which is proper to it," then mortal sin would seem to destroy the very properties that make a person human. The loss of grace by original sin or by mortal sin therefore would constitute a form of "dehumanizing."[206] The corollary to this is that the deification of which Milbank speaks here becomes describable more properly as rehumanization, rather than a transformation in Christ that is freely given to a person by the Holy Spirit and that takes one far beyond what would have been possible on the basis of one's intrinsic resources.[207]

---

201. Levering, "Note," 533. See also Milbank, *Suspended Middle*, 103.
202. Milbank, *Suspended Middle*, 108.
203. Levering, "Note," 533.
204. Aquinas, *Summa Theologica*, I, q. 95, a. 1.
205. Levering, "Note," 533.
206. Levering, "Note," 533.
207. Levering, "Note," 533.

Freedom and "Spirit-Governing"

As we have seen, Milbank maintains that the gift of creation and the gift of grace are already united in one divine gifting. When Milbank applies this view to Aquinas's doctrine of divine governance, he points out that, for Aquinas, created self-governing spirit is never autonomous, but always "is also directly governed by something trans-cosmic and supernatural."[208] This allows him to conclude that to describe created self-governing spirit as "merely natural" would be a mistake because it would give the wrong sense of God's governance.[209] Milbank likewise notes that "Aquinas indicates that the providential mode of dealing with spiritual creatures ultimately includes grace, since such creatures attain the 'ultimate end' of knowing and loving God."[210] Milbank greatly emphasizes the fact that Aquinas never imagines creation without its governing intellect:

> Cosmos requires the government of spirit; spirit is destined to be engraced; therefore in one sense every creature is already for and by grace. After all, how could *charis* be a less original or plenitudinous gift than *esse*?[211]

In addition to the sense that every creature is already "for and by grace," Milbank argues that Aquinas's analogies for an ultimate end that we cannot attain by our own resources alone (analogies such as the oceans' tidal flow being both natural and due to the moon) suggest that grace gives created nature "something of what is proper" to created nature.[212] This view means that "things are 'properly' raised above themselves to a new potential" as opposed to being locked into, by their own created properties, a fulfilment defined by the original potential.[213] Created nature finds itself within what Milbank calls God's "art of spirit-governing" so that the gift of grace cannot in any way be set in opposition to the gift of created nature. God's art is his gifting "gift without contrast."[214] Milbank notes that:

---

208. Milbank, *Suspended Middle*, 105.
209. Levering, "Note," 528.
210. Milbank, *Suspended Middle*, 105.
211. Milbank, *Suspended Middle*, 106.
212. Milbank, *Suspended Middle*, 107.
213. Levering, "Note," 528.
214. Levering, "Note," 528.

since God alone governs our freedom and really turns our freedom towards him, freedom itself is here seen by Aquinas as the natural desire for the supernatural and even as obedience to grace. The gift of supernatural destiny *is* freedom, and it is the gift of our power to shape ourselves with true artistry.[215]

Levering asks whether this gift of grace, which brings about "true artistry," is too individualistic a formulation. Milbank's Aquinas would answer in the negative, because graced action occurs within a human community constituted in and through the mediation or communication of the divine gift.[216] As Milbank notes: "Aquinas puts this supernatural *poesis* in the context of supernatural community: what we do through the influence of a friend we still do properly for ourselves."[217] For Milbank, nature does not "contractually" limit the freedom that is divine-human "gift-exchange," a unified movement of gifting in which the two gifts of nature and grace flow into each other instead of being extrinsic to each other. Freedom means a communion of gifting that breaks down barriers, a communion in which we find created spirit's ultimate end, namely, deification. In this freedom of gift-exchange, we discover divine governance as deification.[218]

Recall Milbank's notion of freedom, as well as his positing the "gift of our power to shape ourselves with true artistry" and "the gift of supernatural destiny." Levering notes that freedom is never neutral toward the good, and thus never neutral toward the ultimate end that God ordains for us as human beings, created in grace. At the same time, if we understand the way that God governs the cosmos, we should be wary of the claim that a rational creature's ability to move in any way toward the good depends in an absolute sense upon God's gratuitous gift of deification. What appears to be at stake is the full variety of modes according to which God works in and through human rational capacities. Certainly, Milbank's insistence on the teleological finality of deification (following de Lubac) is solid ground on which to stand.[219] However, as Levering wisely suggests, perhaps the distinction that Aquinas makes between nature and grace only serves to increase our appreciation of

---

215. Milbank, *Suspended Middle*, 108.
216. Levering, "Note," 529.
217. Milbank, *Suspended Middle*, 108.
218. Levering, "Note," 529.
219. Levering, "Note," 529.

this same teleology as we, at the same time, acknowledge the many modes of participation in God's goodness.[220]

Hans Urs von Balthasar

As much as Milbank maintains that the positions of Pius XII and de Lubac were wholly incompatible, he also claims that the theology of Balthasar, if not directly incompatible with de Lubac's theology, is at least not as consistently brilliant and revolutionary.[221] According to Oakes, Milbank's judgment is likely to be a result of his more "extreme" formulations of de Lubac's achievements. One such claim is that de Lubac is one of the two truly great theologians of the twentieth century and that "it can now be seen that the *Surnaturel* of 1946 was almost as important an event of cultural revision as *Being and Time* or the *Philosophical Investigations*."[222] As we have seen, and despite his criticisms, Milbank's admiration of de Lubac seems based on his judgment that de Lubac was the first advocate "avant la lettre" of Radical Orthodoxy and that it was *Surnaturel* that finally deconstructed the possibility of dogmatic theology as previously understood under neo-scholasticism. It is no wonder then that he should judge Balthasar as not quite measuring up to de Lubac.[223] Ironically, however, Milbank admits early on that the phrase that he used for the title of *The Suspended Middle* comes from Balthasar, and is used by him to describe de Lubac's own fundamental contribution to the debate on nature and grace. Furthermore, Milbank is of the view that Balthasar's capitulation to *Humani Generis* was "more real and substantial than . . . de Lubac."[224] He also maintains that Balthasar reads de Lubac "in a conservative and over-Barthian fashion."[225]

Milbank's desire to contend with Balthasar flows from a desire to pursue answers to the many questions raised by the notion of the natural desire for grace, or, as Max Seckler, a recent student of this issue in Aquinas, puts it: "the natural desire for God is of grace without actually being

---

220. Levering, "Note," 534.

221. Milbank dedicates the entire sixth chapter of his *Suspended Middle* to a comparison of von Balthasar and de Lubac.

222. Milbank, *Suspended Middle*, 64.

223. Oakes, "Paradox," 688.

224. Oakes, "Paradox," 13.

225. Oakes, "Paradox," 73.

grace."²²⁶ Milbank's close reading of Balthasar reveals his "equivocal-tending position" and it seems to "edge de Lubac's position slightly toward a Barthian 'grace over-against nature'" position in which "nature is 'totally locked up' and yet 'totally open to grace.'"²²⁷ In Milbank's opinion, Balthasar's own approach to the notion of the suspended middle offers an alternative that understands created nature as "truly giving something to God."²²⁸ In this way, it accords nature a more robust status than does de Lubac's as it suggests "a more independent ontological space for Creation than de Lubac would allow."²²⁹

Milbank remains generally critical of how Balthasar reads de Lubac, however, claiming that the issue with him is sometimes one of "how much" to grant to grace, and "how much" to grant to nature. This position, he maintains, is a misreading of de Lubac, for whom there can be no such question. He further states that de Lubac was much more consistent than Balthasar in insisting on a dialectical genealogy: for de Lubac, it was not "the properly theological celebration of Man but the pious concern to conserve the gratuity of grace that engendered the monstrous titanic child of atheist humanism."²³⁰ Also, Milbank has concerns that Balthasar missed the most crucial import of de Lubac's work, namely, that the concept of pure-nature had unintentionally given theological justification for secular man's sense that he has no need of God's grace for a happy and fulfilled life.

Oakes points out however that Milbank is confused on two fronts in his treatment of Balthasar, each of which reinforces the other. Balthasar does not abdicate his philosophical responsibilities for the sake of mythology, and instead "accepts the deliverances of philosophical theology for his own work, and in a manner paralleling that of de Lubac, allows theology to instruct philosophy."²³¹ This approach allows the reform of philosophical theology without becoming mythological. It is perhaps Milbank's patently binary approach to de Lubac (that is, pope vs. persecuted Jesuit) that also determines his contrast between de Lubac and Balthasar.²³²

226. Fields, Review of *Suspended Middle*, 748, citing Seckler, *Instinkt*, 213.
227. Milbank, *Suspended Middle*, 73–74.
228. Milbank, *Suspended Middle*, 84.
229. Milbank, *Suspended Middle*, 84.
230. For Milbank's treatment of Balthasar (which I do not mean to replicate here), see Milbank, *Suspended Middle*, 69–84.
231. Oakes, "Paradox," 687.
232. Oakes, "Paradox," 687.

According to Oakes, Milbank has almost totally misunderstood Balthasar. It can be demonstrated that Balthasar in reality accepted de Lubac's point that Aquinas knew only one end for nature (that is, the supernatural one). Balthasar also makes use of an analogy drawn from Christological debates of the fifth century to show how the concept of pure-nature might have evolved in a way that would not have been recognized by earlier theologians, yet which retains its validity although going beyond the intent of Aquinas.[233]

Furthermore, Balthasar can be said to have made a connection that de Lubac never did, namely, that man's nature is a culture-creating nature. Milbank seems to praise de Lubac for *not* making this move:

> More explicitly than de Lubac [Balthasar] saw that the "middle" sphere of continuous event and sign is precisely the sphere of culture. He also was a Christian humanist; without Christian culture, he argued, there is only a nominal, not a mediated grace, which must remain uncomprehended and without real effect.[234]

It is strange that Milbank would count this fact as a criticism of Balthasar as it seems to be a genuine contribution to the nature-grace debate that had been lacking in Augustine, Aquinas, Suárez, Cajetan, Molina, and even perhaps to some extent de Lubac himself. Culture is indeed determinative (though not all-determinative) as part of man's end and arises specifically from man's spiritual nature. It is culture that reveals how one can understand grace as operative throughout the kingdom of nature.[235] Balthasar ultimately (having drawn on the notion of natural manifestations of a kind of "natural" grace in culture) arrives at the same insight that Milbank praises de Lubac for having reached earlier. On this account, Oakes maintains that Milbank's views on the alleged tension between de Lubac and Balthasar are the result of a superficial view of the latter, particularly as compared to his more sympathetic view of the former. Part of the reason for this is that he relies on the outmoded translation of Balthasar's book on Barth by John Drury, published in 1971. That translation left out almost a quarter of the original German (precisely those passages treating of the nature-grace debate), an omission (by Drury) that is known to have incensed Balthasar.[236]

---

233. Oakes, "Paradox," 687.
234. Milbank, *Suspended Middle*, 13.
235. Oakes, "Paradox," 689.
236. Oakes, "Paradox," 692.

Nature, Grace, and Secular Culture

As we have seen, Milbank is critical of de Lubac's ecclesiology given his view that it is a fruit of his capitulation to the papacy after *Humani Generis*. It is on this issue that Balthasar and de Lubac are closely tied in Milbank's mind:

> Yet the lacunae in [de Lubac's] work were partly shaped by his battles with authority. Is there not some contradiction here between his and Balthasar's formal capitulation to papal authority on the one hand, and their ecclesiology on the other, which stressed the primacy of the sacramental influence of the bishops as Eucharistic mediators?[237]

This judgment however only holds if one maintains a position that is common in liberal ecclesiologies, namely, that the institutional and juridical aspects of the church are always and by essence incompatible with the charismatic and sacramental aspects.[238] The fact is that Balthasar dedicates much of the fourth volume of his *Explorations in Theology* to an explanation of why the institutional and the charismatic aspects of the church are both mutually dependent and mutually reinforcing. Similarly, to ignore de Lubac's ecclesiological reflections written subsequent to *Humani Generis* (particularly *The Splendor of the Church*) is to miss an essential part of his theology of grace.[239] One need only refer to de Lubac's critique of the trends following the Second Vatican Council, in which he makes known his fear of a certain tendency that was the mirror opposite of the neo-scholastic extrinsicism that he had battled before the council.[240] Such a tendency, he thought, rather than separating nature and grace (as in extrinsicism), effectively so fuses nature and grace (collapsing the latter into the former) that anything natural becomes, by the fact that it is natural, a form of grace. De Lubac thought that just as the insistence on the preservation of the concept of pure-nature had aided and abetted the rise of secular culture (or the notion of "secular man," without the strict need of religion), so also the tendency after the council to fuse the orders of nature and grace gave rise to exactly the same risk.[241] This "naturalized grace"

---

237. Milbank, *Suspended Middle*, 104.

238. Oakes, "Paradox," 693.

239. Oakes, "Paradox," 693. The title of de Lubac's *Splendor of the Church* in the original French is *Méditation sur l'Église*.

240. For an example of de Lubac's postconciliar reflections, see Lubac, *Brief Catechesis*, 177–234.

241. Lubac, *Brief Catechesis*, 177–234.

merely ends up justifying secular independence from religion, a grave concern of de Lubac after the council. De Lubac states:

> A necessary reaction [to neo-scholasticism], a precondition for the necessary "opening" [of the church, called for by Pope John XXIII], was taken to be revolutionary, and, in public opinion, which was very poorly informed, it was the tradition of the church herself, with all her fertile but misunderstood richness, that seemed to be crushed. Many were no longer attentive to the very work of the Council, to the substance of its teachings, to the spirit that emanated from it: for them, through them, it was a new "modernity," in restless excitement but without a compass, that triumphed over a petrified modernity. What can be said, since then, of the new powers of the day, who, in reverse situation, suffer from a blindness that is more dense and all the more confident![242]

Reading such passages, one clearly sees de Lubac's deep concern for the church. It is unfortunate, therefore, that Milbank sees de Lubac's ecclesiology as the central sticking point that threatens to undo his achievements in *Surnaturel* (as well as Balthasar's own achievements).[243] For Oakes, it is instead Milbank's tendency towards binary opposites that threatens to undo his own critique of de Lubac, not to mention Balthasar, potentially even coming close to Gnosticism himself when he equates the eschatological church with the Godhead.[244]

Karl Rahner and Political Theology

As we have seen, Milbank identifies de Lubac as one of the principal architects of the "integralist revolution," a view favored by the Second Vatican Council.[245] However, Milbank maintains that the council was impeded from teaching this new doctrine properly by the unfortunate necessity of having to distance itself from what he terms earlier "integrist politics."[246] By this, he means to refer to the former (pre–Vatican II)

---

242. Lubac, *At the Service*, 145.

243. Oakes, "Paradox," 695.

244. Oakes, "Paradox," 695. For examples of statements that tend to approach Gnosticism, see Milbank, *Suspended Middle*, 106–7.

245. Milbank, *Theology and Social Theory*, 206.

246. Milbank, *Theology and Social Theory*, 206. Milbank rather confusingly uses the terms "integrist" and "integralist" to denote completely different realities; however, he

"insistence upon a clerical and hierarchic dominance over all the affairs of secular life, founded upon a totalizing theology which presented a complete system, whose details could not be questioned without compromising the whole."[247] It was only after Vatican II that, in Milbank's view, the new "theology of grace" could be fully developed, and this by way of a radically Christian politics; otherwise, no adequate answer to any social question could be found.[248] Milbank credits liberation theology and the experience of "lay apostleship" in "base communities" with showing how the whole concrete life of humanity is always imbued with grace, and that it is not possible to separate political social concerns from the spiritual concerns of salvation.[249] Nevertheless, that is where Milbank's concessions to liberation theology end; beyond this point he is convinced that they go "profoundly wrong."[250] Referencing the "integralist" (intrinsicist) swing in theology, Milbank notes that there were two sources for the momentous change, namely, the French source, which derived from the *nouvelle théologie*, particularly de Lubac (and Blondel), and a German source, primarily from Karl Rahner. Milbank, albeit controversially, maintains that there is a drastic difference between the two versions of integralism. According to Milbank, whereas the French version "supernaturalizes the natural," the German version, "naturalizes the supernatural."[251] The tendency of the German approach is towards a "mediating theology," a universal humanism, or a *rapprochement* with the Enlightenment and the autonomous secular order. Milbank claims that the French version (*nouvelle théologie*), however, proceeds in an entirely different direction, namely, towards a recovery of a premodern sense of the Christianized person as the "fully real person."[252] Milbank points out

does caution the reader about this difference in the original text. His use of the term "integralist" corresponds to my use of "intrinsicist" or "intrinsic."

247. Milbank, *Theology and Social Theory*, 206.
248. Mulcahy, *Aquinas's Notion*, 311.
249. Milbank, *Theology and Social Theory*, 207.
250. Milbank, *Theology and Social Theory*, 207.
251. Milbank, *Theology and Social Theory*, 207.
252. Milbank, *Theology and Social Theory*, 207. See also Rowland, *Culture of the Incarnation*, 64. Here, Rowland notes that the choice (between the French and the Rahnerian schools) presents a choice between a Catholic social theory conscious of both its Augustinian and Thomist heritage and a Thomism that has jettisoned its Augustinian heritage in favor of Kant. "For some, Kant has become a father of the Church" and "the choice is not between reading *Gaudium et spes* with Thomist spectacles versus Augustinian spectacles, but between reading the section on the autonomy of earthly affairs with reference to the account of nature and grace in the work of Karl Rahner and

that the main proponents of political theology in Germany and liberation theology in Latin America accept the Rahnerian, not the French, version of integralism.[253] It is this German option in fundamental theology, Milbank contends, that ensures that their respective political theologies remain trapped within the terms of "secular reason" and its unwarranted foundationalist presuppositions.[254] Given the correlationalist tendencies of the German approach, Marxism is problematically embraced as a discourse that supposedly discloses the "essence" of human beings and presents a fundamental level of human "historical becoming."[255] Milbank claims to have demonstrated that a Marxism of the kind that has been adopted by such theologies can, and has, been critically dismantled, and therefore one should not accept political theology's tendency to hold as inviolable basic Marxist premises simply out of a respect for (and desire to integrate) the autonomy of secular social science. Milbank asserts that it is but a short step from the Rahnerian version of integralism to an embracing of Bonhoeffer's "dialectical paradoxes of secularisation," where the social is an autonomous sphere that does not need to turn to theology for its self-understanding. Yet, despite what these proponents claim, Milbank is of the view (as we have seen) that what is held to be an autonomous secular sphere can already be counted as grace-imbued; thus, for its proponents, "it is *upon* pre-theological sociology or Marxist social theory, that theology must be founded."[256] The consequence of this is that a theological critique of society becomes impossible and,

---

reading the same section with reference to the theme of nature and grace in the work of Henri de Lubac."

253. This is a controversial position, however. Nevertheless, I note that others support the notion that Rahner's theology plays the role of a starting or referential point in liberation theologies (such as those of Metz and Gutiérrez) in that they are pastoral correlational theologies (see Martinez, "Political and Liberation Theologies"; and Komonchak, "Augustine," 114). I would also simply note, as an aside, that Rahner was almost as critical of *Gaudium et Spes* as was Ratzinger. See Peterson, "Critical Voices," and Komonchak, "Augustine." It was Chenu and Congar (French integrist school) who were major contributors to that document. It is also a debatable point as to whether proponents of liberation theology were entirely happy with *Gaudium et Spes* as well. Rowland argues that they viewed it as an expression of middle-class European sensibilities and represented a "bourgeois revolution in modern Catholicism . . . which did not go far enough" (Metz and Segundo). Hugo Assmann even regarded Hans Küng, for example, as a "middle-class reactionary." See Rowland, *Ratzinger's Faith*, 43.

254. For a critique of Milbank's rejection of political theology, see Breyfogle, "Is There Room?," 31–48.

255. Milbank, *Theology and Social Theory*, 208.

256. Milbank, *Theology and Social Theory*, 208. Emphasis in original.

therefore, for Milbank, what is offered is anything but a true theology of the political. Theological beliefs at this point become "but a faint regulative gloss upon Kantian ethics and a somewhat eclectic, though basically Marxist, social theory."[257] For Milbank, the disappointment with political theology, and liberation theology alike, is that rather than attempting to demonstrate how socialism is grounded in Christianity (as is Milbank's own claim), proponents of such theologies have taken the direction of simply another effort to reinterpret Christianity in terms of a dominant secular discourse of the day. For Milbank, it is only the French, not the Rahnerian, version of integralism that provides the possibility for a true political theology, that is, a theological critique of society and politics because only the *nouvelle théologie* "truly abandons hierarchies and geographies in theological anthropology, because it refuses even to 'formally distinguish' a realm of pure-nature in concrete humanity."[258] The political theologies of the Rahnerian brand tend to overlook the fact that there can be no purely natural, secular, or autonomous sphere of thought or action. For Milbank, unless the political reality is conceived in theological terms, it will be conceived unworthily. Liberation theologians have mistakenly supposed that they could learn from (let alone establish a theology from) a science that does not take humanity's supernatural telos into explicit account, instead effectively building their theological houses on the sand of Marxist social theory and upon pre-theological sociology.[259] Milbank points out that liberation theologians (along with Rahner) have built their theologies upon the mistaken supposition that there is "something universal in each individual" such as "his psychology, or rather the epistemic structure of his knowing."[260] In contrast, Milbank notes that in de Lubac's theology, every science learns to build on the rock of grace, because along with Augustine, Aquinas, and Scotus, "one can only specify human nature with reference to its supernatural end."[261] This is one of the main reasons why Milbank eschews a correlationist mode of doing theology. Those that had done so found themselves borrowing explicatory categories from "social theorists" (specifically Freud and Marx). Milbank reminds us that these two archetypal figures of "social theory" are, in actuality, crypto-theologians as each of them, as stated, purports to have

257. Milbank, *Theology and Social Theory*, 208.
258. Milbank, *Theology and Social Theory*, 208.
259. Mulcahy, *Aquinas's Notion*, 311.
260. Milbank, *Theology and Social Theory*, 221.
261. Milbank, *Theology and Social Theory*, 221.

understood the *telos* of the *humanum*. Given this, theologians would do well to be wary of becoming uncritically beholden to their ethos.[262]

CONCLUSION

The concern for the rampant secularization that has been defining and shaping much of the world has provided the impetus for Milbank's theological project. In particular, the tendency in secular culture to reduce the theological to a merely private affair, discredited, and inapplicable to public civic life, is, for Milbank, one of the most challenging aspects of secularization. In answer to this, Milbank seeks to challenge the very possibility of the notion of a reality that is *ab initio* independent from God, and in so doing, to undermine the secularist project. Milbank attempts this by turning to the Platonic ontological notion of participation and especially to the thought of de Lubac and the *nouvelle théologie*, which Milbank deems to be a close ally and, indeed, precursor to his own project. Accordingly, Milbank rejects the notion of extrinsicist reading of nature and grace (and along with it any possibility of pure-nature), and sees this approach, along with de Lubac, as having directly contributed to the rise of secularism. It is de Lubac's recovery of the notion of the supernatural that Milbank thinks is most helpful in challenging the secularist interdependence from God and its concomitant overemphasis on human autonomy, which leads, he observes, to sheer nihilism. It is by means of the Platonic/Christian notion of participation that Milbank thinks postmodern culture can be recovered by the Christian faith. Part of the novelty of Milbank's project is that it seeks to situate itself within postmodernism, while also affirming the importance of metaphysics (specifically, the ontology of participation). This is evidenced especially in Milbank's interpretation of the *ressourcement*. Milbank does not think that the project of the *ressourcement* discloses objective truth and prefers to adhere to the postmodern notion of narrative knowledge, which rejects the categories of subjectivity and objectivity, and which relies on discourse to reveal the true nature of reality. In line with the postmodern narrative approach, Milbank's method presents itself in a narrative of opposition in which the modern history of Western thought is deemed to be nothing more than a genealogy of error accounting for the present challenges of postmodern culture. The blame for the fundamental shift in

262. Burrell, "Radical Orthodoxy: Appreciation," 75.

direction in Western thought, according to Milbank, lies unequivocally with Scotus and his notion of univocity. Utterly rejecting this notion, which he believes has created the possibility for secularism, Milbank insists that participation is that which is able to show that creation is at every moment "suspended" by its Creator, and in this way it cannot ever be entirely separate from him. For Milbank, behind modern, liberal, secular politics stands the epistemology of autonomous reason, which is based in turn on the ontology of univocity and the denial of participation. It is into this notion of participation that Milbank inserts (however controversially) the insights of de Lubac and the *nouvelle théologie*. Milbank re-emphasizes that the Lubacian notion of paradox as applied to nature and grace and the notion of the natural desire for the supernatural are critical insights that must be maintained. Man's primary nature is receptivity to God's gifts, firstly, of being, and secondly, of beatitude. Paradox is in no way inimical to the Christian faith, existing at its very heart in Christ's hypostatic union. For Milbank, Christ stands in a suspended middle between divine and human, the finite and the infinite, because divinity and humanity are not univocal natures that are somehow competing for space, and thus mutually exclusive; rather, Christ is fully both. Relatedly, Milbank resists the extrinsicist idea that seems to pit the gift of grace against the gift of creation, instead stating that the gift of creation and the gift of grace are already united In the one divine gifting. This means that there is nothing lying outside the economy of divine gratuity against which it can be contrasted. Thus, Milbank seeks to recover the Neoplatonic notion of *influentia*, which eschews the notion that grace functions by acting upon man, as if it were some foreign influence, and prefers a paradigm of gratuity in which the recipient of the gift, the gift itself, and the donation of one to the other, establishes a radically and unilateral threefold gratuity. It is only in this way, Milbank thinks, that the gratuity of grace and the proper autonomy of the creature are preserved, all the while rejecting the possibility of pure-nature. Milbank goes even further than the *nouvelle théologie* and equates the notion of participation with grace, such that he is able to say that all creation is "engraced." Likewise, he considers God's original intent to be creation *as* creation and rejects the notion that creation's supernatural destiny *exceeds* the order of creation. Thus, for Milbank, human nature is always already intrinsically raised above itself, while grace always already reaches down to nature. This, as we have seen, is a notion that is certainly not without its problems and in many ways can be said to not only to go beyond, but also to stand at odds with, de Lubac and the *nouvelle théologie*.

Given the central role that participation plays in Milbank's thought, and his rejection of the accepted secular standards of scientific truth or normative rationality, the possibility of correspondence theory in theology is also totally rejected. Milbank's essential idea is that the horizon of Christian theology can confidently include everything in its purview, because everything is numinous in a world made for God in Christ. In this way, Milbank's approach tends to close down any natural space for even a limited non-theological politics or ethics, and secular ways of thought can never be considered normative for Christianity, insisting instead upon a properly theological social theory and a radical Christian politics. Thus, for Milbank, any approach that attempts to deal with postmodern secular culture by means of a correlationist approach, a mediating theology, a universal humanism, or a *rapprochement* with the Enlightenment, is to be rejected because it implies or seems to give credence to the notion that there can be a purely natural, secular sphere of thought or action apart from God, a notion against which Milbank's entire project is aimed.

4

Nature and Grace in the Thought of Joseph Ratzinger

IN HIS 2008 ADDRESS to the Pontifical Council for Culture, Pope Benedict XVI addressed the central theme chosen for the assembly that year, namely, "The Church and the Challenge of Secularisation." In his judgment, secularization is "a fundamental issue for the future of humanity and the church . . . that harshly tries the Christian life of the faithful and Pastors alike." According to Benedict:

> the "death of God" proclaimed by many intellectuals in recent decades is giving way to a barren cult of the individual. In this cultural context there is a risk of drifting into spiritual atrophy and emptiness of heart, sometimes characterized by surrogate forms of religious affiliation and vague spiritualism. It is proving more urgent than ever to react to this tendency by means of an appeal to the lofty values of existence that give life meaning and can soothe the restlessness of the human heart in search of happiness: the dignity of the human person and his or her freedom, equality among all men and women, the meaning of life and death and of what awaits us after the end of our earthly existence.[1]

The Holy Father exhorted the church to confront, with gospel proclamation and witness in the arena of dialogue and the encounter with

---

1. Benedict XVI, *Address to Pontifical Council for Culture*.

cultures, the "disturbing phenomenon of secularisation that enfeebles the person and hinders him in his innate longing for the whole Truth."[2] These remarks make clear just how important the challenge of secular culture has been to him. Throughout his own life and ministry, Joseph Ratzinger had such concerns very much at the forefront of his mind.[3]

For those who have had the opportunity to become familiar with Ratzinger's writings, it becomes evident that he does not attempt to create a theological system of his own. Ratzinger in fact said as much in an interview with Peter Seewald in 1997:

> I have never tried to create a system of my own, an individual theology. What is specific, if you want to call it that, is that I simply want to think in communion with the faith of the church, and that means above all to think in communion with the great thinkers of the faith. The aim is not an isolated theology that I draw out of myself but one that opens as widely as possible into the common intellectual pathway of the faith.[4]

This is why one does not find in Ratzinger's work the presentation of an original theological synthesis but a series of seminal interventions in theological debates thrown up by pastoral crises.[5] If one were to describe Ratzinger's methodology, it would be as follows. Firstly, it tends to take contemporary developments in society and culture as its starting point. Then, in order to offer a response, it seeks out what fellow theologians have had to say on the topic in question. As a next step, Scripture and Tradition are consulted, before finally presenting a systematic answer given in the context of theology as a whole. According to D. Vincent Twomey, Ratzinger's theology, while full of brilliant insights on almost every subject, should be considered to be "fragmentary" rather than a "fixed system."[6]

2. Benedict XVI, *Address to Pontifical Council for Culture*.

3. His many homilies, colloquiums, writings, and interviews (the few that he gave) on this topic evidence this (concerned pastor that he was), including: Habermas and Ratzinger, *Dialectics of Secularization*; Ratzinger, *Values*; Ratzinger and Pera, *Without Roots*; Ratzinger, *Faith and Politics*; Ratzinger et al., *Handing on the Faith*; Ratzinger and Seewald, *Salt of the Earth*; Ratzinger, *Christianity and the Crisis of Cultures*; Ratzinger, *Turning Point*; Benedikt XVI and Seewald, *Benedikt XVI: Ein Leben*; Ratzinger and Seewald, *God and the World*; Ratzinger, *Church, Ecumenism, and Politics*; Benedict XVI and Seewald, *Light of the World*; and Ratzinger, *Christ, Faith, and the Challenge of Cultures*.

4. Ratzinger and Seewald, *Salt of the Earth*, 67.

5. Rowland, *Benedict XVI: Guide*, 1.

6. Rowland, *Benedict XVI: Guide*, 1. See also Twomey, *Pope Benedict XVI*.

This lack of a fixed system obviously presents a challenge for this present enquiry into his thought concerning the nature and grace debate. My approach will require a drawing together of the various strands of his thought as they pertain to nature and grace from his reflections on and reactions to the relevant pastoral and theological issues he has sought to deal with, even though, as we shall see, Ratzinger only in very few instances deals explicitly with the issue of how nature and grace interrelate. In establishing Ratzinger's view of nature and grace, we will firstly situate his thought within the context of the developments in twentieth-century theology, particularly as it stands with respect to neo-scholasticism and the *nouvelle théologie*.[7] It will then seek to extract Ratzinger's view of nature and grace by examining his adoption of theological personalism and Christocentrism, his idea of Christian humanism and the Incarnation, and how he conceives of the church-world relation. Finally, it will examine his work entitled "Gratia Praesupponit Naturam" (a chapter within his *Dogma and Preaching*), which is the most explicit treatment of the topic in Ratzinger's corpus, and thus deserves close examination.

NEO-SCHOLASTICISM AND THE *NOUVELLE THÉOLOGIE*

Over the many years of his theological work, Ratzinger identified various critical fronts within Catholic theology. To his mind, the most urgent of these fronts had been the attempt in Catholic theology to seek a Catholic understanding of the "mediation of history in the realm of ontology." More specifically, according to Ratzinger, theology is yet to give an adequate response to the issues raised by Martin Heidegger's *Being and Time* and indeed to German Idealism more generally. Also of concern to Ratzinger was his desire to overcome the ahistorical temper of neo-scholasticism, without, at the same time, ending up in relativism.[8] According to Tracey Rowland, these issues had been brewing in theology from at least the late eighteenth century with the ascendency of the Romantic movement across Western Europe. The neo-scholastic trend made itself felt within the realm of theological anthropology, particularly concerning the notion of nature and grace and also that of the reception

---

7. As we saw in chapter 2, this is a pertinent question when considering a theologian's approach to the nature-grace question.
8. Rowland, *Benedict XVI: Guide*, 2.

and transmission of Revelation. The decidedly ahistorical character of preconciliar neo-scholastic theology meant that it was hamstrung in entering into the contemporary debates of modern man.[9] Unfortunately, in many instances, those who sought to engage with the questions raised by the Romantic movement were labeled "modernists" and so pushed to the margins of ecclesiastical life, if not expelled entirely. This mode of reacting against those who would challenge the neo-scholastic rationalist, ahistorical hegemony was so pervasive that even those working in patristics worked under a lamentable "cloud of suspicion." It was ultimately the Second Vatican Council that "lifted the lid from this cauldron of theological conundrums," though, it must be said that these same conundrums are far from resolved even in the present day.[10]

The dominant neo-scholasticism, with which so many in Ratzinger's generation were frustrated, had been fostered by the encyclical *Aeterni Patris* (1879) of Pope Leo XIII, which had called for the study of Aquinas as an antidote to prominent forms of rationalism and relativism. This impetus became known as "Leonine Thomism." While this movement did produce works of genuine scholarship in places like Louvain, it nonetheless gave rise to the tendency to rely solely upon secondary sources and manuals, which were proffered to seminarians essentially to rote learn. This approach meant that Aquinas was read abstractly, without regard to his own historical context. Likewise, students would typically read Kant and Descartes through Aquinas rather than engage directly with them in primary sources.[11] In this way, Leonine Thomism, which prided itself on being "perennial" and "above history," became the only framework that was presented to budding theologians and clerics.

After the Second World War, however, theologians sought to challenge the homogeneity and anti-historicism of the neo-scholastic system. Fergus Kerr points out that almost every significant Catholic theologian after the war (including Ratzinger himself) can be said to have been in

---

9. Rowland, *Benedict XVI: Guide*, 2. Pace Rowland, but it does seem ironic that the Thomistic neo-scholastic system should be considered to be *prima facie* inadequate to deal with the concerns of "modern man." It was, after all, understood by Pope Leo XIII to be a formidable intellectual weapon with which to engage nineteenth-century rationalism. See Leo XIII, *Aeterni Patris*. I do, however, take the point that what may have sufficed for nineteenth-century rationalism may not necessarily be effective in addressing postmodern man's concerns in the late twentieth and early twenty-first centuries.

10. Rowland, *Benedict XVI: Guide*, 2.

11. Rowland, *Benedict XVI: Guide*, 2.

one way or another rebelling against the Leonine approach to theology.[12] According to Thomas O'Meara:

> a non-voluntaristic and free theology of grace found in Aquinas was re-formed into a theology of propositional faith, ontology, and church authority. A lack of sophistication in method, a questionable arrangement of disciplines, and absence of history, a moralistic interdiction of other theologies even when based upon Scripture and tradition characterized this theology.[13]

The expression "the Rhine flowed into the Tiber" is a well-known cliché used to explain what happened within the church in the early 1960s. Many ideas that had been circulating in the theology departments of Munich, Lucerne, and Tübingen began to surface as many of the world's bishops came to accept that neo-scholasticism had its limitations. It was the humanists (those who were interested in anthropological questions, were multidisciplinary, but above all, concerned to understand the theological significance of history and tradition) who began to be favored.[14] Rowland points out that one cannot suggest that Ratzinger can be neatly pigeonholed as the Tübingen School's most illustrious heir, or Newman's German apogee, or the Bavarian soul mate of Balthasar. Like all great scholars, Ratzinger defies easy categorization. Nevertheless, one can assert that it is not possible to understand Ratzinger without a certain familiarity with the Catholic wing of the Romantic reaction against the rationalism of the Enlightenment.[15]

Early Impressions of Neo-Scholasticism

Ratzinger would agree with Walter Kasper's assessment that "there is no doubt that the outstanding event in the Catholic theology of our century is the surmounting of Neo-Scholasticism."[16] Ratzinger was very much part of the erstwhile struggle for the integration of spirituality and theology, where the discovery of the living Jesus of the Gospels was the central concern. Ratzinger essentially began his studies in the

---

12. Kerr, *Twentieth-Century Catholic Theologians*.
13. O'Meara, *Church and Culture*, 50.
14. Rowland, *Benedict XVI: Guide*, 23.
15. Rowland, *Benedict XVI: Guide*, 23.
16. Kasper, *Theology and Church*, 1.

midst of this climate of intellectual transition to a different theological sensibility and paradigm.[17]

Ratzinger refers to the fact that he had been taught a "rigid, Neo-Scholastic Thomism" and that he "had difficulties in penetrating the thought of Thomas Aquinas, whose crystal-clear logic seemed to me to be too closed in on itself, too impersonal and ready-made."[18] Ratzinger was taught this neo-scholastic Thomism by Arnold Wilmsen, who himself, after having studied Husserl and phenomenology at Munich, departed dissatisfied to Rome to imbibe the *philosophia thomistica* at the Roman universities. Wilmsen seems to have been in favor of the sort of neo-Thomism that was in favor with the opponents of the *nouvelle théologie*. Despite Ratzinger's dissatisfaction at having been forced to imbibe neo-scholasticism, he nevertheless did not feel required to invent his own version of Thomism.[19] Alfred Läpple (who was Ratzinger's prefect of studies at the Freising seminary) mentions that Ratzinger faulted neo-scholasticism because of its lack of enquiry:

> Man is always asking questions, and when he thinks he's answered one question, a bigger one is already presenting itself. The impulse to consider the truth as a possession to be defended has always unsettled him [Ratzinger]. He didn't feel at ease with neo-scholastic definitions that seemed to him like ramparts, whereby what is inside the definition is the truth, and what is outside is all mistaken.[20]

Läpple points out that, for Ratzinger, neo-scholasticism was not a "theology that kneels [in prayer]," and that "in the dialect of Bavaria we would say: it wasn't his beer."[21]

Ratzinger faults neo-scholasticism for bringing too much order into Aquinas's still inchoate terminology. He thought that too many distinctions were made in subsequent centuries between philosophy and theology.[22] Ratzinger notes that:

> the exclusion of ontology from theology does not emancipate philosophical thinking but paralyses it. The extinction of

---

17. Gaál, *Theology of Pope Benedict XVI*, 25.
18. Ratzinger, *Milestones*, 44.
19. Kerr, *Twentieth-Century Catholic Theologians*, 184.
20. Läpple, Interview by Valente and Azzaro.
21. Läpple, Interview by Valente and Azzaro.
22. Gaál, *Theology of Pope Benedict XVI*, 22.

ontology in the sphere of philosophy, far from purifying theology, actually deprives it of its solid basis. Contrary to the common hostility toward ontology, which is apparently becoming the sole link between contemporary philosophers and theologians, we held that both disciplines need this dimension of thought and that it is here that they find themselves indissolubly linked.[23]

For Ratzinger, the concept of *pure-nature* is a "fata morgana," and so likewise *pure reason* à la Kant does not exist. Only in recognizing this fact can one appreciate Aquinas's position of an effective harmony between faith and reason. Only when faith and reason support each other can the human spirit rise up to knowledge of God, and thus, be able to partake in divine life. A faith without reason ends in fundamentalism, while a reason without faith ends in despair.[24] Leonine Thomism's priding itself on being perennial and above history actually fails to meet the challenge of the "mediation of history within the realm of ontology." Ratzinger frequently called upon his fellow scholars to "look up from their desks and to integrate the faith of nonacademically trained Christians."[25] Taking inspiration from Bonaventure, Ratzinger refers to the *simplex et idiota* (often rendered as the "simple of heart"). Ratzinger's discovery in 1955 of a certain "Bonaventurian anti-intellectualism" led to the notion of the *simplex et idiota* becoming a recurring theme in Ratzinger's oeuvre, particularly as applied to the "hypotrophy of barren intellectualism, typified especially by the Neo-Scholastic rationalist approach to theology."[26]

In a congratulatory note on the occasion of the opening of the Academy of Villa Cavalletti in Grottaferrata in 2003, Ratzinger pondered the meaning of theology. He stated that, through a human being, God entered history as a speaking subject, meaning that the divine Word exists in human words. Therefore, for Ratzinger, one becomes a theologian to the degree to which one nears the sacred authors in their relationship with God and in the manner in which human and divine words collaborate. Theology must first and foremost adopt a threefold posture of listening, believing, and praying. It is by acknowledging God as "Our

---

23. Ratzinger, *Nature and Mission of Theology*, 22.
24. Gaál, *Theology of Pope Benedict XVI*, 22.
25. Ratzinger, *Principles of Catholic Theology*, 160.
26. Gaál, *Theology of Pope Benedict XVI*, 54. See also Komonchak, "Church in Crisis," 11.

Father," that the theologian is freed from reducing God, in a modernist fashion, to the interiority of human subjectivity.[27]

The *Nouvelle Théologie*

As we saw in chapter 1, de Lubac was a major influence on Ratzinger. It should come as no surprise then that, accordingly, one can only best understand Ratzinger by locating him within the *nouvelle théologie*.[28] As we have seen, the *nouvelle théologie* sought to reform the dominant neo-scholastic theology of the time by means of a *ressourcement* that retrieved the theology of the patristic period. Francis Schüssler Fiorenza points out that theologically the *nouvelle théologie* emphasized the integration of nature and grace in such a way that it underscored the importance of a Christian culture. Fiorenza notes that locating Ratzinger within this movement is important because its shows how his theological development is in many ways similar to it and borrows heavily from it.[29] According to Fiorenza, the theologians of the *nouvelle théologie* tended to interpret Aquinas from the perspective of Augustine. Ratzinger however sought a much more direct retrieval of the Augustinian tradition. As we have seen, he wrote his first dissertation on Augustine's understanding of the people of God and his *Habilitationsschrift* on Bonaventure's theology of history. As if evidencing the earlier point concerning accusations of modernism for those challenging Leonine Thomism, Ratzinger's second reader, Michael Schmaus, judged his *Habilitationsschrift* to be defective and containing a "dangerous modernism" that could lead to a "subjectivization of the concept of salvation."[30] Schmaus was so concerned that, in order to prevent Ratzinger and his colleagues from becoming *periti* at the Second Vatican Council, he addressed them disparagingly as "Twen-Theologen" (theologians in their twenties).[31] Despite this opposition, it was precisely their novel understanding of Revelation that would prove revolutionary at the beginning of the council and that would set the tenor for the whole council itself. Ratzinger demonstrated that, for Bonaventure, Revelation is far wider and

27. Wallbrecher, Weimer, and Stötzl, *30 Jahre Wegbegleitung*, 155.
28. Fiorenza, "From Theologian to Pope."
29. Fiorenza, "From Theologian to Pope."
30. Ratzinger, *Milestones*, 106.
31. Gaál, *Theology of Pope Benedict XVI*, 66. Schmaus also attempted to prevent Ratzinger from becoming professor of fundamental theology in Freising, and to sideline him to an insignificant pedagogical college located in Munich-Pasing.

richer than merely that which the human intellect can comprehend or even that which is contained in Scripture. Revelation is both historical and contextual because it is Jesus Christ himself.[32] Following Guardini, Ratzinger also discovered in Augustine and Bonaventure two original theologians unlike the more cerebral Aristotelian, Aquinas, and other later formalistic neo-scholastic thinkers. For Ratzinger, the gravitational center in theology can never be the dogmatic systematization of Revelation for the sake of university lectures, but the historicity of faith and its mystical interiorization by the concrete human person. From this point of view, both Augustine and Bonaventure represent a decidedly salvation-historic perspective that has its roots in Scripture. Thus, for Ratzinger, theological and religious renewal must occur by rediscovering and reawakening the wellsprings of faith.[33] Ultimately, for him, true knowledge is being struck by the arrow of beauty that wounds man, moved by the reality that it is Christ himself who is present and in an ineffable way disposes and forms the souls of men. It is this being struck that is a more real, more profound knowledge than the mere rational deduction of neo-scholastic theology. We must therefore urgently rediscover this form of knowledge, Ratzinger thinks, as it is a pressing need of our time.[34] Ratzinger's theological writings often underscore Augustine's emphasis on spirituality, the role of the Cross, and Christian charity toward one's neighbor, and explicate the Scriptures with reference to patristic images and themes. In this way, says Fiorenza, Ratzinger's writings contrasted sharply with the more arid Scholasticism of his day. For this reason, he was, at the time, perceived as a progressive theologian.[35]

For Fiorenza, Ratzinger's indebtedness to the *nouvelle théologie* comes to the fore in regard to the patristic interpretation of Scripture and the retrieval of Augustine, but also in an emphasis on liturgical renewal and a focus on the centrality of the Eucharist for the life and mission of the church. Fiorenza also asserts that understanding the theological vision of the relationship between nature and grace, and between Christianity and culture, that was central to the *nouvelle théologie* is crucial for understanding Ratzinger's own approach to these issues. In one of his earliest writings on the topic of nature and grace, the chapter entitled "Gratia Praesupponit Naturam" in his *Dogma and Preaching*, Ratzinger

32. Gaál, *Theology of Pope Benedict XVI*, 66.
33. Gaál, *Theology of Pope Benedict XVI*, 66.
34. Bardazzi, *In the Vineyard*, 29.
35. Fiorenza, "From Theologian to Pope," 4.

argues that the focus upon grace perfecting nature should not overlook the Cross of Christ (we will turn to this work more specifically later in the chapter). Ratzinger makes this notion explicit in his understanding of the relation between Christian faith and culture.[36] In his view, Christian faith is not something that exists simply as a set of propositional doctrines; nor does it exist as sheer abstract religion. Instead, as Fiorenza points out, religion and culture are concretely intertwined and cannot be separated. Therefore, Ratzinger says, one cannot simply think of Christianity as independent of culture. Instead, one has to ask how the Christian community is a distinctive Christian culture. Because the Christian faith entails a stance about the meaning of human nature and the affirmation of certain values, it entails a culture of meaning and values. Christianity exists as a social and cultural community called the people of God. Such a community is its own distinctive culture whose beliefs and values stand in tension with other cultures.[37]

Ratzinger is often accused of holding to a high Christology, sacramentality, and ecclesiology. Lieven Boeve is one such interlocutor and holds that Ratzinger is a strong opponent of the Schillebeeckxian way of doing theology (particularly Schillebeeckx's notion of "recontextualization" of the faith to the culture of modernity).[38] Boeve's "bill of indictment" declaims:

> With Ratzinger's theological paradigm we have a subordination of the historical to the eternal, the human to the divine, nature to grace. This also results in a "high" Christology, sacramentality and ecclesiology, in which dialectics is emphasized stronger than dialogue and opposition gets more attention than mediation. It is never from history, nature, reason, or the human that revelation, grace, faith, and the divine can be understood, but decisively the other way around.[39]

According to Rowland, Boeve's use of the notion of "subordination" completely misses the point of the many statements Ratzinger has made about the critical couplets (history and eternity, humanity and divinity, nature and grace). Ratzinger is neither a Monophysite nor a Nestorian and therefore is not attracted to the sharp either/or options typical of

---

36. Fiorenza, "From Theologian to Pope," 4.
37. Fiorenza, "From Theologian to Pope," 4.
38. Depoortere, Boeve, and van Erp, *Edward Schillebeeckx*.
39. Boeve, *Theology at the Crossroads*, 229.

Calvinism, the separations of the Nestorians, or the subordination theories of the Monophysites. In all these areas he is heavily influenced by de Lubac and Balthasar, both of whom were highly critical of Monophysite and Nestorian temptations. A better way of analyzing his ideas would be to say that Ratzinger is hostile to "bastard dualisms such as *pure nature* without grace, *pure reason* without Revelation, or mere history such as a sociological reading of the *signs of the times* without reference to eschatology."[40] When it comes to these critical couplets it is typical of Ratzinger to take the view that we can understand one pole of the couplet only with reference to the other. For example, history is understood only against the backdrop of Revelation, but Revelation itself is historical. Similarly, he argues that faith has the right to be missionary only if it transcends all traditions and constitutes an appeal to reason and an orientation toward the truth itself. Nonetheless, his notion of reason is not the same as the truncated conception typical of eighteenth-century philosophy, but instead encompasses the idea of wisdom and hence must always be open to Revelation.[41] As he writes:

> I am convinced, in fact, that the crisis we are experiencing in the church and in humanity is closely allied to the exclusion of God as a topic with which reason can properly be concerned—an exclusion that has led to the degeneration of theology first into historicism, then into sociologism and, at the same time, to the impoverishment of philosophy.[42]

As we shall see, there is a strong Christocentrism in his theological structure. As he wrote in his best-selling work *Introduction to Christianity*, ontology, represented Christologically by the theology of the Incarnation, and history, represented Christologically by the theology of the Cross, "reveal polarities that cannot be surmounted and combined in a neat synthesis without the loss of the crucial points in each; they must remain present as polarities that mutually correct each other and only by complementing each other point toward the whole."[43] In contrast to the anti-metaphysical animus of contemporary postmodern philosophy, Ratzinger stands for the affirmation of both history and metaphysics, not metaphysics without history (the preconciliar problem) or history

---

40. Rowland, "Ratzinger on Timelessness of Truth," 254.
41. Rowland, "Ratzinger on Timelessness of Truth," 254.
42. Ratzinger, *Principles of Catholic Theology*, 316.
43. Ratzinger, *Introduction to Christianity*, 230.

without metaphysics (the postmodern temptation). He eschews any kind of dualistic choice between the being-Christology of Chalcedon and the event-Christology of the New Testament.[44] In the essay, "Christocentrism in Preaching?" from his *Dogma and Preaching*, Ratzinger states that Chalcedon continues to represent the "definitive ecclesial formulation of Jesus's Divine Sonship" and declares it to be nothing less than "the pivotal truth that decides everything."[45] He further notes that "the ontological character of the Trinity is central for the reality-content of Christianity, but it is not in opposition to the event; rather, it is revealed precisely in the event of God's action toward us."[46] In *Principles of Catholic Theology*, Ratzinger concludes a reflection on the relationship between history and ontology, stating:

> Man finds his centre of gravity, not inside, but outside himself. The place to which he is anchored is not, as it were, within himself, but without. This explains that remnant that remains always to be explained, the fragmentary character of all his efforts to comprehend the unity of history and being. Ultimately, the tension between ontology and history has its foundation in the tension within human nature itself, which must go out of itself in order to find itself; it has its foundation in the mystery of God, which is freedom and which, therefore, calls each individual by a name that is known to no other. Thus, the whole is communicated to him in the particular.[47]

Theological Personalism

Philosophically speaking, Ratzinger's thinking, faith, and prayer life were all inspired by the personalism of Ferdinand Ebner and Martin Buber. They took concrete shape in the Christology of Guardini. Ratzinger's study under Söhngen added the dimension of mystery to his thought. Balthasar and de Lubac gave him the impetus to bring forth a close correlation between Christology and ecclesiology. For Ratzinger, this means that the church cannot be properly apprehended and lived by the believer without first being touched by the mystery of Jesus Christ. These factors

---

44. Ratzinger, *Dogma and Preaching*, 42.
45. Ratzinger, *Dogma and Preaching*, 42.
46. Ratzinger, *Dogma and Preaching*, 46.
47. Ratzinger, *Principles of Catholic Theology*, 171.

blend into a distinctive, inseverable whole that marks Ratzinger as a priest, theologian, and pope.[48] In Ratzinger's view, God is not worshiped and cherished because he can be grasped in exact formulas and demonstrated beyond doubt as the *summum bonum*, as in the neo-scholastic, manualist approach to theology. Instead, for Ratzinger, it is "thrilling and life-altering" to encounter God as a living Thou, who is recognizable as personal and who encourages one to recognize him in return.[49] In this way, Ratzinger is often described as having subscribed to a more "progressive" approach (as opposed to the "conservative" Leonine approach) to theology. He also favored a return to biblical, patristic, and high medieval explications, a fact that very much defines him as a man of the *ressourcement* movement.[50]

Jean Daniélou observes that neo-scholastic theology tends to locate reality in essences rather than in subjects, and by so doing, ignores the "dramatic world of persons, of universal concretes transcending all essence and only distinguished by their existence."[51] It was precisely this dramatic world of persons and subjects who were struggling with their self-identity that was the common ground between nineteenth-century Romantics and twentieth-century existentialists. It was also, it must be said, the concern of ordinary people, at the level of the average parish, who were trying to come to terms with the impact of two world wars and the resulting economic depression on their lives and personal relationships.[52] Ratzinger himself notes:

> People had come back from the war, some from six-year-long participation in the war, and they were now filled with a real intellectual and literary hunger. With questions, too, of course,

---

48. Gaál, *Theology of Pope Benedict XVI*, 44. See also Proniewski, "Joseph Ratzinger's Philosophical Theology," 219–36; and Eller, *Veritas creatrix incarnata*.

49. Gaál, *Theology of Pope Benedict XVI*, 44. In an essay on the notion of the human person, published during the pontificate of John Paul II, Ratzinger was critical of the Boethian definition of the person as the "individual substance of a rational nature," because it neglected the whole dimension of relationality, which makes human persons not merely members of the human race but *unique individual members* of the human race. Both Wojtyla and Ratzinger were driven to develop this dimension of Catholic anthropology as a response to issues thrown up by existentialist philosophy. A theology that has nothing to say about individuality is impotent against the power of nineteenth-century German Romanticism and its twentieth-century developments. See Ratzinger, "Concerning the Notion of Person," 439–54.

50. Gaál, *Theology of Pope Benedict XVI*, 100.

51. Daniélou, "Orientations," 14, cited in Rowland, *Benedict XVI: Guide*, 4.

52. Rowland, *Benedict XVI: Guide*, 4.

questions posed by what they had just lived through. There was a great intellectual élan, and one got swept up with it.[53]

Once after a long, boring lecture from one of his professors on how God is the *summum bonum*, Ratzinger reportedly quipped to Alfred Läpple (one of his seminary professors, who subsequently became one of the most prolific religious writers of our time) that "a *summum bonum* doesn't need a mother." He subsequently turned his attention to the study of Augustine, John Henry Newman, and the mid-twentieth-century personalist scholars such as Martin Buber, as we have already seen.[54] Regarding his study of Augustine, Ratzinger states:

> From the beginning, Saint Augustine interested me very much—precisely also insofar as he was, so to speak, a counterweight to Thomas Aquinas.... What moved me then, however, was not so much his office as shepherd, which I was not familiar with in that way, but the freshness and vitality of his thought. Scholasticism has its greatness, but everything is very impersonal. You need some time to enter in and recognize the inner tension. With Augustine, however, the passionate, suffering, questioning man is always right there, and you can identify with him.[55]

As to his interest in the personalism of Buber, he writes:

> We then found the philosophy of personalism reiterated with renewed conviction in the great Jewish thinker Martin Buber. This encounter with personalism was for me a spiritual experience that left an essential mark, especially since I spontaneously associated such personalism with the thought of Saint Augustine, who in his *Confessions* had struck me with the power of all his human passion and depth.[56]

According to Ratzinger, and reflective of his Augustinian approach, the arid moralism generally associated with Kantian rationalism and Jansenist piety, as well as neo-scholasticism, clashes with the faith. In Ratzinger's funeral eulogy for Luigi Giussani (1922–2005), who founded *Communione e Liberazione*, he said: "Christianity is not an intellectual system, a collection of dogmas, or a moralism. Christianity is instead

---

53. Ratzinger and Seewald, *Salt of the Earth*, 60. See also Juros, "Problems," 145–56.
54. Rowland, *Benedict XVI: Guide*, 4.
55. Ratzinger and Seewald, *Salt of the Earth*, 61.
56. Ratzinger, *Milestones*, 43.

an encounter, a love story; it is an event."[57] Ratzinger emphasizes that Christianity essentially involves a relationship with Jesus Christ. The Suárezean, neo-scholastic overemphasis on doctrinal clarity, he thinks, only serves to obfuscate the spiritual and existential dimensions of the Catholic faith.[58]

When Ratzinger did venture into Scholastic territory, it was Bonaventure who captured his attention, specifically because Bonaventure had a strong interest in the theology of history. Likewise, Ratzinger was interested in the works of the Thomist author, Josef Pieper, who untypically extended his research into the philosophy of history.[59] While Ratzinger was prefect of the Congregation for the Doctrine of the Faith, he gave an address in May 1996 in Guadalajara, Mexico, to the presidents of the Doctrinal Commissions of the Bishops' Conferences of Latin America, stating his opinion that:

> Neo-Scholastic rationalism failed when, with reason totally independent from faith, [it] tried to reconstruct the pre-ambula fidei with pure rational certainty. The attempts that presume to do the same will have the same result.[60]

Clearly, the extant neo-scholasticism was unable to provide Ratzinger and his fellow students with the tools they desired in order to encounter the thought of contemporary man.

In speaking about his intellectual interests, Ratzinger insists:

> We wanted not only to do theology in the narrower sense [neo-scholasticism] but to listen to the voices of man today. We devoured the novels of Gertrude von Le Fort, Elisabeth Langässer, and Ernst Wiechert. Dostoyevsky was one of the authors everyone read, and likewise the great Frenchmen: Claudel, Bernanon, Mauriac. We also followed closely the recent developments in the natural sciences. We thought that, with the breakthroughs made by Planck, Heisenberg, and Einstein, the sciences were once again on their way to God.... In the domain of theology and philosophy, the voices that moved us most directly were those of Romano Guardini, Josef Pieper, Theodor Häcker, and Peter Wust.[61]

57. Ratzinger, "Funeral Homily," 685.
58. Gaál, *Theology of Pope Benedict XVI*, 25.
59. Gaál, *Theology of Pope Benedict XVI*, 25.
60. Ratzinger, *Current Situation*.
61. Ratzinger, *Milestones*, 42.

The challenge was to overcome non-historical theology (specifically neo-scholasticism) without reducing theology to history. This perspective enables a beholding of the earthly Jesus and the gloriously risen Christ as a single person. Ratzinger repeatedly warned against divining an artificial opposition between the Christ of faith and the Jesus of history. There is but one subject in Jesus Christ, in the sovereign *ego eimi*.[62] Referring back to the definitive Jesus enables one to await the risen Christ.

A "CHALCEDONIAN CHRISTOLOGICAL CENTER"

It was from Bonaventure that Ratzinger appropriated his "christocentricity," an approach to theology that was being discovered anew by dogmaticians in the 1950s.[63] Bonaventure pressed Christocentrism to the point of making Christ, who is the center of all, the center even of all the sciences. That is, Bonaventure presses beyond the "literal sense" of any given discipline to its ultimate meaning; thus, the *De reductio artium ad theologiam* (retracing the arts to theology). More specifically, Christ is the *medium distantiae*, the defining center, in his crucifixion: "With his Cross he has uncovered the lost centre of the world's circle, thus giving their true dimensions and meaning to the movement both of individual lives, and of human history as a whole."[64] Ratzinger spoke of his effort "to consider Christology more from the aspect of its spiritual appropriation" and in this way "the classic formulas of Chalcedon appear in the proper perspective."[65]

As de Gaál points out, no matter what area of theology Ratzinger addresses, whether it be liturgy, eschatology, or Mariology, all of his approaches and arguments are grounded in what he terms a "Chalcedonian christological centre." This means that beholding Jesus, in the Christ, enables Ratzinger to dare a synthesis of credal fidelity and scholarly exegesis that oftentimes offers surprising and new insights. This synthesis is not accidental as it draws from the spirit of patristic theology, faithful to the central intuition of the *nouvelle théologie*.[66] Life in its varied over-

62. Gaál, *Theology of Pope Benedict XVI*, 87. Pope Benedict calls for a "Christological hermeneutic" that sees Jesus Christ as the key to understanding the whole Bible as a unity. See Benedict XVI, *From the Baptism*, xix; Staudt, "Reality and Sign," 331–63.
63. Gaál, *Theology of Pope Benedict XVI*, 115. See also Corkery, "Reflection," 19.
64. Ratzinger, *Theology of History*, 146.
65. Ratzinger, *Behold the Pierced One*, 9.
66. Gaál, *Theology of Pope Benedict XVI*, 116.

abundance is far too powerful to be grasped or harnessed by a system (such as neo-scholastic rationalism). This notion is indicative of what de Gaál terms the "Christocentric shift" in Ratzinger's theology. In this sense, one would do great injustice to his theology were one to attempt to press it into a self-contained box containing timeless truths. Ratzinger had always attempted to avoid such a temptation, and his lack of enthusiasm for neo-scholasticism demonstrates this aversion.[67] Importantly, Ratzinger's foundationally Christological approach secures the church's identity as the body of Christ. Even more, it expands the understanding of the mystery of Christ to include his mystical body.[68] As de Gaál notes, in Ratzinger's mind, ecclesiology is essentially Christology.[69] De Lubac's influence on him is clear here, particularly his *Corpus Mysticum*, from which Ratzinger "derived special profit."[70] Ratzinger's Christology is therefore far from any trace of christomonism (the unique focus on the individual, Jesus Christ). The whole Christ embraces the head and the members whose free assent is required for the building up of the body in holiness and truth. Ratzinger's ecclesiological vision therefore is totally pervaded by an eschatological dynamic, a mystery truly present, but whose fulfilment is yet to come (or as Imbelli terms it, "spiritual Christology," because, as Ratzinger notes, "the centre of the person of Jesus is prayer, thus it is essential to participate in his prayer if we are to know and understand him").[71]

Christocentric Anthropology

For Ratzinger, a daring new Christocentric theological anthropology is the medicine that the world needs, and it is the responsibility of the church to administer it. He is critical of interpretations that would transform Christianity into what he calls a "poorly managed haberdashery that is always trying to lure more customers":

> 67. Gaál, *Theology of Pope Benedict XVI*, 300.
> 68. Imbelli, "Christocentric Mystagogy," 124.
> 69. Gaál, *Theology of Pope Benedict XVI*, 65. See also Collins, *Word Made Love*, 88.
> 70. Ratzinger, *Milestones*, 98.
> 71. Imbelli, "Christocentric Mystagogy," 125. See also Galvão, "Mystery of the Church," 708–16. Ratzinger's Christology has been described by Imbelli as a "spiritual Christology," because as Ratzinger notes, "the centre of the person of Jesus is prayer, thus it is essential to participate in his prayer if we are to know and understand him." See Ratzinger, *Behold the Pierced One*, 25. See also McGregor, *Heart to Heart*.

> the Christian faith is rather ... the divine medicine that would never adapt itself to the wishes of its clientele and to what pleases them, for that would be to destroy them utterly. Its role must be to require them to turn away from their imaginary need, which is in reality their sickness, and to entrust themselves to the guidance of the faith.[72]

In Ratzinger's mind, mankind can understand its destiny only through the Revelation of Jesus Christ. This emphasis on Christology is central to Ratzinger's thinking. As we have seen, Ratzinger rejects the formerly dominant view of the "propositional character" of Revelation and argues instead that Revelation is not a mere collection of true statements about God but is Jesus Christ himself, the *Logos*, the all-embracing Word in which God declares himself.[73] Likewise, Ratzinger, with Balthasar, holds that Revelation can only be mediated from a standpoint of "engraced participation" within the horizon of faith. Otherwise, "there are lights, but no Light; words, but no Word. In this situation, religious relativism is inevitable."[74]

For Ratzinger, faith and reason do not collapse into one reality. Like the Christological definition of Chalcedon, the divine and human natures in Christ do not collapse into each other but remain separate and distinct. The two, therefore, while interpenetrating, have their respective autonomous areas. Confronted with grace, human reason experiences purification and transformation. Only faith can provide such sufficient reasonableness for Christianity that can legitimize it in the court of rationality. Human reason however remains essentially bound to history and language. This was, in Ratzinger's judgment, the reason for neo-scholasticism's failure. One cannot reconstruct the preamble of the faith with rationalistic certitude. In this way, Ratzinger avoids the temptations of both fideism and rationalism. Faith needs reason to acknowledge the fullness of Jesus Christ.[75]

---

72. Ratzinger, *Co-Workers of the Truth*, 341.
73. Ratzinger, *On the Way*, 82.
74. Ratzinger, *On the Way*, 65.
75. Gaál, *Theology of Pope Benedict XVI*, 271. See also Renczes, "Grace Reloaded," 273–90.

Morality and Moralism

The term "moralism" generally refers to the Kantian rationalist tendency to reduce Christianity to the dimensions of an ethical framework, or to equate faith with obedience to a law.[76] This can be described as a modern form of Pelagianism (the belief in salvation through good works and obedience), which, according to Lorenzo Albacete, can only be overcome by a proper theology of grace, in which grace is not presented as something added to and external to the natural law itself, as extrinsicists would have it, but rather as the possibility of a personal encounter with Christ.[77] In such a theology of grace, it is not life according to natural law or ethics that is saving, but a relationship and communion with the person of Christ.[78] This essentially is the response that the young Ratzinger gave to his own question in the third of his Münster sermons. He there proposed that the antidote to moralism is the theology of the first letter of St. John, namely, that God is love, and a theology focused on divine love was the solution and the way forward. The same idea was echoed in *Deus Caritas Est*, where he reemphasized that being a Christian is not the result of a lofty idea or ethical choice, but the encounter with an event, a person, "who gives one's life a new horizon and decisive direction."[79] According to Ratzinger, the practice of the faith in the preconciliar era was hampered by moralism. Hence, the problems that arose in the postconciliar era were not simply a result of a spreading secularism but the logical outgrowth of a centuries-long process of separating the true, the beautiful, and the good from each other. Balthasar used the term "perichoresis" to refer to the unity of these three transcendentals and saw that their severance from each other was one of the unfortunate outcomes of the Reformation. Thus, in the absence of a Christian culture in which the mutual relationship of transcendentals is clearly visible and culturally embodied, the temptation to moralism is strong.[80] In the post-Tridentine church, the Kantian emphasis upon duty and the notion of the moral as that which is done out of a sense of obligation rather than affection (or even tradition) shares a logical affinity with Jansenism. Ratzinger well understood this problem and was disturbed by the spiritual pathologies that Kantian

---

76. Rowland, *Ratzinger's Faith*, 66.
77. Albacete, "Pope against Moralism," 85.
78. Albacete, "Pope against Moralism," 85.
79. Rowland, *Ratzinger's Faith*, 66.
80. Rowland, *Ratzinger's Faith*, 66.

and Jansenist tendencies generated among the faithful. Ratzinger (along with Balthasar) made the point that there could not have been such an implosion of Catholic moral practices within such a short time frame after the council unless there was something so deeply flawed about the motivations behind preconciliar practices. Ratzinger concluded that in preconciliar times the tendency was to live prescriptively, not because Catholics were convinced that the moral commands were life-giving, nor because they could apprehend the truth, goodness, and beauty in them, but because they feared going to hell. Once the fear of hell was eliminated, the motivation holding up the practice dissolved.[81] Ratzinger emphasized that becoming a Christian is not about taking out a sort of spiritual "insurance policy," or the "private booking of an entry ticket to heaven"; rather, it is about "reaching that point in love at which we recognize that we, too, need to be given something."[82] As we have seen, Ratzinger has been strong in his criticism of the neo-scholastic manualist tradition for its "decided rationalism," which marginalized Scripture and Christology. He lamented the fact that this system no longer allowed people to see the "great message of liberation and freedom given to us in the encounter with Christ" but instead the negative aspect of so many prohibitions and noes rather than presenting them as what they really are, namely, the actualization of a great "yes." The casuistry of these manuals may have suited those with a positivist or legalistic mindset, or those simply fearful of committing sin and looking for moral certitude, but it did not give a deep understanding of the intrinsic beauty, truth, and goodness of the Christian moral life.[83] Against these tendencies, Ratzinger held that the Ten Commandments are not to be interpreted first of all as law, but rather as a divine gift, a dynamic that is open to an ever greater and deeper understanding.[84]

THE INCARNATION AND CHRISTIAN HUMANISM

A common attribute of theologians who have been influenced by the Romantic movement is an interest in culture, understood in all three German senses of the term, namely, as *Kultur* meaning "civilization,"

---

81. Rowland, *Ratzinger's Faith*, 68.
82. Ratzinger, *What It Means*, 75.
83. Ratzinger, "Renewal of Moral Theology," 358.
84. Rowland, *Ratzinger's Faith*, 70.

Geist meaning "the spirit or ethos of institutions," and *Bildung*, meaning "self-cultivation or education."[85] Neo-scholasticism tended to ignore the concept of culture altogether and to respond to the rationalism of the Enlightenment with a Scholastic counter-rationalism. The Romantics, on the other hand, were more interested in understanding the social and liturgical embodiment of Christian ideas, or what Rowland calls "the lifestyle implications of the choice for or against Christianity."[86] Whereas neo-scholasticism tried to prove that Christianity was more rational than the alternatives, the Catholic romantics tried to demonstrate that the opportunities for *Bildung* (self-cultivation and development) were greater with the Catholic Christian option. Erich Przywara observed that there is a tension or polarity between religion and culture that has run through the whole history of Christianity. He noted that their opposition might be categorized as the either/or between religion as the ultimate strength of culture, and culture as religion's opponent. Przywara observes that such polarities fed into the chaos of the Reformation when the contrast was between the culturally resplendent church of the high Renaissance and later Baroque period, and the iconoclastic imperceptive and invisible God of the Protestants.[87] Nineteenth-century intellectual history was characterized by a division between the idea of the pursuit of scientific and cultural knowledge as a kind of religion in itself, and the gradually ascendant ideals of the Catholic romantics of science and culture that have their immanent ideals in religion (particularly Christianity).[88] According to Rowland, Przywara's summary might be updated by observing that in the postconciliar church, there has been a division between those who want to baptize contemporary mass culture and those who regard this strategy as a major cause of the dramatic decline in numbers of those participating in the sacramental life of the church. Indeed, it seems that these two poles have drifted so far apart that it is no longer accurate to describe them as poles held in tension at all. Rowland points out that while whole diocesan liturgical offices and commissions spend their time trying to make the liturgical practices of the church resemble those elements of contemporary pop culture, others like Cardinal James Stafford claim that "every world religion is trembling before the advances of American pop culture" and thus pop culture is actually toxic to the

---

85. Rowland, *Benedict XVI: Guide*, 25.
86. Rowland, *Benedict XVI: Guide*, 25.
87. Rowland, *Benedict XVI: Guide*, 26.
88. Rowland, *Benedict XVI: Guide*, 26.

flourishing of the faith.[89] The distinction today is no longer between austerity and sensual splendor but between those who regard beauty as something objectively discernible and those who regard it as a mere matter of taste or preference. Ratzinger is firmly on the side of those who think like Stafford, and as Rowland notes, his opposition to the project of accommodating the cultural life of the church to that of contemporary mass culture is possibly the element of his intellectual work for which he is most famous. Ratzinger therefore is one of the very few theologians of his generation who does not follow the so-called "correlationist" pastoral strategies associated with the likes of Rahner, Chenu, Schillebeeckx, and Tracey, which sought to attach the faith to *pierres d'attente* that jut out from modern cultural formations.[90]

Ratzinger is of the view that the uniqueness of Christian culture is rooted in the Incarnation and that all of its specific characteristics disintegrate when this belief is eclipsed.[91] The Incarnation means that the invisible God enters into the visible world so as to be known and loved by those bound to matter. As *Gaudium et Spes* §22 states:

> The Truth is that only in the mystery of the incarnate Word does the mystery of man take on light. For Adam, the first man, was a figure of Him who was to come, namely Christ the Lord. Christ, the final Adam, by the revelation of the mystery of the Father, and his Love, fully reveals man to man himself and makes his supreme calling clear.[92]

Ratzinger was particularly critical of the first section of *Gaudium et Spes*, expressive of a strong extrinsicism and attachment to the "pure-nature" notion, as it fosters the fiction that it is possible to construct a rational philosophical picture of man intelligible to all and on which all men of goodwill can agree. The actual Christian doctrines were then merely added to this as a crowning conclusion. This approach prompted the question of "why exactly the reasonable and perfectly free human being described in the first articles was suddenly burdened with the story of Christ."[93] Notwithstanding this criticism, Ratzinger strongly praised paragraph 22, which was to become one of the most quoted paragraphs

---

89. Rowland, *Benedict XVI: Guide*, 26.
90. Rowland, *Benedict XVI: Guide*, 26.
91. Ratzinger, *Co-Workers of the Truth*, 18.
92. Vatican II Council, *Gaudium et Spes*, §22.
93. Ratzinger, "Dignity," 120.

of all the documents of the Second Vatican Council by John Paul II. According to Ratzinger, paragraph 22 treats of Christ's assumption of human nature in its full ontological depth:

> The human nature of all men is one; Christ's taking to himself the one human nature of man is an event which affects every human being; consequently human nature in every human being is henceforward Christologically characterized.[94]

Ratzinger went on to say that this outlook is important because it opens a bridge between the theology of the Incarnation and that of the Cross (a point to which I will return):

> A theology of the incarnation situated too much on the level of essence, may be tempted to be satisfied with the ontological phenomenon: God's being and man's have been conjoined . . . . But since it is made clear that man's being is not that of a pure essence, and that he only attains his reality by his activity, it is at once evident that we cannot rest content with a purely essentialist outlook. Man's being must therefore be examined precisely in its activities.[95]

The International Theological Commission under Ratzinger's leadership echoed his fundamentally Christological position in the following paragraph of its 1988 document, *Faith and Inculturation*:

> In the last times inaugurated at Pentecost, the risen Christ, Alpha and Omega, enters into the history of peoples: from that moment, the sense of history and thus of culture is unsealed and the Holy Spirit reveals it by actualizing and communicating it to all. The church is the sacrament of this revelation and its communication. It re-centers every culture into which Christ is received, placing it in the axis of the world which is coming, and restores the union broken by the Prince of this world. Culture is thus eschatologically situated; it tends towards its completion in Christ, but it cannot be saved except by associating itself with the repudiation of evil.[96]

---

94. Ratzinger, "Dignity," 120.

95. Ratzinger, "Dignity," 160. Here Ratzinger is opening up what in other places he has referred to as the mediation of history in the realm of ontology. Both he and Karol Wojtyla converge in their interest in the uniqueness of human persons caused by their particular location within history. For this reason they share a mutual interest in what is called relationality, or that dimension of the human person that is determined by his or her relations with other persons, including the Persons of the Holy Trinity.

96. International Theological Commission, *Faith and Inculturation*, §28.

In this paragraph one finds all the key elements of a Catholic humanism and its associated culture, namely, that the Incarnation restores the union broken by Satan at the time of the Fall, and it recenters culture eschatologically, that is, with a view to the return of Christ in glory and the consummation of the world, even though this does not happen automatically. What is required is a repudiation of evil, and thus the potentiality of the Incarnation stands always under the shadow of the Cross. The Holy Spirit and the church are responsible for the communication of the possibilities thrown open to the world by the Incarnation.[97] The same notions can be seen in the work of Guardini, who was one of the most important figures in the years of Ratzinger's seminary formation. In his main address at the *akademische Feier* for Guardini, Rahner described him as a Christian humanist who led Germany's Catholics "out of an intellectual and cultural ghetto [and] into the contemporary age."[98] Balthasar said of Guardini that he believed that "it is not Christ who is in the world, but the world is in Christ" and, further, that the "immensity of this reversal" was "the very basis" of Guardini's thought. Guardini was also highly critical of the extrinsicist account of the relationship between nature and grace. In his *Welt und Person* (which predated de Lubac's *Surnaturel* by seven years) Guardini wrote:

> Seen in the fullness of its energy as Paul proclaimed it and Augustine unfolded it, grace means something that is, not added on to the nature of man for his perfection, but rather the form in which man finally is himself. This presupposes, however, that we understand by the term "man" what Paul and Augustine mean: not some being artificially let loose in a "pure nature" but rather that human being whom God intends and of whom scripture speaks.[99]

Ratzinger also observes that the Incarnation is properly understood only when it is seen within the broader context of creation, history, and

---

97. Rowland, *Culture of the Incarnation*, 155.

98. Krieg, *Romano Guardini*, 197. See also Katholische Akademie in Bayern, *Akademische Feier*.

99. Guardini, *Welt und Person*, 161. My translation. Original as follows: "In ihrer vollen, von Paulus verkündeten und von Augustinus entfalteten Energie gesehen, bedeutet Gnade nicht etwas, was zur Vollständigkeit des Menschen hinzukäme, sondern die Form, wie der Mensch endgültigerweise er selbst ist—vorausgesetzt allerdings, dass unter Mensch das verstanden wird, was wiederum Paulus und Augustinus darunter verstehen: keinen künstlich herausgelosten, rein natürlichen, sondern jenen Menschen, den Gott meint und von dem die Schrift redet."

the new world. It is only then that it becomes clear that the senses belong to the faith, and that the new seeing does not abolish them, but leads them to their original purpose.[100] Aidan Nichols summarizes the metaphysical foundations of what Ratzinger termed the "humanism of the Incarnation" in the following manner:

> This polarity structure of all existence, while manifesting the ontological difference between the being of the creature and that of the Creator, also suggests a positive moment where the creature displays a certain likeness and so comparability with its God. For between these poles there plays a fullness of inner life—a continuous epiphany of the divine likeness.[101]

Not every variety of Catholic culture, however, has accepted this humanism. There are spiritual movements that periodically arise, and that exaggerate humanity's fallen condition. The concern these movements have is that people will grow to love the world too much or claim too much for human nature. Jansenism is one such example, which had a particularly destructive effect on Catholic culture in eighteenth-century France and nineteenth-century Ireland and countries of the New World that were under the influence of Irish orders of religious. According to Rowland, the two areas that were most affected by Jansenism were liturgy and sexuality. The Jansenists favored austerity in both of these areas of social life and were to cause what French psychiatrists termed "La Maladie Catholique" (an inability to successfully integrate one's sexuality into one's overall personal development, producing what Nietzsche thought were weak, submissive individuals who were tortured in conscience and incapable of self-development).[102] Liberation theology, on the other hand, also had a tendency to suppress the role of the sensual in Catholic culture and to treat an interest in the transcendental of beauty as a peculiarly bourgeois vice, inconsistent with a preferential option for the poor.[103]

In *The Spirit of the Liturgy*, Ratzinger reflects on the earliest disputes within the church about art and beauty, observing that:

> iconoclasm rests on a one-sided apophatic theology, which recognizes only the Wholly Other-ness of the God beyond all images and words, a theology that in the final analysis regards

---

100. Rowland, *Benedict XVI: Guide*, 28.
101. Nichols, *Say It Is Pentecost*, 3.
102. Rowland, *Benedict XVI: Guide*, 28. See also Murphy, *Christ, Our Joy*, 22.
103. Murphy, *Christ, Our Joy*, 29.

revelation as the inadequate human reflection of what is eternally imperceptible.[104]

He concludes:

> What seems like the highest humility toward God turns into pride, allowing God no word and permitting him no real entry into history . . . matter is absolutised and thought of as completely impervious to God, as mere matter, and thus deprived of its dignity.[105]

Ratzinger even goes so far as to suggest that a theologian who does not love art, poetry, music, and nature can be dangerous, because "blindness and deafness toward the beautiful are not incidental: they necessarily are reflected in his theology." Further, he states that "the only really effective apologia for Christianity comes down to two arguments, namely, the saints the church has produced, and the art which has grown in her womb."[106] Ratzinger also states that "therefore, nothing can bring us into close contact with the beauty of Christ himself other than the world of beauty created by faith, and light that shines out from the faces of the saints, through whom his own light becomes visible."[107]

Ratzinger stands in the long tradition of others including Augustine, Bonaventure, Hugh of St. Victor, Newman, and Balthasar in regarding the aesthetic moment as essentially theophanic. Evidently, what stands behind this position is the influence of Platonism, for which the beautiful and the good are coincidental. Ratzinger, quoting Nicholas Cabasilas (a Byzantine theologian), points to the rediscovery of Plato's experience:

> When men have a longing so great that it surpasses human nature and eagerly desire and are able to accomplish things beyond human thought, it is the Bridegroom himself who has wounded them. Into their eyes he has sent a ray of his beauty.[108]

Ratzinger is quick to add that beauty "wounds," but that is precisely how it awakens man to his ultimate destiny. This Platonic position, he adds, has nothing to do with superficial aestheticism and irrationality or with the flight from clarity and from sober reason. This is because

---

104. Ratzinger, *Spirit of the Liturgy*, 124.
105. Ratzinger, *Spirit of the Liturgy*, 124.
106. Ratzinger, *Report*, 129.
107. Ratzinger, *Message to Communion and Liberation*.
108. Ratzinger, *On the Way*, 35.

"true knowledge," he says, "is being struck by the arrow of beauty that wounds man: being touched by reality, by the personal presence of Christ himself."[109] Ratzinger continues:

> Who has not heard Dostoyevsky's oft-quoted remark: "Beauty will save us"? Usually people forget to mention, however, that by redeeming beauty Dostoyevsky means Christ. He it is whom we must learn to see. If we cease to know him only though words but are struck by the arrow of his paradoxical beauty, then we will truly come to know him and will no longer merely know about him at second-hand. Then we will have encountered the beauty of truth, of redeeming truth.[110]

In *The Spirit of the Liturgy*, Ratzinger applies his Platonic approach to a broad-brush history of Western art. He argues that in the art of icons, as well as in the great Western paintings of the Romanesque and Gothic periods, this aforementioned experience has gone from being an interior event to being an external form and thus has become communicable. Today, he argues, the task of Christian art is to:

> oppose the cult of the ugly, which says that everything else, anything beautiful, is a deception and that only the depiction of what is cruel, base, and vulgar is the truth and true enlightenment. And it must withstand the deceptive beauty that diminishes man instead of making him great and that, for that very reason is false.[111]

Christian art, he asserts, must always emphasize the paschal mystery as a whole, and it must be plainly evident so as to guarantee its epiphanic potential. While Ratzinger laments the diminution of this potential in the post-Renaissance era of art and painting, he thinks that music suffered an even worse regression that harkens back to the paganism of Dionysian cults. Ratzinger rejects the notion that form and substance can be easily separated (contrary to evangelical Protestants and some Catholic liturgists). That is, he does not accept the argument that the problem with rock music is merely explicit lyrics, for he finds the music itself objectionable and claims that it has no place in the liturgy. Ratzinger uses the phrase "utility music" to describe popular music that is used in the liturgy,

---

109. Ratzinger, *On the Way*, 36. See also Cirelli, "Christian Realism," 709–36.
110. Ratzinger, *On the Way*, 36.
111. Ratzinger, *On the Way*, 40.

the defense of which is normally given to be "pastoral pragmatism."[112] Ratzinger takes Adorno's point that "the fundamental characteristic of popular music is standardization" and, as such, he describes it as "incompatible with the culture of the Gospels, which seeks to take us out of the dictatorship of money, of making, of mediocrity, and brings us to the discipline of truth, which is precisely what pop music eschews."[113] Ratzinger even more forcefully asserts that the trivialization of the faith by following the trends of mass culture "is not a new inculturation, but the denial of its culture and prostitution with the non-culture."[114] Furthermore, he observes that disputes about music are at least as old as the conflict between Dionysian and Apollonian music in classical Greece, and that while "Apollo is not Christ," Plato's concern about the music of the Dionysian cults remains relevant today, since contemporary musical forms have become a "decisive vehicle of a counter religion."[115] In Ratzinger's view, rock concerts are "anti-liturgies where people are yanked out of themselves and where they can forget the dullness and commonness of everyday life,"[116] and are also enterprises to make money out of the human need for an experience of self-transcendence:

> People are, so to speak, released from themselves by the experience of being part of a crowd and by the emotional shock of rhythm, noise and special lighting effects. However, in the ecstasy of having all their defenses torn down, the participants sink, as it were, beneath the elemental force of the universe. The music of the Holy Spirit's sober inebriation seems to have little chance when the self has become a prison, the mind is a shackle, and breaking out from both appears as a true promise of redemption that can be tasted at least for a few moments.[117]

In contrast, Ratzinger has specifically referred to the idea of Basil the Great that when Christianity meets a pre-Christian culture it must make a slit (or wound) in that culture, as one would in the bark of a tree

---

112. Ratzinger, *Spirit of the Liturgy*, 130. See also Ratzinger, *Feast of Faith*; Ratzinger, *New Song*; and Rowland, "Joseph Ratzinger as Doctor."

113. Rowland, *Benedict XVI: Guide*, 33, citing Ratzinger, *New Song*, 108.

114. Rowland, *Benedict XVI: Guide*, 34, citing Ratzinger, *New Song*, 109.

115. Rowland, *Benedict XVI: Guide*, 34, citing Ratzinger, *New Song*, 109.

116. Rowland, *Benedict XVI: Guide*, 34, citing Ratzinger, "Liturgy and Sacred Music," 387.

117. Rowland, *Benedict XVI: Guide*, 34, citing Ratzinger, "Liturgy and Sacred Music," 387.

in order to graft another on to it; it must be done, however, extremely delicately at the right time, in the right place, at the correct angle. This slit is also a kind of purification.[118] He cautions against hurriedly seeking to adapt the liturgy to customs and cultic traditions of peoples, where the same has been created overnight by decisions of conferences of bishops. It is not, he thinks, until a:

> strong Christian identity has grown up in the mission country in question that one can begin to move, with great caution and on the basis of this identity, toward christening the indigenous forms by adopting them into the liturgy and allowing Christian realities to merge with the forms of everyday life.[119]

While it is true that Ratzinger was influenced by the new liturgical movement of the first half of the twentieth century and enthusiastic about the potential for liturgical renewal in the early 1960s, he came to regard the liturgical experiments of the postconciliar period in a negative light. He argues in *The Spirit of the Liturgy* that liturgists who sought to bring God down to the level of the people were engaging in behavior analogous to the Hebrews' worship of the golden calf, which was nothing less than apostasy.[120] Elucidating Ratzinger's thought, Aidan Nichols states:

> The Liturgy as saving action is "catabatic" coming down from God to human beings. What by contrast is anabatic—going up to God—about the liturgy is the glorification of God by men. But notice that, while the catabatic aspect of the Liturgy must come first, it is to such anabatic glorification that the sanctifying divine action is ultimately directed. The example of our great High Priest tells us so. Christ's entire life and passion was directed chiefly to the glorification of the Father: even the salvation of the human race was subordinated to this goal. So also in the Liturgy the soteriological intent of the rite, aiming as it does, at our sanctification, is itself subordinated to its doxological purpose. This may seem an unnecessary exaltation of God at the expense of man, shades indeed, of a Feuerbachian nightmare. But we see that things cannot be otherwise, once we realize that our sanctification is nothing other than our incorporation into the glorification of God through Jesus Christ Our Lord.[121]

---

118. Ratzinger, *On the Way*, 46.
119. Ratzinger, *Feast of Faith*, 82.
120. Ratzinger, *Spirit of the Liturgy*, 22.
121. Nichols, "St Thomas," 590.

Thus for Ratzinger, what some may deem merely to be matters of form are for him frontline issues in the battle for the reevangelization of the West. Thus, everything associated with the Eucharist must be marked by beauty, as he states in *Sacramentum Caritatis*, §35:

> The beauty of the liturgy is part of this mystery; it is a sublime expression of God's glory and, in a certain sense, a glimpse of heaven on earth. The memorial of Jesus's redemptive sacrifice contains something of that beauty which Peter, James, and John beheld when the Master, making his way to Jerusalem, was transfigured before their eyes (cf. Mark 9:2). Beauty then, is not mere decoration, but rather an essential element of the liturgical action, since it is an attribute of God himself and his revelation. These considerations should make us realize the care which is needed, if the liturgical action is to reflect its innate splendor.

Ratzinger's focus on the transcendental of beauty is therefore part of his Augustinian heritage and also one of the many points where his thought converges with that of Balthasar and Newman. It is in his works on the liturgy that one finds most of Ratzinger's views on the importance of beauty.[122] For Ratzinger, the marketing of vulgar art, music, and literature, and the generation of low mass culture is one of the serious pathologies of contemporary Western culture. Thus, clerics who think they can win young people to the church by adopting the marketing strategies of public relations firms and attempting a transposition of the church's cultural patrimony into the idioms of mass culture are only further diminishing the opportunities of youth for an experience of genuine self-transcendence.[123] Ratzinger states in the *Feast of Faith*:

> The church is to transform, improve, "humanize" the world—but how can she do that if at the same time she turns her back on beauty, which is so closely allied to love? For together, beauty and love form the true consolation in this world, bringing it as near as possible to the world of the resurrection. The church must maintain high standards; she must be a place where beauty can be at home; she must lead the struggle for that "spiritualization" without which the world becomes the "first circle of hell."[124]

---

122. Rowland, *Ratzinger's Faith*, 9.
123. Rowland, *Ratzinger's Faith*, 9.
124. Ratzinger, *Feast of Faith*, 124.

Contrary to what traditionalists are inclined to believe, for Ratzinger, the Second Vatican Council is perfectly capable of orthodox and what Rowland terms "hostile-to-philistinism" interpretation, provided one uses what he calls a "hermeneutic of continuity" as opposed to a "hermeneutic of disruption" in its interpretation.[125] He does not accept (as traditionalists also do) that the mere interest in the question of the relationship between history and ontology inevitably means dangerous modernist and nihilist dispositions. Ratzinger maintains that it is not possible to defend tradition while eschewing the importance of history. His response to the nihilist Romantics of the nineteenth-century (it should be noted that Romanticism can be developed in either a Catholic or a nihilist direction; Ratzinger obviously occupies the former), and to the nihilism and philistinism of the twentieth and twenty-first centuries, is precisely the humanism of the Incarnation:

> The Magi of the Gospel are but the first in a vast pilgrimage in which the beauty of this earth is laid at the feet of Christ: the gold of the ancient Christian mosaics, the multi-colored light from the windows of our great cathedrals, the praise of their stone, the Christmas songs of the trees of the forest are all inspired by him, and human voices like musical instruments have found their most beautiful melodies when they cast themselves at his feet. The suffering of the world too—its misery—comes to him in order, for a moment, to find security and understanding in the presence of the God who is poor.[126]

This humanism is dynamic since it is generated by the work of grace in the lives of Christians, and thus, its potential for social and cultural achievements is almost infinite. Ratzinger's approach is far from fostering a traditionalist, anachronistic museum-piece Catholic culture or ghetto, and states that Catholics cannot live in some kind of spiritual nature reserve.[127] Nevertheless, what is immutable are the theological foundations that comprise the creation of the world, the Incarnation, and the paschal mysteries, which make possible the intimacy between the divine and the human, and between nature and grace, and the sacramental presence of God in the world.[128]

---

125. Rowland, *Benedict XVI: Guide*, 46.
126. Ratzinger, *Co-Workers of the Truth*, 16. See also Carola, "Academics," 65–93.
127. Ratzinger, *Christ, Faith, and the Challenge of Cultures.*
128. Rowland, *Benedict XVI: Guide*, 46.

In the person of Christ, human beings encounter the fullness of reality. Their own personhood is woven into a trinitarian reality. For this reason, there can be no pluralistic theology of religions but only a Christocentric theology of history and anthropology. Alarmed by an unnuanced reading of *Gaudium et Spes*, Guardini advised Paul VI against an optimistic understanding of the world's autonomy. He stated that what can convince modern people is not a historical or psychological or ever modernizing Christianity, but only the unrestricted and uninterrupted message of Revelation. Ratzinger repeated the same idea in various ways constantly. Revelation is not a construction of the human intellect, but the divine message entrusted to man.[129] God makes himself accessible to mankind in Christ Jesus and thereby liberates it from all the fallacious proposals to fulfil humanity. Human wholeness is Jesus Christ alone. Thus, by emulating this unity of Jesus's volition with that of his Father, human beings find the foundation and core of their own being. Human freedom, in other words, finds a goal.[130]

As de Gaál points out, predication and the essence of Jesus's person are identical. In Jesus, one must apprehend both human forsakenness and divine sovereignty, earthly imprisonment and divine freedom; one who is suffering his passion and glorification on the Cross. In the one person of Jesus, a heretofore unknown, paradoxical, coincidence occurs.[131] As Ratzinger notes:

> The inner unity between Jesus' lived *kénosis* (cf. Phil 2:5–11) and his coming in glory is the constant motif of his words and actions; this is what is authentically new about Jesus, it is no invention—on the contrary, it is the epitome of his figure and his words.[132]

As the true offering, he becomes not only the true template for every human being but, even more profoundly, "he is not just one individual, but rather he makes all of us 'one single person' (Gal 3:28) with himself, a new humanity."[133] Thus the complete response to all human questions, wishes, and hopes lies in Jesus Christ, who *is* life.[134]

129. Rowland, *Benedict XVI: Guide*, 80.
130. Benedict XVI, *From the Baptism*, 149.
131. Gaál, *Theology of Pope Benedict XVI*, 82.
132. Benedict XVI, *From the Baptism*, 330.
133. Benedict XVI, *From the Baptism*, 334.
134. Gaál, *Theology of Pope Benedict XVI*, 82.

For Ratzinger, only God ultimately defines who the human person is. He insists constantly that Christianity is not the acceptance of a logical structure of truths but of a divine person as the fullness of being. The fact that Jesus is defined as God-man must necessarily have anthropological implications.[135] Ratzinger likewise observes that there is an intrinsic connection between matter and spirit, between body and soul. Therefore, in the eschaton, there must be both an individual and a communal aspect, because one cannot conceive of eternal bliss without the fellowship of human beings with God and, therefore, with one another.[136] The goal of the Christian is not private bliss, but the whole.

In Jesus, human volition acquires a divine form, and an "alchemy of being" occurs.[137] According to de Gaál, in evangelization, the incarnational nature of Christianity should be explained. Our joy is in becoming the body of Christ. Being a Christian means offering earthly realities as the place of the Word. These are the implications of the Word's *descendit de caelis* and the meaning of Vatican II: "in reality it is only in the mystery of the Word made flesh that the mystery of man truly becomes clear" (*Gaudium et Spes*, §22). Thus, all forms of terrestrial expression are "saved" in Christ's eternal being. All human matters can become eternal (as Balthasar would put it). Evangelization means overcoming the dualism of God and creation that leads merely to the soulless and godless world of deism. The church must be discerning as, too often, her members may be tempted to live under the spell of Descartes's bifurcation between *res cogitans* and *res extensa*. Ratzinger's spiritual Christology seeks to overcome this dichotomy, which has confounded intellectual history ever since Descartes.[138]

One central insight for Ratzinger is that there is an inner tension that depends on the objective vault connecting dogma, Scripture, the church, and the present age. Each serves as a foundational column that may not be dismantled.[139] Dogma may not be left on the sidelines. Ratzinger was particularly concerned in the 1970s about the issue of correlating personal experience to the faith of the church. The fundamental question was: how do experience and faith relate to one another? Ratzinger's analysis, particularly as set out in *Dogma and Preaching*, insisted on restoring the

---

135. Ratzinger, *Introduction to Christianity*, 226.
136. Gaál, *Theology of Pope Benedict XVI*, 142.
137. Ratzinger, *Behold the Pierced One*, 34.
138. Gaál, *Theology of Pope Benedict XVI*, 220.
139. Ratzinger, *Dogma and Preaching*, 7.

centrality of content over method.¹⁴⁰ Ratzinger has great concerns over the inductive method that had brought about a pauperization of the faith among children in particular. This pauperization occurred because such a method places experience first (e.g., "seeing-judging-acting") in overreaction to the intellectualism prevalent in the theological and catechetical programs of the neo-scholastic system in the nineteenth and the first half of the twentieth centuries. While it is important that children recognize that the Christian faith is important in understanding and mastering life, Ratzinger warns that such a correlation between the content of the faith and concrete life experience runs the danger of shortchanging (or eliminating) the kerygma of the faith.¹⁴¹

GRATIA PRAESUPPONIT NATURAM

Despite his vast corpus of theological writings, interestingly, Ratzinger only directly and explicitly treats of the notion of nature and grace in the twelfth chapter of his text, *Dogma and Preaching*, entitled "Gratia Praesupponit Naturam."¹⁴²

Ratzinger calls attention to Söhngen, who points out Karl Barth's reaction to what he terms "an undifferentiated optimism about nature" and the tendency of "harmonizing theology" that brought the Reformation critique of Catholic nature-theology to bear on Aquinas's claim. For Ratzinger, Aquinas should be discussed especially as a contrast to Bonaventure.¹⁴³ This approach is in contrast to a truncated Thomism that, according to Ratzinger, had rightly become an object of polemical attack in the Reformation. This approach also attempts to defend the right of nature in faith against Barth's one-sidedness. Ratzinger emphasizes that since Thomas can no longer be presupposed, he should now be discussed, especially as a contrast to Bonaventure.¹⁴⁴

Ratzinger notably points out that there are two aspects of the problem of nature and grace that affect Christianity today. On the one hand, the theological denial of nature has regrettably been easy to combine with eschatological Marxism, which is ignorant of "nature" per se, but

---

140. Gaál, *Theology of Pope Benedict XVI*, 221.
141. Gaál, *Theology of Pope Benedict XVI*, 230.
142. Ssennyondo, *Christianity*, 215. See also Billeci, *Gratia supponit naturam*.
143. Ssennyondo, *Christianity*, 215.
144. Ratzinger, *Dogma and Preaching*, 144.

instead only turns to facts that must be changed in order to carry the world forward to the desired utopia. Essentially this involves a subordination of the facts of nature to political ideology. Connected to this, he notes, is Sartre's existentialist nihilism, which asserts that man has no essence, only existence, and as such, each individual is free to create his own essence as desired. Thus, man is decided by only what he makes.[145]

Concerning Ratzinger's text *Introduction to Christianity*, de Gaál makes the point that the notion of *gratia praesupponit naturam* is of fundamental importance in understanding the same. In this text, Ratzinger does not so much explicitly address the issue of nature and grace as rely on it implicitly. In another work, where he addressed the habilitation of a priest member of the Catholic Integrated Community (an apostolic community canonically established by respective local bishops and recognized in several dioceses in Germany, Austria, Italy, and Tanzania), he did, however, write a few lines on the relationship between nature and grace.[146] Ratzinger there observes that even in Jesuit and Dominican theologies, grace was considered as restraining freedom. Ratzinger observes that in the drama of humanity's seeking emancipation and greater freedom during the Enlightenment and up to and including the present age, God's fatherly love was (and is) considered a burden upon man's freedom. God is perceived no longer as enabling one's life, but as impeding it. The Enlightenment was glad to liberate mankind from this unwelcome burden. It is little wonder then that in modern discussion, including that of liberation theology, the notion of grace is completely absent. Genuine freedom is conceived of as self-created freedom and is relational only in the negative sense of the word. Ratzinger points out that modernity leads into the cul-de-sac that is the absurdity of autonomous freedom. He holds that mankind must discover anew that grace does not compete with freedom but enables it.[147] Grace is the tool by which God establishes a kingdom of freedom and charity. Grace and freedom, for Ratzinger, are interrelated. Freedom is thereby liberated from its individualistic abstraction and brought into the human community convoked by God, which is the church. The church in turn enables genuine freedom through grace, and indeed the church is the place of freedom par excellence.[148]

---

145. Ratzinger, *Dogma and Preaching*, 144.
146. Ratzinger, "Foreword," 5.
147. Ratzinger, "Foreword," 5.
148. Ratzinger, "Foreword," 6.

The Nature and Grace Debate: Problems and Challenges

As Charles Ssennyondo points out, Ratzinger identifies two extremes that can occur in the consideration of the relationship between nature and grace. One extreme is a certain "supernaturalism" that tends to downplay or even to deny the existence of nature, and ironically, in so doing, makes grace meaningless as well. The other extreme is a certain "naturalism" that tends to collapse grace into nature, ignoring any distinction between the two so as to eschew the building up of an ultimately meaningless supernatural world.[149] In Ratzinger's mind, both extremes ultimately lead to the same end, which is either a minimization, or indeed a flat denial, of the role and value of God's grace.

Ratzinger notes that the axiom *gratia praesupponit naturam* had almost become a slogan during the early twentieth-century German Youth Movement.[150] This slogan seemed to capture the religious sentiment of early twentieth-century (particularly young) Catholics who had a desire for a less bourgeois formality and a new undisguised naturalness that challenged all convention. This sentiment was reflective of a more general cultural shift away from the stifling old conventions of society, particularly after the impact of the First World War, towards a greater freedom, and appreciation of nature and the natural. Ratzinger points out that there is a good dose of Nietzschean thinking in this ethos (particularly the scorn for the "virtue of the virtuous"), and of Nietzsche's desire to prove ultimately vacuous the many anxiously guarded formulas that had constituted erstwhile cultural norms.[151] It was in this context, Ratzinger notes, that the axiom *gratia praesupponit naturam* was rediscovered as a saving power, opening up a new possibility of Christian consciousness, specifically that being a Christian does not mean breaking with nature at all; on the contrary, it means heightening and perfecting it. This evidences Catholicism as a religion that embraces the possibility of "both/and," that is, spirit *and* body, God *and* man, grace *and* nature, in a great universal harmony.[152] Ratzinger emphasizes that this new emphasis was

---

149. Ssennyondo, *Christianity*, 216.

150. Ratzinger, *Dogma and Preaching*, 145. Ratzinger translates *gratia praesupponit naturam* as "grace presupposes nature" (as it is rendered in the English version of *Dogma and Preaching*). He adds the alternative version of the axiom, "*Gratia non destruit, sed supponit et perficit naturam*" ("Grace does not destroy but supposes and perfects nature"). See also Beumer, "Gratia supponit naturam," 535–52.

151. Ratzinger, *Dogma and Preaching*, 145.

152. Ratzinger, *Dogma and Preaching*, 146.

in fact a *rediscovery* of "true Catholicism," as opposed to the short-lived asceticism of the nineteenth century. He notes that:

> this Yes to the beautiful purity of nature had always been alive, this joyful affirmation that was just starting again to make headway against a supernaturalism that supposed it was honoring God by crucifying man. The theology of the previous era was being read with new eyes . . . people reflected once more on the sacred mystery of the incarnation, on this unfathomable fact that God became "flesh" and thus "world" and that from then on the flesh, the world, desires to be the expression and the dwelling place of the divine, that therefore the orientation of religious living can no longer be a flight into the spirit, but, rather, leads straight into corporeal matters, in which God still wants to become flesh once more.[153]

Catholicism recalled again the doctrine of the Greek church fathers who spoke of the consecration of the world in the flesh of Christ, particularly the ideas of Irenaeus concerning the recapitulation of the world in Christ, bringing the world back to its real home in the body of the Lord.[154] Ratzinger notes that this shift in sentiment was focused as though by a magnifying glass into the axiom *gratia praesupponit naturam*, in which the theology of the *analogia entis* found its central expression. In his view, the word "catholic" seemed to express the basic idea of the all-embracing, great, universal Yes of the analogy of being.[155]

Interestingly, at the same time that these ideas were reestablishing themselves within early twentieth-century Catholicism, Ratzinger notes that a renewal was also taking place within Protestantism, albeit with diametrically opposed premises. Specifically, Barth gave expression to a completely different experience of man and God. Barth certainly did acknowledge a nature in which the grace of Christ is internal and natural; however, he thought that man as he really lives in history does not live in his true nature. Instead, he proposed that an unnatural state had become man's nature. This meant that, for Barth, to continue to attempt

---

153. Ratzinger, *Dogma and Preaching*, 146.

154. I would also point to St. Irenaeus's oft quoted maxim in his *Against Heresies* IV, 20: "For the glory of God is a living man [or 'man fully alive,' as it is alternatively rendered]; and the life of man consists in beholding God. For if the manifestation of God *which is made by means of the creation*, affords life to all living in the earth, much more does that revelation of the Father which comes through the Word, give life to those who see God." My emphasis.

155. Ratzinger, *Dogma and Preaching*, 147.

to "perfect" that "natural state," man would simply be accomplishing only his self-destruction, canonizing "misery instead of leading him into salvation."[156] Thus, as we saw in chapter 2, for Barth, grace cannot be a continuation of the perfection of nature, but only the disruption, contradiction, and thwarting of it. This position led Barth to ultimately reject the *analogia entis* (indeed stating in his *Church Dogmatics* that it was the "invention of the Antichrist"[157]). In Ratzinger's assessment, such a position is obviously inimical to Catholic theology. He cites the work of Willem Hendrik van de Pol on the notion of sin to illustrate the differences between Catholic and Reformation theology. A Catholic understands sin, in general, to be an action that is contrary to the will of God, and as an action, it may be circumscribed and defined such that one might confess it in the context of the sacrament of penance. The Reformed Christian, on the other hand, rejects this notion of sin as too pointillistic and moralistic, and believes instead that individual acts of transgression only serve to instantiate a deeper and more underlying general condition. Thus, individual sins express only the *real* sin that precedes them.[158] Ratzinger summarizes this position by stating that for the Reformed Christian, man's sin consists of the fact that, in the end, he seeks himself in everything, that selfishness is the secret driving force of all his activity. This fundamental selfishness, he thinks, does not even exclude a morality that otherwise is quite orderly but that does mean that even the best moral attitudes are somehow corroded by man's underlying general condition of sin that cannot be jettisoned. The Reformed Christian might cite the example of the Pharisees to illustrate this point, as while they fulfilled every moral prescript of the law, it was not enough to overcome their basic, and insidious selfishness, which in the final analysis is *the* sin of man, of which individual sins are merely secondary outgrowths. Ratzinger notes that these differences are not just an instance of theological bickering but concern "the very heart of Christian existence in the world: the very concrete question of the kind of stance that the Christian should take in this world and toward this world."[159]

---

156. Ratzinger, *Dogma and Preaching*, 147.

157. Karl Barth, *Kirchliche Dogmatik*, vol. 1, part 1, xiii, cited in Ratzinger, *Dogma and Preaching*, 147.

158. Ratzinger, *Dogma and Preaching*, 148.

159. Ratzinger, *Dogma and Preaching*, 149.

Proposals for a Solution

Considering these differences in approach to the nature-grace question, that is, between a "supernaturalist" or a "naturalist" approach, and between the Catholic and Reformed traditions, Ratzinger sets out in *Dogma and Preaching* to propose a way forward. Firstly, he notes the difference in meaning attributed to the word "nature" between the "world-friendly" theology of the analogy of being, and the "stern dialectic" of the thought of early Barth.[160] In the world-friendly theology of the analogy of being, "nature" means the opposite of man-made things and denotes that which is original and in keeping with creation. In the case of the stern dialectic of Barth, the word denotes the historically determined condition of man, which includes the features of his unholy history beginning from Adam. Ratzinger questions whether such an elucidation is actually necessary, given that Barth would only have to say to theologians who support the analogy of being that this is precisely their error: that they believe in a pure-nature without artifice as it was at creation (a state that Barth thinks has never existed), because in this era of the world, all human "nature" has become an artifice, that is, distorted beyond recognition by its errant history. In order to address this, Ratzinger firstly turns to what Scholasticism originally meant when it proposed the axiom *gratia praesupponit naturam*.[161]

When this axiom first appears, he notes, it has a very simple ontological meaning. It is meant to denote that grace is not a self-subsistent, independent creature, but rather an act of God upon a creature that already exists. Specifically, grace is not intended to be a substance in itself, but rather *an event* that presupposes a bearer, or point of reference.[162] Ratzinger points out that this intended meaning of the axiom does not imply a value judgment about nature, but instead is a statement about the ontological status of grace. Bonaventure formulates the axiom as *gratia praesupponit naturam sicut accidens praesupponit subjectum* (grace presupposes nature as an accident presupposes a subject). Ratzinger points to Bonaventure's version of the axiom as not only more precise, but also more illuminating. Nature on this reading is regarded purely in terms of its status as a subject, in its formal capacity to become the bearer of qualities and the goal of actions. It is not viewed in terms of material

---

160. Ratzinger, *Dogma and Preaching*, 149.
161. Ratzinger, *Dogma and Preaching*, 149.
162. Ratzinger, *Dogma and Preaching*, 150.

characteristics that could in some way determine the modality of grace; in fact, Bonaventure specifically rejects this notion.[163]

Ratzinger declares at this point that "nature" in the Scholastic axiom means the formal definiteness of what is human, or rather, the particular man in his humanness as such, which is to be the point of reference for the grace event. Essentially it says nothing on the question of how man concretely is constituted with regard to grace. Bonaventure distinguishes repeatedly between the natural course of worldly things and a miraculous course with which God interrupts the course of nature. Thus, nature, with its normal laws, and God's freedom are contrasted. Bonaventure, in the interests of exactitude, actually recognizes three "courses": the natural course, the voluntary course, and the miraculous course. According to Ratzinger, this means that the human will is presented as a separate middle order between mere nature and God's own freedom, which means that between the general realm of nature and the divine realm is the interpolated realm of the distinctly human. Likewise, man's personhood falls between the general realm of nature and God's revelatory actions.[164] According to Ratzinger, Bonaventure's position means that the human soul is entirely beyond the realm of mere nature. For him, a merely natural soul is not possible, as an essential feature of a soul is that it cannot subsist in itself alone and must be preserved by something that is greater than itself, namely, something "supernatural."[165] This supernatural thing does not thereby cease to be a freely given grace nor does it cease to be "supernatural," and therefore it is something that cannot be derived from mere nature. Ratzinger cites Bonaventure's example of healing. That is, the principle of bodily healing is nature, while the principle of spiritual healing must be something *above* nature, that is, something *supernatural*, namely, grace. Nature, according to Bonaventure, is still preserved in the case of bodily sickness and can thus bring about recovery. Grace, however, is lost through sin, therefore a new infusion of divine grace by the mercy of God is required to restore life to the soul.[166] Ratzinger points out that the unique structure of the soul cannot be overlooked. Specifically,

---

163. Ratzinger, *Dogma and Preaching*, 150. Bonaventure goes on to note that where nature is better, there is often less grace, and someone who is less meritorious today will perhaps be the greater tomorrow.

164. Ratzinger, *Dogma and Preaching*, 152. Ratzinger here sets out a very helpful diagram to elucidate Bonaventure's position on the matter.

165. Ratzinger, *Dogma and Preaching*, 153.

166. Bonaventure, *Sentences*, II, d. 28, a. 1, q. 1, ad 2, cited in Ratzinger, *Dogma and Preaching*, 153.

its immediate relation to God is so intimately essential to it that it cannot exist properly except in being preserved immediately by God at every moment, meaning that spirit surpasses pure-nature. He concludes that in contrast to all attempts in the past or present to "naturalize spirit," Bonaventure's position makes clear the unique structure of the soul, which can "exist only in the manner of dialogue and freedom."[167]

Certainly, it is not possible to define the nature of man without also taking into account his freedom, and as such, one must also take into account man's history. As Ratzinger states, "there is no ahistorical naturalness of man."[168] This Bonaventurian position is conscious of the imprint of history upon "nature." According to Ratzinger, post-Tridentine theology usually knew of only two domains of norms (both of which are unhistorical), being firstly, *natura*, that is, the natural law, and secondly, the *supernatural*, that is, super-nature with its supranatural system of laws. Bonaventure on the other hand, following tradition, set out a triad that is instead historical in character. Bonaventure speaks of three "eras," which proceed sequentially in ascent. These are: the era of the natural law, the era of the written law, and finally, the era of the law of grace.[169] Likewise, Ratzinger points to Bonaventure's teaching on original sin as being that which was "not personal but natural." This approach then logically allows him to speak about man's "natura corrupta," which does not prevent him from distinguishing between the "nature" of man that Christ assumed and sin, which he did not assume. This idea supports Bonaventure's position that the nature of man is marked by history, even though there is at the same time "an inmost core of imperishable order" through which "creation gleams, which makes it possible for this nature to become a space of grace to work, ultimately even to be the locus of the Incarnation."[170]

Ratzinger concludes his treatment of the Scholastic notion of nature by turning to Bonaventure's observations of nature with the view "from above." Bonaventure states that if we observe nature from above, that is, from God's perspective, then it becomes evident that in the end all nature is "grace" and that the *cursus naturalis* is at bottom a *cursus voluntarius*.[171]

---

167. Ratzinger, *Dogma and Preaching*, 153.

168. Ratzinger, *Dogma and Preaching*, 153.

169. Bonaventure, *Sentences*, IV, d. 8, p. 1, a. 1, q. 2c, cited in Ratzinger, *Dogma and Preaching*, 153.

170. Ratzinger, *Dogma and Preaching*, 154.

171. Bonaventure, *Sentences*, I, d. 44, a. 1, q. 1, ad 4: "Hoc totum quod fecit, fuit gratia"; cited in Ratzinger, *Dogma and Preaching*, 154.

As Ratzinger concludes, for Bonaventure, all nature is ultimately in its inmost depth an outpouring of the will: it is voluntaristically structured in terms of God's primordial creative will, to which alone it owes its existence.[172] What remains is the fact that nature in man is encompassed by a twofold freedom, namely, God's freedom and man's own freedom. It is marked by the:

> dual-single history that results from the partnership of man with God: by the vocation from God that calls man to surpass himself and, thus, to come into his true authenticity as well as by the refusal of man who wants to be only a man, who is afraid to set out beyond himself, and, thus, fails to achieve himself.[173]

At this point, Ratzinger turns to ponder what Scripture has to say about *nature* and the *natural*. He firstly calls attention to the writings of St. Paul that seem pertinent to the present discussion, in particular, his use of the word *physis*. Ratzinger points out that one finds in Paul's writings a concept of nature that corresponds to the Jewish roots of his own thought. For a Jew, race (specifically, the lineage of those who were descended from Abraham) was also a theological category, as salvation is fundamentally tied up with the children of Abraham. Having attributed a theological meaning to the notion "race," it follows therefore that the term should become significant, albeit in a negative way, when applied to gentiles. Given that the gentiles do not descend from Abraham, they do not belong to the covenant, and thus do not come under God's promises. Ratzinger points to Rom 2:27 and 11:21 in support of this argument.[174] In both instances Paul uses *physis* to denote a racial understanding of nature. There is also a passage in Paul's writings in which he uses a concept of nature that, according to Ratzinger, appears to have been borrowed from popular Stoic philosophy. In this context, nature is given the meaning of an essential structure that is rationally understood. Ratzinger points out that this is evidence of the Greek roots of Paul's thought.[175]

There are other examples of the use of the word *physis* in Paul's writings which denote a legal meaning. That is, *physis* is also used to suggest

---

172. Ratzinger, *Dogma and Preaching*, 154.

173. Ratzinger, *Dogma and Preaching*, 155.

174 Rom 2:27, ἡ ἐκ φύσεως ἀκροβυστία, "Then those who are physically uncircumcised but keep the law will condemn you who have the written code and circumcision but break the law"; Rom 11:21, τῶν κατὰ φύσιν κλάδων οὐκ ἐφείσατο, "For if God did not spare the natural branches, neither will he spare you."

175. Ratzinger, *Dogma and Preaching*, 156.

the law to the gentiles, that is, the natural law. Those who according to their biological *physis* are gentiles and therefore do not have the law by that title, are nevertheless inspired by *physis* (metaphysically understood) to follow the law.[176] An example of this is Rom 1:26, which speaks about "natural" and "unnatural" sexual relations, corresponding to heterosexual and homosexual relations respectively. Paul makes clear here that man's "nature" is understood to be a genuine guidance for him.

Ratzinger also points to the fact that, with the coming of Christianity, there arose a new situation in which, on the one hand, the biological concept of nature became a theological concept. Nature is now understood not in terms of biology or rational metaphysics but in terms of the concrete history that has taken place in the interactions between God and man.[177] Ratzinger refers to Eph 2:3, in which Paul, speaking to his fellow Jews, using the pronoun "we," denotes that indeed even Jews have sinned, like the rest of mankind.[178] This is a new use of the term in Paul, denoting a biological usage (meaning on account of one's birth or biological origins, Ratzinger explains) that applies also to the Jewish race of the redeemed. In effect, Paul establishes a new universality in the use of the term that abolishes the racial notion that was still present linguistically, replacing it with this new usage. This is to say that Paul, as a Christian, no longer takes a natural, racial concept as his point of departure, instead preferring that salvation comes from the spiritual event of believing. Merely natural, racial existence, in and of itself, is without salvation. No one is saved by birth alone, he says. Thus, Ratzinger concludes that, for Paul, concrete nature as it is in fact bestowed on man is not a salvific order.[179] Ratzinger states:

> If we try to summarize the Pauline data, we find that Paul no doubt attributes to nature a certain guiding character, but it by no means assumes the status of an unambiguous and absolute norm. Man receives true enlightenment about his being, not from "nature," but rather from his encounter with Christ in faith. Nature can very well be the sign of the Creator, but it is not so with perfect clarity, because it is also the expression of

---

176. Ratzinger, *Dogma and Preaching*, 156.
177. Ratzinger, *Dogma and Preaching*, 157.
178. Eph 2:3, "Among these we all once lived in the passions of our flesh, following the desires of body and mind, and so we were by nature children of wrath, like the rest of mankind."
179. Ratzinger, *Dogma and Preaching*, 157.

man's highhandedness. Once again we find, as in Bonaventure's writings, the nature of man in tension between two freedoms: God's and man's. But Paul's letters reveal even more momentously the resulting conflict, the peculiar tension of the human being, which announces itself in a nature that is just as much the expression of God's call (Romans 2:14) as it is that of his wrath (Ephesians 2:3).[180]

Ratzinger's Synthesis: A Paschal Relation between Nature and Grace

Ratzinger begins his attempt at a synthesis on this matter by asserting that the axiom *gratia praesupponit naturam* is "correct and fully biblical" in saying that grace, which is the encounter of man with God, does not destroy what is truly human in man, but rather "salvages and fulfils it."[181] The genuine humanity of man is not at all extinguished by the encounter with grace, and lies at the very basis of every single human person, and in different ways it continuously has its effects on man's concrete existence, summoning and guiding him. Ratzinger however points out that man has nonetheless acquired for himself "a second nature" (citing Pascal), which is a susceptibility to egoism, namely, concupiscence. Ratzinger goes on to point out that this is why in both ancient and modern languages the word "man" has a peculiarly ambiguous set of connotations, in which both man's nobility and man's baseness seem strangely intertwined. This strange paradox is nowhere better epitomized than by *the* man who remains the standard, goal, and perfection of all humanity, namely, the "Son of Man," Christ Jesus. It is, after all, in Christ that we see a united expression of both man's exaltation and his lowliness in a span that reaches from the glory of God down to the utter abyss of ultimate rejection.[182] For Ratzinger, it seems clear that the way that grace travels to reach man is by passing through the "second nature," breaking open his prideful shell that covers the divine glory within him. Thus, he says, "there is no grace without the Cross."[183] Ratzinger here cites de Lubac:

---

180. Ratzinger, *Dogma and Preaching*, 158.
181. Ratzinger, *Dogma and Preaching*, 158.
182. Ratzinger, *Dogma and Preaching*, 159.
183. Ratzinger, *Dogma and Preaching*, 159.

> The whole mystery of Christ is a mystery of resurrection, but it is also a mystery of death. One is bound up with the other, and the same word, Pasch, conveys both ideas. Pasch means passing over. It is a transmutation of the whole being, a complete separation from oneself which no one can hope to evade. It is a denial of all natural values in their natural existence and a renunciation even of all that had previously raised the individual above himself.[184]

Importantly, Ratzinger states that the humanity of Christ, as the second Adam, is the true humanity as only the humanity that has endured the Cross brings man to true light. Any humanism that is based simply on the "nobility" of man's nature eventually leads to man's self-assertion and self-idolization and the refusal of God. Ratzinger cites de Lubac once again:

> Christian humanism must be a *converted humanism*. There is no smooth transition from a natural to a supernatural love. To find himself, man must lose himself, in a spiritual dialectic as imperative in all its severity for humanity as for the individual, that is, imperative for my love of man and of mankind as well as for my love of myself. *Exodus* and *ecstasy* are governed by the same law.[185]

Ratzinger emphasizes that although the created order of true humanity is no longer the concrete order of man, it is no mere abstraction either. It continues to intrude into reality such that it serves as a "permanent warning against an eccentric spirituality."[186] Ratzinger reminds us that there is a certain "common sense," a "sound human understanding" by which the created order makes itself known, and man should allow himself to be corrected repeatedly by this awareness in order to be called back to the ground of reality. This awareness of the abiding power of the created order should give the Christian ethos of the Cross a certain sobriety that is a safeguard against any religious fanaticism, eccentricity, or extravagance. Ratzinger notes that he had earlier made the point that it is the nature of spirit to be constantly surpassing itself, to be pointing beyond itself. According to him, "being related beyond oneself which is constitutive of the essence of spirit is typified especially in the Revelation to Abraham in the perpetual fundamental law of exodus and perfected

---

184. Lubac, *Catholicism*, 367.
185. Lubac, *Catholicism*, 368. Emphasis in original.
186. Ratzinger, *Dogma and Preaching*, 160.

in the Christian mystery of the Pasch."[187] This "going forth" is the fundamental law of Revelation and, at the same time, it is also the fundamental law of the spirit, the genuine fulfilment of the cry of its nature. Beautifully, Ratzinger then concludes that, contrary to Nietzsche, who held that the Cross was the "crucifixion of man," instead, it is his true healing, which saves him from his deceptive self-sufficiency in which he ultimately loses himself in the "bourgeois mush of his supposed naturalness."[188] The paschal way of the Cross, he says, "breaks down all earthly assurances with their false satisfactions and leads to man's true homecoming, the true cosmic harmony, in which God will be everything to everyone."[189] Ratzinger continues:

> In fact, the Cross is not the destruction of man, but, rather, the foundation of true humanity, about which the New Testament says the unfathomably beautiful words: "The goodness and loving kindness of God our Savior appeared" (Titus 3:4). The humanity of God—this is indeed the true humanity of man, the grace that fulfils nature.[190]

According to Corkery, Ratzinger's theology is marked by what he terms "a paschal pattern of authentic Christian existence." This notion means that there is a pattern to the way in which Ratzinger sees the relationship between nature and grace, Christ and humanity, and the Kingdom of God and history. The way in which grace relates to nature therefore is always converting and transformative, that is, ultimately paschal. Grace purifies nature as does Christ humanity, and the Kingdom history.[191]

For Corkery, this "paschal pattern" is best grasped according to the notion of "discontinuity." Ratzinger himself draws attention to the fact of the divergent lines in Christian theology between what is termed the "theology of the Incarnation," which sprang from Greek thought and dominated the Catholic tradition of East and West, and the "theology of the Cross," which based itself on St. Paul and is more typical of Reformation thought. Ratzinger notes that the former speaks of "being" and centers around the fact that here a man *is* God, and that, accordingly, at the same time God is man, a fact which is an all decisive one. For this

---

187. Ratzinger, *Dogma and Preaching*, 160.
188. Ratzinger, *Dogma and Preaching*, 160.
189. Ratzinger, *Dogma and Preaching*, 161.
190. Ratzinger, *Dogma and Preaching*, 161.
191. Corkery, *Ratzinger's Theological Ideas*, 33.

theological approach, all the individual events that followed pale before the event of God's Incarnation. The interlocking of God and man is truly the decisive, redemptive factor, as the real future of man, on which all lines must finally converge.[192] On the other hand, the theology of the Cross eschews ontology of this kind, and speaks instead of the event, following the testimony of early days, when people "enquired not about being but about the activity of God in the Cross and Resurrection," an activity that conquered death and pointed to Jesus as the Lord and the hope of humanity.[193] Ratzinger notes that the differing tendencies of these two theologies result from their respective approaches. The theology of the Incarnation tends towards a static, optimistic view. For this approach, sin appears as a transitional stage of fairly minor importance. The decisive factor is not that man is in a state of sin and must be saved; the aim goes far beyond any such atonement for the past and lies in making progress toward the convergence of man and God. The theology of the Cross, on the other hand, leads rather to a "dynamic, topical, anti-world interpretation of Christianity, which understands Christianity only as a discontinuously but constantly appearing breach in the self-confidence and self-assurance of man and of his institutions, including the church."[194]

In Corkery's judgment, Ratzinger can be placed firmly within the Reformation-leaning "theology of the Cross."[195] Corkery notes that in the period after the Second Vatican Council, there was a struggle to find a correct balance between the theology of the Incarnation and the theology of the Cross. Corkery points to Ratzinger's 1966 talk in Bamberg at the *Katholikentag* (German Catholic Diet), but also what "lay at the heart of his celebrated book *Introduction to Christianity*."[196] He asserts that following this pattern, and anchoring it in a fuller theological synthesis, Ratzinger's *Introduction to Christianity* offers not so much an incarnational theology but rather a "newly emphasized *theology of the Cross*" that, in Walter Kasper's view, was deserving of further exploration.[197] This theology of the Cross situates conversion at the center of man's relationship with God, Corkery notes, treading the paschal path, receiving a forgiveness that we cannot bestow on ourselves. In Kasper's judgment,

192. Ratzinger, *Introduction to Christianity*, 229.
193. Ratzinger, *Introduction to Christianity*, 229.
194. Ratzinger, *Introduction to Christianity*, 230.
195. Corkery, "Reflection," 22.
196. Corkery, "Reflection," 22.
197. Corkery, *Ratzinger's Theological Ideas*, 34.

Ratzinger draws out the dynamic of the theology of the Cross "in contradistinction to a one-sided and static theology of the Incarnation."[198] According to Corkery, as Ratzinger's thinking unfolded, "it became clearer that his theological leanings were very close to what he had referred to as 'the eschatological phase' in his Bamberg talk."[199] During his 1966 Bamberg conference, Ratzinger had voiced critical words of caution. He warned against a naïve postconciliar triumphalism, stating that as long as the church is a pilgrim on earth, she has no reason to pride herself on her own works. He continues:

> A turning of the church toward the world, which would entail turning away from the cross, cannot lead to the church's renewal, but [only] to her demise. The purpose of the church's turning toward the world cannot be to dispense with the scandal of the cross, but exclusively to render its nakedness accessible anew, by removing all secondary scandals [that is, sins committed by members of the church], which have been interposed and have unfortunately oftentimes covered up the folly of the love of God with the folly of human self-love.[200]

According to Corkery, these aforementioned sentiments are typical of Ratzinger: "The world contaminates. Purification, about-turn, decontamination are needed."[201] Faith is its antidote, according to Corkery, which purifies, converts, and turns us towards God and away from what

---

198. Kasper, "Wesen des Christlichen," 182–88.

199. Corkery, "Reflection," 22.

200 Ratzinger, "Katholizismus," 317. My translation. Original as follows: "Eine Weltzuwendung der Kirche, die ihre Abwendung vom Kreuz darstellen wurde, konnte nicht zu einer Erneuerung der Kirche, sondern nur zu ihrem Ende fuhren. Der Sinn der Weltzuwendung der Kirche kann nicht sein, den Skandal des Kreuzes aufzuheben, sondern allein der, ihn in seiner ganzen Bloße wieder zuganglich zu machen, indem alle sekundären Skandale weggeräumt werden, die sich dazwischengeschaltet haben und leider oft genug die Torheit der Liebe Gottes mit der Torheit der Eigenliebe der Menschen verdecken."

De Gaál notes that there is an unconfirmed report given by Hans Küng, a former colleague of Ratzinger at Tübingen, that portrays an image of Ratzinger being shouted down by students during the student revolt. Whether or not this single event occurred as Küng claims, Ratzinger appears to have been quite popular among the students during those "heady times." During a podium discussion with Professors Seckler, Küng, and Neumann, students demanded: "Ratzinger must speak! Ratzinger must speak!" See Seewald, *Benedict XVI: Intimate Portrait*, 86. Valente (a former student) describes listening to Ratzinger's words at Tübingen as having "had the accent of prayer." See Valente, "Difficult Years," 42.

201. Corkery, "Reflection," 26.

is ungodly (*fides purgans*). The path of the Christian, for Ratzinger, thus is the path of Christ, that is, walking the paschal way, bearing the Cross, dying to self. Corkery notes that this emphasis on the Cross of Christ and on grace (understood as fundamentally healing) is essential, and it is, he thinks, what makes Ratzinger closer to Reformation theologians rather than most other Catholic ones. Grace does not so much "build" on nature created as "good" as "*reverse* it (following a sin-aware tradition rooted in Augustine). The *discontinuities* between nature and grace and the fact that the latter is much more a healing than an elevating divine gift are obvious, given our condition."[202]

For Corkery, Ratzinger had already grasped, with de Lubac, that there cannot be any grace without the Cross, and also why he rejoiced that *Gaudium et Spes* in paragraph 22 managed to present a corrective to what Ratzinger thought was *Lumen Gentium*'s neo-Pelagian tendency in its emphasis on human activity (that is, that we could be agents of our own salvation).[203] As stated, according to Corkery, Ratzinger's view of how nature and grace relate favors:

> discontinuity over continuity; it indicates that the way of grace is the way of the cross; it puts stress on grace healing and transforming nature (*gratia sanans*) more than on grace elevating and perfecting nature (*gratia elevans*).[204]

For Corkery, Ratzinger's view on nature and grace is unsurprising, "given Ratzinger's preference for Augustine and Bonaventure over Aquinas."[205]

In *Dogma and Preaching*, as we have seen, Ratzinger shows how different understandings of nature exist in Catholic and Protestant theologies. He then seeks to move beyond these by probing the original

---

202. Corkery, "Reflection," 23. Emphasis in original. One might pause here to ask, however, whether there can actually be said to be a difference between "elevating" and "healing" grace, for fear that we should fall back into the minutiae of distinctions typical of neo-scholasticism. Surely, God's "healing" is at once and the same time also "elevating"? I also note that Corkery makes mention of grace "building" on nature. This, as we have seen, is typical of the extrinsicist account of nature and grace. It must be pointed out, however, that this is not what Ratzinger means by "praesupponit."

203. Corkery, *Ratzinger's Theological Ideas*, 34. For an appreciation of de Lubac's view on *Gaudium et Spes*, see Portier, "What Kind of World?," 136–51.

204. Corkery, *Ratzinger's Theological Ideas*, 44.

205. Corkery, *Ratzinger's Theological Ideas*, 44. De Gaál notes, however, that in Ratzinger's judgment Bonaventure is neither anti-Aristotelian nor Augustinian, and Ratzinger has expressed sympathy for Aquinas quite frequently, both in his *Habilitationsschrift* and later on. See Gaál, *Theology of Pope Benedict XVI*, 70; see also Ratzinger, *Theology of History*, 157.

meaning of the axiom *gratia praesupponit naturam*, and also looks at what Scripture has to say about the notion of nature. In his synthesis, he holds that what is truly human in man is not fully extinguished but becomes covered with the dirty covering of Pascal's notion of "a second nature." This means that the notion of "human" imported a two-sidedness of meaning, namely, the high and the low, the noble and the base, the *grandeur et misère*. Here we see what Corkery terms Ratzinger's "fidelity to sin-awareness and creation-faith" and, consequently, the importance he attaches to the necessity of preaching about the topic of sin and repentance.[206] Corkery points also to Bonaventure's influence on Ratzinger in terms of how grace is related to created nature (rather than historical nature). Ratzinger shows that Bonaventure falls foul of a fear of ascribing more to nature than it is owed but less to God than is God's due by collapsing nature into grace and so eclipsing the divine at the expense of the human.[207] According to Corkery, this leads him to tend towards emptying nature of positive content, reducing it to nothing, though his intention was actually to celebrate its excellence. This approach means then that nature falls into a double disregard, where *historical* nature, sullied by sin, is in need of transformation, and as *created* nature, thanks to Bonaventure's inclination to say that all that God has made is in itself already grace (*hoc totum quod fecit fuit gratia*), its excellence is eclipsed or erased.[208] According to Corkery, the concept of *nature* in the hands of Bonaventure fares poorly in the end: as *historical* it "demands reversal" and as *created* "it is trumped by grace"; therefore he thinks that, either way, it has a tendency to disappear, either through transformation or through dissolution. Corkery suggests that these emphases have all been found in Ratzinger too and refers to the fact that, in Ratzinger's mind, "we approach God empty; we rely on receiving, not on anything we bring or do" and "there is an eclipsing here of the goodness of created nature, a wariness about the human contribution—think only of Ratzinger's legendary nervousness about praxis theologies" and also what he terms an "excessive emphasis on the *divine* side in the divine-human reality that is grace, Incarnation, and even church." For Corkery, Ratzinger (like Bonaventure) tends to "spiritualize . . . and to be world-wary"—"the link from these tendencies to an Augustinian tradition and outlook is

---

206. Corkery, *Ratzinger's Theological Ideas*, 46.
207. Ratzinger, "Wortgebrauch von Natura."
208. Corkery, *Ratzinger's Theological Ideas*, 46.

discernible."[209] Avery Dulles observed that at the Extraordinary Synod of 1985, there were two schools of thought present, the first of these led by Ratzinger and Hoeffner had a "markedly supernaturalistic point of view, tending to depict the church as an island of grace in a world given over to sin." This outlook he termed "neo-Augustinian" as opposed to the "communitarian" and "humanistic" tendencies of the second school of thought.[210] Corkery surmises therefore that if, earlier, the idea had been that the church could value the world and even learn from it, that time had passed such that the church had allowed itself to be contaminated through its openness to the world. The Ratzingerian remedy to this contamination, therefore, is faith in God (because sin is a loss of faith in God), which humbles and purifies, as against the proud insights of the philosopher, and which is ultimately a gift of God. It is this faith that functions as *fides purgans* by means of the Incarnate *Logos* of the Father. For Ratzinger, it is the purified reason (the pure in heart) that can see God. This means that becoming a Christian involves being purified and converted (*metanoia*) by Christ. Ratzinger eschews any suggestion of a Pelagian notion where nothing from the excellence of our rational capacities and nothing from our own powers of action bring about this purification. Instead, each of these powers stands in need of purification. Corkery however asks whether it would not be more "heartening, more encouraging" if Ratzinger were instead to acknowledge more forcefully "that we can be purified by first falling in love with the One who purifies."[211] He notes that Ratzinger's "Augustinian and Bonaventurian roots" could be grasped more clearly if his anthropology were to be juxtaposed to that of Rahner, who, he adds, was "more Thomist and more friendly towards the world than Ratzinger."[212] Ratzinger did not accept Rahner's notion that being Christian is not some sort of "special case" of being human. Rahner had instead proposed the notion that being Christian is simply accepting "man as he is."[213] Ratzinger was decidedly unhappy also with Rahner's notion of the "anonymous Christian." For Ratzinger, "man as he is" is specifically that which is in need of conversion and purification "the thing to be risen above, mastered and transcended," says Corkery.[214]

209. Corkery, *Ratzinger's Theological Ideas*, 47.
210. Dulles, *Reshaping of Catholicism*, 191.
211. Corkery, *Ratzinger's Theological Ideas*, 49.
212. Corkery, *Ratzinger's Theological Ideas*, 49.
213. Corkery, *Ratzinger's Theological Ideas*, 49.
214. Corkery, *Ratzinger's Theological Ideas*, 49.

In Corkery's judgment, Ratzinger's anthropological approach is stark, reflecting a spirit of discontinuity between nature and grace, as opposed to the spirit of continuity inherent in Rahner's thought. For Rahner, "man as he is" can be trusted, and he can trust the world. Whereas, asserts Corkery, Ratzinger's "man as he is" cannot trust his own life and is himself not to be trusted.[215] This, he thinks, indicates a flight *from* the world, as opposed to Rahner's flight *to* the world, and that "Ratzinger's approach underplays the *particularity* of human goodness" in his "stark, reversing, radically self-emptying anthropology."[216]

Given this assessment, we ask, however: Is this truly the case? Is a sober acknowledgment of the biblical notion of original sin and man's need of God's forgiveness and grace really such a discontinuous way to conceive of nature and grace? Does it also imply a rejection of the theology of the Incarnation and a flight, in hatred of the world, to the theology of the Cross? Are the two always and everywhere mutually exclusive?[217] *Pace* Corkery and Kasper, does Ratzinger truly favor a "theology of the Cross," with its concomitant anti-world attitude, at the expense of the "theology of the Incarnation"?

The notion that one may favor a theology of the Cross with its concordant categorization as "discontinuity" at the expense of a theology of the Incarnation (or vice versa), is reminiscent of the thought of the Belgian Jesuit Léopold Malevez (1900–1973), whose work is known for its identification of a division between incarnational and eschatological approaches to history. As we have seen, for those who favor the eschatological approach, the emphasis is on the discontinuity between profane history and the final reign of God after the renewal of creation. For those however who favor the incarnational approach, the proposal is that all good human actions prepare for the coming age beyond the

---

215. I am reminded here of St. Mark's words: "Repent [μετανοεῖτε] and believe in the Gospel" (Mark 1:15).

216. Corkery, *Ratzinger's Theological Ideas*, 49.

217. Philipp Renczes, SJ, points out that in *Caritas in Veritate* nature is submitted to a far-reaching evaluation in Benedict's thought, i.e., he uses "nature" not to indicate a verifiable depository of an "ethical code" but to highlight human beings' reception of their own being from God, out of which follows the principle of gratuitously giving. In other words, nature has been graced to receive more grace. According to Renczes, we see in Benedict's thought a firm rejection of the notion of "pure-nature" and the "two-tier" system of nature and grace in neo-Thomism. Ratzinger adopts these insights from de Lubac and thus inherits John Paul II's notion of nature as both "vocation" and as "gift of the Creator who has given it an inbuilt order" that is lived in nature's dynamic realization. See Renczes, "Grace Reloaded," 285. See also Strand, "Method," 835–52.

consummation of the world.[218] The eschatological approach is usually identified with an emphasis on the theology of the Cross, while the incarnational approach is identified, obviously, with the theology of the Incarnation.[219] Malevez had been influenced by a fellow Belgian theologian, Gustave Thils (1909–2000), who was a *peritus* at the Second Vatican Council and a member of the Secretariat for Christian Unity.[220] Thils is generally remembered for his doctrinal history of the ecumenical movement, published in 1955, and for his criticism of the theology of Jean Daniélou for being too far down the eschatological end of the spectrum.[221] In an article on the interventions of Cardinal Josef Frings in the debates of the Second Vatican Council, Ratzinger observed that Frings was keen to emphasize one general principle:

> For the Christian life in the world three revealed truths are always to be kept before us: creation, which teaches us to love the things of the world as God's work; the incarnation, which spurs us on to dedicate to God all the things of the world; the cross and resurrection, which leads us in the imitation of Christ to sacrifice and continence with regard to the things of the world.[222]

Consistent with Ratzinger, Abbot Christopher Butler made the point that Christian eschatology and Christian incarnationalism are not mutually exclusive and that the division identified by Malevez between the two, that is, between the incarnational and the eschatological approach to history, should not be a real division but rather two poles held in tension. According to Butler:

> Eschatology without incarnation is not Christian at all, but Jewish. Incarnation without eschatology is—I know not what; Buddhism, perhaps, or Platonism. Born within the Jewish tradition and of Jewish spiritual stock, Christianity has been eschatological from the beginning . . . . But its novelty was not that it simply lodged the idea of incarnation within an eschatological framework, but that it proclaimed a real, "mystical," "sacramental" anticipation of the Last Things as the unique gift

---

218. Rowland, *Culture of the Incarnation*, citing 146, Malevez, "Deux théologies catholiques," 225–40.

219. Rowland, *Culture of the Incarnation*, 146.

220. Rowland, *Culture of the Incarnation*, 146.

221. Rowland, *Culture of the Incarnation*, 146, citing Thils, *Histoire doctrinale*.

222. Rowland, *Culture of the Incarnation*, 149, citing Ratzinger, "Cardinal Frings' Speeches," 143.

that God was bestowing on man in the Gospel—and of this real anticipation the Incarnation is the epitome and the fountainhead.... Incarnation, for us, is eschatological, and eschatology is incarnated.[223]

As Christopher Collins points out, it is within the very identity of Jesus as Son of the Father (referring to Ratzinger's "Son Christology"[224]) that this tension is ever present and has existed throughout the entire Christian theological tradition. Ratzinger himself acknowledges that this tension, between theology built primarily from the Incarnation and that built from the Cross, cannot be easily resolved, nor is there the possibility of any easy synthesis.[225] As Ratzinger sets out:

> Anyone at all familiar with these two great historical forms of Christian self-comprehension will certainly not be tempted to try his hand at a simplifying synthesis. These two fundamental structural forms of "Incarnation" theology and "Cross" theology reveal polarities that cannot be surmounted and combined in a neat synthesis without the loss of the crucial points in each; *they must remain present as polarities that mutually correct each other* and only by complementing each other point toward the whole.[226]

Ratzinger then surmises that the foregoing reflections perhaps have given a glimpse of the ultimate unity, which makes these polarities possible and prevents them from falling apart as contradictions. Ratzinger states, "For we have found that the *being* of Christ ('Incarnation' theology!) is *actualitas*, stepping beyond oneself, the exodus of going out from self; it is not a being that rests in itself, but the act of being sent, of being son, of serving."[227] Ratzinger notes that this *doing* is not just doing but *being* as it reaches down into the depths of being and coincides with it:

> This being is exodus, transformation. So at this point a properly understood Christology of being and of the incarnation must pass over into the theology of the Cross and become one with it; conversely, a theology of the Cross that gives its full measure must pass over into the Christology of the Son and of being.[228]

---

223. Rowland, *Culture of the Incarnation*, 150, citing Butler, "Value of History," 294.
224. Collins, *Word Made Love*, 83. See also Ratzinger, *Introduction to Christianity*, 168.
225. Collins, *Word Made Love*, 83.
226. Ratzinger, *Introduction to Christianity*, 230. My emphasis.
227. Ratzinger, *Introduction to Christianity*, 230.
228. Ratzinger, *Introduction to Christianity*, 230.

While acknowledging the difficulty of the synthesis, we can see, given these comments, that Ratzinger strove to hold both poles in tension. Rather than attempting to place him in one camp or the other (that is, wholly within a theology of Incarnation versus a theology of the Cross), Ratzinger is best understood as walking the middle way between the two poles.

According to Rowland, "a tabloid caricature of Ratzinger is that he has imbibed too much of the thought of St. Augustine, leaving him with a neo-Manichean stance of hostility to the world."[229] This caricature, she states, draws Catholics into two camps, namely, that of "grace sniffers" and that of "heresy sniffers," with Ratzinger firmly in the latter. Another caricature, she suggests, is that Ratzinger was so shocked by the student demonstrations at Tübingen in 1968 that he developed a pathological fear of "the world," which had remained ever since.[230] These caricatures are not only simplistic, but they fail to engage with Ratzinger's actual academic work on the issue of the relationship between the church and the world and the church and modern culture.[231]

As we have seen, the young Ratzinger appropriated the thought of Augustine as mediated through the scholarship of Erich Przywara, Fritz Hofmann, Romano Guardini, Gottlieb Söhngen, and Henri de Lubac. Hofmann, a professor of theology at the University of Würzburg, published in 1933 a seminal work on the ecclesiology of Augustine, which Ratzinger read in preparation for his own doctoral dissertation on the concepts of the People of God and the House of God in the works of Augustine. This work was followed in 1940 by Hofmann's reflection of the theme "God is Love," a topic that was adopted by Benedict XVI in his first encyclical, bearing the same title.

In the interbellum period, Przywara was publishing material on Augustine and was one of the most influential German-speaking Jesuits of the twentieth century. He was also spiritual director to the Carmelite-martyr Edith Stein and taught both Karl Rahner and Hans Urs von Balthasar. Przywara was also the editor of the influential journal *Stimmen der Zeit* and translated the works of Newman into German. Among his many works (more than sixty books and six hundred articles), he wrote *Crucis mysterium: Das christliche Heute* (1939), a work that Ratzinger

---

229. Rowland, "World," 109.
230. Rowland, *Culture of the Incarnation*, 2.
231. Rowland, "World," 109. See also Rowland, *Culture of the Incarnation*, 7–48.

later praised.²³² For Przywara, the most perfect modern reincarnation of Augustinianism is found in the works of Newman. Przywara concluded that Newman had settled accounts with the Reformation more thoroughly than Hegel and Kierkegaard ever did, and saw that the Reformation could not be overcome by negotiations of any kind, but only by the reversal of its first principles. In other words, as Rowland observes, there is nothing remotely Reformational about Przywara's appropriation of Augustine.²³³ Przywara in fact speaks of a "triple Augustinianism" (*dreifachen Augustinismus*), or three dominant ways in which Augustine has been appropriated.²³⁴ It will assist us to bear these in mind as we speak of Ratzinger's own appropriation of Augustine, via Przywara.

First, Przywara speaks of the "idealist Augustine" (*idealer Augustinismus*), whose accent on truth and the intelligent world appears to relate him to the spirits of Descartes and Kant. There is also an affinity between Augustine and Goethe in their mutual contemplative openness to the truth of light, and an affinity between Augustine and Hegel in their mutual appreciation of the pathos of wholeness, as one finds in fragments from Augustine.²³⁵

The second Augustinianism Przywara mentions is that of an emphasis on hereditary sin and redemption, as found in Augustine's *Retractationes*. Here the "idealist Augustine" of the first interpretation receives measure and judgment from the Augustinianism of the "supernatural eye" (*übernatürlichen Auges*).²³⁶ In this work, the Augustine "of critical and idealist truth," that is, the Augustine of an ideal humanity of insight and freedom, is inwardly transformed by the more critical Augustine of the *praevaricatores, redite ad cor*, that is, the Augustine of the "repenting retreat into the abyss of soundness that oozes from the original sin" (*der bussenden Einkehr in den Abgrund der Sündhaftigkeit, die aus der Erbsünde quillt*).²³⁷ Similarly, the correlation between sight and light in the

232. Rowland, "World," 110.
233. Rowland, "World," 111.
234. Rowland, *Beyond Kant and Nietzsche*, 149, citing Przywara, *Augustinisch*, 93–94.
235. These include: "Deus sub quo totum, in quo totum, cum quo totum"—*Soliloquiorum*, I, 4; "Contrariorum oppositione saeculi pulchritudo componitur"—*De Civitate Dei*, XI, 18; and "Deus, per quem universitas etiam cum sinistra parte perfecta est"—*Soliloquiorum*, I, 2. Fragments (and the corresponding bibliographic details of Augustine's works) from Rowland, *Beyond Kant and Nietzsche*, 149.
236. Rowland, *Beyond Kant and Nietzsche*, 150, citing Przywara, *Augustinisch*, 93.
237. Rowland, *Beyond Kant and Nietzsche*, 150, citing Przywara, *Augustinisch*, 93.

contemplative Augustine knows that the "smoke of greed can cloud one's vision and therefore that the true light of grace must burn fiery bright" (*diesen Qualm als Licht ansieht, und wie darum tötend hell das wahre Licht der Gnade hineinbrennen muss, bis der Mensch, durch die Blindheit des Glaubens sehend geworden*).[238]

Finally, Przywara proposes the Augustine who acknowledges the incomprehensibility of the relation between *iustitia* and *misericordia*, and between heaven and hell, "which do not enter into any aesthetically shimmering formula" (*die in keine ästhetisch schimmernde Formel eingehen*), because these relationships belong inside the territory of divine prerogatives. They are, in Przywara's idiom, "the crown prerogatives of God," who said: "My thoughts are not your thoughts and My ways are not your ways."[239]

Przywara concludes that, compared to the critical idealistic Augustinianism of the "spirit," the deeper Augustinianism of the curse of the "flesh" remained conscious of the effects of original sin. However, this second Augustinianism, the Augustine who is acutely conscious of the reality of concupiscence, is still not as deep as the third Augustinianism, the Augustine of the "Verbum-Caro," the "Eternal Truth that became flesh and lives on in the flesh of humanity as the body of Christ."[240] As Rowland notes, consistent with his "polyphonic counter-point metaphysics,"[241] Przywara concluded that "it is not merely that the Augustinianism of the spirit is humiliated by the Augustinianism of the flesh . . . or that the Augustinianism of light is humiliated in the Augustinianism of the night" (*Es ist nicht einfachhin so, dass der Augustinismus des Geistes nur in einen Augustinismus des erbsündigen Fleisches gedemütigt wäre . . . Es ist nicht einfachhin so, dass der Augustinismus des Lichtes gedemütigt wäre in den Augustinismus der Nacht*).[242] While these humiliations are a fact, the story does not end here on a low note with "paradise lost" and the victory of death. Rather, the diminuendo of the Fall is followed by the crescendo of the Redemption.[243] In Przywara's words:

---

238. Rowland, *Beyond Kant and Nietzsche*, 150, citing Przywara, *Augustinisch*, 93.
239. Rowland, *Beyond Kant and Nietzsche*, 150, citing Przywara, *Augustinisch*, 94.
240. Rowland, *Beyond Kant and Nietzsche*, 150, citing Przywara, *Augustinisch*, 95.
241. Rowland, *Beyond Kant and Nietzsche*, 150.
242. Przywara, *Augustinisch*, 94–95.
243. Rowland, *Beyond Kant and Nietzsche*, 150.

It is not the torn state of the human being in this night of struggle that is the deepest, but the deeper Augustinianism of the night that raises its head in the middle, the Augustinianism of the "light of the world" that rose into the "darkness" where the darkness is finally overcome in the Eternal Light of Easter in his church.[244]

This third Augustinianism is the "Augustinianism of glory" (*Augustinismus die Glorie*),[245] the form favored by Ratzinger. Przywara reads this third form of Augustinianism as the solution to the contrast or polarity between ecstatic Neoplatonism and demonic Manicheanism and between an Antiochene Christianity of an ethical-rational perfection (right down to Pelagianism) and an Alexandrian Christianity of the merciless absorption into the life and work of God (until one falls into Jansenism and Docetism).[246]

Towards the end of his analysis of Augustinian polarities, Przywara could not resist finding one last paradoxical contrast to "entice the interest of an already intellectually dizzy reader."[247] Przywara noted that owing to the fact that Augustine became the one in whom all the theology of the Scriptures and the fathers culminated, and from whom all the theology of Scholasticism emanated, he was at the same time humiliated as the source from which all the great heresies of the subsequent period derived, so that the condemnations of the church seemed directed against him.

Having offered an account of the hallmarks of the three appropriations of Augustine and their internal polarities, Przywara then moves on to examine the poles represented by the names Augustine and Aquinas. Here he suggests that the two poles need to be studied from the perspective of three questions: Does perception go from top to bottom or from bottom to top, that is, in *a priori* intuition or in real experience (*in apriorischer Intuition oder in realer Erfahrung*)? Second: Does perception go from the inside out or from the outside in, that is, in primary self-knowledge or in primary knowledge of the world (*in primärer*

---

244. Przywara, *Augustinisch*, 95. My translation. Original as follows: "Aber nicht die zerrissene Zuständlichkeit des Menschen in dieser Nacht des Kampfes ist das Tiefste, sondern der tiefere Augustinismus der Nacht erhebt mitten darin sein Haupt, der Augustinismus des Lichtes der Welt, das in die Finsternis stieg, um sie auf sich zu nehmen bis in die Finsternis des Karfreitags und so zu überwinden in das Ewige Licht der Ostern in Seiner Kirche."

245. Przywara, *Augustinisch*, 96.

246. Przywara, *Augustinisch*, 96–97.

247. Rowland, *Beyond Kant and Nietzsche*, 151.

Selbsterkenntnis oder in primärer Welterkenntnis)? Third: Does perception go from beyond to beyond or from this side to beyond, that is, is it primarily theological or primarily philosophical (*Geht das Erkennen von jenseits nach diesseits oder von diesseits nach jenseits, d.h. primär theologisch oder primär philosophisch*)?[248] Przywara then gives an account of the differences between Augustine and Aquinas concerning abstraction and intuitive wisdom,[249] before pointing out a difference in the temperaments of two of the most prominent names in Catholic theology, to which he gave poetic expression:

> In Augustine [we have] the longing for bridal love, in Thomas her quiet celebration . . . in Augustine therefore the burning, anticipating and therefore gladly fearful and exaggerating of such a longing (through highs and lows),—in Thomas the impersonal silence and daring sobriety of such a celebration, up to the rigidity of a "ceremonial"; in Augustine, therefore, the fear of the night of the divine light in the midst of being swept away,—in Thomas, the quiet worship (*Adoro te devote, latens deitas*), until a formula of confession is said.[250]

For Przywara, Augustine shows that what is metaphysically ultimate is neither an absolute immanence nor an absolute transcendence,

---

248. Przywara, *Augustinisch*, 99.

249. Przywara, *Augustinisch*, 99. In Augustine, especially in his *De Trinitate*, Przywara found a "looping duplicity of intuitive wisdom and inductive science (de Trin XII 2; 2–14; 22), just as Aquinas distinguished between the sensually indirect way of factual perception (*quantum ad apprehensionem . . . per species quas a sensibus abstrahimus*) and the immediacy of the judgmental mind to pure truth (*quantum ad iudicium . . . intuemur inviolabilit veritater* Ver q 10 a 8 corp)." Conversely, Przywara found that the abstraction of Aquinas "seems to so decisively bind the mind to the limits of the sensory world, that the spontaneity of the mind (*intellectus agens*) has the formal task of abstraction (S.Th. 1q 84 a 6 corp)" and that the "first principles, in which all knowledge and all wisdom are contained (*primum a quo . . . ultimum in quod.* Ver q 14 a 1 corp etc.), are so decided in the senses (in Boeth de Trin a 4 corp) that they have their 'instance' in it (*resolutio in sensibile*: Ver q 12 a 3 ad 2 et 3)."

250. Przywara, *Augustinisch*, 99. My translation. Original as follows: "in Augustinus die Sehnsucht der bräutlichen Liebe, in Thomas ihr ruhiges Feiern . . . in Augustinus darum das Brennende, Vorwegnehmende und darum gern Angsthafte und Übersteigernde einer solchen Sehnsucht (durch Hohen und Tiefen),—in Thomas die unpersönliche Stille und abwägende Nüchternheit eines solchen Feierns, bis zur Starre eines Zeremoniells; in Augustinus darum das Bangen um die Nacht des göttlichen Lichtes mitten im Hineingerissensein,—in Thomas das ruhige Anbeten (*Adoro te devote, latens Deitas*), bis zum Hersagen einer Bekenntnisformel."

but a dynamic rhythm between them, that is, between the poles of divine immanence and divine transcendence.[251] According to Przywara:

> the great idea of Augustine, which constitutes the, so to speak, formal principle of his thought, and bears implications even for the subtlest branches of Christian ethics is this: *Deus interior et exterior*, God in all and above all, God more inward than we are to ourselves, and yet transcending and surpassing us as the one who is infinite and incomprehensible.[252]

Betz points out that, conversely, the problem since the Reformation has been that modernity is unable to maintain the two in productive tension, in terms of what Przywara calls *Spannungseinheit*. That is, the tendency is to either absorb immanence into transcendence, and all creaturely objectivity and mediation into divine subjectivity (theopanism), or alternatively, to collapse transcendence into immanence, divinity into humanity, grace into nature (a form of pantheism).[253] In both cases, according to Przywara, the concept of God is dissolved—whether it be in the name of divine immanence (à la Schleiermacher) or in the name of a dogmatic theology of divine transcendence (à la Barth).[254] Przywara, years later, strikingly said that:

> all that is left [once the *analogia entis* is denied] is an either-or between a piety toward God that is hostile to the world and a piety toward the world that is hostile toward God. Such is the either-or between the Reformation taken to its logical conclusion (as in early Karl Barth) and secularism taken to its logical conclusion (as with Lenin and Stalin).[255]

Przywara suggests that both extremes are, in the end, equally remote from a true understanding of God, and that the one leads as much

---

251. Betz, "*Analogia Entis*," 90.

252. Przywara, *Ringen der Gegenwart*, 543. My translation. Original as follows: "Es ist der Große Gedanke Augustins, der bei ihm bis in die feinsten Verzweigungen christlicher Ethik hinein sozusagen das Formprinzip bildet: *Deus interior et exterior*, Gott in allem und über allem, Gott uns innerer als wir selbst, und doch uns übersteigend und überragend als der unendliche und unbegreifliche."

253. Betz, "*Analogia Entis*," 91.

254. Betz, "*Analogia Entis*," 92.

255. Przywara, *Logos*, 112. My translation. Original as follows: "Es bleibt nur das Entweder-Oder zwischen welt-feindlicher Gott-Frömmigkeit und gott-feindlicher Welt-Frömmigkeit. Es ist das Entweder-Oder zwischen zu-ende-gedachter Reformation (wie Karl Barth sie zuende denkt) und zu-ende-gedachter Säkularisation (wie Lenin-Stalin sie zu Ende denken)."

to the denial of God as the other. Thus, Przywara posits that Augustine remains "the thinker of Christian balance," which is to say, according to Betz, the first great thinker of the *analogia entis*, since one finds in him both "the God of blessed intimacy" (divine immanence) and the God who, "if you comprehend him, is not God" (divine transcendence).[256]

As we have earlier seen, it was Söhngen who also greatly influenced Ratzinger, particularly as he approached both Augustine and Bonaventure. Ratzinger points out that Söhngen's writings on the *analogia entis* and the *analogia fidei* sought to do justice to Barth's critique of a superficially held optimism about nature that liked to base itself on Aquinas. Söhngen sought to hold fast to the seriousness of the Protestant critique, while at the same time not giving up on Catholic theology's yes to the ontological dimension in its creation-faith.[257] Corkery observes that Ratzinger follows this general direction (typical of a Bonaventurian direction, especially as we see in Ratzinger's anthropological writings), given he always strove to maintain the seriousness of sin and the biblical call to repentance, while at the same time, not abandoning creation-faith (the fundamental goodness of creation) on the other. On the topic of the *analogia entis* and *analogia fidei*, as we have seen, Ratzinger had a great admiration for the work of Przywara, which he describes as "masterful" and as possessing a "salutary sobriety." Ratzinger demonstrates a profound grasp of Przywara's doctrine of the *analogia entis* but also illustrates how Przywara's understanding of the *analogia fidei* (the analogy between the two covenants centered in Christ) is ultimately connected to his understanding of the *analogia entis*.[258] For the ever-greater God of the *analogia entis*, Ratzinger points out that nowhere is this so manifest as in the crossing oppositions of the admirable commercium of the Cross. It is in the glory of the Cross that we see precisely a coincidence of a *theologia analogiae fidei* and a *theologia analogiae entis*. In Ratzinger's view, Przywara's late work also demands serious attention, constituting a

---

256. Betz, "*Analogia Entis*," 91. Further, Betz cites Augustine, Sermon 117, 5: "Si comprehendis non est Deus"; and he suggests comparing this with Augustine, Sermon 52, 16: "Quid ergo dicamus, fratres, de Deo? Si enim quod vis dicere, si cepisti, non est Deus: si comprehendere potuisti, aliud pro Deo comprehendisti. Si quasi compregendere potuisti, cogitatione tua te decepisti. Hoc ergo non est, si compregendisti: si autem hoc est, non comprehendisti. Quid ergo vis loqui, quod comprehendere non potuisti?"

257. Corkery, *Ratzinger's Theological Ideas*, 45.

258. Przywara, *Analogia Entis*, 10. See also Betz, "*Analogia Entis*," 92; and Gertz, "Kreuz-Struktur," 555.

significant theological prolegomenon whose objective weight is in every respect comparable to his *analogia entis*.[259]

With respect to the doctrine of the *analogia entis*, Przywara concluded that there are basically two models: the Christian-Platonic model associated with Augustine, and the Christian-Aristotelian model, exemplified in St. Thomas:

> The first is, on the one side, the type that chiefly affirms God as "All in all," and yet, just because God is, so to speak, the essence or summary of the world, it is, on the other side, the type which chiefly affirms the comprehensible nearness of God. The second, on the one side, is the type which chiefly affirms the "reality of the creature," but yet, just because in doing so it recognizes the difference between God and the world, is, on the other side, the type which chiefly affirms the incomprehensible aloofness of God. Nevertheless . . . in the Augustinian *homo abyssus*, *Deus-caritas*, and *Deus incomprehensibilis* are given the fundamentals of the Christian Aristotelian type; while conversely in Aquinas the Augustinian passion for truth, with its "ideas of life" and its *Deus-veritas*, lives on.[260]

Notwithstanding the harmonious relationship between the two, they do represent two different emphases: the Platonic Augustinian on the relative *likeness* between God and the person, and the Aristotelian Thomistic on the relative *unlikeness* between God and creation. Przywara describes this situation as giving rise to a "dual kind of rhythmical motion within the one *analogia entis*."[261]

Ratzinger's fundamentally paschal notion of the relation between nature and grace can also be clearly seen in his first encyclical as pope, *Deus Caritas Est*. In this document, Pope Benedict lays out paradigms for the relations between *eros* and charity and between charity and justice. In relating charity and justice, Benedict delves deep into four themes: the nature of the human person, the meaning of prudence, the relation between social justice and ideology, and the relation between church and state. According to Stephen Fields, the relationality between these elements is indicative of and structured upon an implicit paradigm of nature's relation to grace.[262] The core of this paradigm, according to Fields,

259. Przywara, *Analogia Entis*, 10.
260. Przywara, *Analogia Entis*, 10.
261. Przywara, *Analogia Entis*, 10.
262. Fields, "Nature and Grace," 826.

is lodged in Ratzinger's understanding of the sacramentality of charity. Charity, as an efficacious sign of the church, is the pouring forth of the life of the Spirit, who conforms the church evermore to Christ's pierced side. As an efficacious sign, charity constitutes the essence of grace, the transformation of humanity that the church as the body of Christ offers the world, both directly through baptism and indirectly through the charitable activity of Christians everywhere.

Following de Lubac's work that the Second Vatican Council incorporated, Ratzinger posits the church as the prime sacrament that vivifies the seven sacraments as channels of the grace that leads to glory.[263] Fields points out that the notion of "universal charity" raises deep suspicions in Ratzinger, as he fundamentally considers it an ideal whose fruition here and now is as delusional as that of human perfectibility, as it can only be realized here and now by acts of concrete brotherly love.[264] Ratzinger's distrust of universal ideals by no means arises from an inherent cynicism about the futility of human endeavors in the face of unending problems in the world, but from the virtue of Christian hope that is grounded in the eschatology that powerfully shines through in the Gospel of John (and likewise in *Deus Caritas Est*). As Fields points out, the Christian must accordingly own a dual vocation, namely, to live for Christ in this age and for the age to come.

For Ratzinger, therefore, grace is both sacramental and eschatological. It is against the background of this concept of grace that he develops a flexibly analogical notion of nature. This notion, as we have seen, is that grace serves to purify (and perfect) nature, a concept that comes out clearly in *Deus Caritas Est*. Given the paradox of the Christian vocation, nature is both recalcitrant to grace, and yet charged with it. For Ratzinger, this means that until the full fruition of the eschaton, history will ever demand a *metanoia* within individual persons.[265] Thus, unless human freedom is truly and fundamentally liberated from sin, no social communion, based either on justice or charity, will ultimately prevail. This liberation obtains as a function of the church's sacramentality. As Ratzinger points out, unless mankind accepts God's gratuitous offer of friendship and redemption, even the most ambitious and humane solidarity movements will "succeed only in miring man more deeply in his

---

263. Ratzinger, *Principles of Catholic Theology*, 47.
264. Ratzinger, *Principles of Catholic Theology*, 54.
265. Ratzinger, *Principles of Catholic Theology*, 51–52.

tragic situation."²⁶⁶ For Ratzinger, the path deep into inward conversion is the purification that grace first offers nature. This path and "the path that draws [humanity] together [into communion] are [thus] not in conflict; on the contrary, they need and support each other."²⁶⁷

Fields notes that not only does nature need purifying from sinfully hardened hearts, but it "also stands in need of elevating so that it can ever more represent the kingdom that is to come."²⁶⁸ To enact this, grace purifies nature in two further senses. On the one hand, natural prudence, even when cleansed of sin, still requires further guidance. This guidance is supplied by the Holy Spirit's gift of counsel, which, according to Aquinas, inspires an intuitive sense of truth that transcends prudence's ability to assess options for action.²⁶⁹ According to Benedict, "faith enables reason to do its work more effectively and to see its object more clearly," and Catholic social thought is the point where "politics and faith meet."²⁷⁰ On the basis of the church's reading of natural law in the light of grace, it offers counsel to practical reason. This does not entail the church's direct involvement in politics but only that the church preach its understanding of justice. This understanding, according to Ratzinger, is natural, although evinced under the influence of grace. Reason can reach its own integrity under grace's influence, even when reason does not accept the truths of grace in an act of faith.²⁷¹

It is by situating nature squarely within the "Johannine tension between realized and future eschatology" that Ratzinger gives nature a "dynamic adaptability."²⁷² Even when nature is incorporated into the Kingdom by the church's justifying work, it nonetheless requires further growth and development. Even when justified and awaiting the fullness of its future transcendence, nature expands under the influence of prudence. Nonetheless, whether exercised by the Christian or the secular humanist, prudence must further dilate into the counsel given by the Holy Spirit, says Fields. By grafting the promotion of justice onto prudence growing into counsel, as set out in *Deus Caritas Est*, Benedict incorporates Aquinas's virtue theory into his Johannine development of

266. Ratzinger, *Principles of Catholic Theology*, 53.
267. Ratzinger, *Principles of Catholic Theology*, 52.
268. Fields, "Nature and Grace," 828.
269. Fields, "Nature and Grace," 828.
270. Benedict XVI, *Deus Caritas Est*, §28.
271. Fields, "Nature and Grace," 829.
272. Fields, "Nature and Grace," 829.

Augustine.[273] It is the Johannine *eros* of Christ's pierced side that inspires Benedict's view that nature, even when prosperously graced by wisdom, still needs drawing into the plenitude of love. From Christ's wounded side, love flows forth towards sinners, not asserting its rights, but offering only self-sacrifice. Buried in the church's sacramental mysticism, this love, which alone incarnates the City of God, so drives nature into grace that, for all intents and purposes, the limits between them will ultimately be lost.[274]

For Fields, the subtlety with which Ratzinger develops his own vision of love and justice in the light of the church's tradition and his reading of the signs of the times is bold, flexible, and nuanced. Fields questions whether this schema nonetheless leaves us questioning whether a state of pure-nature, disconnected from grace, exists. In other words, are there, in Ratzinger's estimation, a natural justice, prudence, and love that, conditioned by original sin, remain untouched in their origins by the gratuity of divine life? As we have seen, there are aspects of Aquinas's thought that can be interpreted as lending weight to such a theory; however, this notion has been challenged by more recent scholarship. Like his *nouvelle théologie* peers, Ratzinger understands nature and grace as "dialectically analogous," says Fields. Although nature continues to be riddled by sin and its effects, it retains "a plasticity" that expands under "grace's ubiquitous accessibility and likewise contracts under the influence of evil."[275] The Fall however was not so cataclysmic as to eradicate the vestiges in nature of the divine life. Consequently, postlapsarian nature retains some similarity with its former state. This is evident, according to Balthasar, because nature forms the basis in Jesus for the Word's Incarnation.[276] This event joins nature and grace into a unity-in-diversity, such that there can be no "slice of pure-nature in this world." Nevertheless, nature retains an analogous similarity with its postlapsarian subsistence. Ratzinger reminds us that although nature will finally realize the eschaton, it now embodies "the world [that] hates you, [even as] it has hated me" (John 15:18). The dialectical tension between grace and nature remains even while it awaits its future resolution in the eschaton. Consequently, although natural justice, prudence, love, and all other virtues can be practiced without a directly conscious connection to grace, Fields notes that their existence

---

273. Fields, "Nature and Grace," 829.
274. Fields, "Nature and Grace," 829.
275. Fields, "Nature and Grace," 833.
276. Balthasar, *Theology of Karl Barth*, 283.

is ontologically impossible without some connection, however seminal, with the grace that leads to glory. This connection cannot be conceived as such a theoretical remainder that it suffices for justification in light of original sin or that it discounts sin's perduring corrosiveness. At the same time, Fields notes that "it cannot be conceived as so diastatic that it loses its original congeniality with the Word."[277] It is, after all, the self-same divine *Logos* who redeems what his creative agency brings forth. It is he who restores the luster of nature's disfigured face by the beauty of his crucified and resurrected own. There can be no pure-nature that would render the Word himself equivocal. Derived therefore from a common source in the gratuity of the divine love, nature and grace originate in an analogy, Fields surmises. For Ratzinger, in the created order, nature and grace sustain this analogy in a dialectical series that accounts for nature's prelapsarian and postlapsarian states, its redeemed subsistence, and the anticipation of its finality when grace may be all in all (1 Cor 15:28).[278]

CONCLUSION

The challenge of secularization in the West remained of paramount concern for Ratzinger, and constituted, in his view, the fundamental issue for the future of humanity and the church. Part of Ratzinger's approach to dealing with this issue involved the encounter with culture by the church's gospel proclamation and witness in a dialectical process inspired by charity. Following de Lubac, Ratzinger was convinced that the limits of the neo-scholastic extrinsicist account of nature and grace, along with its dry, manualistic, and rationalistic approach to theology, proved wholly ineffectual in addressing these concerns. It is instead by means of a Christocentric, personalist approach to Christianity that the church has in her hands a much more potent tool with which to engage modern culture and to stand any hope in effectively bringing Christ to man in our own times. Ratzinger's "Chalcedonian" Christocentric approach, while eschewing invalid dualisms, seeks to hold in paradoxical tension the two polarities of the Incarnation and of the Cross, straddling what Ratzinger himself termed a "difficult synthesis," but one that, in our view he maintains successfully. This paradoxical tension (drawing from the *nouvelle théologie*), while eschewing any correlationist approach to culture on the

277. Fields, "Nature and Grace," 833.
278. Fields, "Nature and Grace," 833.

part of the church, nonetheless, maintains the value of Christian culture and the critical importance of the three transcendentals, appropriating a Przywaraian reading of Augustine. Ratzinger's work is deeply steeped in a Catholic humanism, an influence of the German Romantic movement no doubt, but (in his mind) nonetheless firmly anchored in the Incarnation. His many pages written on the importance and role of music, art, and culture evidence this fact, which, to his mind, proves to be theophanic. Being "wounded" by the experience of beauty, he thinks, can open man to reality, to the personal presence of Christ. It is this specifically Catholic Christian humanism that recenters culture eschatologically, always under the shadow of the Cross. Christ's taking to himself human nature is the event that affects every human being, and that means that all human existence is henceforth characterized Christologically. Ratzinger points out that a theology of the Incarnation, however, is too much on the level of essence and runs the risk of being too self-content, as it struggles to pass beyond the ontological phenomenon of God's becoming man. Importantly, because man's being is not pure essence, it follows that he only attains his reality by means of his activity, and that, therefore, man's being must be examined precisely in its activities. It is against this temptation to self-contentment in Incarnationalism that Ratzinger holds up the theology of the Cross as a necessary corrective, taking Christ's own being as the guiding star. It is the new Christological constitution of humanity that opens up a bridge between the theology of the Incarnation and the theology of the Cross. It is Christ's constantly lived kenosis, and his coming glory, that also provides the template for every human being, and constitutes in his own person, a new humanity. In living Jesus's unity of volition with the Father, man finds the foundation, the core, and the ultimate goal of his own being. It is therefore to be expected that in Ratzinger's theology we find an emphasis on dialectics over dialogue, on Revelation over personal experience, and on content over method.

Ratzinger cautions against the extremes of either "naturalism" (collapsing grace into nature) or "supernaturalism" (collapsing nature into grace) in the approach to the nature-grace debate. Working from Bonaventure's principle of *gratia praesupponit naturam*, Ratzinger shows that this axiom has been rediscovered as a saving power, an opening up of new possibilities of Christian consciousness in that being a Christian does not mean eschewing nature at all, but, on the contrary, heightening and perfecting it. This, for Ratzinger, is the fundamentally paschal mode of relation between nature and grace—that by means of man's exodus from self-sufficiency into self-donation in love to Christ, man's nature is perfected by means of God's grace acting in and upon him. Man remains fully human, but it is a humanity, a human nature, that is perfected, healed and therefore elevated. Ratzinger stresses that this fact evidences that Catholicism is a religion of "both/and," that is, spirit and body, God and man, nature and grace, as opposed to the short-lived, Jansenistic, Calvinist asceticism of the nineteenth century.

The principle *gratia praesupponit naturam* likewise gave voice to the *analogia entis*, and expresses the basic idea of the all-embracing, universal "yes" to the analogy of being, against a supernaturalist tendency, which supposed it was honoring God by crucifying man. Contrary to the Nietzschean sentiment that the Cross is merely the crucifixion of man, Ratzinger maintains that it is instead his true healing, saving him from the deception of self-sufficiency, and leading him to his true homecoming, the true cosmic harmony in which God is all in all. The Cross for Ratzinger is, consequently, not man's destruction, but the foundation of true humanity. The fundamental law of exodus, perfected in the Christian mystery of the Pasch, is the fundamental law of Revelation and also the fundamental law of the Spirit. For Ratzinger, the being of Christ is *actualitas*, a going forth, an exodus from self, in loving service, that constitutes true transformation. The Christology of being and the Incarnation must "pass over" into the theology of the Cross and become one with it: this stands at the core of Ratzinger's notion of nature and grace.

5

Milbank and Ratzinger Compared
Nature and Grace, Church and World

THE QUESTION OF HOW Christianity relates to postmodern secular culture, that is, Christianity's position within the culture, is a specifically Christian question. It would never have occurred to any ancient philosopher to enquire as to the position of Greco-Roman religion to public life or how it relates to the *polis*.[1] In ancient cultures, the "gods" pervaded every aspect of life, whether private or public. To question this status quo meant to question, and indeed even to endanger, the cosmic and political order. Those that did so found themselves labeled as impious enemies of the state and were punished accordingly. So much was the fate of many early Christians, and even of Socrates.[2]

Within the scope of Christian theology, as de Lubac has made plain, the question of how nature and grace relate to each other has direct consequences for the way in which a theologian will conceive of how the church should relate to the world—in this case, a Western world dominated by secular culture. Both Ratzinger and Milbank have been exercised by this state of affairs and have sought, in their own particular ways, to give a theological response to the perceived challenge that secularism presents to the church. Accordingly, we will see in this chapter how Ratzinger's and Milbank's respective approaches to the nature and grace question translate into their varying conceptions of both the status and

---

1. Kasper, "Nature, Grace, and Culture," 33.
2. Kasper, "Nature, Grace, and Culture," 33. See also Justin Martyr, *First Apology*.

genealogy of secular culture, and consequently how the church should understand and interact with the same.

In this chapter, we will firstly compare Ratzinger's and Milbank's respective approaches to the nature and grace question through the lens of participation and the *analogia entis*, followed by de Lubac's concept of the paradox and their respective adherence to, or departure from, the *nouvelle théologie* more generally. Following this comparison, and drawing upon these insights, we will turn to a comparison of Milbank and Ratzinger on the church-world relation. We will approach this question by firstly setting out their respective approaches to the issue of secularism, including an examination of their respective genealogies of the same. Following this, we will briefly examine Ratzinger's approach to *Gaudium et Spes* in order to further elucidate his approach to the church-world relation, then examine Milbank's notion of the church as Social Theory. A comparison of Ratzinger and Milbank on the question of correspondence theory and the value (or lack thereof) of the concept of secular truth for the church then follows. Finally, we will pursue an in-depth comparison of Ratzinger's and Milbank's approaches to the question of theology and politics as applied to the reality of secular culture.

NATURE AND GRACE

Participation and the *Analogia Entis*

As we have seen, Milbank takes the notion of participation to be at the core of Radical Orthodoxy's thought such that it forms its foundational notion. Indeed, according to Milbank, it is precisely Western philosophy's forgetting of the notion of participation that has led to the loss of meaning and depth in the world, the possibility of secular culture, and ultimately nihilism. The advantage Milbank sees in the notion of participation is that it eschews the possibility of any reserve of created territory apart from God in which secular culture might dwell.[3] As shown, Milbank points to Scotus as having caused the shift away from medieval ontology towards univocity of being and the rejection of participatory metaphysics and the *analogia entis* of Aquinas. Milbank's project seeks to recover participation as a foundational notion, asserting that creation does not stand alongside God, or indeed even *outside* God, but is, at

---

3. Milbank, Pickstock, and Ward, "Introduction," 3.

every moment, "suspended over the nihil" and held in existence by participating in existence itself. Scotus's univocity, in Milbank's view, opens up space for modernity because of the immanentization and subsequent flattening of the world, as opposed to the Platonic notion of *methexis*, which has led to the separation of the creature from the Creator, making possible a discrete secular order.

In attempting his synthesis of nature and grace, and in order to set up his counternarrative and genealogy against the secularity of modernity, Milbank draws from the Blondelian and Lubacian notions of nature and grace. In so doing, Milbank seeks to elaborate a suspended discourse of relational participation of the natural in the supernatural.[4] On one hand, Gonzales points out that this position opens Milbank up to attack from both sides, that is, that it wholly usurps philosophy and the secular sphere, allowing them no independence and autonomy from God; and on the other hand, the discourse is far more philosophical, cultural, and political than theological. This, as we have seen, however, is exactly the intention of Milbank, who attempts to propose a new sort of ontology, a "non-ontology" as it were, articulated between the discourses of philosophy and theology, fracturing both their respective autonomies.[5] Milbank's position bears a similarity to that of Przywara's analogical relationality between philosophy and theology. His view of non-ontology arises from an attempt to articulate a Christian metaphysical grammar that sees grace as inherently incarnational and thus needing history, culture, politics, and philosophy. Without the mediation of the same, grace would remain incomprehensible and without any real effect.[6] Milbank, like Przywara, can be said to be a theologian of culture and thus thinks about the mediation of grace. This marks Milbank's thought as a "between," "suspended," and "hovering" discourse that plays back and forth between the relational and participatory site of mediated analogical exchange, and as between philosophical and theological discourses. This site of non-ontological space between thus seeks to think of the event of grace as a "paradoxical mediatory interruption."[7] The interruption of the Word, in history, transfigures and changes all cultural discourses, but in a way that the Word truly and authentically mediates himself within these discourses, thereby fulfilling and completing them. This interruption,

4. Gonzales, *Reimagining the Analogia Entis*, 265.
5. Milbank, *Suspended Middle*, 5.
6. Milbank, *Suspended Middle*, 13.
7. Gonzales, *Reimagining the Analogia Entis*, 266.

Gonzales points out, creates a genuine Christian culture whereby Christian experience, thought, and practice are made incarnate (mediated), as grace does not destroy, but presupposes and perfects nature, and, in this case analogously, culture. This mediated interplay between nature and grace prompts Milbank to speak from both sides of the philosophical and theological divide. This speaking is never precisely a pure philosophical or a pure theological speaking. It is, rather, a speaking within the always already trans-natural and analogically relational exchange between the two discourses. Milbank's discourse, following Przywara, is thus a radically "suspended middle" discourse, one that is a thinking of the event of the "between."[8] Milbank, as stated, has recourse to a participatory analogical metaphysics. In so doing, like Przywara, he strongly believes that theology must be metaphysical, and simply demurs at the proclamation of the death of metaphysics. Milbank thinks, again like Przywara, that metaphysics must analogically participate in the theological and become a theological metaphysics. This means two things for his narrative counter-genealogy and the notion of the suspended discourse on nature and grace. Firstly, to hold a narrative-style theology does not mean that the metaphysical is excluded. Secondly, metaphysics is wholly necessary to narrative in order to explicate the beliefs in this narrative.[9] Milbank more fully develops the narrative impulse that is extant in Przywara's work and expressed in the latter's accenting of the one concrete history of grace and redemption. Milbank's approach essentially walks a fine line between a purely propositional and dogmatic understanding of Christianity, and a totally experiential interpretation of it. Milbank thus does not desire to establish a sharp distinction between narrative and metaphysics, because all stories are ultimately stories of being.[10] Analogical metaphysics is important for Milbank's narrative theology, because only an analogical metaphysics respects the harmony and mediation of unity within difference. This analogical harmonious difference is ultimately rooted in the trinitarian God, a God who is dynamic mediation. According to Gonzales, the Trinity is analogical insofar as the unity between the Father and the Son is given in and through the gift of the difference, which is the Holy Spirit. It is the Holy Spirit that opens a between that is a dynamic mediation of unity and difference.

8. Gonzales, *Reimagining the Analogia Entis*, 266.
9. Milbank, *Theology and Social Theory*, 392.
10. Gonzales, *Reimagining the Analogia Entis*, 268.

Contrary to the thought of Scotus, and in line with the Augustinianism of Przywara, Milbank affirms that man is a mystery, or *homo abyssus*. Furthermore, like Przywara, this inherent mystery is rooted in an analogical metaphysics of creation *ex nihilo*. The utter giftedness of creation does not make creation a "mere chimera" but, along with Przywara, the analogical paradox is invoked whereby man's relative and participatory autonomy is what allows man to share in creation and make the human world.[11] For Milbank, creatures can and do mediate, share, and pass on the good. This is what the *analogia entis* respects and proposes, namely, the utter contingency and giftedness of creation and the unsurpassable glory of God, as this God gives creation its own glory as a genuine sharing in God's glory. This notion finds its culmination in Milbank's interpretation of Przywara's *analogia entis* as bespeaking the same truth, and same reality, as de Lubac's *Surnaturel*.[12] As Milbank sets out:

> In his book on Barth, von Balthasar brought together de Lubac's account of the supernatural with Erich Przywara's restoration of the *analogia entis* to refute both a liberal theology starting from a human foundation below, and a Barthian commencement with a revelation over against a nature at once utterly depraved and merely passively open to the divine (in the sense of passivity "opposed" to human activity, not a radical passivity with respect to God in the heart of the active self). These two refutations imply a "suspended middle" and a non-ontology, since Przywara's analogy and de Lubac's supernatural belong neither to natural theology nor to doctrine, while at the same time they belong to both and encompass both. Natural analogies for God remotely anticipate even the divine essence, while the discourse of grace must perforce still deploy names that initially refer to the created order.[13]

Such remarks demonstrate the importance of Przywara and the *analogia entis* for Milbank's thinking, so much so that he uses Przywara's phrase (adopted via Balthasar), the "suspended middle," for one of his most important works. That is, an analogical discourse of the "suspended middle" as bespeaking the truth of the one concrete order of sin/grace and redemption seeks to think of the paradox of grace in its mediatory

---

11. Gonzales, *Reimagining the Analogia Entis*, 271.

12. Gonzales, *Reimagining the Analogia Entis*, 271. Gonzales notes that Milbank is here following Balthasar's bringing together of Przywara and de Lubac as set out in his *Theology of Karl Barth*. See Milbank, *Suspended Middle*, 31.

13. Milbank, *Suspended Middle*, 31.

and relational interaction with being. This is the heart of Milbank's narrative theology, namely, to overcome any and all dualistic understandings of nature and grace that result in the possibility of secularity. This means, as for Przywara, taking up a participatory analogical metaphysics rooted in the one concrete order of sin and redemption, where philosophy is shown to be insufficient unto itself.[14] Likewise, neither can theology deny or exclude metaphysics, as both metaphysics and theology (analogically conceived) become a thinking of the event of relation between the two discourses. It is a middle discourse, a between discourse of analogical paradox and, as such, it is true to both discourses in their inherent and historic relationality. Milbank's story is a Christian story and thus an analogical story of paradox, a story of the mediation of being through grace, and of grace through being. This mediation occurs within a participatory and performative narrative theology situated within the one concrete order of sin and grace and redemption.[15]

Ratzinger likewise relies upon the insights of Przywara (principally through Söhngen), specifically, the *analogia entis*, upon which Ratzinger's central axiom, *gratia praesupponit naturam*, rests. Ratzinger prized Przywara greatly. However, unlike Milbank, he draws attention to the fact of his understanding of the *analogia fidei* and how it is connected to the *analogia entis*. In line with his paschal notion of nature and grace, Ratzinger points to the Cross as the place of utmost coincidence between the *theologia analogiae fidei* and a *theologia analogiae entis*. Unlike Milbank, Ratzinger also does not specifically turn to the notion of participation to ground his theology. What is evident in Ratzinger's thought is a certain revitalization of Christian realism, based upon his conviction that the culture of the West originates with the creative power unleashed by commitment to Christ Jesus, Word of God.[16] According to Cirelli, the key to understanding Ratzinger's realism is the Platonic and patristic context from which it derives. This in turn is determined by a metaphysical vision of reality that is grounded in form (*eidos*). One finds in Ratzinger a focus on the transformation of the Platonic *eidos* from an impersonal principle of reality set out by Plato, to a personal and Christocentric principle of creative power as developed by the fathers.[17] According to Ratzinger, this transformation is the galvanizing principle

14. Gonzales, *Reimagining the Analogia Entis*, 273.
15. Gonzales, *Reimagining the Analogia Entis*, 273.
16. Cirelli, "Christian Realism," 709.
17. Cirelli, "Christian Realism," 709.

behind the creative forces that shaped Western culture, particularly regarding the understanding of the person and culture as *forma Dei*.

Ratzinger's thought is grounded in the *philosophia perennis et universalis*, that is, the traditional metaphysics that extended from Plato to the medieval and early modern periods. The identification of the Platonic notion of "form" with the person of Jesus Christ is for Ratzinger the watershed moment in the history of ideas and culture. This moment recognizes that Christ is not only the *Logos* but also the *forma Dei*, and hence the source of perfection of all beings. Christ is the dynamic, galvanizing center of human creativity. We are, in turn, performative agents of the *Logos* by virtue of participation, and so we are builders of Christian culture to the extent, greater or lesser, of our participation in Christ. This deliberately and specifically Christocentric emphasis is what makes Ratzinger's approach different from that of Milbank.

In essence, Ratzinger's realism can be said to be Platonic-patristic. This position demands that the Christian be able to believe in the necessity of form as the key to knowledge of the truth of Being, a knowledge that grasps form as the source of life for all beings. This belief permits one to know and understand (and thus interpret reality correctly), hence the turn to Christ, the *forma Dei*, rather than oneself, as the key to individual and cultural fulfilment. This understanding, taken up by the fathers, is the essential point in understanding Ratzinger's realism.[18] The fathers understood Christ to be creative reason, the *Logos*, for all creatures, since all have their being precisely through participation in him. Christ is the form of all forms, the perfecting power that makes things to be what they are precisely as the *forma formarum humanarum*.[19] In Christ, therefore, one sees the truth of all Being. The linkage of form and *Logos* in a personal rather than a purely speculative manner, however, is not unique to the Christian fathers. Rather it constitutes, according to R. M. Price, a cosmic vision common to all of the major intellectual movements of the patristic era, and indeed even of the entire ancient world.[20] Ratzinger's Christian realism should be understood in the light of this tradition, which asserts that man must continually turn to God in a continual act of love and adoration in order to find healing, sanctification, progress, and ultimately his perfection as a human being. The implication of this realism is that Christ, in perfecting humans (that is,

---

18. Cirelli, "Christian Realism," 720.
19. Cirelli, "Christian Realism," 724.
20. Price, "'Hellenization' and *Logos* Doctrine," 18.

making them saints), releases creative possibilities through those that work towards the establishment of the greater realization of a Christian culture. Without this Christocentrism, Western culture is in danger of being lost. For Ratzinger, Christ not only sanctifies and perfects human beings, but also inspires and enables them to create. This vision is at risk of being lost where God is not permitted in public life.[21] That the truth of one's being rests with God in his *Logos* therefore entails the necessity of turning to the *Logos* in an act of love, for only by this means can one be fully one's self, free and alive.[22] Ratzinger, following Origen, states that only in love, that is, only in a passionate observance of, devotion for, and availability to, Christ, can one know the truth of one's self.[23]

Specifically, the way and mode of being Christian for Ratzinger is by means of participation in a person, the Word of God, who constitutes the liberation, justice, sanctity, and salvation of all human beings.[24] It is only when human beings choose to open themselves to the infinite God who is *Logos*, and thus refuse to remain closed in on themselves as the fundamental way of being in the world, of being human, that culture will reach high degrees of progress.[25] Eschewing any form of Pelagianism, Ratzinger takes the point of Gregory of Nyssa that ever greater participation (*methexis*) in God is the key to development in individual and communal life, rather than obsession with our own activities. Relatedness to God alone, which is determined by loving assent, and takes the form of complete gift of self to God, is the way to effect positive change in human life and culture. In his General Audience of June 25, 2008, Pope Benedict cited Maximus the Confessor, noting that we must live united to God in order to be united to ourselves and to the cosmos, giving the cosmos itself and humanity their proper form. Ratzinger noted that it is Christ who shows us how to put all values in the right place. He states:

> We think of values that are justly defended today such as tolerance, freedom and dialogue. But a tolerance that no longer distinguishes between good and evil would become chaotic and self-destructive, just as a freedom that did not respect the freedom of others or find the common measure of our respective

---

21. Cirelli, "Christian Realism," 713.
22. Ratzinger, *In the Beginning*, 47.
23. Benedict XVI, *Church Fathers*, 39.
24. Cirelli, "Christian Realism," 713.
25. Ratzinger, *In the Beginning*, 45.

liberties would become anarchy and destroy authority. Dialogue that no longer knows what to discuss becomes empty chatter.[26]

Ratzinger concedes that while these values are important and fundamental, they can only remain true values if they have the point of reference that unites them and gives them true authenticity. This reference point, he notes, is the synthesis between God and the cosmos, the figure of Christ, "in which we learn the truth about ourselves and thus where to rank all other values, because we discover their authentic meaning."[27] It is Jesus Christ who is the reference point that gives light to all other values.

Ratzinger's linking of the Platonic *eidos* to the personal and Christocentric principle is a point of fundamental difference from Milbank. Whereas Milbank maintains the importance of *methexis*, he does not link it to any dogmatic principle or indeed even to the person of Jesus Christ in the manner contemplated by the fathers. For Ratzinger, however, what comes to the fore is a philosophical theology of the person that points to relational complementarity. According to Proniewski, Ratzinger's approach to philosophical theology is both original and creative because he argues that, based on his dialogical understanding of the human person, the individual must transcend him- or herself, because relationship and dialogue are as primordial a form of being as substance itself.[28] Ratzinger's theology of the person is also deeply biblical and highlights man's unique dialogical relationship to God.[29] Ratzinger turns to the personalism and existentialism of the twentieth century in order to arrive at an understanding of the human person. Basing his reflections on the assumptions of philosophical theories that understand the person as a finite being, Ratzinger takes Revelation (and thus, God himself) as the starting point of his theology. This personal approach leads to a concept of man that is based in theology and has its origins in the doctrine of the Trinity and the two natures of Christ.[30] Ratzinger's theology of the person is ultimately based on the biblical image of the person, which affirms man's unique and dialogical relationship to God, in which is found the essence of personalism.

---

26. Benedict XVI, *General Audience, 25 June 2008*.
27. Benedict XVI, *General Audience, 25 June 2008*.
28. Proniewski, "Joseph Ratzinger's Philosophical Theology," 234.
29. Proniewski, "Joseph Ratzinger's Philosophical Theology," 219.
30. Proniewski, "Joseph Ratzinger's Philosophical Theology," 220.

In contrast, one does not find in Milbank a strong notion of relationality or personalism concerning his notion of man's relation to God and the nature-grace couplet. The closest Milbank comes to a personalist notion is in his discussion about the "ontological gift-exchange" and the importance of gratitude on the part of man. What is lacking in Milbank's theological project is a strong conception of the notion of love as it pertains to the nature-grace question. Ratzinger was at pains to emphasize the importance of the love of God as the fundamental driving force in the life of the Christian and as the principle that stands at the heart of theology itself. At the vigil on the occasion of the international meeting of priests in 2010, Pope Benedict decried theologies that are satisfied to be merely academic and scientific and that forget the vital reality of the presence of God. This he termed an "abuse of theology":

> There is a theology that comes from the arrogance of reason, that wants to dominate everything, God passes from being the subject to the object of our study, while he should be the subject who speaks and guides us. There is really this abuse of theology, which is the arrogance of reason and does not nurture faith but overshadows God's presence in the world.[31]

Against this "arrogance of reason," Ratzinger contrasts an approach to theology that is instead motivated by a love that seeks to know more of the beloved. This, for Ratzinger, is the correct approach to theology, namely, that which truly comes from love of God, of Christ, and wants to enter more deeply into communion with him. He continues:

> In reality, temptations today are great. Above all, it imposes the so-called "modern vision of the world" (Bultmann, Weltbild), which becomes the criterion of what would be possible or impossible . . . . So, have the courage to resist the apparently scientific approach, do not submit to all the hypotheses of the moment, but really start thinking from the great faith of the church, which is present in all times and opens for us access to the truth.[32]

Leaving aside the fact that Milbank's writings are often criticized for being too complicated and obscure, they often lean towards a certain intellectualism that tends to treat God as merely an object to be studied rather than the subject of loving contemplation. One of Ratzinger's major

---

31. See also Ratzinger, *Principles of Catholic Theology*, 323–30.
32. Benedict XVI, *Vigil.*

strengths is that he kept the Bonaventurian notion of the *simplex et idiota* in mind as he developed his corpus.

Paradox and the *Nouvelle Théologie*

As we have seen, both Ratzinger and Milbank hold the insights of the *nouvelle théologie* and specifically those of de Lubac as fundamental to their respective theologies. Both authors share a disinclination towards neo-scholasticism and view it as not only dry and too formulaic but also as wholly inadequate to respond to the questions of contemporary man, and the challenges presently facing the church, especially that of secularism.

As stated, Ratzinger, unlike Milbank, insists on a Christological emphasis in his theology, borne out particularly by his turn to personalism. One does not find in Milbank's thought either a Christological emphasis, or indeed a personalist perspective. Milbank is far more conceptual and systematic in his thought, however lacking in dogmatic emphasis.

While both draw heavily from the insights of de Lubac, Milbank tends to radicalize de Lubac's position in his view of nature and grace and tends to see both as phases within a single extension. Ratzinger, on the other hand, while acknowledging an interplay between nature and grace, seeks to maintain more clearly than Milbank the integrity of each.[33] According to Kucer, Milbank's position on nature and grace reveals a marked tendency towards hylozoism, such that natural law and hylomorphism are seen as incompatible with de Lubac's "true intentions."[34] In this way, nature and grace in Milbank's view can be seen as radically integrated. Milbank is at such pains to preserve the gratuity of grace that he even goes so far as to state that grace must presume nothing, not even creation. For Milbank, it cannot be the case that creation *ex nihilo* established a pure-nature to which grace is later added, but instead, a "gift without contrast" was brought into being. That is, there are "modes" or "distinctions of gift" but there is nothing outside the economy of divine gratuity against which it can be contrasted. This radical understanding of the gratuity of grace means that God's gifting is radically unilateral, and natural spirit is linked so much to grace such that the possibility of pure-nature is totally eschewed. Milbank disallows even any relative

---

33. Kucer, *Truth and Politics*, 212.
34. Kucer, *Truth and Politics*, 212.

perfection of nature within its own order, as would be the case in a more moderate interpretation of de Lubac.

As stated, for Milbank, the way in which the natural and the divine are integrated are by means of "phases within a single extension."[35] This is particularly evident in Milbank's assertion that unless intellectual disciplines are "explicitly ordered to theology . . . they are objectively and demonstrably null and void, altogether lacking in truth."[36] The same is evident in his integration of the church with Christ, even to the extent of prioritizing the "place" of the church over the person of Christ.[37]

In contrast to Milbank, Ratzinger would wholly reject the notion of creation as being internal and external to God, and human correspondence a participation in God's internal creation. Ratzinger resists attempts such as Milbank's to integrate the divine with the created world. These attempts were prevalent after the council, according to Ratzinger, who states:

> The feeling that, in reality, there were no longer any walls between church and world, that every "dualism": body-soul, church-world, grace-nature and, in the last analysis, even God-world, was evil—this feeling became more and more a force that gave direction to the whole. In such a rejection of all "dualism," the optimistic mood that seemed actually to have been canonized by the words *Gaudium et spes* was heightened into the certainty of attaining perfect unity with the present world and so into a transport of adaptation that had sooner or later to be followed by disenchantment.[38]

Ratzinger cautions against two extremes in the nature-grace debate, namely, a certain "supernaturalism" that downplays the role of nature, and a "naturalism" that collapses grace into nature. Both extremes ultimately lead to the same end, which is either a minimization or a denial of the role and value of grace. Measuring Milbank against Ratzinger in this regard, we would concur with Kucer's assessment that one finds in Milbank a definite tendency towards a certain supernaturalism that

---

35. Milbank and Pickstock, *Truth in Aquinas*, 21.

36. Milbank, *Future of Love*, 306. Kucer points out that it is possible that Milbank could be in the process of modifying this extreme position away from hylozoism and the notion of nature and grace being simply phases on one single extension to a position closer to Ratzinger's, i.e., as parallel realties, each with its own proper integrity. So much was evident during his Stanton lectures in 2011.

37. Milbank, *Word Made Strange*, 158.

38. Ratzinger, *Principles of Catholic Theology*, 383.

clouds the clear distinction between nature and grace, and ironically, in so doing, undermines the importance Milbank attaches to de Lubac's notion of the paradox. Ratzinger's *gratia praesupponit naturam* stands as a helpful counterbalance against either a supernaturalist or a naturalist weighting in how one conceives of the nature-grace couplet. Ratzinger is at pains to emphasize that being Christian does not mean breaking with nature at all, but rather heightening and perfecting it.[39] This "perfecting" of course does not in any way imply that nature ceases to be itself, such that its own integrity might be compromised, only that it is perfected. Milbank's notion that every intellectual discipline must be *explicitly* ordered to theology runs the risk of compromising the integrity of the notion of nature, leaving only a resulting supernaturalism that, to Ratzinger's mind, ultimately, and ironically, only compromises the same grace that Milbank is trying to exult. Interestingly, even though Milbank acknowledges the role and value of the *analogia entis* and takes it as a starting point in his theology, his attempt to expose de Lubac's "true intentions" by going beyond what de Lubac actually says only ultimately undermines him. The idea of paradox, after all, is a delicate balance, and theologians can easily fall into either the supernaturalist or the naturalist camp without explicitly intending as much.

In this same vein, Milbank's equivocation of the notion of "participation" with "grace" is another instance of contrast with Ratzinger. As we have seen, in attempting to promote a "theo-ontology" and the notion of man's creaturehood, Milbank asserts that, in man, "grace goes all the way down."[40] For Milbank, therefore, nature *is* only insofar as it participates in God, and thus is suffused with grace. Everything, therefore, including all of creation, by virtue of the fact that it participates in God by existing, is said to be "engraced." It should come as no surprise that this position goes far beyond what Ratzinger would hold to be acceptable (likewise de Lubac). Milbank's notion of "engraced nature" seems to collapse into one not only the orders of nature and grace, but also, importantly, the notions of creation and redemption, such that the Fall is downplayed almost entirely. Milbank would argue that he pushes this line in order to preserve the notion of the gratuity of grace, and therefore is happy to risk eschewing further distinctions such as between creation and election, or creation and Incarnation. Ratzinger, however, would insist that, in so

---

39. Ratzinger, *Dogma and Preaching*, 146.
40. Milbank and Pickstock, *Truth in Aquinas*, 51.

doing, not only would the notion of paradox collapse into incoherence, but so also would the entire Christian narrative itself. The remedy to this is to reassert the distinction between created and graced participations in God's goodness, despite the fact that both have their source in God. As Levering has shown, without this distinction, one would be forced to conclude that the loss of grace by sin would mean the loss of the properties that make a person human, leading to a certain de-humanization. While Ratzinger does assert that those who sin "are living in untruth and unreality" and that they "stand in the sway of death," he would not go so far as defend a position such as that of Milbank.[41] For Milbank, sin and death are seen as distortions of creation's original harmony, and redemption in Christ is seen as the restoration of creation *as* creation.[42] Thus, for Milbank, the process of deification takes the form of "re-humanization" rather than a transformation in Christ by means of the Holy Spirit. For Milbank, God's original intent in creating the cosmos was creation *as* creation. This intent, he thinks, was fulfilled within creation itself, because creation originally already participated in the Immanent Trinity to the fulness of its capacity to do so. Thus, Milbank does not posit creation's supernatural destiny as exceeding the order of creation.[43] This means that, for Milbank, grace and the supernatural do not mean passage to a different order that exceeds that of nature. As we have seen, Milbank attempts at all costs to avoid undermining the notion of the gratuity of grace. While he himself cautions against tendencies in theology that attempt to either supernaturalize nature or naturalize the supernatural, it is difficult to view Milbank's approach as being anything other than the "supernaturalization" of nature, if there can be no possibility of exceeding or passing beyond to a different order. No matter how full of the supernatural Milbank construes nature to be, if there is no notion of passing to a different order, it remains but nature and not yet supernatural.

In contrast to Milbank's position, and seeking to maintain the distinctions inherent in the paradox, Ratzinger, following de Lubac more closely, would distinguish between the man's creation in *imago Dei* and

---

41. Ratzinger, *In the Beginning*, 71. Ratzinger not only conceives of the notion of sin as being the rejection of creatureliness and the refusal of truth and reality but also couches it in relational terms, using the Patristic notion of a rupture of relation between man and God, and man and others. See also Benedict XVI, *Spe Salvi*, §14.

42. Milbank, *Word Made Strange*, 229.

43. Milbank, *Word Made Strange*, 229.

the supernatural *resemblance* to which he is called, and which exceeds the order of creation. As we have seen, Ratzinger proposes a paschal relation between nature and grace such that grace salvages and fulfils what is truly human in man, perfecting it. This paradoxical perfection is expressed above all in man's call to supernatural love, exemplified by Christ's sacrifice on the Cross. Ratzinger emphasizes that any humanism based solely on man's nobility ultimately only leads to nihilism. Instead, he is called to a converted humanism based on the supernatural love of Christ. Nevertheless, Ratzinger reminds us that the abiding power of the created order stands as the ground of reality for man, and as a sobriety that is a safeguard against religious fanaticism and eccentricity. Ratzinger asserts that the genuine fulfilment of the cry of man's nature is a certain "going forth," which paradoxically is also the fundamental law of Revelation and of spirit, and which comes to fruition in man by means of the Cross. The Cross is the foundation of man's true humanity. It is in the humanity of God that we see the true humanity of man, and the grace that fulfils and perfects nature.[44] For Ratzinger, grace is that which purifies, converts, and transforms nature. Thus, in contrast to Milbank, Ratzinger holds to the principle that grace and redemption not only remedy the consequences of sin, but also bring humanity to the fulfilment of its supernatural vocation, namely divine filiation, and not merely to the restoration of its original state.

Milbank attempts to preserve the gratuity of grace so as to eschew any possibility of a reserve of pure-nature that might give rise to a phenomenon such as atheist humanism. As well-intentioned as this attempt is, Milbank pushes the Lubacian paradox beyond breaking point such that nature collapses into grace. This presents issues not only with respect to the integrity of the Christian narrative, but also with respect to beatitude and sanctification, which, as we have seen, are conceived of as discontinuities of state *within the same order of creation*. Thus, like Ratzinger, Milbank posits an essential continuity between human nature and supernatural destiny; however, unlike Ratzinger, Milbank states that both nature and grace consist in (diverging) degrees of participation in God. This means that, for Milbank, human nature (and indeed all of creation) is always already intrinsically raised above itself, while grace is always already reaching down to nature.

---

44. Ratzinger, *Dogma and Preaching*, 161.

This difference in principle between Ratzinger and Milbank also has implications for the way in each author conceives of the Christ-event. While both Ratzinger and Milbank (following de Lubac) would agree that it is within history (rather than outside or above it) that Christian theology finds the substance of its truth, and that God is constantly at work in creation (thus sociohistorical context is important), each has a different interpretation of the notion of the Christ-event's interruption of history. For Ratzinger, the Christ-event marked the turning point in the Christian dialectic, and an introduction of a new principle that transfigured creation. For Milbank, the Christ-event, while marking a discontinuity of states, does not entail a passage to a different order or a transfiguration of creation.[45] This difference, as we shall see in the section that follows, has major implications for the way in which the church conceives of herself in the world, and her role and duties towards it.

CHURCH AND WORLD

The Problem of Secular Culture

In his 1993 meeting with the Doctrinal Commissions in Asia, Ratzinger reflected on the meaning and role of culture and the challenge of secularism that was facing Europe and the West. In highlighting the origins of secularism, he noted that it was modern Europe that first originated the concept of culture in which it appeared as its own domain, distinct from, or even in opposition to, religion. After all, it was religion that determined the structure of values and thereby forms of culture's inner logic, formed its veritable inner core. Ratzinger lamented that by removing from a culture its own religion that begets it (in the case of Europe, Christianity) is to "rob it of its heart." Ratzinger noted that culture, as a general principle, has to do with knowledge and values, and marks an attempt to understand the world and man's existence in the world that passes beyond mere theory. It is, rather, ordered to the fundamental

---

45. This difference is also borne out in each author's respective notion of Revelation. Ratzinger views Revelation ultimately as the act of self-disclosure of the *Logos* to man within history. Milbank, however, does not accept that Revelation should be thought of as God's "putting new information about God and what God has done before our minds." Rather, it is an "intensification of human understanding, and a special illumination of the intellect." Ratzinger's notion of Revelation would for Milbank imply an unacceptable dualism between human reason and Revelation. See Milbank, "Intensities," 445.

interests of human existence, showing us how to be human and how man is meant to take his proper place in the world.[46] This question is not to be pondered individualistically, Ratzinger notes, because man can only succeed with others. Therefore, it is right and fitting that as a community mankind develop the understanding and knowledge that give rise to praxis, incorporating thus the dimension of values and morals. This fundamental enquiry, given man's nature, must include the notion of the divine. Ratzinger asserts that one can neither understand the world nor live uprightly if this question remains unanswered. Culture in the classical sense, he points out, means going beyond the visible and apparent, to actual causes, and thus the notion of culture, at its core, is directed toward God. Relatedly, the individual transcends him- or herself in culture, and finds him- or herself carried along in a larger social project whose insights he can borrow, continue and develop further. Ratzinger notes that:

> the common subject conserves and develops insights which exceed the capacity of the individual, insights which can be termed pre-rational and super-rational. In so doing, cultures appeal to the wisdom of the "ancients," who stood nearer to the gods; they appeal to primordial traditions which have the character of revelation, that is to say, they do not stem from men's probing and deliberating but from an original contact with the ground of all things. In other words, cultures appeal to a communication from the divine. The crisis of a culture ensues then when the culture is no longer able to bring this super-rational heritage into a convincing connection to new, critical knowledge. In such a case, inherited truth becomes questionable; what was once truth becomes mere habit and loses its vitality.[47]

Viewed in this light, one can see why Ratzinger thinks that the postmodern secular culture of Europe is in crisis. The fact that the West is beset by a culture that simply cuts off the notion of religion and the divine from public life and the common cultural consciousness means that, to use Ratzinger's expression, it has lost its heart; something essential is fundamentally missing. Furthermore, the inability of secular culture to

---

46. Vatican II Council, *Gaudium et Spes*, §53, wherein the council attempts to explicate the meaning of the world "culture": "The word 'culture' in its general sense indicates everything whereby man develops and perfects his many bodily and spiritual qualities; he strives by his knowledge and his labor, to bring the world itself under his control."

47. Ratzinger, *Christ, Faith and the Challenge of Cultures*.

recall its own "super-rational heritage" in the explicit form of the faith means that what has erstwhile formed the basis of its identity is now entirely open to question and deconstruction. For Ratzinger, faith itself is culture. There is no such thing as naked faith or mere religion. Insofar as faith tells man who he is and how he should begin being human, faith creates culture, and indeed it is itself culture. In eschewing this aspect, secular culture can only limp along with one leg, as it were, presenting to each generation the inheritance of the insights of rational inquiry (positivist, as it tends to be), but entirely leaving out the richness of religion and the notion of the divine. It is for this reason that theologians such as Ratzinger and Milbank, and indeed the church generally, perceive secularism to be such a threat and a challenge. If culture is meant to "show man how to be human" and how to "understand the world and man's existence in the world,"[48] then it is incumbent upon the church to seek to engage with this truncated culture in order to proclaim that it is Christ who reveals to man not only the nature of the divine but, indeed, who man is in himself.

Communio theologians such as Ratzinger have long held that the problem of secularization was fostered by the intellectual positions of the church's own scholars, in particular by the two-tiered or extrinsicist understanding of nature and grace that came to prominence after the Council of Trent. As we saw in chapter 2, this understanding underplayed the patristic heritage of Thomism in order to defend the faith within Kantian parameters, and by extrinsicist accounts of the relationship between the world and the church.[49] This same extrinsicism fostered the distinction between the secular and sacred realms, encouraged by Catholic scholars dedicated to a synthesis of the Liberal and Catholic traditions. Communio scholars generally argue that at least since the Reformation, Catholic theology has been set on several trajectories: nature and grace, faith and reason, the secular and the sacred, Scripture and Tradition, all of which have tended to be isolated and analyzed as separate compartments.[50]

In his homily during the Mass for the election of the Roman pontiff in 2005, Ratzinger, as dean of the College of Cardinals, expressed his concern at the regnant relativism of modern society, and sought to reassert that Christ remains the true measure for mankind:

---

48. For more on Ratzinger's theology of culture, see Casarella, "Culture and Conscience," 63–86.

49. Rowland, *Ratzinger's Faith*, 25. See also O'Shea, "Nature or Grace," 2.

50. Rowland, *Ratzinger's Faith*, 25.

> Today, having a clear faith based on the Creed of the church is often labelled as fundamentalism. Whereas relativism, that is, letting oneself be "tossed here and there, carried about by every wind of doctrine," seems the only attitude that can cope with modern times. We are building a dictatorship of relativism that does not recognize anything as definitive and whose ultimate goal consists solely of one's own ego and desires.[51]

Ratzinger was also greatly concerned at the challenge that forms of secular humanism present to the church, and remarked, also on the same occasion, that "we, however, have a different goal: the Son of God, the true man. He is the measure of true humanism."[52] For Ratzinger, an "adult" faith is not a faith that follows the trends of fashion and the latest novelty but is deeply rooted in friendship with Christ. It is this friendship, for Ratzinger, that "opens us up to all that is good and gives us a criterion by which to distinguish the true from the false, and deceit from truth."[53]

The current environment in which the church finds herself seems to be a curious combination of postmodern relativism, particularly in the area of private morality, and eighteenth-century Enlightenment conceptions of freedom and truth, which form the basis of the dominant political cultures of the West.[54] Ratzinger, particularly as pope, sought to navigate through the paradoxical waters of eighteenth-century-style attacks on the rationality of the faith, and the nineteenth-century attacks on Christian notions of human dignity and morality. He constantly sought to point out to his interlocutors that philosophy had always been nourished by religious traditions, and he was convinced that the church should never simply retreat (whether willingly or unwillingly) into her own ghetto, "[enclosing] men and cultures in a kind of spiritual nature reserve."[55]

---

51. Ratzinger, *Mass "Pro Eligendo Romano Pontifice."* See also Benedikt XVI and Seewald, *Benedikt XVI: Ein Leben*, 1074. Here, Benedict speaks about what he perceives to be a worldwide dictatorship of humanist ideologies, and an anti-Christian creed formulated by modern society. Those who resist this creed, he observes, are punished with "social excommunication" (gesellschaftlich exkommuniziert).

52. Ratzinger, *Mass "Pro Eligendo Romano Pontifice."*

53. Ratzinger, *Mass "Pro Eligendo Romano Pontifice."*

54. This state of affairs is perplexing because postmodernism tends to reject grand narratives, and yet it seems to comfortably, and uncritically, exist alongside ideologies such as neo-Marxism, scientism, and, indeed, even the fundamental Enlightenment principles that underpin secular society.

55. Ratzinger, *Christ, Faith and the Challenge of Cultures*. On this point, Nichols observes that when reason is made to subvert faith, it only undermines its own foundations and is locked within a certain positivism. The scandal is when theologians,

Where an author stands on the issue of the culture of modernity depends on how they view the genealogy of the same. There are accordingly several schools of interpretation of modernity, but most thinkers can be placed into one of three academic categories, which are not necessarily always closed or exclusive. The first school of interpretation views modernity as the severance of the classical-theistic synthesis: all that remains presently are free-floating concepts that have lost their meaning once separated from the whole. The second is that modernity represents a mutation of the classical-theistic synthesis, since key concepts, once severed from their Christian roots, are given new meanings. The third is that modernity is an entirely new culture based on concepts and values that were specifically developed to take the place of the defunct Greek and Christian concepts.[56] Milbank can be firmly placed within the second category, with his notion of the emergence of the liberal, secular state importing its own heretical soteriology. Ratzinger, on the other hand, as is typical of his unsystematic theological corpus, has not sought to present a comprehensive genealogy of modernity. What can be said, however, is that he has no sympathy at all for the third category (that is, that secular modernity is altogether something completely new), nor does he favor the Hegelian belief in constant progress to which it is closely allied. Ratzinger, after all, rejects all materialistic and deterministic theories of history. For Ratzinger, there is no "philosophy of history" in the strict sense, but only a Christian theology of history.[57] This was the position Ratzinger took in his *Habilitationsschrift* and echoes the position of Pieper, as well as that of the whole Christocentric trajectory of Balthasar. Revelation, for Ratzinger, is an event of total originality and the foundation of a new history that, paradoxically, is experienced as the end of all history:

> The beginning and end of this new history is the Person of Jesus of Nazareth, who is recognized as the last man (the second Adam), that is as the long-awaited manifestation of what is truly human and the definitive revelation to man of his hidden nature; for this very reason, it is oriented toward the whole human race

---

hoping to acquire parity with their non-theological colleagues by being good positivists, pursue a historicist reconstruction of the original meaning to their texts, and in so doing renounce the most distinctive task of theology, namely, the quest for the whole. As a consequence, students look elsewhere for a truer theology, finding it in the practical action of an option for a better-world future on the basis of the principle that orthopraxy precedes orthodoxy. See Nichols, "Joseph Ratzinger's Theology," 382.

56. Rowland, *Ratzinger's Faith*, 106.
57. Rowland, *Ratzinger's Faith*, 107.

and presumes the abrogation of all partial histories, whose partial salvation is looked upon essentially as absence of salvation.[58]

Ratzinger therefore rejects all philosophies of history that would find in the historical process some dynamic outside of the theo-drama of God's offer of grace and the human response to this offer.[59] He describes secular theories of historical progress, particularly the Marxist and liberal accounts, as examples of ideological optimism and a secularization of Christian hope.[60] Much like Milbank, Ratzinger rejects the notion that modernity can be completely severed from all Christian roots. It is entangled with Christian heritage irrespective of how much secularists may deny this fact. According to Rowland, Ratzinger offers a "double helix" genealogy with reference to two sets of three intellectual moments in which the Hellenic component of the culture was severed from the Christian and in which the Christian was fundamentally undermined by the mutation of the doctrine of creation. When faith in creation is lost, the Christian faith is transformed into gnosis, and when faith in reason is lost, wisdom is reduced to the empirically verifiable, which cannot sustain a moral framework.[61] Ratzinger identifies the first moment of severance with the philosophy of Giordano Bruno (1545–1600) and acknowledges that, at first sight, it might seem strange to accuse him of undermining faith in creation, but it was precisely his reversion to the notion of a "divine cosmos" that brought about the recession of faith in creation. He concludes that this is the authentic prelude to an increasingly prominent idea that the human dependency implied by faith in creation is unacceptable.[62] The second moment for Ratzinger arrives with Galileo Galilei (1564–1642), in which there is a return to the mathematical side of Platonic thought. In other words, the God of creation is overtaken by the God of geometry, wherein the study of geometry allows one to touch the traces of God. While this is partially true, the effect it had was to turn the knowledge of God into the knowledge of mathematical structures of nature: the concept of nature in the sense of the object of science takes the place of the concept of creation.[63]

---

58. Ratzinger, *Principles of Catholic Theology*, 155.
59. Rowland, *Ratzinger's Faith*, 107.
60. Ratzinger, *Yes of Jesus Christ*, 46.
61. Ratzinger, *Yes of Jesus Christ*, 46.
62. Ratzinger, *In the Beginning*, 84.
63. Ratzinger, *In the Beginning*, 84.

The third form of deviation from the classical-theistic idea of creation came with Luther, who, unlike Bruno and Galileo, went in the opposite direction, seeking to purge Christian thought of its Greek heritage, particularly the notion of the cosmos as it relates to the question of being, and consequently, creation. Luther's notion of redemption imports the idea that man must be liberated from the curse of the existing creation and thus grace exists in radical opposition to creation (in other words, he posits a radical separation of the orders of grace and nature). Ratzinger resists the Hegelian attempt to resolve this extreme dualism by a completely new idea of God and history, and does not accept, as Marx does (the greatest of the left-wing Hegelians), that redemption should take a political form.[64] For Ratzinger, man is created for worship (not work, as in Marx), and thus "the only goal of the Exodus was worship which can only occur according to God's measure."[65] According to Ratzinger:

> the danger which confronts us today in our technological civilization is that we have cut ourselves off from this primordial knowledge which serves as a guidepost and which links the great cultures, and that an increasing scientific know-how is preventing us from being aware of the fact of creation . . . [as a consequence] those who reject God's rest, its leisure, its worship, its peace and its freedom, fall into the slavery of activity.[66]

Ratzinger also identifies three moments in the subversion of the Greek strand of the helix, set out especially in his Regensburg address. Ratzinger focuses on Luther as the main culprit for the severance of the Greek component from Christianity.[67] Kant followed two centuries later, continuing the same program of severance. Ratzinger points out that the modern project of "dehellenization" first emerged in connection with the postulates of the Reformation in the sixteenth century. The principle of *sola scriptura* sought faith in its pure, primordial form, as originally found in the biblical word. Metaphysics, he notes, appeared as a premise derived from another source, from which faith had to be liberated in order to become once more fully itself. According to Ratzinger, "when Kant stated that he needed to set thinking aside in order to make room for faith, he carried this program forward with a radicalism that

---

64. Rowland, *Ratzinger's Faith*, 109.
65. Ratzinger, *Spirit of the Liturgy*, 16.
66. Ratzinger, *In the Beginning*, 28.
67. Rowland, *Ratzinger's Faith*, 110.

the Reformers could never have foreseen."[68] In this way, he notes, Kant anchored faith exclusively in practical reason, "denying it access to reality as a whole."[69]

Ratzinger also points to Adolf von Harnack's (1851–1930) contribution to the process of dehellenization. Harnack sought to distinguish between the God of the philosophers and the God of Abraham, Isaac, and Jacob. The God of the philosophers effectively therefore put an end to worship in favor of morality. Thus, according to Ratzinger, the scope of science and reason had been so severely narrowed that the question of God is made to appear to be either unscientific or, at best, prescientific. A third moment within this trajectory Ratzinger identifies as the anti-European attitude that surfaced in the aftermath of the two world wars, as well as with the rise of Asian and African nationalism in the 1960s. This has meant that the synthesis of Greek and Christian thought, while considered to have been an important project for the first few centuries after Christ, is no longer relevant to contemporary non-European cultures.[70] Ratzinger nonetheless believes that the relationship of faith to reason arose providentially from the junction of the Greek and Hebraic cultures, and thus is indispensable. The effect of Luther and Kant has thus been to force a choice between scripture alone and so called "pure-reason," meaning that Christianity effectively became instrumentalized moralism for those proceeding down the route of reason (which formed the basis for secular society). As we can see, Ratzinger's genealogy of modernity thus takes the form of severance and mutation, and that once the relationship between nature and creation and consequently nature and morality has been severed, the way is cleared for the Nietzschean project of the transvaluation of the Judeo-Christian heritage. This means that, politically, the result is that the church must contend with the argument that only Enlightenment secular culture can be constitutive for the identity of Europe—and the Western world more generally.[71]

Ratzinger emphasizes that the French Revolution was a watershed moment that led to the shattering of the spiritual framework that had formed the basis of Europe since its inception. This shattering had a major impact on both ideals and politics.[72] In terms of ideals, it destroyed

68. Benedict XVI, *Meeting Representatives of Science*.
69. Benedict XVI, *Meeting Representatives of Science*.
70. Rowland, *Ratzinger's Faith*, 111.
71. Rowland, *Ratzinger's Faith*, 111.
72. Ratzinger and Pera, *Without Roots*, 62–63.

the sacred foundation of both history and the state. Ratzinger notes that history is no longer measured on the basis of an idea of God that had preceded and molded it; instead, the state came to be understood in purely secular terms, grounded in rationalism and the will of citizens. The secular state here arose for the first time in history, and abandoned and excluded any divine guarantee or legitimation, declaring that God is a private question that does not belong in the public square, or is in any way relevant to the democratic formation of the public will. Ratzinger points out that public life accordingly came to be considered the domain of reason alone, leaving no place for a seemingly unknowable God, meaning that the question of religion belonged more properly to the domain of sentiment rather than reason. The question of God, and his will, became thus irrelevant to public life.[73] As Ratzinger points out:

> Since "secularity" also means free thinking and freedom from religious constrictions, it also involves the exclusion of Christian contents and values from public life. This exclusion leads to the tendency on the part of the modern conscience to treat the entire realm of faith and morals as "subjective."[74]

Ratzinger praises the efforts of philosophers and theologians of the last two hundred years whose insights were incorporated into the Second Vatican Council, and who had attempted to "open the gates that had divided the faith from the learning of the Enlightenment and embark on a fertile exchange between the two."[75] Such a position, however, would be entirely untenable for Milbank, who, as we shall see later, cannot abide the notion that the church can learn anything from Enlightenment secular culture.

For the strict secularist, religions can coexist with their respective rights (although it must be said that these rights are increasingly being eroded by secular states the world over) only on the condition and to the degree to which they respect the criteria of secularism, and importantly, are subordinated to it.[76] Ratzinger however believes that the church can never uncritically accept this state of affairs, which in effect amounts to a marginalization of the church. He points to the early Christians who

---

73. Ratzinger and Pera, *Without Roots*, 116. See also Ratzinger, *Yes of Jesus Christ*, 76.
74. Ratzinger and Pera, *Without Roots*, 116.
75. Ratzinger and Pera, *Without Roots*, 116.
76. Rowland, *Ratzinger's Faith*, 112. See also Colosi, "Ratzinger, Habermas, and Pera," 148–69.

would not allow Christ into the pantheon of pagan gods, nor would they accept the *polis* as the highest good. He states:

> In our country no one disputes the right of Christianity, like any other group in society, to promote its values and to develop its lifestyles, in other words, to function as one societal force among others. But this retreat into the private sphere, this inclusion in the Pantheon of all possible value systems, contradicts faith's claim to truth, which is per se a public claim.[77]

On this point Ratzinger is influenced by Robert Spaemann, who "speaks about the fatal tendency of the Christian Churches to view themselves as one part of the ensemble labelled 'societal forces.'"[78] This, according to Ratzinger, means a withdrawal of the church's claim to truth and thus cancels out precisely what the church is about and what also makes her "valuable" to the state. Ratzinger observes that, for Spaemann, the church must not fall back to the position of representing a "religious need" but, rather, must realize that she is "the locus of an absolute public dimension that surpasses the state under the legitimizing claim of God." Spaemann realizes that this same self-understanding cannot find adequate expression in the sphere of civil law, which presents a dilemma, as Ratzinger points out: "if the church gives us this claim, she no longer accomplishes for the state what it needs from her. Yet if the state accepts this claim, it abolishes its own pluralistic character and thus both church and state are lost."[79]

Ratzinger notes that in the Western church there has been a struggle to strike a balance between these two extreme possibilities. This balance depends on the freedom of the church and the freedom of the state, where the danger of erring toward one or another pole depends on the historical situation. Ratzinger is of the view that today the danger of a theocracy (at least in the West) is minimal, although he notes that the "misalliance" between Christianity and Marxism can lean in this direction with its notion that utopia (typically equivocated with the Kingdom of God) is to be created politically.[80] Ratzinger notes that faith's claim to be a public force must not be detrimental to the pluralism and religious tolerance of the

---

77. Ratzinger, *Church, Ecumenism, and Politics*, 206.
78. Ratzinger, *Church, Ecumenism, and Politics*, 206.
79. Ratzinger, *Church, Ecumenism, and Politics*, 206.
80. Ratzinger, *Church, Ecumenism, and Politics*, 206. See also Ratzinger, *Turning Point*, 88.

state. This does not mean however that the state is neutral when it comes to values. The state must recognize that a fundamental system of values based on Christianity is the precondition for its existence. In this sense it simply has to know its historical place and the ground from which it cannot detach itself without completely falling apart. The state must instead learn that there is a fund of truth that is not subject to consensus but rather precedes it and makes it possible.[81]

It is on this point that Ratzinger is very close to Milbank's notion of the fallacy and illusion of the claim that the secular state is neutral, and thus devoid of any theological presuppositions and foundations. In his November 2004 interview with *La Repubblica*, Ratzinger stated:

> [The notion of secularism] is beginning to transform itself into an ideology that imposes itself through political means and does not concede public space to the Catholic or Christian vision. [This vision] thus is at risk of becoming a purely private matter, and as such, mutilated. In this regard, a struggle exists, and we must defend religious liberty against the imposition of an ideology that presents itself as if it were the only voice of rationality, when in reality, it is merely the expression of a certain "rationalism."

Asked then what he thought secularism was, Ratzinger responded:

> Secularism is freedom of religion. The state does not impose a religion but gives space to religion[s] with a responsibility towards civil society, and thus permits these religions to be factors in the construction of social life.[82]

Similarly, in an interview on *Rai Uno* on Luigi Giussani and the *Comunione e Liberazione* movement, and reported in *La Repubblica*, Ratzinger said:

---

81. Ratzinger, *Church, Ecumenism, and Politics*, 206. See also Ratzinger, *Values*, 67–70. Here Ratzinger reaffirms this point and notes that the state is not itself the source of truth and morality. It cannot produce truth from its own self or via majority. It must receive from outside itself the essential measure of knowledge and truth of the good.

82. Politi, "Laicismo." My translation. Original as follows: "Comincia a trasformarsi in un' ideologia che si impone tramite la politica e non concede spazio pubblico alla visione cattolica e cristiana, la quale rischia così di diventare cosa puramente privata e in fondo mutilata. In questo senso una lotta esiste e noi dobbiamo difendere la libertà religiosa contro l' imposizione di un' ideologia che si presenta come fosse l' unica voce della razionalità, mentre invece è solo l' espressione di un 'certo' razionalismo . . . La laicità giusta è la libertà di religione. Lo Stato non impone una religione, ma dà libero spazio alle religioni con una responsabilità verso la società civile, e quindi permette a queste religioni di essere fattori nella costruzione della vita sociale."

> We must avoid a secularism that excludes the faith, that excludes God from public life and transforms it [the faith] into a purely subjective matter and thus also, arbitrary. If God does not have public value, and is not an instance for all of us, he becomes then solely a manipulatable idea. We must oppose, therefore, this kind of radical secularisation.[83]

Similarly, in his subsequent address to the participants in the plenary assembly of the Pontifical Council for Culture, Pope Benedict, remarking on secularism, observed:

> [Secularisation] is a fundamental issue for the future of humanity and of the church. Secularisation that often turns into secularism, abandoning the positive acceptance of secularity, harshly tries the Christian life of the faithful and pastors alike, and during your Assembly you have additionally interpreted and transformed it into a providential challenge in order to propose convincing answers to the questions and hopes of man, our contemporary.[84]

Here we see that Benedict admits of the distinction between "secularisation" and "secularism," with the latter presenting great challenges for the church in that it seeks to banish religion to the private sphere. Benedict is not consistent in the use of his terminology here, often using the term "secularism" to denote something positive, as we shall briefly see. The point however is that Benedict is prepared to admit of a certain valid secularity as opposed to a form thereof that is manifestly hostile to religion.[85] The fact that Benedict makes this distinction, or at least seeks to nuance the term, differentiates him from Milbank, who, as we have seen, does not allow that the secular realm could ever be valid. Benedict, in fact, in his interview with the French journal *Le Figaro*, states that "we are in favor of secularism, correctly understood." Benedict develops his point as follows:

> Naturally, the pope is also concerned about the ideological secularism that is manifesting itself strongly today. We are for [a]

---

83. *Repubblica*, "Secolarismo." My translation. Original as follows: "Dobbiamo evitare un secolarismo che esclude la fede, che esclude Dio dalla vita pubblica e lo trasforma in un fattore puramente soggettivo e quindi anche arbitrario. Se Dio non ha un valore pubblico non è un'istanza per noi tutti, diventa allora un'idea manipolabile. Quindi opporsi a questa secolarizzazione radicale."

84. Benedict XVI, *Address to Pontifical Council for Culture*.

85. On this point, see also Ossewaarde-Lowtoo, "Resurrecting Democracies," 224–49.

secularism [that is] correctly understood. But we are opposed to an ideological secularism that risks locking the church in a ghetto of subjectivity. This current of thought wishes that public life would not be affected by Christian and religious reality. Such a separation, which I would describe as absolute profanity, would certainly be a danger to the spiritual, moral, and human physiognomy of Europe.... It is necessary to understand—with full respect for cultural pluralism, religious freedom and sound secularism—that the Christian faith has something to say for common morality and for the composition of society. Faith is not a purely private and subjective matter. It is a great spiritual force that must touch and illuminate public life.[86]

In his address at the Elysée Palace in Paris, on the occasion of his visit to France in 2008 for the one hundred and fiftieth anniversary of the apparitions at Lourdes, Pope Benedict pointed out that Christ had already offered the basic principle for a just solution to the problem of relations between the political sphere and the religious sphere, citing Mark 12:17: "Render to Caesar the things that are Caesar's, and to God the things that are God's." He noted that the church in France currently benefits from a "regime of freedom," and remarked:

> You yourself, Mr President, have used the fine expression *"laïcité positive"* to characterize this more open understanding. At this moment in history when cultures continue to cross paths more frequently, I am firmly convinced that a new reflection on the true meaning and importance of *laïcité* is now necessary. In fact, it is fundamental, on the one hand, to insist on the distinction between the political realm and that of religion in order to preserve both the religious freedom of citizens and the responsibility of the State towards them; and, on the other hand, to become more aware of the irreplaceable role of religion for

---

86. De Ravinel, "'Haine de soi.'" My translation. Original as follows: "Naturellement, le pape est aussi préoccupé par le laïcisme idéologique qui se manifeste fortement aujourd'hui. Nous sommes pour la laïcité, bien entendu. Mais nous sommes opposés à un laïcisme idéologique qui risque d'enfermer l'Eglise dans un ghetto de subjectivité. Ce courant de pensée souhaite que la vie publique ne soit pas touchée par la réalité chrétienne et religieuse. Une telle séparation, que je qualifierais de 'profanité' absolue, serait certainement un danger pour la physionomie spirituelle, morale et humaine de l'Europe. Il faut comprendre—dans un plein respect du pluralisme culturel, de la liberté religieuse et d'une saine laïcité—que la foi chrétienne a quelque chose à dire pour la morale commune et pour la composition de la société. La foi n'est pas une chose purement privée et subjective. Elle est une grande force spirituelle qui doit toucher et illuminer la vie publique."

the formation of consciences and the contribution which it can bring to—among other things—the creation of a basic ethical consensus in society.[87]

In his 2010 address to the representatives of British society, given at Westminster Hall, Benedict also lamented the marginalization of religion in secular culture and noted that religion is not a problem for legislators to solve, but a vital contributor to the national conversation. Benedict voiced his concerns to those in attendance about the increasing marginalization of religion, particularly of Christianity, that takes place in some quarters, even in nations that purportedly place a great emphasis on tolerance. Benedict went on to note that there are those who would advocate that the voice of religion be silenced, or at least relegated to the purely private sphere. Also, there are those who argue that the public celebration of festivals such as Christmas should be discouraged, "in the questionable belief that it might somehow offend those of other religions or none" and that "there are those who argue—paradoxically with the intention of eliminating discrimination—that Christians in public roles should be required at times to act against their conscience."[88] Benedict concluded that these are worrying signs of a failure to appreciate not only the rights of believers to freedom of conscience and freedom of religion, but also the legitimate role of religion in the public square.[89]

As we see therefore, Ratzinger is no opponent of secularism that is rightly and properly understood. He instead laments instances where secularism becomes so aggressive that it seeks to banish religion from public life, relegating it to the private realm. Ratzinger recognizes that there are serious anthropological consequences to this:

> [A] society that turns what is specifically human [that is, religion] into something purely private and denies itself in terms of a complete secularity (which moreover inevitably becomes a pseudo-religion and a new all-embracing system that enslaves people)—this kind of society will of its nature be sorrowful, a place of despair: it rests on the diminution of human dignity.[90]

Along these same lines, in *Caritas in Veritate* §29 Benedict notes that the deliberate promotion of religious indifference or practical atheism

---

87. Benedict XVI, *Welcome Ceremony*.
88. Benedict XVI, *Meeting Representatives of British Society*.
89. Benedict XVI, *Meeting Representatives of British Society*.
90. Ratzinger, *Yes of Jesus Christ*, 76. See also Benedict XVI, *Visit to the Bundestag*.

in many countries serves to obstruct the true development of peoples, depriving them of spiritual and human resources. Benedict asserts that God is the guarantor of man's true development because man is created in his image and likeness, willed by God, loved by God, and not the product of blind chance or necessity. Benedict also warns of the dangers that economic development can present to morality and religion, distinguishing between what he terms "superdevelopment" and "authentic development." He notes that when the state promotes, teaches, or actually imposes forms of practical atheism, it deprives its citizens of the moral and spiritual strength that is "indispensable for attaining integral human development and it impedes them from moving forward with renewed dynamism as they strive to offer a more generous human response to divine love."[91] He cautions that in the context of cultural, commercial or political relations, economically developed or emerging countries may export this "reductive vision of the person and his destiny" to poorer countries. This is the damage, Benedict thinks, that "superdevelopment" causes to "authentic development" when it is accompanied by "moral underdevelopment."[92]

According to Chryssavgis, Ratzinger builds on Augustine, arguing that Christianity created the secular as a new phenomenon in history by positing a difference between religion and the state, thereby dethroning political theocracy and allowing for the secularity of the state with its lay character.[93]

In a 2001 interview with *Le Figaro*, Ratzinger emphasized that the notion of secularism must be properly defined. He noted that there is a positive notion of secularism in the sense that, as a new phenomenon in history, Christianity has created the difference by recognizing the distinction between religion and state. For Ratzinger, this distinction between the domain of God and that of Caesar is the source of the concept of freedom that has developed in the West. It implies that religion gives man a vision for his whole life, not just for his spiritual life. At the same time, the religious institution is not totalitarian: it is limited by the state. Likewise, the state cannot take everything into its own hands: it is limited by the freedom of religion. Ratzinger noted that:

---

91. Benedict XVI, *Caritas in Veritate*, §29.
92. Benedict XVI, *Caritas in Veritate*, §29.
93. Chryssavgis, *Primacy in the Church*, 813.

> The state is not everything, and the church in this world is not everything. Secularism is deeply Christian . . . . Political institutions and religious institutions have their own spheres. However, the fundamental values of faith must be manifested publicly, not by the institutional strength of the church, but by the strength of their inner truth. If secularism wants to exclude religion, it is a mutilation of the human being.[94]

For Milbank, however, to propose the notion that "secularism is deeply Christian" in support and defense of secular culture is a grave error. After all, Milbank maintains the notion that "once there was no secular" but now there is proof positive of Christian heresy.[95] As Hovdelien points out, Ratzinger is not here advocating for a theocratic government. Instead, he favors a "healthy" approach to the state without any attempt to "deify the church's role."[96]

Pope Benedict also notes that while the church faces a great challenge in the face of a rampant and hostile secularism, paradoxically, and rather worryingly, it exists also within the church. This secularization, he notes, is not only an external threat to believers, but "has been manifest for some time in the heart of the church herself. It profoundly distorts the Christian faith from within, and consequently, the lifestyle and daily behavior of believers."[97] Ratzinger observes that as believers live in the world, they are often marked, if not conditioned, by the cultural imagery that impresses contradictory and compelling models regarding the practical denial of God. The temptation, accordingly, is to think that "there is no longer any need for God, to think of him or to return to him."[98] Ratzinger notes that the prevalent hedonistic and consumeristic mindset regrettably fosters in the faithful and in pastors "a tendency to superficiality and selfishness that is harmful to ecclesial life," where the

---

94. Sévillia, "Exclure la religion." My translation. Original as follows: "L'Etat n'est pas tout, et l'Eglise dans ce monde n'est pas tout. Prise dans ce sens, la laïcité est profondément chrétienne . . . Les institutions politiques et les institutions religieuses possèdent leurs sphères propres. Cependant les valeurs fondamentales de la foi doivent se manifester publiquement, non par la force institutionnelle de l'Eglise, mais par la force de leur vérité intérieure. Si la laïcité veut exclure la religion, c'est une mutilation de l'être humain." For an example of the application of the principle that secular and religious institutions have their own spheres, see Ratzinger, "Church and Economy," 199–204.

95. Milbank, *Theology and Social Theory*, 9. See also Zatwardnicki, "Radical Orthodoxy," 121–47.

96. Hovdelien, "In Favour of Secularism," 241.

97. Benedict XVI, *Address to Pontifical Council for Culture*.

98. Benedict XVI, *Address to Pontifical Council for Culture*.

phenomenon of secularization "enfeebles the person and hinders him in his innate longing for the whole Truth."[99]

In his audience with Queen Elizabeth II, Benedict called upon the peoples of the United Kingdom to resist aggressive forms of secularism that also seek to undermine traditional values, noting that while today the United Kingdom strives to be a modern and multicultural society, the challenge is always to maintain its respect for traditional values and cultural expressions that more aggressive forms of secularism no longer value or even tolerate. Benedict emphasized the importance of never obscuring the Christian foundation that underpins the United Kingdom's freedoms, such that this Christian patrimony, "which has always served the nation well, constantly inform the example your Government and people set before the two billion members of the Commonwealth and the great family of English-speaking nations throughout the world."[100]

Ratzinger commented likewise, as prefect of the Congregation for the Doctrine of the Faith:

> We are living in a situation of great transformation. The ethnic composition of Europe is also changing. Above all, we have passed from a Christian culture to an aggressive, intolerant secularism. And yet, although the churches are empty and many can no longer believe, faith is not dead. I am sure that even in the context of a multicultural society, and amid great contrasts, the Christian faith remains an important factor, capable of providing moral and cultural strength to the continent.[101]

Referencing Joseph Pieper, Ratzinger warned of a kind of lethargy that is a symptom of secularization, particularly the banishment from public life of the Christian faith. In this way, Christianity begins to lose its characteristic of public obligation and a "profound, existential inertia" can set in. In the face of these challenges, Ratzinger reminds the church that it must have the courage to be bold and to underline the public status

---

99. Benedict XVI, *Address to Pontifical Council for Culture*.

100. Benedict XVI, *Audience with H.M. the Queen*.

101. Politi, "Laicismo." My translation. Original as follows: "Viviamo in una situazione di grande trasformazione. Denatalità e immigrazione—ci confida il porporato—mutano anche la composizione etnica dell' Europa. Soprattutto siamo passati da una cultura cristiana ad un secolarismo aggressivo e a tratti persino intollerante. E ciò nonostante, sebbene le chiese si svuotino e tanti non riescano più a credere, la fede non è morta. Sono sicuro che anche nel contesto di una società multiculturale, e fra grandi contrasti, la fede cristiana rimanga un fattore importante, capace di fornire forza morale e culturale al continente."

of its image of man, so as to be "salt of the earth ... light of the world, the city set on a hill."[102]

While it is obvious, given the many preceding examples that secularism was of great concern to Ratzinger, for Milbank, the same is of such great importance that it stands at the heart of his theological project. This is so much the case that Milbank opens his foundational text, *Theology and Social Theory*, with the following words: "once, there was no secular." According to Milbank:

> for several centuries now, secularism has been defining and constructing the world. It is a world in which the theological is either discredited or turned into a harmless leisure-time activity of private commitment.... And today the logic of secularism is imploding. Speaking with a microphoned and digitally simulated voice, it proclaims—uneasily, or else increasingly unashamedly—its own lack of values and lack of meaning. In its cyberspaces and theme-parks it promotes a materialism which is soulless, aggressive, nonchalant, and nihilistic.[103]

For Milbank, in premodern times the secular could not be considered a latent reality that was waiting to burst into the empty space created by the relaxation of the sacred in public life after the Enlightenment. Instead, as he points out, there was one single community of Christendom comprised of the dual aspects of *sacerdotium* and *regnum*. The *saeculum* in the medieval era was not a domain but a time that is the interval between the Fall and the eschaton where "coercive justice, private property, and impaired natural reason must make shift to cope with the unredeemed effects of sinful humanity."[104] Milbank rejects the notion that the secular emerged from the ruins of the medieval consensus and offers in his *Theology and Social Theory* a theological challenge to the standard thesis of the secularization of the West.[105] For Milbank, the secular is not simply that which is left behind once society has rid itself of religion and theology. This standard thesis, as Oliver points out, is that the secular is a sphere of neutral and autonomous reason that developed through the simultaneous retreat of religion and theology, meaning a *de*sacralization of public life. In other words, "the clutter of theology

102. Ratzinger, *Yes of Jesus Christ*, 76–77.
103. Milbank, Pickstock, and Ward, *Radical Orthodoxy*, 1.
104. Milbank, *Theology and Social Theory*, 9.
105. It is a noteworthy (but altogether unsurprising) fact that Milbank (an Anglican) eschews apportioning blame to the Reformation for the phenomenon of secularization.

and religion in antiquity and the Middle Ages was swept aside to reveal the cool, clear air of natural and autonomous reason."[106] For secularists, "desacralization" means clearing away the debris of superstition, ritual, and tradition that dominated medieval Europe in order to open the new possibilities directed by the neutral hand of reason, expressed above all in the natural sciences. In this way, the advent of the secular is seen by its advocates as a result of the inevitable progress of human knowledge and thinking. Milbank notes that secular sociology tends to regard Christianity not as the discernment of reality but as the *addition* of the sacred to an essentially neutral bedrock, and as such, it is a superfluous addition and not at all intrinsic to the natural order. As we have seen, Milbank follows de Lubac in diagnosing the inherent dangers of separating existence into dual realms ("bastard dualisms," he calls them) that stand over and against each other on a univocal plane (Scotus). For Milbank, like Ratzinger and the Communio school, it is ultimately thanks to the dualistic conception of nature and grace promoted by neo-scholasticism that the secular became possible. The secular thus is not a neutral, dispassionate, or objective view of the world and man, and had to be created as a positive ideology. According to Milbank, the modern notion of the secular imports its own assumptions and prejudices concerning human society and nature that are no more objective or justifiable than those of the ancient and medieval philosophers and theologians. Instead, "the secular" had to be instituted and imagined through theology, philosophy, politics, and the arts.

In this way, thinks Milbank, the secular is not simply the rolling back of a theological consensus to reveal a neutral territory where we all become equal players, but the replacement of a certain view of God and creation with a different view that still makes *theological* claims, that is, claims about origins, purpose, and transcendence. The problem is that this "pseudo-theology" is bad theology. For Milbank, secularism is, quite literally, a Christian heresy; it is an ideological distortion of theology.[107] He also notes that "the secular *episteme* is a post-Christian paganism, something in the last analysis only to be defined negatively, as a refusal of Christianity and the invention of an 'anti-Christianity.'"[108] This *episteme* in other words is not value-neutral. For Milbank, it is a prejudiced way of organizing our world and our thinking and is full of undisclosed

106. Oliver, "Henri de Lubac," 395.
107. Oliver, "Henri de Lubac," 395.
108. Milbank, *Theology and Social Theory*, 280.

value-judgments. Given the chance, it would impose its will upon us and exclude all other ways of being in and valuing the world.[109] This means that secularization is not merely a neutral observable process in which beliefs and faith-based institutions are supplanted by those based on science and reason alone. Milbank thinks the secular itself is based on a leap of faith, driven by authoritative pronouncements of worldly powers that find it convenient to relegate religious claims to the private realm, so as to neuter them.

For Milbank, secular liberalism is not a scientifically based, objective view of the world, but is, in fact, an alternate religion, one that cannot peacefully coexist with Christianity because it offers a fundamentally different view of the world. Milbank associates secularism with pagan religion, principally because of the fact that, like paganism, secularism is concerned with the worship of power for its own sake. It accepts the basic forces of the world as brute facts that are given by fortune, fate, or chance. That is, the self-interest of nation-states, the individual's drive for survival, the impersonal working of market forces are in so many ways like the will of the gods in pre-Christian Greek myth. All of these forces are not directed towards any harmonious vision of the good or any reconciliation of the different parts of our life, and exist as expressions of a blind will-to-power.[110] This blind pursuit of power however is nothing new, as Augustine had already made a contrast between the earthly city (in the form of the Roman empire) whose *Pax Romana* was achieved by violent conquest, and the heavenly city, represented by the church, which embodies peace without violence.[111] According to Milbank:

> secular "scientific" understanding of society was, from the outset, only the self-knowledge of the self-construction of the secular as power. What theology has forgotten is that it cannot either contest or learn from this understanding as such, but has either to accept or deny its object.[112]

Milbank claims that social science is anything but scientific (that is, based on empirical evidence alone and free of any ideological bias). Instead, social science only exists as the surface expression of a deeply questionable set of prejudices and ideas about value and truth. As

---

109. Shakespeare, *Radical Orthodoxy: Critical Introduction*, 9.
110. Shakespeare, *Radical Orthodoxy: Critical Introduction*, 9.
111. Shakespeare, *Radical Orthodoxy: Critical Introduction*, 10.
112. Milbank, *Theology and Social Theory*, 10.

Shakespeare points out, by bracketing out ideas of the transcendent, divine or supernatural, it presents us with a world that makes sense without reference to the truth claims of theology or the reality of grace. This it can only do, however, by supplanting the idea of God with some other overriding order or principle, in order to ensure that secular knowledge can be said to have a foundation. Such examples may include Darwinism, capitalist theory, blind forces of nature, self-interest, Marxism and the "inevitable march of history" towards civilization or revolution, and so on. As Milbank notes, in each case, what are supposed to be neutral facts accessible to any reasonable observer are revealed rather to be value judgments asserted with all the dogmatism that one would otherwise associate with religious fundamentalism. This, for Milbank, reveals that, at bottom, these overriding orders or principles are founded on nothing other than the force of power, violence, and domination itself.[113] This is why he applies the couplet "ontology of violence" versus "ontology of peace" to secular culture and the church, respectively. For Milbank, the Enlightenment dream of unbiased reason and universal values, free from interminable theological squabbles and wars of religion, ironically shelters a horrible violence in its heart. As Milbank points out, the so-called "age of progress" has been incredibly violent. As history attests, this dream coexists with European imperialism, racism, concentration camps, gulags, and ultimately genocide. Nazi paganism and Stalinist "scientific" socialism are but the most obvious examples of what happens when all value and truth are located in the power games of the world, and human value and dignity are forgotten. For Milbank, Kantian liberal humanist logic and Nazi logic are seamlessly linked, whereby Nazism was nothing but an unhindered attempt to raise man as a god "to unleash and perfect the power of human freedom," and "the Holocaust was the supreme consummation of secularity."[114]

Milbank therefore seeks to challenge the orthodoxy of the academy, that is, that secularity offers a purely objective, neutral account of human life untainted by faith perspectives. Milbank sees the notion of the secular as a *mythos*—and a late one at that.[115] Rejecting modern dualisms (particularly as between nature and grace) and the myth of the neutrality of secularity allows theology in mainstream discourse to be "unapologetically confessional" and Christian research across the disciplines to be

113. Shakespeare, *Radical Orthodoxy: Critical Introduction*, 13.
114. Milbank, *Being Reconciled*, 179–80.
115. Smith, *Introducing Radical Orthodoxy*, 74.

"unapologetically theological." Milbank hopes that once the theoretical foundations of secularity are dismantled (and demonstrated as such) the spaces for public discourse (in both politics and in the academy) will provide new opportunities for the expression of a properly theological (Christian) account of reality.[116]

As we have seen, Ratzinger is prepared to accept a certain form of secularity that may be considered valid. He makes a distinction between a form of benign secularism that he terms "positive" and "healthy," and an aggressive secularism that seeks to drive the church out of the public sphere.[117] Milbank, on the other hand, draws no such distinction, and views any form of secularism as hostile, violent, and essentially the product of Christian heresy. Milbank would say that Ratzinger has not "correctly understood" the challenge of secularism and in admitting any validity whatsoever for the secular is merely to add legitimacy to the errors of Scotus. Milbank would also view Ratzinger's attempts to draw a distinction between forms of valid and invalid secularism as an unacceptable concession to a culture that is fundamentally flawed from its inception. Ratzinger, on the other hand, would say that Milbank has collapsed nature into grace, in effect supernaturalizing nature, and as such, taken de Lubac and the *nouvelle théologie* too far.

The Church and Correspondence Theory

Ratzinger on Gaudium et Spes

In his *Principles of Catholic Theology*, Ratzinger lamented that "despite many attempts to clarify it in section two of *Gaudium et spes*, [the concept of the world] continues to be used in a pre-theological stage." According to Ratzinger:

> by "world" the Council means the counterpart of the church. The purpose of the text is to bring the two into a relationship of cooperation, the goal of which is the "reconstruction of the

---

116. Smith, *Introducing Radical Orthodoxy*, 74.

117. While acknowledging the challenges that Christianity is facing there, an example of "positive secularism" for Ratzinger is the United States of America, where "the religious sphere . . . acquires a significant weight in public affairs and emerges as a pre-political and supra-political force with the potential to have a decisive impact on political life." See Ratzinger and Pera, *Without Roots*, 72. In contrast to this, Ratzinger could be said to have had France in mind in speaking of a secularism that is unhealthy. See Fourest, "Piège."

world." The church cooperates with the world in order to build up the world—it is thus that we might characterize the vision that informs the text.[118]

Ratzinger notes however that it is not clear whether the world that cooperates and the world that is to be built up are one and the same world. This is because, he points out, what is intended by the word "world" is not clear in every instance. What seems, however, to be clear is that the authors, speaking for the church, were acting on the assumption that they themselves were not the world, but its counterpart. The authors also took the view that the church had a relationship to the world that was, in fact, unsatisfactory, where it existed at all. Ratzinger notes:

> To that extent, we must admit, the text represents a kind of ghetto mentality. The church is understood as a closed entity, but she is striving to remedy the situation. By "world," it would seem, the document understands the whole scientific and technical reality of the present and all those who are responsible for it or who are at home in its mentality.[119]

This definition of the notion of "world" gives the impression of a concept that embraces all those social institutions in which the church has little or no influence. Consequently, *Gaudium et Spes* sounds like "a plea from the ghetto" to be offered the occasional invitation into the hallowed halls of secular academies.[120] In the view of E. Michael Jones, the council occurred at the "high-noon of the Catholic inferiority complex" and at a moment in history when Catholic intellectuals, tired of being regarded as reactionary and anti-intellectual, "lusted after modernity."[121] Ratzinger points out that *Gaudium et Spes* appeared to be operating within not only a church-world dualism but also a church-humanity dualism. Ratzinger also laments the use of the term *genus humanum* to refer to the church's dialogue partner in the modern world.[122] He notes that the church is part of the *genus humanum* and, therefore, cannot be contradistinguished from it. For Ratzinger:

> the church meets its *vis-à-vis* in the human race . . . . But it cannot exclude itself from the human race and then artificially

---

118. Ratzinger, *Principles of Catholic Theology*, 379–80.
119. Ratzinger, *Principles of Catholic Theology*, 379–80.
120. Rowland, "World," 116. See also Ratzinger, *Theological Highlights*, 9.
121. Jones, *Living Machines*, 42.
122. Rowland, "World," 116.

> create a solidarity which in any case is the church's lot. The lack of understanding shown in this matter by those who drafted the text can probably only be attributed to the deeply rooted extrinsicism of ecclesiastical thought, to long acquaintance with the church's exclusion from the general course of development and to a retreat into a special little ecclesiastical world from which an attempt is then made to speak to the rest of the world.[123]

At the foundation of the "deeply rooted extrinsicism" of which Ratzinger speaks is a tendency to think of the church canonically or bureaucratically rather than mystically, and in so doing, to presume an ecclesiology based more on the Tridentine-era theology of Bellarmine than the multi-dimensional outlook one finds in de Lubac and Balthasar upon which postconciliar Communio theology was built.[124] He continues:

> The text of this article was particularly hotly disputed, precisely because it involved a decision about the whole theological approach and therefore the structure of the entire schema . . . . Nevertheless it seemed to many people, especially theologians from German-speaking countries, that there was not a radical enough rejection of a doctrine of man divided into philosophy and theology. They were convinced that fundamentally the text was still based on a schematic representation of nature and the supernatural viewed far too much as merely juxtaposed.[125]

Both de Lubac and Balthasar preferred to present the church as a "symphonic interplay" of "different spiritual missions and relationships."[126] For Ratzinger, the conclusion to be drawn from Communio ecclesiology (which he thought was one of the great advances of the Second Vatican Council) is that any assessment of the relationship between the church and the world requires something much more theologically complex than a merely juridical understanding of the church and a merely sociological understanding of the world.[127] In the early 1960s, when Communio ecclesiology was still in its infancy, those responsible for drafting *Gaudium et Spes* struggled to articulate a coherent analytical framework for a subject as complex as the church's relationship with the world. In his commentary on *Gaudium et Spes*, Ratzinger noted that §2 of the Zurich

---

123. Ratzinger, "Dignity," 119.
124. Rowland, "World," 117.
125. Ratzinger, "Dignity," 119.
126. Rowland, "World," 117.
127. Rowland, "World," 117.

text of the document had attempted to justify the whole notion of the church's dialogue with the world by means of the scriptural reference to reading the "signs of the times" (Matt 16:3; Luke 12:56). An earlier draft had regarded epochs as a sign and a voice to the extent that they involve God's presence or absence, and consequently it was argued that the voice of the age must be regarded as the voice of God.[128]

In response, Ratzinger argues that it would have been much better to begin *Gaudium et Spes* with the notion of Revelation in Christ. This would have demonstrated that even a construction such as "pure-reason" ultimately depends on theological presuppositions. The mystery of the Incarnation is not a superfluous addition to the secular description of an otherwise perfectly self-sufficient humanity. The two-tiered neo-scholastic presuppositions that Ratzinger objects to are evidenced when examining *Gaudium et Spes* §36 in isolation, because it advocates in favor of the "autonomy of earthly affairs."[129] While it is true that Aquinas does state that creation is endowed with stability, goodness, and order on its own, he cautions that at the same time, varying degrees of stability, goodness and order exist. This relative goodness does not come about on its own but is created by the triune God. The world on its own evidences "vestigia," that is, traces of the Trinity as Augustine had argued in *De Trinitate*.[130]

It is because of this notion of creation's goodness and stability that those who read *Gaudium et Spes* as the church's embrace of the culture of modernity claim the authority of Aquinas (normally, via Rahner) to support their position and suggest that those who oppose this reading *de facto* operate according to an Augustinian or some other non-Thomist line.[131] This reading however ignores Aquinas's starting point of cre-

---

128. Rowland, "World," 118.

129. Gaál, *Theology of Pope Benedict XVI*, 107.

130. Gaál, *Theology of Pope Benedict XVI*, 108. For a contrasting view, see Kasper, "Theological Anthropology," 129–40.

131. Rowland, *Ratzinger's Faith*, 35. As we saw in chapter 2, given Aquinas's lack of ultimate clarity on the matter, it seems that he can be adduced in support of either an intrinsicist or an extrinsicist relationship between nature and grace. Those advocating for the "autonomy" of earthly affairs, strictly speaking, are adhering to a more extrinsicist position. An example of the Augustine/Aquinas dichotomy can be found in Komonchak, "Vatican II," 86. It must, however, be noted that here Komonchak does acknowledge the fact that the traditional opposition thought to exist between Augustinians and Thomists might not be entirely fair and risks being a "considerable oversimplification." I would also point out that neither the Augustinian nor the Thomistic traditions can be considered to be monolithic, and that there are numerous contemporary Thomists

ation and emphasizes only the secondary clause, which exudes, when severed from this fundamental starting point, a radical autonomy and extrinsicism. Reading Aquinas in this way can be used in extreme cases as a basis for the creature to turn his back on the Creator while pursing autonomous or "purely natural" ends. This clause, regrettably, is also commonly taken to mean that there is no relationship between theology and politics, economics, and the other social sciences. According to Kasper, for example, *Gaudium et Spes* was the "church's recognition of the autonomy of secular fields of activity" and that the council had accepted the "fundamental concept of the modern age" that "secular matters are to be decided in a secular fashion, political matters in a political fashion, economic matters in an economic fashion."[132] As we shall see, such a position is wholly untenable for Milbank.[133]

Paradoxically (without further qualifications), such a reading requires a neo-scholastic extrinsicism, and an almost extreme severance of the church from the world, even though, ironically, *Gaudium et Spes* is regarded as a general call to Catholics to be more engaged in the life of the world. More significantly, such a view is inconsistent with the Thomistic understanding of the hierarchical arrangement of goodness in the cosmos, such that individual goods are ordered toward their final good in God.[134] Both Augustine and Aquinas emphasize the notion of the analogy of being and a related hierarchy of goodness.[135] There is arguably no suggestion in their thought of an extrinsicist separation of nature and grace and, consequently, of the sacred and the secular. As demonstrated earlier,

---

who remain critical of *Gaudium et Spes*. See also Komonchak, "Augustine," 109, 112; and Komonchak, "Church in Crisis." For a counter point to Rowland's position, see Komonchak, "Postmodern Augustinian Thomism," 123–46. For a neo-Thomist reading of the reputed differences between Augustine and Aquinas, see Fortin, *Classical Christianity*. For further commentary on this issue, which goes beyond the scope of the present work, see Rowland, *Culture of the Incarnation*, particularly chapter 3. Rowland here notes that these two trajectories—on the one hand, the suppression of the patristic dimension of Aquinas (in favor of man's rational will and intelligence, i.e., separating philosophical Aquinas from theological Aquinas), and on the other, a neo-Manichean reading of Augustine—"are on the wane in contemporary scholarship, though they continue to be presented as popular caricatures of the two traditions."

132. Kasper, "Nature, Grace, and Culture," 4.

133. Milbank's specific mentions of *Gaudium et Spes* are very few; see, e.g., Milbank, "How Democracy Devolves." Consistent with his non-correlationist approach, Milbank here is critical of the Second Vatican Council, and specifically of *Gaudium et Spes*, for being "over-accepting of modern liberal democracy and market economics."

134. Rowland, *Ratzinger's Faith*, 35.

135. Aquinas, *Summa Theologica*, I, q. 85; Augustine, *Trinity: Trinitate*, VI, 12.

anyone influenced by de Lubac, such as Ratzinger, would not accept that an extrinsicist reading is possible on a proper reading of Aquinas. Similarly, anyone who wishes to read *Gaudium et Spes* as endorsing a simplistic correlationist accommodating of the church to the culture of modernity would be relying on the same account of nature and grace as defended by the likes of Garrigou-Lagrange. This notion illustrates what de Lubac controversially saw to be two sides of the same coin, namely, that the turn-of-the-century modernists and the neo-scholastics were operating from the same nature and grace first principles. To assert the necessity of a radical autonomy of the world from the church, would mean that dialogue ends in each sphere speaking to itself.[136] A non-theological reading of parts of *Gaudium et Spes* (particularly §36) may lead to a false optimism concerning the ability of the world to perfect its ways without grace. This is evidenced by the fact that some argued, after the document's publication, that the church had recognized the inherent goodness of modern culture. For others, the sacraments could be considered to be mere customs. This interpretation was favored by many in France who considered it to be the church's final accommodation of the nation's laicist constitution and of the French Revolution, whereas in Germany, the nineteenth-century *Kulturkampf* was considered definitively over, with Catholic Germans becoming mainstream Germans.[137] The notion of the utopia of a good world achieved without God was popularized in Germany in the 1960s by the Marxist philosopher Ernst Bloch (who, while not strictly a member of the Frankfurt School, nonetheless enjoyed a certain influence with them) in his three-volume compendium, *The Principle of Hope*. He was very much an ally of the 1968 movement, more even than Herbert Marcuse. Ratzinger saw in this work the looming danger of a deified society and self-perfecting history. Proponents of political theology (most notably, Johann Baptist Metz and Juan Luis Segundo) supported a proletarian revolution and naturally thought that *Gaudium et Spes* justified such a new view, which inaugurated a definitive break with Pius IX's unqualified opposition to modernity. In contrast to this, Ratzinger saw that *Gaudium et Spes* §22 was stating that the remedy for all of mankind is Christ, and it is likewise the responsibility of the church to administer this medication.[138]

According to Fields, following *Gaudium et Spes*, Ratzinger posits a correct and appropriate autonomy to nature and to grace, and likewise,

136. Rowland, *Ratzinger's Faith*, 36.
137. Gaál, *Theology of Pope Benedict XVI*, 150.
138. Gaál, *Theology of Pope Benedict XVI*, 150.

to the church and to the secular order. In exploring this autonomy, Ratzinger hearkens to a framework broadly put forth in Augustine's *De Civitate Dei*. That is, the church embodies the divine city as its sacramental image in history, where it is nonetheless placed squarely in the midst of the secular city, which is deeply marred by "traducianism." For Augustine, the church stands as an uncompromising alternative to an alien and hostile world and serves as a refuge from it. Nevertheless, as Fields notes, Augustine envisages a salutary traffic between nature and grace. That is, sinful members of the human city can nevertheless occupy positions in the church and rightly order it, and likewise, sanctified members of the church can perform the same function in the human city.[139] This demonstrates that the effects of original sin are ubiquitous, strewn even throughout the church, which nonetheless offers the means of *metanoia*. Converted people, availing themselves directly of the means of grace, can strengthen the vestigial presence of divine providence in the human city's natural order, but ultimate love lodges in the church as the representation of the heavenly city that is still fully to come. Individuals fortified by grace are thus able to draw forth and strengthen what Aquinas calls the good of utility, in that they lead natural human virtue "ever closer to the baptism that justifies."[140]

While Augustine beheld the world as something transitory and only the *Civitas Dei* as worth celebrating, it was Joachim of Fiore who paved the way to the "immanentisation of the eschaton." This led to the notion of "progress," a presumption to which numerous socialists and liberal capitalists subscribe.[141] De Gaál notes that two tendencies continue to emerge in Ratzinger's thought. All attempts to create a perfect society devoid of a notion of transcendence are doomed to bring about an impersonal society beholden to economic or political perfectionism, disregarding the inalienable dignity of the individual human person and society as one of mutual respect and solidarity. This insight confirms the need for Christianity to play a foundational role in modern society as the latter strives to bring about a just and harmonious society. The understanding of a tension-filled relationship between the body politic and the church is specific to the Catholic vision of the church-state relation, but

---

139. Fields, "Nature and Grace," 831.

140. Fields, "Nature and Grace," 831. See also Lee, "Benedict XVI and Modernity," 89–110.

141. Gaál, *Theology of Pope Benedict XVI*, 149.

in Ratzinger's mind, it is indebted in a particular way to Augustine.[142] As Ratzinger argued in his doctoral dissertation, "The People of God and God's House in Augustine's Doctrine of the Church," the tension between temporality and celestial permanence is not resolved but restated. *De Civitate Dei* is Ratzinger's guide in relating to modern society. His thesis is that the City of Man and the City of God can never be conflated. This world necessarily remains incomplete and imperfect. To ignore this fact ultimately only means doing violence to the created order. It is sin that colors the landscape of this world, and no economic, technical, or political ideology or program can ever ultimately cancel out this reality.[143] For Ratzinger, it is precisely appreciating this world as imperfect and yearning for a perfection that is not self-made that allows the genius of the arts to arise and personal charity to triumph over injustice. It also avoids the inevitable pitfall of disillusionment. Ratzinger thinks that the aim to create an all-just society suggests that the state can be the good moral agent, supplanting the individual's responsibility to labor for the good. Yet, invariably, political projects will succumb to some form of utilitarianism, rather than relying on moral norms that defy scientific verification. The remedies to these dangers, according to Ratzinger, are found in Christianity. Society is called to acknowledge the transitory nature of this world and to (as much as man may not want to) accept its imperfections. This honesty (and humility) allows society to consciously live the supernatural virtue of a hope anchored in eternity. Mankind is then able to work to improve this world as a way to give expression to charity. The Christian faith can then provide society with the moral consensus it is in dire need of.[144] This consensus can then become the source for moral norms that provide orientation for a society's politics and economics. While never reaching divine justice, human justice is able to evaluate what is good and bad.[145] Thus there should remain a creative difference between the Christian faith and the political and economic spheres, where, as Pope Gelasius (492–496) proposed, both kingship (*regnum*) and the priesthood (*sacerdotium*) are considered to be of divine origin.[146]

It is because justice is a sacrament of love that the church acts so to change the hearts of humanity and strives that "love will enfold justice."

142. Gaál, *Theology of Pope Benedict XVI*, 149.
143. Gaál, *Theology of Pope Benedict XVI*, 149.
144. Gaál, *Theology of Pope Benedict XVI*, 149.
145. Gaál, *Theology of Pope Benedict XVI*, 150.
146. Ziegler, "Pope Gelasius I," 412–37.

Nature, Grace, and Secular Culture

This means that natural justice will spring from love and lead to love, even while retaining its ground in nature and remaining subject to prudence. This pattern reflects Ratzinger's fundamental notion of grace purifying nature. He also believes that the transformation of justice by love finds its source in the church, from which it can exercise an elevating effect on the secular order. As Fields notes, this effect is both dialectical and synthetic. As dialectical, the church shows the natural order that a communion of love constitutes both the basis for and the finality of the natural order's promotion of justice. Without the church's eschatological witness, the ensuing loss of transcendence would evoke, according to Ratzinger, the flight into utopia and its ideological delusions, such as Marxism.[147] As synthetic, the church leavens the prudence of consciences by its own vision of justice. Consequently, the church is able to draw the secular order into its own immediate ambit, even while respecting its autonomy.[148]

Ratzinger is aware of the fact that an outright divorce between church and state would compromise the authentic humanism of nature (as opposed to the secular varieties of humanism), and accordingly does envisage a public role for the church. This role should be executed, he thinks, by robust preaching and educating. Furthermore, Ratzinger is not insensitive to the need to change those social structures that embody injustice. However, Fields thinks that he is too steeped in Augustinian realism to give these a priority over the actions of individuals. Ironically, this realism gives him tangential contact with some postmodern thinkers, such as Jean-François Lyotard, who, as a typical postmodernist, is skeptical of all grand schemes and narratives. Ratzinger remains "temperate" in his expectations of the fruit that practical reason will bear in the secular state, and knows that structures do not change themselves. Change, he thinks, only results ultimately from converted human hearts.[149]

Milbank's Church as Social Theory

As we have seen, the notion of participation stands at the heart of Radical Orthodoxy, whereby all creation shares in the nature of God. Milbank shares with Eastern Orthodoxy the notion of "deification" and speaks

---

147. Ratzinger, *Church, Ecumenism, and Politics*, 206.
148. Fields, "Nature and Grace," 829.
149. Fields, "Nature and Grace," 829. See also Ratzinger, "Eschatology and Utopia," 227.

of the beatific vision. However, he interprets deification as more than simply contemplating the divine perfection. For Milbank, deification involves becoming part of God's life. Milbank's notion of humanity is inseparable from this end point. Final beatitude is not individualistic, and Radical Orthodoxy stresses the social as much as possible. Milbank strongly adheres to the metaphor of the city as a sign that human reality is always political and communal. This is so much the case that, according to Milbank, without this communal dimension, Christianity would become merely a pale reflection of selfish liberalism.[150] For Milbank, the practice of forgiveness is that which marks and founds the community of the church as an alternative political structure, that is, as an "alternative city." It is the church that establishes the link between God and creation and cannot ever be considered to be an optional extra, but is the means by which reconciliation of God and mankind is realized. Shakespeare points out that, on the one hand, Milbank's vision is universal: all creation exists to participate in God. On the other hand, it is highly specific: it is the particular story of Jesus that demonstrates what it means for God and man to be reconciled. It is the church that makes this story a living reality through the way it worships and lives. Milbank is adamant than no "universal reason" could ever justify these claims. People are drawn to the church only by means of the inner "attractiveness" of the stories and practices offered by her.[151] For Milbank, the church is a social formation that renders intelligible all other formations and is the way in which all truth can be encountered and judgments made upon all other worldviews. Milbank's participatory ontology counters the ontological atomism of ontologies of immanence (which are based on univocity) and, as such, counters the social atomism of secular modernity by generating an alternative account of sociality rooted in participation.[152] For Milbank, mankind was created for communion, and thus the goal of redemption is the renewal and restoration of community. The primary site of this renewed sociality is the *ecclesia*, the body of Christ.[153] The relationship between theory and practice is thus reciprocal. The possibilities of a participatory or creational ontology and its attendant account of sociality are unfolded in and by the formation of the liturgy and the practice of

---

150. Shakespeare, *Radical Orthodoxy: Critical Introduction*, 30.

151. Shakespeare, *Radical Orthodoxy: Critical Introduction*, 31. This is typical of Milbank's postmodern "narrative" approach to Christianity.

152. Smith, *Introducing Radical Orthodoxy*, 232.

153. Milbank, Pickstock, and Ward, *Radical Orthodoxy*, 184.

being the community of God. For Milbank, there can be a distinguishable Christian social theory only because there is also a distinguishable Christian mode of action, a definite practice. The theory is first and foremost an ecclesiology.[154]

Recalling Hauerwas, Milbank states that the church does not have a social theory; it *is* a social theory.[155] According to Milbank, Christian social theory:

> is first and foremost an *ecclesiology*, and only an account of other human societies to the extent that the church defines itself, in its practice, as in continuity and discontinuity with these societies.[156]

Milbank's notion of social theory refers to what is normative regarding human relationality within communities (somewhat in the vein of Marx or the Frankfurt School). For Milbank, every sociology already presumes a social theory, which in turn requires an *a priori* account of human nature and relationships. Such a theory is in turn necessarily rooted in theology, meaning that social theory is fundamentally "confessional." Mankind was created with a natural unity, grounded in the *imago Dei*, which grounds mankind's participation in God and one another.[157] The disruption of this unity was introduced by the Fall, beginning with Adam's attempt to blame Eve for sin, and continuing with the murderous narratives of Genesis chapters 3 to 11. Thus, contrary to modern secular narratives, mankind was not originally at war as part of a kind of natural opposition between individuals but only as a result of its postlapsarian condition. For Milbank, part of redemption means the restoration of original unity and communion. This happens by means of participation in Christ's Body and only in Christ's Body. The *ecclesia* is the site of the renewed union that existed before the Fall but it is only an anticipation of the "eschatological gathering of all the nations to Israel."[158] While Milbank does not identify the church with the heavenly Jerusalem, nevertheless, he does think that the true commonwealth is located not in the empire but in the *ecclesia*. It is on this point that Milbank (and also Ward and

---

154. Milbank, *Theology and Social Theory*, 380.

155. Milbank, *Theology and Social Theory*, 380. Emphasis in original. See also Hauerwas, *Peaceable Kingdom*, 99.

156. Milbank, *Theology and Social Theory*, 380.

157. Milbank, Pickstock, and Ward, *Radical Orthodoxy*, 184.

158. Milbank, Pickstock, and Ward, *Radical Orthodoxy*, 185.

Pickstock) suggest a substantial constructive agreement between Radical Orthodoxy and Hauerwas in that the latter's project is allied with that of Radical Orthodoxy in viewing the church as *polis*.[159]

The account of the Fall underpins Milbank's critique of secular modernity and the state. The Fall, after all, was for Milbank the beginning of social atomization and individualism, and the modern state, basing itself on pseudo-soteriology, attempts to effect peace but ends up only with a parody of the *ecclesia* insofar as it attempts to construct a community without calling into question the supposed naturalness of individualistic opposition and without the redemption brought by Christ.[160] In other words, the modern state falsely attempts to ensure peace merely by striving for the absence of conflict. In this respect, Milbank views the state as a form of pseudo-*ecclesia* and the *ecclesia* as the only authentic *polis*.[161] For Milbank, the shape of the *ecclesia* as the authentic community and sociality is centered around *agape*, a fact that challenges the power-centered false *ecclesia* of the state.[162] The church is a community of peace, an *authentic positive peace*, not merely the negative peace of the absence of war. True society, Milbank reflects, "implies absolute consensus, agreement in desire, and entire harmony amongst its members, and this is exactly what the church provides."[163] For Milbank, therefore, the Christian community is, firstly, a unique *polis* that is demarcated by a distinct narrative (Scriptures), recounted in distinct practices (liturgy); secondly, a different *telos* that transcends the contemporary order; and thirdly, the common presence of the Spirit at work among its members through Word and sacrament.[164]

By conceiving of the church as a *polis*, Milbank calls into question the naïve assumption regarding the secular state's "neutrality" and highlights the antithesis between the kinds of people that the state wants to create, versus those that the Spirit forms through the church. Milbank specifies that for the Christian community, the norms of social life and ethical action are specified by a distinct *telos*, communion with God and

---

159. Smith, *Introducing Radical Orthodoxy*, 236.

160. Smith, *Introducing Radical Orthodoxy*, 237.

161. This idea is very much in line with that of Hauerwas, who views the church as a form of alternative polity, both like and unlike any other. See Hauerwas, *Peaceable Kingdom*, 102.

162. Milbank, *Theology and Social Theory*, 393.

163. Milbank, *Theology and Social Theory*, 404.

164. Smith, *Introducing Radical Orthodoxy*, 239.

neighbor, which is itself specified only in the distinct Christian story embodied in Revelation.[165]

Milbank emphasizes the primacy of ecclesiology because the church is seen as the locus for the realization of freedom, as people learn a way of being that is not defined by the dead-end and destructive laws of secular modernity. Milbank states that "without community, without its self-sustaining affirmation of objective justice, 'excellence' and transcendental truth, goodness, and beauty, one must remain resigned to capitalism and bureaucracy."[166] The church, in contrast, embodies the practice of forgiveness and reconciliation, unlike the "violence" of secular modernity. Beyond empty individualism and the indifference of secular freedom, Milbank notes:

> The universality of the church transcends the universality of enlightenment in so far as it is not content with mere mutual toleration and non-interference with the liberties of others. It seems in addition a work of freedom which is none other than a perfect social harmony, a perfect consensus in which every natural and cultural difference finds its agreed place within the successions of space and time.[167]

For Milbank, Christianity is inherently social and political. It cannot become a private, individualistic or apolitical spirituality without abandoning the world, and in so doing, betraying itself. The church ultimately realizes the harmonious and peaceful form of community that is God's original will for creation. This is what sets it apart from all other associations in society. Milbank is adamant that if the church accepts the notion of pluralism, then it has effectively allowed secular skepticism and its capitalist powers to win the day.[168]

For Milbank, the most fundamental of all events is Christ's and the church's "interruption" of history. This is by its nature a social event:

> The *logic* of Christianity involves the claim that the "interruption" of history by Christ and his bride, the church, is the most fundamental of events, interpreting all other events. And it is *most especially* a social event, able to interpret other social

---

165. Smith, *Introducing Radical Orthodoxy*, 240.
166. Milbank, *Word Made Strange*, 282.
167. Milbank, *Word Made Strange*, 154.
168. Shakespeare, *Radical Orthodoxy: Critical Introduction*, 84.

formations, because it compares them with its own new social practice.[169]

The social nature of Christianity for Milbank is of fundamental importance and reflects a wider belief about the nature of being itself. Reality, after all, participates in the nature of the trinitarian God. Thus, the church, as a social event, reveals what creation is intended to be, and what God is like. It is for this reason that Milbank spends much time attacking secular social science. To his mind, these disciplines are not neutral, scientific observations, as man is already caught up in social relationships, and adopts (often uncritically) contemporary philosophical assumptions, and, in the final analysis, such disciplines produce their own vision of society, which is no less ungrounded and mythical than that of any religion.[170] For Milbank, the story of the state begins with a distorted theology in which there is no participation of mankind in God. God (if he is admitted) is a commanding power, and power is necessary to bring people together. Milbank however views the state as a modern invention that is devised to serve certain interests of power, whereby the creed of tolerance serves only to foster an indifference to working out the common good. The role of the state is ultimately to claim for itself a monopoly of violence so that its citizens do not take the law into their own hands. This monopoly, in turn, allows it to transcend the differences that might lead its citizens into conflict with and violence against each other. Thus, the notion of "liberal tolerance" that is at the heart of the secular state seeks to contain reasonable differences. The consequence of this so-called "tolerance" is that "intolerant" people and ideologies (such as the church) need to be tamed or excluded, whereby the end result is not harmony and cooperation, but essentially competition contained by law.[171]

For Milbank, the dualism that was produced by an extrinsicist conception of nature and grace meant that the church adopted a view that separated politics from religion. In other words, the church looked after the soul, and the state looked after the body.[172] As already stated, for Milbank, Christianity is the true politics and the true polity, providing an alternative to the challenges of what he perceives to be the capitalist status quo. It also means that the church embodies the true form of human

---

169. Milbank, *Theology and Social Theory*, 390. Emphasis in original.
170. Shakespeare, *Radical Orthodoxy: Critical Introduction*, 85.
171. Shakespeare, *Radical Orthodoxy: Critical Introduction*, 86.
172. Shakespeare, *Radical Orthodoxy: Critical Introduction*, 86.

social, political, and economic organization, meaning that the church is not confined or limited to the religious sphere. Its claim about how human life should encompass every dimension of that life. Politics and economics should not therefore be despised as "worldly" and therefore impure. Nor, Milbank contends, should they be left to secular experts, because those experts will in fact be guided by their own (anti-Christian) ideologies. The church is ordered ultimately by its liturgy, of its worship of the triune God, wherein the liturgy, being a work of the people, orders human work, relationships, and creativity towards the divine. Milbank also points to the fact that "the church itself, as the realized heavenly city, is the *telos* of the salvific process."[173] The church is more than merely a means to an end, and is instead an end in itself. The church, therefore, can never be merely an optional extra, nor is it possible for one to be a Christian and not attend church; hence the notion of being an "anonymous Christian" is completely rejected. A certain way of being *in community* is the essential content of the Christian faith. For Milbank, *believing* without *belonging* is merely the outcome of the secular world's privatization of religion into a domestic, individual sphere that poses no threat to the status quo. Secularism can tolerate any amount of private faith, but it can in no way tolerate a community that seeks to embody an alternative to secularism in any material way.[174] For Milbank, the church must take seriously its call to perfection because:

> unless the textual and ecclesial representation of Jesus—and so its relationship to Jesus, which must be a kind of "incarnation" of the procession of the Holy Spirit—is in some sense "perfect," how could Jesus's perfection be at all conveyed to us?[175]

It is by means of the perfection and infallibility of the church that we are guaranteed an encounter with the true Christ. Were this not the case, the church and its message would be relegated to the level of just another story, among a sea of others. Milbank is aware of the high calling of the theologian and the damage that is done when theology goes awry. He states that theology is "tragically too important" because "we remain uncertain as to where today to locate true Christian practice."[176] Therefore, according to Milbank:

173. Milbank, *Theology and Social Theory*, 405.
174. Shakespeare, *Radical Orthodoxy: Critical Introduction*, 91.
175. Milbank, *Word Made Strange*, 162.
176. Milbank, *Word Made Strange*, 1.

in his or her uncertainty as to where to find this, the theologian feels almost that the entire ecclesial task falls on his own head: in the meagre mode of reflective words he must seek to imagine what a true practical repetition would be like. Or at least he must hope that his merely theoretical continuation of the tradition will open up a space for wider transformation.[177]

As Shakespeare points out, this view imports a certain dualism, because as true politics must reside within the church, outside the church there can be only darkness. In Milbank's mind, the potential for meaningful alliances with bodies outside the church seems to be pointless, if not to be actively discouraged. Thus, ironically, it seems that in being so keen to avoid "bastard dualisms," Milbank can be said to fall into the same trap. That is, the church, the continuation of the Incarnation as the mystical body of Christ, has to be separated from the world, which is fallen and utterly ruined. If the church reveals God to us, then this means that God has to be separated from the world too.[178]

Milbank eschews the idea that the church may lord its position over the world, as this would make it merely the pale reflection of modern states. In addressing this issue, Milbank proposes the notion of "complex space":

> Better, then, that the bounds between church and State be extremely hazy, so that a "social" existence of many complex and interlocking powers may emerge, and forestall either a sovereign state, or a statically hierarchical church.[179]

The notion of the complex space for Milbank is an attempt to resist the aspirations of modern capitalist and state socialist nations to have effective control over all forms of human association. Milbank concedes that this sort of complex space had been endorsed in Catholic teaching; however, it runs uncomfortably close to fascism, even going so far as to suggest that the social teaching of Pope John Paul II would lead to "soft fascism."[180] The reason for this is that it endorses capitalist property rights, and calls on firms to ensure workers' welfare, but it can undermine the true free association of workers in unions. Thus, paternalism and

---

177. Milbank, *Word Made Strange*, 1.
178. Shakespeare, *Radical Orthodoxy: Critical Introduction*, 94.
179. Milbank, *Theology and Social Theory*, 413.
180. Milbank, *Word Made Strange*, 284.

totalitarianism can work hand in hand.[181] By way of contrast, Milbank favors what he terms to be a "socialism by grace," which is not a socialism rooted in Marxist atheism and the notion of the inevitable march of history, but a form of Christian socialism.[182] This, he thinks, can offer a progressive alternative to capitalism and dictatorship.

For Milbank, the church has something to offer the entire human race, and therefore its vision is political to the core. This means that it cannot turn in on itself and away from the world. As we have seen, this does not mean that Milbank proposes a "theocratic" solution in which the church governs all aspects of society. Power must be dispersed, such that "socialism need not retreat to a premodern contemplation of eternal positions and pre-given hierarchies."[183] Milbank also thinks (in agreement with John Paul II) that democracy can become a slave to propaganda, and also warns that the church needs to be self-critical and held to account for its "collusion with capitalism and fascist ideology."[184]

Shakespeare observes that Milbank's vision of the "haziness" of the boundary between church and state sounds very much like Anglicanism (which should come as no surprise, given that Milbank is Anglican), particularly evidenced by resistance to a centralized authority, such as in the form of the Holy See.[185] Milbank explicates this haziness in his response to the dialogue between Radical Orthodox and Roman Catholic theologians:

> Ever since the Gregorian reforms, the Roman Catholic Church has arguably over-insisted on clerical control of a specifically "spiritual" social space, which (as Charles Péguy argued) has left the laity, disenfranchised as Christians, with nothing left to do but invent their own sphere of securely "secular" operations.[186]

Milbank goes on to note that Anglicanism has usually made the opposite and equally modern error of ultimate control of ecclesial institutions by power organized for secular ends. Nevertheless, in his view, the blurring of boundaries in Anglicanism is congenial to Radical Orthodoxy:

---

181. Shakespeare, *Radical Orthodoxy: Critical Introduction*, 101.
182. Milbank, *Being Reconciled*, 162.
183. Milbank, *Word Made Strange*, 283.
184. Milbank, *Word Made Strange*, 285.
185. Shakespeare, *Radical Orthodoxy: Critical Introduction*, 103.
186. Milbank, "Programme," 36.

It is in this blurring, this non-duality of reason and faith, secular and social, which I want to emphasize, because it has often been misunderstood. Radical Orthodoxy favors no theocracy, because theocracy is predicated upon the very dualism it rejects: for the sacred hierophants to be enthroned there must be a drained secular space for them to command. But for Radical Orthodoxy there is no such space.[187]

For Milbank, the sacral interpenetrates everywhere and if it descends from above, this descent is also manifest through its rising up from below.[188] As Kerr notes, Milbank's attempt to push de Lubac even further in the direction of theology's overcoming of metaphysics cannot but arouse disquiet.[189] Even the inheritors of transcendental Thomism and the continuators of Cajetanian Thomism (utterly opposed as they are to each other's viewpoints) would be united to repudiate Milbank's project of a fully Christianized ontology, and would resist his binary choice between either nihilism (expressed in secular culture) and Christian Platonism (in the form of his own project), which Milbank seems to present us.

Correspondence Theory

In Milbank's theology, truth is not a simple correspondence of one's words and ideas with reality. Instead, truth is a dynamic relationship, and constitutes participation in the "beautiful in the beauty of God."[190] Milbank even goes as far as to suggest that the relationship of God to the world becomes, after Christianity, a rhetorical one, and ceases to be anything to do with "truth" per se. Milbank, after all, eschews fixed substances, and instead, for him, truth, like language itself, is made up of shifting differences. It is out of this material that we have to construct meaning. In creating this meaning, in becoming creators, we discover too that we are also creatures. God's creativity is discovered in the things that we produce as they take on meaning and power beyond what we can imagine.[191] Thus, when Milbank speaks of the church being "first and foremost neither a program nor a real society, but instead an enacted

187. Milbank, "Programme," 36.
188. Milbank, "Programme," 37.
189. Kerr, "Catholic Response," 57.
190. Milbank, *Theology and Social Theory*, 430.
191. Shakespeare, *Radical Orthodoxy: Critical Introduction*, 105.

serious, fiction,"[192] what is being signaled is the way in which we make and receive truth. Truth is not just correspondence, nor the projection of human ideas onto the world. It is instead a relationship, an event, an openness to the creative unfolding of differences.[193] Milbank notes that the Trinity, after all, is an absolute that is *itself* difference, inclusive of all difference.[194] This notion has implications for how Milbank conceives of the church in the modern world. Given that God is inclusive of difference, the church too is similarly inclusive. For Milbank, "Revelation is not in any sense a layer added to reason. It is lodged in all the complex networks of human practices, and its boundaries are as messy as those of the church itself."[195] As already stated, Milbank uses the notion of *poesis* (creative making) as a key to understanding human culture and divine Revelation. For Milbank, Revelation happens when our own attempts to create meaningful works slip free from our control and our limited intentions. At their best, the things we make are not merely objects or commodities whose only future is to be used up, bought and sold, but instead are able to communicate, to bring people into relationship with one another, and with God. We meet God and share in God's creation through the work of our hands and minds.[196] The danger with such an idea of course is that it tends towards salvation by works. Furthermore, it creates a problem if Milbank is proposing that we must create a perfect church in order for God to be revealed. Milbank denies however that he sees the church as a utopian, perfect society, because the peace of Christ is already given, but not yet realized in the world.

Milbank in his *Theology and Social Theory* notes that the church continues what began in the Incarnation, particularly through the Eucharist. The church is "other-governed," a lived project of universal reconciliation, and must never mistake herself for God. The reconciliation brought by the church is already perfected in Christ, but not in history. Thus, the church is not just another flawed institution, but neither is it utopia. It continues to exist through the "mess" of institutional debate and conflict.[197] It is, however, questionable as to whether Milbank has always maintained this balance. He does, after all, seem at times to place

192. Milbank, "Enclaves," 342.
193. Milbank, "Enclaves," 342.
194. Milbank, *Theology and Social Theory*, 430.
195. Milbank, *Being Reconciled*, 122.
196. Shakespeare, *Radical Orthodoxy: Critical Introduction*, 103.
197. Milbank, *Theology and Social Theory*, xxxi.

too much faith in the perfection of what seems to be a rootless, timeless, and idealized church and its sacraments. Milbank does nevertheless seek to affirm that truth is made known through the open-ended story of history, rather than simply appeal to a static perfection.[198]

As we have seen, Milbank is extremely resistant to the notion that the church can receive anything from the world, asserting that only Christianity can redeem the world, and present the truth. Milbank makes this plain when he writes:

> Christianity's universalist claim that incorporation into the church is indispensable for salvation assumes that other religions and social groupings, however virtuous-seeming, were, in their own terms alone, finally on the path of damnation . . . . [It] is absolutely integral to the nature of the Christian Church, which itself claims to exhibit the exemplary form of human community. For theology to surrender this claim, to allow that other discourses—"the social sciences" for example—carry out yet more fundamental readings, would therefore amount to a denial of theological truth. The *logic* of Christianity involves the claim that the "interruption" of history by Christ and his bride, the church, is the most fundamental of events, interpreting all other events.[199]

Milbank apparently eschews any possibility of dialogue with secular culture, even going so far as to say that non-Christians cannot be good by definition, on *a priori* grounds. This position would be entirely repugnant to Ratzinger as it seems to rule out any possibility of any meaningful cooperation or conversation with the "unredeemed." Milbank elsewhere states that all morality outside the church is in league with scarcity and death. Secularism cannot overcome death, only vainly try to hold it in check.[200] Milbank writes that "given the death-fact, the best we can do is to be virtuous, not kill and not cause to suffer, become doctors and firemen and so forth."[201] As Shakespeare notes, comments such as these tend to indicate Milbank's rather petty way of writing off secular callings, which makes Radical Orthodoxy sound "arrogant and detached."[202]

---

198. Shakespeare, *Radical Orthodoxy: Critical Introduction*, 109.
199. Milbank, *Theology and Social Theory*, 390.
200. Shakespeare, *Radical Orthodoxy: Critical Introduction*, 111.
201. Milbank, *Word Made Strange*, 224.
202. Shakespeare, *Radical Orthodoxy: Critical Introduction*, 111.

Nature, Grace, and Secular Culture

Milbank is also resistant to the idea of dialogue between religions, set out especially in his text "The End of Dialogue." Milbank argues that the idea that there is an abstract and general notion called "religion" is a Western invention, which cuts the huge variety of human religious practices to fit the same template. It assumes that all religions are about the same thing directed to the same end.[203] Radical Orthodoxy however asserts that there is "no view from nowhere," that is, purported claims of "neutrality" are purely nonsensical. The idea that dialogue partners are equal is idealistic; however, in reality, one can assume this in advance only if one also assumes that all parties are speaking about the same thing. Milbank argues that this position empties religion of its content, and in the case of Christianity, this would mean that the church is ignored because religion is treated as a set of beliefs rather than a social project. Milbank insists on the uniqueness of the church: "no other religious community comprehends itself (in theory) as an international society" in which all are equal and committed to "perfect mutual acceptance and co-operation."[204] For Milbank, the notion that religions can be brought together on the basis of shared values and practice, to the exclusion of particular beliefs, is simply naïve. Practice and belief are inseparable and shape each other. Thus, for Milbank, where consensus exists, it is usually because people of faith have abandoned their own traditions and replaced them with the values of Western liberalism. To claim the high moral ground by arguing that no religion can have a monopoly on the truth leads only to a liberal Western monopoly. Milbank also thinks that there is nothing wrong with judging the practice of another culture to be wrong in some respect, provided that one admits that this judgment is made from one's own cultural reading of the world.[205] For Milbank, "if it were accepted that all cultures (religions) have equal access to the (religious) truth, then all critique, including critique of sexist and racist constructs, would become impossible."[206] Pluralism, therefore, cannot deliver justice because the idea of justice is tied to the notion of the ultimate Good. Milbank thinks that justice cannot be established on the basis of "universal human reason" as, in attempting to do this, we just set the bad version of Western liberalism above criticism, which, in turn, promotes an indifferent tolerance rather than a real encounter with the Other.

203. Milbank, "End of Dialogue," 177.
204. Milbank, "End of Dialogue," 179.
205. Shakespeare, *Radical Orthodoxy: Critical Introduction*, 113.
206. Milbank, "End of Dialogue," 184.

Pluralism is not the same as trinitarian difference and harmony. Pluralism, likewise, does not lead to real reconciliation. Versions of pluralism in other religions are still based on conflict and offer no way beyond it.[207] Milbank points out that, unlike Eastern religions, only Christianity can value the other precisely *as other*. Milbank therefore suggests replacing dialogue with a hermeneutic of "mutual suspicion" and a commitment to the church's specific project of reconciliation.[208] Part of Milbank's objection to dialogue is that it masks an essentially oppressive approach that is unable to respect the other as genuinely other. For him, it is ironic that dialogue assumes that everyone is the same, which is an unsafe foundation upon which to begin encountering differences.[209]

According to Shakespeare:

> by setting up the terms of engagement in this way, it [Radical Orthodoxy] refuses all dialogue and so refuses any accountability to standards other than those internal to itself. The irony is that the picture of the world that is created is one of incompatible, competing discourses, locked in a war to the death—precisely the kind of agonistic account of reality for which secularism is condemned. Whilst celebrating the participation of time in eternity, infinite in finite, Radical Orthodoxy cannot extend the logic of this sacramental view beyond its own barriers. Outside the Christian language and field of vision, there is only war and death.[210]

Concerning the notion of objective knowledge, Milbank is most at odds with Ratzinger. Unlike Ratzinger, Milbank rejects the notion of objective knowledge, detached reasoning, and universally accessible evidence. Such evidence and sources are invoked mainly for their value as "actors" in the drama of the Radical Orthodoxy story. That story appeals to a truth that lies not in the correspondence of thought to reality but in the doctrine of the Incarnation of the eternal Word in a human discourse.[211] In this respect, Milbank is unwilling, and indeed unable, to admit a dialectic in relation to other approaches, nor to invite dialogue with scholarly perspectives or points of view. Its core message, after all, is that the horizon of Christian theology can confidently include

---

207. Shakespeare, *Radical Orthodoxy: Critical Introduction*, 113.
208. Milbank, "End of Dialogue," 190.
209. Shakespeare, *Radical Orthodoxy: Critical Introduction*, 114.
210. Shakespeare, *Radical Orthodoxy: Critical Introduction*, 114.
211. Janz, "Radical Orthodoxy," 325.

everything in its purview, as everything is numinous in a world made for God in Christ.[212]

While Ratzinger also warns against correlating the faith to the intellectual fashions and social practices of the times, he certainly does not adopt a position as against the world as extreme as that of Milbank. As Rowland observes, the correlationist project reached the zenith of its popularity in the 1970s, though it has never completely died out and enthusiasm for the project can still be found among clergy and schoolteachers who came of age during the 1960s, when the project was first promoted. As we have seen, for Ratzinger, the church cannot be likened to a haberdashery shop that updates its windows with each new fashion season, and described such projects in the field of liturgical practices as "infantile claptrap."[213]

According to Fiorenza, Ratzinger's theological vision gives a foundational role to a metaphysical view of human dignity and to the importance of truth claims. In his view, democracy, pluralism, and human rights rest upon such claims. Ratzinger has argued that this view of Christianity points to the possibilities for dialogue in a democratic and pluralist world. Unlike Milbank, such a vision, he argues, is pluralist but not relativist, because it affirms basic values. Ratzinger's confrontation with liberation theology makes the important point that religion can become an ideology of political policy unless it is mediated through a political ethics and assessed in terms of Christian values. Likewise, he insists that in interreligious dialogue, one must keep in mind the possibility of the ideological distortions and consequences of religious beliefs.[214] This vision of Christianity as a community with a distinctive culture stands behind Ratzinger's choice of Benedict as the name to express the direction of his papacy. Just as Benedictine monasteries were resources of Christian culture, seeding Christian culture throughout Europe, so too today the Catholic Church should be a community of a clearly identifiable Christian culture and tradition. In this respect Ratzinger and Milbank would agree, namely, that the church should be marked by a distinct and identifiable culture of its own, in contradistinction to that of the world. For Ratzinger, any attempt to engage in religious and cultural dialogue must proceed out of a community with its own clearly

---

212. Janz, "Radical Orthodoxy," 325.

213. Rowland, *Culture of the Incarnation*, 2.

214. Fiorenza, "From Theologian to Pope." See also Proniewski, "Joseph Ratzinger's Philosophical Theology."

defined cultural identity. Unlike Milbank, however, and in contrast to some of the negative characterizations of him, Benedict does envision the Catholic Church in dialogue with others, but he is convinced that such dialogue should not rest on some generic understanding of religion and culture. Instead, it should stem from a community that brings its vision into the dialogue.[215]

Ratzinger possesses an understanding of the theological virtue of hope that is different from that of secular social theorists, especially from the ideas, for example, of Bloch. Bloch did influence certain Catholic theologians, most notably Johann Baptist Metz. Ratzinger, however, was most definitely not in favor of his ideas. One reason for Ratzinger's opposition to secularist analogues for the theological virtue of hope and to the whole correlationist project is that he believed that social theories are not theologically innocent.[216] Many contemporary social theories are secularist mutations of classically Christian or Jewish ideas, and thus, to correlate the faith to them is to engage in a project of "self-secularization." This notion bears great resemblance to Milbank's opposition to the claim of neutrality that secular culture makes. As we have seen, Milbank is not prepared to accept that secularism is in any way theologically, philosophically, or even ideologically neutral. The correlationist project runs the risk of confusing the faithful by giving the impression that mutated concepts passing themselves off as "neutral" are consistent with Christian concepts when, in fact, they may not be. Each time this is done, something of the richness and complexity and even multidimensional nature of the Catholic vision is lost.[217]

Concerning the Second Vatican Council, Ratzinger noted with some concern that the commentary of most observers seemed unfortunately more concerned with the notion of how the church might accommodate herself with contemporary culture. These observers seemed to think that this was the single most important characteristic of the

---

215. Fiorenza, "From Theologian to Pope."

216. Fiorenza, "From Theologian to Pope."

217. Rowland, *Culture of the Incarnation*, 2. Komonchak also points out that the postmodern critique of universal reason and of foundationalism and its insistence on the incommensurability of linguistically mediated worlds is often considered to resemble Ratzinger's more Augustinian approach, with its "abandonment of the myth of pure reason and its insistence on the unbridgeable gulf that the Cross of Christ digs with regard to the very notion of rationality." Komonchak, interestingly, also notes that, "in this line, Dossetti and Ratzinger would appear, at least temporarily, to have won the victory." See Komonchak, "Augustine," 116.

council, perceiving it in terms of the political categories of "progressive" and "conservative," rather than to "behold the inner aspects, the spiritual profile of the church."[218] Ratzinger stresses that it is the Christ-filled reality of the church that transcends such clichés. All renewal ultimately is measured according to Christ, to whom Scripture is a witness.

Ratzinger reinforces this idea:

> To link the Roman proverb on time as the voice of God with Jesus's eschatological warning against the blindness of his nation which though on the look-out for signs, was not able to interpret him, God's eschatological sign to that age, or his message, was considered not only exegetically unacceptable but of doubtful validity in itself. Since Christ is the real "sign of the time," is he not the actual antithesis to the authority of *chronos* expressed in the proverb "*vox temporis vox Dei*"?[219]

Repeatedly, Ratzinger emphasizes that early Christianity drew its primordial strength from transforming Greek philosophy and not from accommodating the then existing pagan religions. In this way, Christianity was able to create a singular synthesis of reason, faith, and life.[220] He cautions his readers not to dismiss Augustine's Platonic understanding of the world as the reflection of a more valuable reality beyond itself. He does, however, acknowledge a lack of appreciation on the part of Augustine for the intimate involvement of God with and in the world. Ratzinger acknowledges the tension in Augustine between *sarx* and *pneuma*. Not appreciating this Pauline tension of the world and spirit leads to not only a naïve view of life, but also to an undervaluation of the Incarnation.[221] Only later in life did Augustine become more nuanced and speak of worldly life *secundum Deum*, that is, in keeping with divine precepts. The radical Neoplatonic separation of the world and God is either overcome, or fails to be overcome, by accepting or rejecting the divine will and the joy of the Incarnation.[222]

---

218. Rowland, *Culture of the Incarnation*, 2. See also Komonchak, "Church in Crisis," 15.
219. Ratzinger, "Dignity," 115.
220. Gaál, *Theology of Pope Benedict XVI*, 54.
221. Gaál, *Theology of Pope Benedict XVI*, 63.
222. Gaál, *Theology of Pope Benedict XVI*, 63.

Political Theology vs. Theology of Politics

Given Ratzinger's view of nature and grace, which seeks to maintain the integrity of each order without falling into the tendency to supernaturalize nature (as in Milbank), Ratzinger resists those theologians after the Second Vatican Council who "sought to transform de Lubac's theology of Catholicity into a political theology that sought to put Christianity to practical use as a catalyst for achieving political unity."[223] According to Ratzinger, this transformation does not follow de Lubac's thought to its logical conclusion. This does not mean that Ratzinger is advocating an individualistic mode of Christianity in which grace mediated by the church alone has relevance for the individual soul and not also for the human being as a whole, and indeed human society.[224] According to Ratzinger, de Lubac's notion of nature and grace does not lead to the promotion of a political theology in which particular political expressions are best expressive of faith. Instead, de Lubac's notion of salvation concerning not only the individual but also drawing people into communion with God does not refer to the political, but to the church considered as a sacrament.[225] Ratzinger notes:

> Two things are important here: the sacrament we call church does not directly establish man's secular, political unity; the sacrament does not replace politics; and theocracy, whatever its form, is a misunderstanding.[226]

For Ratzinger, therefore, the church is not a principle of unity considered in merely political terms, but is instead centered around the Eucharist:

> Now at last we have reached the inmost core of the concept "church" and the deepest meaning of the designation "sacrament of unity." The church is *communion*; she is God's communing with men in Christ and hence the communing of men with one another—and, in consequence, sacrament, sign, instrument of salvation. The church is the celebration of the Eucharist; the Eucharist is the church; they do not simply stand side by side; they are one and the same. The Eucharist is the *sacramentum*

---

223. Ratzinger, *Principles of Catholic Theology*, 51.
224. Kucer, *Truth and Politics*, 223.
225. Kucer, *Truth and Politics*, 223. See also Lubac, *Catholicism*, 12.
226. Ratzinger, *Principles of Catholic Theology*, 54.

Christi and, because the church is *Eucharistia*, she is therefore also *sacramentum*.[227]

Contrary to Milbank (as we shall see), the church as communion is not primarily or directly concerned with political realities, but rather with God, who transcends the boundaries of love of fellow man. Through the Eucharist "the church draws people together into a community of faith that is different from every club or political party."[228] For the church to surrender to politics would mean that it would ironically also lose its "political interest because no spiritual force emanates from her."[229] This force can only be retained by maintaining a clear distinction between her eschatological truths of faith and her eucharistic sacramental identity, on the one hand, and political goals and political reasoning, on the other. Likewise (unlike Milbank, with his clearly articulated preference for "Christian socialism"), the church cannot identify a political system that best represents the truth of faith. At this same time, this does not imply that the church should avoid engagement with the world, but instead, it is meant to engage in the world by addressing the spiritual and material needs of humanity. Addressing these needs should not mean however that the church is to formulate a political theology, or an ideal political system that is meant to best serve those needs.[230] For this reason, notes Kucer, Ratzinger strongly rejects the political theologies of both Alfons Auer and Metz. These two theologians, according to Ratzinger, confused truths of faith with truths that reason is capable of adequately grasping by proposing the "ecclesialisation of everything" (*Verchristlichung des Alls*).[231] Ratzinger is adamant that salvation must never be politicized, because it is primarily directed to the heavenly world. Political theologies instead merely attempt to liberate the world within its worldliness, and in this way, collapse grace into nature. In his *Introduction to Christianity*, Ratzinger argues that the politicization of theology is contrary to the trinitarian faith since God is triune in himself and not merely as manifested in history.[232] Ratzinger notes that due to the freedom and incomprehensibility of the world, no one political system can be promoted

---

227. Ratzinger, *Principles of Catholic Theology*, 53.
228. Ratzinger, *Principles of Catholic Theology*, 83.
229. Ratzinger, *Principles of Catholic Theology*, 116.
230. Kucer, *Truth and Politics*, 225.
231. Ratzinger, *Neue Volk Gottes*, 296–97.
232. Ratzinger, *Introduction to Christianity*, 112.

as definitive, as in Hegelianism or Marxism. Rejecting the notion that the faith is a political norm of political activity, Ratzinger writes:

> The Kingdom of God which Christ promises does not consist in a modification of our earthly circumstances.... That Kingdom is found in those persons whom the finger of God has touched and who have allowed themselves to be made God's sons and daughters. Clearly, such a transformation can only take place through death. For this reason, the Kingdom of God, salvation in its fullness, cannot be deprived of its connection with dying.[233]

He notes that the notion of a man-made terrestrial paradise (without the aid of God) has been particularly popular over the last four decades in both Western Europe and North America. Likewise, this *political* hope has been imposed on peoples by dictators in Eastern Europe, Asia (especially Communist China), and Latin America.[234] These sentiments were also echoed in an earlier work penned by Ratzinger for Cardinal Josef Frings (then archbishop of Cologne, president of the German Bishops' Conference) that was presented in the form of a lecture in preparation for the Second Vatican Council. The lecture (given by Frings) was titled *Uber das Konzil vom dem Hintergrund der Zeitlage im Unterschied zum Ersten Vatikanischen Konzil* ("On the Council: The Background of the Current Intellectual Climate Compared to the First Vatican Council"). The final point made in the lecture concerns certain ideologies, such as Marxism, existentialism, and neoliberalism. All these express the human heart's yearning for a great, sustaining hope. The promise may not be only for an individual: it should be one capturing the heart and the imagination of all mankind. With these considerations as a background, the (then) upcoming Second Vatican Council appeared as one with an overriding pastoral concern, intending to point to Jesus Christ as the only object worthy of placing such hope in. It is the church (rather than man's political efforts alone) that is the Father's house in which human beings find such hope not disappointed.[235]

Ratzinger noted in his *Introduction to Christianity* that "in 1968 there was a fusion of the Christian impulse with secular and political action and an attempt to baptize Marxism."[236] This project, labeled as "liberation

233. Ratzinger, *Eschatology*, 62.
234. Ratzinger, *Eschatology*, 71.
235. Gaál, *Theology of Pope Benedict XVI*, 90.
236. Ratzinger, *Introduction to Christianity*, 14. See also Nichols, "Joseph Ratzinger's Theology."

theology," was particularly strong in countries that were formerly Spanish or Portuguese colonies, such as the Philippines, Honduras, Nicaragua, Argentina, and Brazil. It was also popular among Catholic intellectual elites throughout Europe and the Anglophone countries. Ratzinger spent many of his early years as prefect of the Congregation for the Doctrine of the Faith contending with so-called "theologies of liberation." This does not mean however that Ratzinger should be characterized as a "neo-conservative," that is, that he attempts to tie together Christianity and liberal market economics.[237] Ratzinger acknowledged the existence of great poverty and economic injustice in many countries and even described as "astounding" the notion that market forces could be considered to be inherently good.[238] Nevertheless, he thought that "whoever makes Marx the philosopher of theology adopts the primacy of politics and economics" and, as a result, the redemption of mankind is pursued through the vehicles of economics and politics."[239] Ratzinger concluded that "the real and most profound problem with liberation theologies is their effective omission of the idea of God, which, of course, also changed the figure of Christ fundamentally."[240] That is, while liberation theologians did not formally declare themselves to be atheists, their "God had nothing to do" and so Jesus Christ was transformed (and reduced) into a mere political agitator. For Ratzinger, the notion of a God with nothing to do, has been around for at least a century, so it was no surprise that there arose these theologies of political and economic liberation. He observes that over the last century:

> Christian consciousness acquiesced to a great extent—without being aware of it—in the attitude that faith in God is something subjective, which belongs in the private realm and not in the common activities of public life where, in order to be able to get along, people all have to behave now *esti Deus non daretur*.[241]

237. Rowland, *Benedict XVI: Guide*, 6.

238. Ratzinger, "Church and Economy," 200.

239. Ratzinger, *Introduction to Christianity*, 15. See also Congregation for the Doctrine of the Faith, *Instruction on Christian Freedom*; and Congregation for the Doctrine of the Faith, *Instruction on "Theology of Liberation."* These documents were published at the time that Ratzinger was prefect of the Congregation for the Doctrine of the Faith and deal with so-called "theologies of liberation"—in particular, the danger inherent in an uncritical acceptance by theologians of theses and methodologies that come from Marxism.

240. Ratzinger, *Introduction to Christianity*, 16.

241. Ratzinger, *Introduction to Christianity*, 16. In the face of this, Ratzinger calls

Ratzinger concludes:

> It did not take any particular negligence, and certainly not a deliberate denial, to leave God as a God with nothing to do, especially since his name had been misused so often. But the faith would really have come out of the ghetto only if it brought its most distinctive features with it into the public arena: the God who judges and suffers; the God who sets limits and standards for us; the God from whom we come and to whom we are going. But as it was, it really remained in the ghetto, having by now absolutely nothing to do.[242]

It was not only liberation theologians who contributed to this marginalization of God from public significance, but Catholics inspired by liberal philosophy were also complicit. According to Rowland, it suited their "upward social mobility prospects" to privatize their faith or to promote what Marcel Gauchet called a "superstructural faith" that does not penetrate to the core of a person or culture itself.[243] In effect, both groups allowed their political and social interests to transform their theology, rather than allow their theology to transform their political and social interests. With so many internal problems, it should not be surprising that Christianity was unable to present itself as a viable alternative to the various Marxist and Freudian inspired ideologies in 1968 or to the nihilist currents in postmodernism in 1989 and beyond.[244] With such challenges (including the emergence of postmodern theologies that challenge the notion of Christianity as a master narrative, valid for all ages and cultures), Ratzinger states in his *Principles of Catholic Theology* that the fundamental crisis of our age is the development of a Catholic understanding of the mediation of history in the realm of ontology.[245] This, for Ratzinger, became the central problem around which and upon which so much of the structure of the narrative depends. So many of his

---

for the reversal of this Enlightenment axiom: "even if one who does not succeed in finding the path to accepting the existence of God ought nevertheless to try to live and to direct his life *veluti si Deus daretur*, as if God did indeed exist." See Ratzinger, *Christianity and the Crisis of Cultures*, 50.

242. Ratzinger, *Introduction to Christianity*, 17.
243. Gauchet, *Disenchantment*, 164.
244. Rowland, *Benedict XVI: Guide*, 8.
245. Ratzinger, *Principles of Catholic Theology*, 158–63.

theological interventions relate to this notion, and it is expressive of his distaste for neo-scholastic systems of theology that claim to be "above history."[246]

The faith has the primary objective of causing conversion in individual persons through their transformation in Christ and not in bringing about structural political change. Ratzinger asserts that it is an illusion to hold:

> that a new man and a new world can be created, not by calling each individual to conversion, but only by changing the social and economic structures, for it is precisely personal sin that is in reality at the root of unjust social structures. Those who really desire a more human society need to begin with the root, not with the trunk and branches of the tree of injustice.[247]

Given that Ratzinger views the source of all systemic injustices as being personal sin, it follows then that the church's role must be to effect individual conversions and not to directly bring about structural changes to political systems. The latter is proper to the political order, not to the ecclesial.[248] By means of focusing on individual conversion, rather than structural change, the church remains faithful to her origin, since "from the beginning it has insisted on leaving politics in the sphere of rationality and ethics. It has taught mankind to accept the imperfect and has made this possible."[249] Christianity, therefore, proposes ethics for politicians to follow and not a structural model for them to implement. Ratzinger notes that:

> the Scriptures always reject the fanaticism that tries to set up the kingdom of God as a political project. It is still true that politics is the province, not of theology, but rather of ethics, which of course, can only be substantiated theologically. In precisely this way, the New Testament remains true to its repudiation of

---

246. Ratzinger, *Principles of Catholic Theology*, 158–63. A truly in-depth treatment of the notion of the "mediation of history in the realm of ontology" is beyond the scope of this book (particularly as it relates to Ratzinger's study of Bonaventure). Nevertheless, this is an area that invites further examination, particularly as the notion relates to the present theme regarding secular culture and evangelization. Works that treat of this notion include: Collins, *Word Made Love*; Rowland, *Culture of the Incarnation*; Healy and Schindler, *Being Holy*; Sweeney, *Sacramental Presence*; Rowland, *Catholic Theology*; and Rowland, *Benedict XVI: Guide*.

247. Ratzinger, *Report*, 190.

248. Kucer, *Truth and Politics*, 236.

249. Ratzinger, *Church, Ecumenism, and Politics*, 204.

justification by works, for political theology in the strict sense of the word says that perfect justice in the world must be produced through our work, that justice comes about as work and only in that way.[250]

Ratzinger asserts that if the church were to abandon her claim, based on faith, of having a special relationship to truth, she would no longer accomplish for the state what it needs from her. At the same time, if the state were to accept this claim, it would abolish its own pluralistic character and thus both church and state would be lost.[251] Kucer observes that this raises an interesting question in that it seems to imply that the state cannot retain its proper identity if it acknowledges the church's claim to truth. It seems, therefore, that Ratzinger means that the state, in order to retain its identity, cannot formally accept the church's truth claims but can "implicitly and non-formally do so."[252]

For Ratzinger, two extremes threaten the moderately integrated relationship between the church and the political realm. The first is a dualism, promoted by an extrinsicist reading of nature and grace, in which the church is viewed as having no relevance for public life and politics. The second is a radical integralism in which the church and state form a theocracy. The danger of theocracy, he thinks, begins to appear "where the misalliance between Christianity and Marxism brings about a pre-figuration of the kingdom of God that is supposed to be created politically."[253] When either extreme occurs, the transcendence of the faith becomes obscured, and then "the myth of the divine state rises again, because man cannot do without the totality of hope."[254] This myth can be resurrected by either extreme; when it is brought to life by a theocracy, the Kingdom of God is considered to be "the outcome of politics" and faith is twisted "into the universal primacy of the political."[255] This blatantly contradicts the Christian faith that "destroyed the myth of the divine state, the myth of the earthly paradise or utopian state and of a society without rule. In its place it put the objectivity of reason."[256]

250. Ratzinger, *Church, Ecumenism, and Politics*, 204.
251. Ratzinger, *Church, Ecumenism, and Politics*, 206. See also Nichols, "Joseph Ratzinger's Theology," 388.
252. Kucer, *Truth and Politics*, 237.
253. Ratzinger, *Church, Ecumenism, and Politics*, 203.
254. Ratzinger, *Church, Ecumenism, and Politics*, 144.
255. Ratzinger, *Church, Ecumenism, and Politics*, 144.
256. Ratzinger, *Church, Ecumenism, and Politics*, 146.

In other words, the Christian faith makes the claim that regardless of political affiliation, each person, by means of reason, can apprehend universal truth.

For Ratzinger, high-minded orthopraxis becomes the plaything of ulterior motives with little regard for the gospel, and by means of a rebellion of the human intellect against the faith. This can only be explained by favoring utopia at the expense of Christian eschatology.[257] Nothing short of opting for self-redemption versus grace occurs in such a theological current as liberation theology.[258] In this way, for Ratzinger, liberation theology, is more a "liberation from theology" than anything else. It appears that Ratzinger is arguing that the Christian eschatological vision must be upheld for the sake of a realistic, humane, and Christian utopia.[259] A reinterpretation of Christianity along the lines of liberation theology is unbiblical and defies the praxis of Christ. The Marxist position of class struggle clashes with Christ as the Lamb of God. It undermines the meaning of truth and presents the notion of class struggle as an objective, necessary law of history, evading the call to personal conversion.[260] Instead, Ratzinger emphasizes that the adoration of the crucified Christ in the Eucharist is the point of departure for all communion, and also for genuine solidarity with the disenfranchised. Saints like Teresa of Calcutta and Martin de Porres make this abundantly clear.[261] Communion with Christ is communion with God himself, who, in turn, urges Christians to practice solidarity. In this respect, Ratzinger was particularly influenced by de Lubac. He strove to overcome the dangers of either an exaggerated glorification of the church, or likewise, her overspiritualization. The world, and indeed even more so, the church, receives unity from Christ's person and work. The mystery of Christ is, for the fathers, inherently and entirely a mystery of unity.[262]

---

257. Kissler, *Deutsche Papst*, 162.

258 Ratzinger notes that the peril of succumbing to the temptation of "self-redemption" has always been present in Christian history, most notably in the heresy of Pelagianism. It is in liberation theology that Ratzinger divines the danger of instrumentalizing theology for worldly ends (and, in so doing, collapsing grace into nature). This Pelagian danger looms at every stage of history and must be rejected time and time again. Liberation theology, according to Ratzinger, is just the latest variant of this constant threat. See Gaál, *Theology of Pope Benedict XVI*, 157.

259. Gaál, *Theology of Pope Benedict XVI*, 153.
260. Gaál, *Theology of Pope Benedict XVI*, 153.
261. Gaál, *Theology of Pope Benedict XVI*, 153.
262. Ratzinger, *Unity of the Nations*, 23.

Selfless and disinterested Christian charity far surpasses anything a Marxist or socialist model will ever be able to evoke. Thus, Christ is the solution to social problems. The Eucharist, specifically, is the sacrament of transformation to Christ and therefore to one another. It is in Christ's passion that suffering and violence and death are transformed into an act of love.[263] This is faithful to the principle of *gratia praesupponit naturam* in that the Eucharist is seen as transforming pagan religious customs into the memory of the life-sacrifice of Jesus Christ and the church's sacrifice. The liturgy is not of marginal interest to Ratzinger but is a profoundly Christological and therefore central concern.[264]

For Ratzinger, there is an intimate connection between political and Christological issues. His essays in *Politics and Redemption* essentially center on Marxist thought and its attendant derivatives in Western society and in Christianity until the collapse of the Soviet Union. The central issue is whether mankind is able to heal and redeem itself. For Marxists, redemption is no longer a theological category or religious term, but rather a stage in history that is organized by human beings. For Ratzinger, development without being mindful of the cultural, transcendental and religious dimension of mankind never offers the prospect of genuine liberation. He saw that Marxism takes up the divinization of utopian thoughts of all possible and impossible variations of reality and inverts them into history. Without God, utopia becomes the actual creedal content, and history becomes the true deity. In this way, individuals evaporate into the anonymous collective whole and the spiritual dimension of humanity is lost.[265] This problem, according to Ratzinger, is not entirely novel. As de Gaál observes, the early church fathers "developed the distinction between the supernatural and natural realms, which finds its correspondence in the distinction between the church and the world."[266] In Ratzinger's view, while the *nouvelle théologie* presented a new understanding of the relationship between nature and grace (that is, that one cannot speak of two levels of reality, one being unrelated to the other), in some quarters (obviously influenced by Kantian epistemology) the terms "supernatural" and "supernature" were judged to be artificial. This eventually led, he observes, to the supernatural being eschewed in favor of the concrete human being and a

---

263. Gaál, *Theology of Pope Benedict XVI*, 153.
264. Gaál, *Theology of Pope Benedict XVI*, 262.
265. Gaál, *Theology of Pope Benedict XVI*, 154.
266. Gaál, *Theology of Pope Benedict XVI*, 156.

completely horizontalized history. The obvious conclusion drawn was that "the Christian must then become worldly in order to be truly Christian, and the church must open to, or even merge with, the world to conform to this movement of history."[267]

Ratzinger observes that over the course of the second half of the twentieth century:

> the main thing affecting the status of Christianity in that period was the idea of a new relationship between the church and the world. Although Romano Guardini in the 1930's had coined the expression *Unterscheidung des Christlichen* [distinguishing what is Christian]—something that was extremely necessary then—such distinctions now no longer seemed to be important; on the contrary, the spirit of the age called for crossing boundaries, of reaching out to the world, and becoming involved in it.[268]

Hegel inspired both Feuerbach and Marx, who proposed that in history, difference always implies opposition, and therefore, conflict. In contrast, for the Christian, difference does not invariably entail opposition, as not every distinction produces dualism and opposition. For Ratzinger, a duality of principles guarantees social unity. He gives the example of Scholastic hylomorphism, which distinguishes between body and soul, yet this tension actually safeguards the integrity of the human person.[269] We have earlier seen the limitations of an extrinsicist rendering of nature and grace. Nevertheless, Ratzinger cautions strongly against collapsing the orders of nature and grace into one another, as the dissolution of the metaphysical into history runs the risk of having theology serve an ideology or of closing rational gaps in economic or political logic.[270] As he states in his *Introduction to Christianity*:

> All these plans for an epoch-making synthesis of Christianity and the world had to step aside, however, the moment that the faith collapsed into politics [as grace into nature] as [the primary] salvific force.... Man is indeed, as Aristotle says, a "political being," but he cannot be reduced to politics and economics. I

---

267. Ratzinger, *Politik und Erlösung*, 13. My translation. Original as follows: "Der Christ muss dann weltlich werden, um wahrhaft Christ zu sein, und die Kirche muss sich zur Welt öffnen oder sogar mit ihr verschmelzen, um dieser Bewegung der Geschichte zu entsprechen."

268. Ratzinger, *Introduction to Christianity*, 13.

269. Ratzinger, *Introduction to Christianity*, 26.

270. Gaál, *Theology of Pope Benedict XVI*, 157.

see the real and most profound problem with liberation theologies in their effective omission of the idea of God, which, of course, also changed the figure of Christ fundamentally.... Not as though God had been denied—not in your life! He simply was not needed in regard to the "reality" that mankind had to deal with. God had nothing to do.[271]

Ratzinger instead advocates for the Aristotelian model of politics, which provides for the relative autonomy of politics. He is also in agreement with Aquinas. Consistent with Augustine's position, Ratzinger insists on the two *civitates* as important in safeguarding the ineffable independence of God and the serene autonomy of theology vis-à-vis ideologies and politics. For Ratzinger, either completely blending the two realms of church and world (or nature and grace) or radically separating them is incorrect.

It is precisely the independence of these realms that demonstrates the specific nature of faith, and the inability of politics to substitute for it as a source for values and orientation beyond pragmatic, penultimate human desires.[272] For Ratzinger, the church is an ethical court of appeal *sui generis*, and does not create truth, but receives it as Revelation. The church does not posit truth: she herself is posited by it.[273] On the other side of this tension-filled arc lies the state, which must acknowledge that it has no authority concerning either religious or ethical matters.[274] It can but evidence secular truth as a constantly fluctuating consensus such as a parliament or the electorate may reach. In this sense, as de Gaál notes, a healthy tension exists between church and state, whereby both benefit. The individual and the state need to be aware of the intrinsic imperfection of the human condition per se.[275] Without God as the highest and nondisposable good, every value becomes totalitarian. In sum, Ratzinger's position is that while the church and the state differ regarding their respective natures, the church may not be deprived of her legal form proper to an institution. That is, the church's sacramentality does not occasion her spiritualization. For this reason, the notion of the church as *Corpus Christi* does not deprive her of her worldliness and world-transforming nature, nor, however, may it be reduced to an exclusively juridical entity.

271. Ratzinger, *Introduction to Christianity*, 16.
272. Gaál, *Theology of Pope Benedict XVI*, 157.
273. Nichols, "Joseph Ratzinger's Theology," 383.
274. Nichols, "Joseph Ratzinger's Theology," 383.
275. Gaál, *Theology of Pope Benedict XVI*, 184.

Only a balanced approach between the ideational and the pneumatic, between the sacramental and empirical, enables a proper appreciation of Augustine's notion of *Civitas Dei*.[276]

In his early work *The Unity of the Nations*, Ratzinger shows that Christianity, in its universal sense, could inspire a supranational ethics that cannot be justified only from the political economic realms. Ratzinger describes the early church's attitude towards the political realm and writes that Christianity did not aim at a "political, but an ethical revolution, at changing man rather than changing his relationships."[277] The moral revolution that Christians wanted to bring about was based upon their conviction that salvation does not come from earthly politics, but from outside of the temporal realm. This notion was contrary to the Roman notion of salvation coming from within the Roman empire, since the whole universe was considered as united as the body of Zeus: "As already mentioned, the whole world was Zeus's body; the hidden divine unity that characterized the world was converted into political reality by the Roman *princeps*," which was typified at the time of Christ by the *Pax Romana* of Caesar Augustus.[278] Christianity, on the other hand, saw that salvation and earthly unity are not tasks for one in this world but are part of an eschatological hope that will be fulfilled ultimately in heaven. This eschatological hope, Ratzinger notes, "allowed Christian martyrs to set their faith-filled conviction over against the authority of the state, the internal strength of truth over against the external force of earthly powers."[279] The early Christians distinguished their theology from the political theology of the Romans and also that of the Gnostics, who viewed creation as evil. As Ratzinger sets out, the early Christians knew that:

> the present world was not altogether bad but only stood in need of transformation whereby it was supposed to rise to eternal glory. For this reason it was not difficult for them to see that, although it was transitory, the world order that they knew nonetheless possessed a relative goodness and hence deserved respect when it stepped outside this framework and absolutised itself. They found this expressed in the Lord's words, "Render

---

276. Gaál, *Theology of Pope Benedict XVI*, 186.
277. Ratzinger, *Unity of the Nations*, 5.
278. Ratzinger, *Unity of the Nations*, 7.
279. Ratzinger, *Unity of the Nations*, 5.

under Caesar the things that are Caesar's, and to God the things that are God's" (Mark 12:17).[280]

This perspective stands midway between the univocal Roman view and the equivocal Gnostic view, and is typical of Ratzinger's analogy of being. It does not see the world and the political affairs of the people as a divine end in itself, and at the same time, by recognizing creation's relative value, it does not reject the entire cosmos as evil and unrelated to God.[281]

Given Ratzinger's interpretation of Augustine, he notes that the church is in a "painful 'between' state," in that the church must relate in some fashion with the political, despite reservations. This manner of relating, however, must not threaten the essentially non-political nature of faith.[282] In *Jesus of Nazareth*, Ratzinger explicitly argues that the essence of the church is non-political because the "essence of his [Christ's] new path" is having "actually achieved a separation of the religious from the political."[283] Ratzinger identifies the moment that this separation occurs, namely, at the crucifixion. Ratzinger writes:

> But this separation—essential to Jesus's message—of politics from faith, of God's people from politics, was ultimately possible only through the Cross. Only through the total loss of all external power, through the radical stripping away that led to the Cross, could this new world come into being. Only through faith in the Crucified One, in him who was robbed of all worldly power and thereby exalted, does the new community arise, the new manner of God's dominion in the world.[284]

In his *Faith and the Future*, Ratzinger describes Christ as principally having taken on flesh in order "interiorly to share in the passion of mankind" and:

> not as a *deus ex machina* to set everything in order, but as the Son of Man in order interiorly to share in the passion of mankind . . . [and] to share in the passion of mankind from within, to extend the sphere of human being so that it will find room for the presence of God.[285]

---

280. Ratzinger, *Unity of the Nations*, 21.
281. Kucer, *Truth and Politics*, 239.
282. Kucer, *Truth and Politics*, 230.
283. Benedict XVI, *From the Entrance*, 169.
284. Benedict XVI, *From the Entrance*, 170.
285. Ratzinger, *Faith and the Future*, 96–97.

Ratzinger continues:

> The Kingdom of God will be the city of man. The New Testament concludes with a vision of this city. It is true that this city spells the end of all our planning and its collapse. It comes down from above. But it only comes because and when man has run and suffered the whole course of his human existence to the limits of his capacities. And so in the meantime we are left simply with the task of corroborating the affirmation of faith that in Christ man has become the hope of humanity, by living our own lives in terms of this model, seeking to become one another's hope and to set upon the future the seal of Christ's features—the features of the coming city that will be completely human because it belongs completely to God.[286]

In the church's "painful 'between' state" on earth, she shares in the suffering of mankind from within by relating to the world non-politically. She does so by offering moral norms for politics and not by presenting herself as an ideal norm of political activity.[287]

As opposed to Ratzinger, Milbank favors a political theology that is informed by his close integration of nature and grace, such that a political theology is basically required. Milbank is of the view that without political theology, Christian social action is inauthentic and useless. For Milbank, this inauthenticity arises when political and economic factors are not seen as an essential aspect of how Christians relate to each other. Thus, the right ordering of these factors is fundamental to Christians' relationship with each other in accordance with the social nature of the Trinity, where unity arises from the trinitarian differences.[288] Based upon the insights of de Lubac, Milbank argues for a politicized version of the nature and grace relationship. As we have seen, Milbank draws a contrast between French integralism (intrinsicism) and the German variety, most notably represented by Karl Rahner and expressed in political theology and liberation theology.

---

286. Ratzinger, *Faith and the Future*, 98–99.

287. Ratzinger, *Eschatology*, 59. Even though Ratzinger does not advocate any political ideology, he is favorable toward democratic socialism, as, in his view, it is close to Catholic social doctrine, and in any case it has contributed toward the formation of social consciousness. Ratzinger is quick, however, to distinguish democratic socialism from totalitarian socialism, as in the former USSR and its "false economic dogmatism" and erroneous concept of human rights. See Ratzinger, *Europe*, 28–29.

288. Kucer, *Truth and Politics*, 244.

In the early twentieth century, there arose in France two ways of integrating the social order with the religious order. On the one hand, there were the "intransigent" Catholics who adhered strictly to the *Syllabus of Errors* and pledged to root out heretics and who collaborated politically with the monarchical, ultramontaine political organization run by the agnostic, Charles Maurras. Maurras's *Action Française* advocated a restoration of the traditional alliance between monarchy and church. On the other hand, there were those who had been inspired by Blondel, and advocated for a more democratic form of government transformed by a Christianization of the social order.[289] According to Kucer, both groups claimed that they represented the correct integration of politics and faith, with Milbank belonging to the latter group. Milbank not only opposes the version of integralism advanced by French traditionalists but also rejects the German form as inspired by Rahner. In comparing the two, Milbank notes "a difference that can be crudely indicated and misleadingly summarized by saying that whereas the French version supernaturalizes the natural, the German version naturalizes the supernatural."[290] As we have seen, the autonomous secular order proposed by Rahner is a variation of the concept of a pure state of nature developed by Suárez and the neo-scholastics and is considered to already be "grace-imbued."[291] Therefore, it is upon pre-theological sociology that theology must be founded. As in liberation theology, this autonomous "pre-theological" sociology is Marxism.[292] In contrast, French integralism refuses even formally to distinguish a realm of pure-nature in concrete humanity.[293] An encounter with grace does not occur, as in Rahner, at the margins of every individual's knowing, but rather in the confrontation with certain historical texts and images that have no permanent place whatsoever, save that of their original occurrence as events and their protracted repetition through the force of ecclesial allegiance. No social theory can set limits to the capacity of these events to become fundamental for human

---

289. Kucer, *Truth and Politics*, 246.

290. Milbank, *Theology and Social Theory*, 207.

291. Milbank, *Theology and Social Theory*, 207.

292. Ratzinger observes that, like positivism, Marxism rejects the primacy of *logos* and sees reason as "dialectically" generated by matter, by the irrational, and therefore must regard truth simply as a human postulation. See Nichols, "Joseph Ratzinger's Theology," 382.

293. Milbank, *Theology and Social Theory*, 208.

history any more than it can in the case of any other events.²⁹⁴ Milbank notes that this version of integralism that "supernaturalizes the nature," is, therefore, also the more historicist in character, because it does not identify with the supernatural as any permanent "area" of human life. But neither does it locate "nature" in the supernatural. According to Milbank, "where the supernatural impinges as the cultural recurrence of an event, it is at once recognizable as 'different', and, at the same time, limitlessly capable of transforming all other cultural phenomena."²⁹⁵ One, therefore, can conclude:

> In avoiding any hypostatization of human nature, in stressing the historical, by insisting that the later and superseding may assume priority over the earlier and apparently more "basic," the French version of integralism points in a "postmodern" direction which has more contemporary relevance than the view of Rahner.²⁹⁶

It is upon this view of integralism, observes Kucer, that Milbank builds his political theology as a better alternative to liberation theology and its precursor, namely, the political theology that began in Germany. Milbank further develops French integralism in a more radical direction by broadening the concept of salvation as socially understood. Following Blondel, de Lubac sought to integrate the social order with the salvific order by demonstrating that salvation is necessarily social. As Milbank explains, in contrast with German integralism, salvation for de Lubac is not dualistically divided into individual salvation and salvation of social structures, but rather entails a salvation mediated by the church in which humans are reconciled with God and with each other.²⁹⁷ Milbank however points out that de Lubac "does appear finally to insulate ecclesial history from secular and political history in general."²⁹⁸ This leads in turn to an insufficient integration of the social and religious realms that in turn causes the religious realm to be insufficiently relevant to the social.²⁹⁹ In this regard, Milbank observes that in the final chapter of *Catholicism*, entitled "Transcendence," de Lubac "imperils his

---

294. Milbank, *Theology and Social Theory*, 208.
295. Milbank, *Theology and Social Theory*, 209.
296. Milbank, *Theology and Social Theory*, 209.
297. Kucer, *Truth and Politics*, 248.
298. Milbank, *Theology and Social Theory*, 228.
299. Kucer, *Truth and Politics*, 248.

conclusions hitherto by asserting: 'There is in man an eternal element, a "germ of humanity," which always breathes the upper air, and which always, *hic et nunc*, evades the temporal society.'"[300] That is, the truth of man's being transcends his being itself. According to Milbank, when talking about the church, de Lubac is careful to avoid what Milbank defines as "the sociological illusion" of making society and the individual spatially external to each other, and yet, he observes, this care is forgotten when it comes to distinguishing the church from secular concerns. Milbank notes that:

> here de Lubac rediscovers the evasive spark of purely psychic life and makes the contrast of church/secular society in terms of the contrast individual/social, despite the fact that the preceding chapters had argued that the church is *also* a society. In this light, Marx's supposed "dissolution of the human being into the social being" ought to be an entirely illusory specter, yet, for de Lubac, this is what must be, above all, exorcised.[301]

According to Milbank, by invoking this specter, de Lubac actually implies that, in the manner of Weberian sociology, there *is* a realm that is merely "social" and that the individual might stand outside. Furthermore, this realm is an autonomous realm that the church, as church, should not interfere with, even in terms of advice, "except at points where social actions impinge on the ethical and religious sphere, which now appears especially 'individual.'"[302]

As we see, therefore, by completely eliminating any concept of the social order having some degree of autonomy from the supernatural order as mediated by the church, Milbank radicalizes de Lubac's integralism. This way of understanding the interaction of nature and grace, and consequently, the church and the world, leads Milbank to integrate politics with faith to the extent that the church is seen as a political norm.[303]

Milbank refers to the nineteenth-century French socialist Philippe-Joseph-Benjamin Buchez, and in so doing conceives of "the church (thought of as an amalgam of voluntary associations), rather than the sovereign state, as the site of a new social order."[304] This manner of

---

300. Milbank, *Theology and Social Theory*, 228.
301. Milbank, *Theology and Social Theory*, 228.
302. Milbank, *Theology and Social Theory*, 228.
303. Kucer, *Truth and Politics*, 249.
304. Milbank, *Theology and Social Theory*, 198.

conceiving a theology with "the church itself as the ultimate location of the just society" is, according to Milbank, properly in accordance with de Lubac's view of nature and grace, and the supernaturalization of the natural. In Milbank's post-political theology, the project of the church is the establishment of "a new, universal society, a new civitas."[305] Milbank distinguishes his post-political theology from political theology, as represented by Metz, and from various forms of Latin American liberation theology, by grounding his version of political theology in de Lubac's French integralism, rather than in the German form of integralism, typified by Rahner. By refusing to acknowledge any clear boundary between the religious order, in which grace is bestowed, and the social order, Milbank conceives the church, in accordance with his interpretation of Augustine, as herself a political reality.[306] As Milbank states:

> They [the Donatists] fail to see that the unity and inter-communion of Christians is not just a desirable appendage of Christian practice, but is itself at the heart of the actuality of redemption. The church itself, as the realized heavenly city, is the *telos* of the salvific process. And as a *civitas*, the church is, for Augustine, itself a "political reality."[307]

Since, according to Milbank, the church is to be the norm for politics, he asserts that "all political theory" in the antique sense is to be relocated by Christianity as thought about the church. When all political theory is conceived of as thought about the church, then a social political reality will emerge characterized by forgiveness, where "truly just economic exchanges occur."[308] In order for the church to be the church, she must not attempt to contain this social-political sphere of reconciliation within herself, but rather must seek to extend the sphere of socially aesthetic harmony within the state where this is possible.[309]

Milbank notes that on the Cross, Jesus inaugurated a "new politics of harmony" shaped by the concrete "practice of forgiveness; forgiveness as a mode of government and social being."[310] For Milbank, this means that "since we are situated on the far side of the Cross—the event of the

---

305. Milbank, *Theology and Social Theory*, 230.
306. Kucer, *Truth and Politics*, 250.
307. Milbank, *Theology and Social Theory*, 407.
308. Milbank, *Theology and Social Theory*, 424.
309. Milbank, *Theology and Social Theory*, 424.
310. Milbank, *Word Made Strange*, 161.

judgment of God—no return to law, to the antique compromise of inhibition of violence, remains possible."[311] This means that the church, when presenting the faith, is not to instruct political reason with specific moral laws understood as ahistorically universal; rather, faith, in the form of a new practice convertible with truth in the church established through Christ's death on the Cross, is to be the site and norm for a new political practice to emerge, based on nonviolence and the blending of differences that emerge by means of these differences, not despite them.[312] The harmonization of difference in a nonviolent manner occurs through ecclesial consensus. In explaining this, he writes that "the consensus sought by the church is not a consensus on the abstract, concerning a list of the desirable individual virtues. And if it *has* an abstractly specifiable goal, this is now consensus itself, meaning a society without violence and unjust domination."[313] This means that, for Milbank, the consensus achieved by the church is not based on universally valid moral laws, but rather upon the practice of reconciliation and the appreciation of difference. The church is furthermore to oppose an approach to morality defined by ahistorical moral laws. This is because, according to Milbank, Christianity refuses to treat reason and morality as ahistorical universals, but "instead asks, like Hegel, how has Christianity affected human reason and human practice?"[314] For Milbank, the church should abandon all Scholastic attempts to "graft faith onto a universal base of reason," and instead should turn to the church fathers, and indeed go beyond them, "in seeking to elaborate a Christian *logos*, or a reason that bears the marks of the incarnation and Pentecost."[315] At the same time, the church should seek to define a Christian *Sittlichkeit*, a moral practice embedded in the historical emergence of a new and unique community. Both tasks, he thinks, are "in turn situated in the re-narration of Christian emergence, a story which only constitutes itself as a story by re-narrating previous stories, both of past history and of the relation of creation to Godhead."[316]

Milbank nevertheless points out that the church has often failed in its mission to extend the different "story" of forgiveness in the world. Instead, in imitation of the political practice before the Cross, Christianity

311. Milbank, *Theology and Social Theory*, 442.
312. Milbank, *Word Made Strange*, 155.
313. Milbank, *Word Made Strange*, 155. Emphasis in original.
314. Milbank, *Theology and Social Theory*, 383.
315. Milbank, *Theology and Social Theory*, 383.
316. Milbank, *Theology and Social Theory*, 383.

has "helped to unleash a more naked violence."³¹⁷ This process began in the Middle Ages, when the "attempts of people to rule directly over people in small communities without recourse to an elaborate formal mechanism of law, gradually failed."³¹⁸ The church failed in her mission precisely because she failed to displace this old political practice, and instead promoted the multiplication of "new legal forms" in order to bind people together.³¹⁹

As we have seen, in order to regain the original political mission of the church, Milbank argues that the church must embrace a form of "ecclesial socialism" as its proper political form, in contrast to the prior political forms based on law and the containment of violence.³²⁰ Milbank is careful however to distinguish Catholic socialism from Marxism, which he describes as "standing almost alone in the nineteenth century as a 'modernist' Enlightenment variant of socialism, which in the final vision of the *Grundrisse* envisages social cooperation in a purely utilitarian fashion, and subordinates this to the single value of a full realization of individual liberty."³²¹ In Milbank's version of socialism, individual liberty is always conceived within the context of "sacramental and charitable bonds" as founded on trinitarian freedom in eternal, loving, creative relationship.³²² Milbank goes on to differentiate his ecclesiastical socialism from centrally planned state socialism (e.g., Stalinism) and even agrees with the capitalist Friedrich Hayek's rejection of central planning. Milbank prefers decentralized socialism that relies on "syndicalism or cooperativism," in imitation of the medieval guilds, which would encourage a professional ethos that upholds a standard of quality for all practitioners to reach. In such a socialism, products are to be manufactured not only for profit, but also, and principally, to maintain a degree of quality. This allows the product to take on the aspect of a gift. Socialism conceived in this way with the central role of upholding values other than for profit, is not, according to Milbank, "to 'limit' the market, but rather to reconstrue exchange according to the protocols of a universal gift-exchange: that is to say, in every negotiated transaction, something other than profit and

---

317. Milbank, *Theology and Social Theory*, 434.
318. Milbank, *Theology and Social Theory*, 434.
319. Milbank, *Theology and Social Theory*, 435.
320. Kucer, *Truth and Politics*, 253.
321. Milbank, *Theology and Social Theory*, 198.
322. Milbank, *Theology and Social Theory*, 435.

loss must be at issue."³²³ According to Milbank, a consensus on quality is fundamental and must be brought about by guilds and like associations. If this does not occur, then within any political system, "there can only be market mediation of an anarchy of desires—of course ensuring the triumph of a hierarchy of sheer power and the secret commanding of people's desires by manipulation."³²⁴

In contrast, Ratzinger, while maintaining that one cannot separate Christ from the Holy Spirit—that is, a Christ-centered, institutional church, from the pneumatic-prophetic one—remained adamant that the necessary tension between and relative autonomy of religion and politics be maintained. If this were not to be the case, the attendant danger would be twofold: mockery would be made of God, and the state would become inhumane.³²⁵ Ratzinger gave an address in 1980 at St. Ludwig's Church in Munich (having been forced there from the lecture hall due to unruly university campus communists), at which he addressed the students as follows:

> Render unto God what is God's and unto Caesar what is Caesar's—these seemingly so simple words inaugurated a new phase in the history of the relationship between politics and religion. Until then, it was commonly held that the political was also the sacred. Jesus cut apart this identification of the state's claim on man with the sacred claim of the divine will in the world. This placed into jeopardy the ancient idea of the state and it is understandable that the ancient state considered this negation of its totality as an attack on the very foundations of its existence, punishable on pain of death. If Jesus's word is valid, then indeed the Roman state could not continue in its previous construction. At the same time, it must be stated that this separation of state and sacred authority—and the new dualism inherent in it—represents the origin and abiding foundation of the Western idea of freedom.³²⁶

In *Jesus of Nazareth*, Pope Benedict points out that—in contrast to the ancient Roman rulers, who had declared themselves to be the "Son of the Divine Caesar" and therefore Son of God—Jesus Christ defined his kingship in entirely different terms. Authentic divine sonship rests on

323. Milbank, *Being Reconciled*, 186.
324. Milbank, *Future of Love*, 248.
325. Gaál, *Theology of Pope Benedict XVI*, 145.
326. Wallbrecher, Weimer, and Stötzl, *30 Jahre Wegbegleitung*, 43.

the unity of the Son with the Father with the Spirit. Given this, therefore, for Benedict:

> the fundamentally apolitical Christian faith, which does not demand political power, but acknowledges the legitimate authorities (cf. Romans 13:1–7), inevitably collides with the total claim made by the imperial political power. Indeed, it will always come into conflict with totalitarian political regimes and will be driven into the situation of martyrdom, into communion with the Crucified, who reigns solely from the wood of the Cross.[327]

While Jesus does enter into the drama of human existence, he does not disavow his divine identity or redefine himself in any other way. Nothing "political" or "material" may replace Jesus's divine commission and eternal origin with the Father, lest "the things of God fade into unreality, into a secondary world that no one really needs."[328] This is the importance of the temptation narratives, whereby the devil attempts to lure Jesus into the trap of seeking merely worldly power and sustenance. Jesus is not indifferent to human suffering; however, the proper priorities are called for if one is to truly satisfy man's thirst for happiness, beatitude, and fulfilment. Genuine humanism hinges on listening to God and living with God, where orthodoxy leads to orthopraxis.[329] For Benedict, religion, especially Christianity, may never be instrumentalized to sanction or canonize a body politic as Paul Althaus and the National Socialists did. Ancient pagan religions succumbed naturally to this temptation. Yet, for the Christian, the world and thus the *polis* remain essentially transitional and therefore alien terrain. However Christianized a society may be, the church points to the world yet to come.[330] With the advent of Christianity, religion could no longer be used *nolens volens* to sanction a particular political reality. For Ratzinger, the church does not simply become an uncritical companion to the world. Rather, oriented to God as the *Bonum diffusivum sui*, the church lives in the trinitarian mystery that has opened itself to her in Christ.[331]

Ratzinger considered this uncritical adoption of worldly politics the danger of reading Rahner's *Grundkurs des Glaubens*. In it, Ratzinger

---

327. Benedict XVI, *From the Baptism*, 339.
328. Benedict XVI, *From the Baptism*, 29.
329. Gaál, *Theology of Pope Benedict XVI*, 146.
330. Gaál, *Theology of Pope Benedict XVI*, 147.
331. Ratzinger, *Neue Volk Gottes*, 283–84.

divines something of a pseudo-Hegelian reduction of God to a self-becoming of the Absolute Spirit in time and space. Likewise, the concept of Rahner's supernatural existential runs the risk of being misunderstood as the grace-free self-becoming of humanity in history. This, as de Gaál points out, is latently and acutely accented in Metz's political theology. Instead, for Ratzinger, the solution lies in "Christification" (not "justification" in the Western Protestant sense). For Ratzinger, salvation history as Revelation history may not be collapsed into world history in a Hegelian sense of the progressive self-explication of mankind.[332] Humanity is redeemed by Christ *in* history but not *through* history. Nature and grace (and likewise faith and reason) interact without becoming dialectic entities within a larger, faceless automatic process.[333]

Ratzinger develops a theology of politics that, while recognizing some overlap of faith with political reason, also maintains a certain degree of integrity of each realm. Consistent with his more moderate view of the integration of nature and grace, Ratzinger asserts that the site where the truth of faith overlaps political reason is solely concerned with specific moral teaching. In this moral *locus*, faith as lived out by the church is normative for politics, but its normative dimension does not go far beyond specific moral teachings.[334] As we have seen, for Ratzinger, faith is not "a political norm of political activity."[335] The transformation that faith is directly concerned with in the political realm therefore is with personal conversion and not with structural change. This does not mean, however, that believers are not individually entitled to express their political views, or that particular ideologies are prima facie forbidden (Ratzinger, after all, expresses his preference for democratic socialism).[336] For Ratzinger, what is essential is that clear boundaries between politics and the doctrinal truths of the faith be maintained. He maintains that the faith is beneficial to politics, since it allows the church to be an open space of reconciliation among parties. As a result, Catholics possess the

332. Gaál, *Theology of Pope Benedict XVI*, 149.
333. Ratzinger, *Principles of Catholic Theology*, 166.
334. Kucer, *Truth and Politics*, 256.
335. Ratzinger, *Eschatology*, 59.
336. Kucer, *Truth and Politics*, 256. See also Ratzinger and Pera, *Without Roots*, 72, where he makes this plain; and Ratzinger, *Neue Volk Gottes*, 386–88. Here Ratzinger adds that, rather than structural change, the church's missionary proclamation is the historical execution of divine salvation. See also Ratzinger, "Eschatology and Utopia," 227. Here Ratzinger emphasizes that the stronger the underpinning of *mores*, the fewer *instituta* are needed.

interior freedom to judge a political party according to the supranational ethics of the church, founded in universal truths, which, in turn, encourage Catholics to ultimately transcend their political party.[337] In contrast, Milbank develops a political theology and presents the boundaries between the church and state as being "extremely hazy."[338] This state of affairs he terms "post-political theology" in order to distinguish it from the German variants that integrate faith with political reason, such as liberation theology. In accordance with his radical integration of nature and grace, Milbank differs from Ratzinger in that he does not see the church's role as preaching unchanging moral truths but is instead *herself* a political norm for political activity, a position that Ratzinger repeatedly and explicitly rejects.[339] For Milbank, the faith is to transform the political not by upholding specific moral truths, but rather by forming a site of ecclesial socialism. This ecclesial socialism would take the form of a complex, non-centrist and non-Marxist socialism based upon the social aspects of the trinitarian persons in harmony through their differences, and not despite them.[340] There are, nevertheless, a number of similarities between Ratzinger's theology of politics and Milbank's political theology. Both affirm the relevancy of faith for the political. They differ, however, on the degree to which this is to be held. Also, both seem to affirm socialism. This is important, as Milbank criticizes the church for having taken "fright at socialism" after the European revolutions of 1848.[341] This fright obviously does not include Ratzinger. Nonetheless, unlike Milbank, he does refuse to identify any political ideology (including socialism) as being constitutive of the faith.[342]

CONCLUSION

The question of the church's position within secular culture remains a central concern for both Ratzinger and Milbank. The fundamental theological question that pertains to this issue is the relationship between nature and grace. In order to address this problem, Milbank builds his

---

337. Ratzinger, *Called to Communion*, 100; and Ratzinger, *Faith and the Future*, 56.
338. Milbank, *Theology and Social Theory*, 410.
339. Ratzinger, *Eschatology*, 59.
340. Kucer, *Truth and Politics*, 257.
341. Milbank, *Word Made Strange*, 273.
342. Kucer, *Truth and Politics*, 258.

theological project upon the Platonic notion of participation (*methexis*), which enables him in turn to eschew any possibility of a reserve of territory apart from God in which the secular may dwell. Milbank points to Scotus as the initial cause of the modern-day rejection of the *analogia entis* and the notion of participation. Ratzinger, like Milbank, relies upon the insights of Przywara in adherence to the *analogia entis* and anchors his central thesis of *gratia praesupponit naturam* upon the same. Ratzinger goes further than Milbank in seeking to connect the *analogia entis* with the *analogia fidei* and notes that it is the Cross that presents the most obvious and profound coincidence of these two notions. Ratzinger, also unlike Milbank, seeks a revival of Christian realism, based upon the notion that the culture of the West originates with the creative power unleashed by commitment to the *Logos*, which passes from the Platonic *eidos* to the Christocentric principle, present in the fathers, and recognized as *forma Dei*. This Christocentric emphasis is one of the major distinguishing features between the thought of Ratzinger and that of Milbank. For Ratzinger, the specific mode of being Christian involves participation in the person of Christ Jesus, Word of God. Thus, we see that the notion of participation is important in both authors; however, it is only in Ratzinger that we find a clearer and more distinct personalist, Christological emphasis. Ratzinger and Milbank both draw from the insights of de Lubac and the *nouvelle théologie* and tend to eschew the dry and formulaic theology of neo-scholasticism. Milbank however tends to radicalize de Lubac's position and is inclined to view nature and grace as phases within a single extension, rather than clearly defined realities. Ratzinger, on the other hand, while acknowledging the interplay and interaction between nature and grace, seeks to maintain the integrity of each much more robustly than Milbank. Thus, nature and grace tend to be radically integrated in Milbank, whereas in Ratzinger the stability of each is more evident. In this way, Milbank leans towards a certain supernaturalism, which downplays the role of nature. Ratzinger's *gratia praesupponit naturam* however provides a useful counterbalance to such a tendency, while at the same time avoiding a naturalist interpretation that would collapse grace into nature, thus downplaying grace. Ratzinger emphasizes that being Christian does not mean breaking with nature at all, but instead, by means of one's cooperation with grace, heightening and perfecting it. Milbank, in contrast to Ratzinger, also tends to equivocate the notion of participation with the notion of grace, and in this way seeks to provide a "theo-ontology," in which grace goes all the way down to man's core. Everything, thus, for Milbank, is "engraced." This position however is greatly problematic for Ratzinger as it not only purports to collapse the notions of grace and nature, but also those of creation and redemption, risking the elimination of the entire Christian narrative itself. For Milbank, sanctification involves a certain "re-humanization," that is, a restoration of original justice, and life as it was before the Fall. For Ratzinger, however, and more in line with de Lubac, sanctification involves a transformation in Christ by the working of the Holy Spirit. Thus, for Ratzinger, man's supernatural telos exceeds the order of creation, whereas for Milbank it does not. While Ratzinger successfully preserves the Lubacian paradox, Milbank pushes it beyond breaking point such that nature collapses into grace.

Concerning the problem of secularism, both Ratzinger and Milbank are in agreement that it was fostered, at least initially, by theological positions adopted by the church's own scholars, that is to say, extrinsicist modes of considering the nature and grace relation. Milbank views the phenomenon of secularism as a mutation of the classical-theistic synthesis, which when severed from its Christian roots is given new meanings. Ratzinger is largely in agreement with this position and does not admit of any philosophy of history (particularly in the Hegelian sense) outside the Christian theology of history and the notion of the theo-drama of God's offer of grace to man, and man's response. Both Ratzinger and Milbank seek to demonstrate that secular culture is not devoid of theological presuppositions and foundations, thus undermining the notion of its supposed "neutrality," particularly apropos of religious matters. Ratzinger is prepared however to admit of a distinction between a positive kind of secularity and a negative form that seeks to banish religion from public life and into the private sphere, locking the church into a "ghetto of subjectivity." Milbank, on the other hand, does not allow for the validity of secularity at all, and considers it to be a form of Christian heresy, based on what he terms an "ontology of violence," as opposed to the church's "ontology of peace." Ratzinger and Milbank both similarly reject the possibility of correspondence theory, although Ratzinger is much more moderate in this sense. Milbank, after all, does not consider that the Christian Church can learn anything at all from secular sources of knowledge. Following *Gaudium et Spes*, Ratzinger posits a correct and appropriate autonomy of the church and of the secular order, reflective of his interpretation of the relationship between nature and grace, which seeks to preserve the integrity of each while allowing for interaction between the two. Milbank, on the other hand, consistent with his tendency to supernaturalize nature, envisages the church as a form of social theory and an alternative political structure. That there could be the possibility of distinct realms of church and state is completely eschewed by Milbank. This leads him to develop a political theology as the church is herself a political norm for political activity, a position that Ratzinger completely rejects. For Milbank, the faith is to transform the political not merely by preaching and upholding moral truths but by forming a site of ecclesial socialism. Ratzinger, on the other hand, is adamant that there be maintained clear boundaries between politics and the doctrinal truths of the faith. Nevertheless, these same truths are beneficial to politics and allow that the church might be an open space for a wide political spectrum. Ratzinger instead is much more concerned with the idea of personal conversion rather than the notion of structural change.

Conclusion

THE EVANGELIZATION OF CULTURE stands at the center of the Christian missionary vocation. The manner in which one conceives of the relationship between nature and grace directly impacts how one understands the church's relation to culture.

Chapter 1 provided a biographical outline of both Ratzinger and Milbank as well as a brief introduction to the main features of their thought. Chapter 2 traced a historical outline of the nature and grace debate as it had unfolded in the years since the Reformation, in order to establish a context for the theological comparison of Ratzinger and Milbank. We saw there that Catholic theologians had, at the time of the Reformation, attempted to steer a middle ground through the opposing extremes of Calvinism, which largely denigrates human nature, and Baianism, which elevates it such that man can purportedly attain to God by means of his natural merits alone. Theologians of the time proposed the theory of the *Duplex Ordo* in order to contend with these challenges, which was based upon the work of Aquinas and Aristotle. While the *Duplex Ordo* was able to buttress traditional Catholic teaching against the challenges of the heretics, it did, regrettably, lead to the tendency to see reality as a separation into natural and supernatural realms. In the mid-nineteenth century, in order to respond to the ongoing challenges of the Enlightenment, Leo XIII encouraged a revival of this same Thomism by means of his encyclical, *Aeterni Patris*, which, accordingly, led to a revival of the Suárezian notion of the *Duplex Ordo* and the extrinsicist separation of nature and grace. One of de Lubac's most important insights was to note that this separation directly and indirectly led to the possibility of secularism and the encouragement of secular humanists in their cutting the church off from public life. In this way, theology had colluded in its own banishment from the public life of the state. Taking a different approach from that of the erstwhile regnant neo-scholastic Thomism, the *nouvelle théologie* sought a greater engagement and theological appropriation of the categories of history, concrete philosophy, and politics. Basing itself upon the insights of Blondel, and setting out upon a project of *ressourcement*, the theologians of the *nouvelle théologie* offered a counter-theology to that of neo-scholasticism. Drawing from the fathers and medieval sources, these theologians, de Lubac principal among them, engaged with the modern philosophical, theological, and political concerns of their contemporaries in ways that exceeded the possibilities of the rationalistic categories of the typically manualist theology that preceded it. Accordingly, their method involved rereading the ancient sources in light of the present challenges and renouncing traditional apologetics in favor of fundamental theology. As opposed to the extrinsicism of neo-scholasticism, the *nouvelle théologie* has, at its core, an intrinsicist conception of the relationship between nature and grace, based principally upon the notion of the paradox. This approach to theology can provide the church with more effective tools in answering the challenge of secularism, because it is better able to engage with the concerns of contemporary man and eschews the possibility of a neat separation of the realms of the "worldly" and the "spiritual."

Chapter 3 showed that Milbank bases his theological project upon the insights of the *nouvelle théologie*, especially those of de Lubac. One of Milbank's motivating factors was the challenge that liberal secular culture presents to the church, in particular the secularist tendency to reduce religion merely to a private affair, with no relevance to public life. For Milbank, the fruit of the genius of de Lubac was to reject any possibility of a reserve of reality that could be counted as independent of God. In this way, Milbank sought to make plain the theological presuppositions of secular culture and, in so doing, he undermines any notion that the same could be considered to be "above" the theological squabbles of warring religious groups, and in this way validly considered to be properly "neutral." Secularism contains just as many theological presuppositions as any mainstream religion. Milbank sustains his theological project by relying on the Platonic notion of participation, and, as stated, he sees himself as the inheritor of the Lubacian project, charging himself with the task of continuing it to its logical conclusion. In particular, de Lubac's notion of the paradox and the natural desire for the supernatural are fundamental insights of the *nouvelle théologie* that Milbank wants to defend. To those (principally neo-Thomists) who would seek to denigrate as nonsensical the centrality of the Lubacian "paradox," which serves his interpretation of nature and grace, Milbank points to the hypostatic union. This union, Milbank reminds his readers, is itself a mysterious paradox. Christ stands in a "suspended middle" between the divine and the human, the finite and the infinite, because divinity and humanity are not univocal natures that are somehow competing for space, and thus mutually exclusive. Christ is, after all, fully both. In order to allay neo-scholastic charges of having abolished the notion of the gratuity of grace, Milbank emphasizes that the gift of creation and the gift of grace are already united in one divine gifting. Thus, he resists the attempt to put the gift of creation against the gift of grace. There is nothing outside the economy of divine gratuity against which it can be contrasted. Recovering the Platonic idea of *influentia*, Milbank proposes that grace functions by acting upon man not as though it were some foreign influence but by means of a paradigm of gratuity in which the recipient of the gift, the gift itself, and the donation of one to the other establish a radically unilateral threefold gratuity. In this way, the notions of the gratuity of grace and the autonomy of the creature can be held together without contradiction, and, importantly, without having to make concessions to the extrinsicists by relying on the idea of "pure-nature." While Milbank relies heavily on de Lubac's insights, he exceeds them in some respects. Notwithstanding his own cautions against supernaturalizing tendencies in the relation of nature and grace, one finds in Milbank the very same tendency, that is, of collapsing nature into grace. In this same vein, Milbank also controversially tends to conflate the notions of "participation" and "grace" such that he maintains that all creation is "engraced." This conflation presents problems when one considers the possibility of the loss of grace by means of sin. Furthermore, Milbank considers God's original intent to be creation specifically *as* creation, and thus rejects the notion that creation's supernatural destiny *exceeds* the order of creation. This position, likewise, presents problems for the traditional Catholic understanding of grace and sanctification and goes far beyond what de Lubac and Ratzinger would maintain. Milbank also rejects the possibility that secular standards of scientific truth and rationality could ever be truly normative for the church because of the central importance of participation. Rejecting correspondence theory, Milbank asserts that it is specifically because participation is to be held to be foundational, and because participation is equated with grace, that Christian theology accordingly can and indeed must confidently include everything within its purview. In this way, Milbank does not allow for any so-called "neutral" space for even a non-theological politics or ethics and rejects any suggestion that secular ways of thought could ever be considered normative for Christianity, insisting instead upon a theological social theory and a radical Christian politics. For Milbank, to attempt to contend with the problem of secular culture by appeasing it, or creating intellectual space for it, is to have failed *ab initio*. Thus, any notion of a correlationist approach, a mediating theology, a universal humanism, or a *rapprochement* with the Enlightenment is to be rejected because such approaches are based upon the premise that there can validly exist a purely natural, secular sphere of thought or action apart from God with which the church must dialogue. Such an approach is symptomatic of an extrinsicist conception of nature and grace, a concept that has regrettably given impetus to secular humanists.

Ratzinger, likewise, is deeply concerned with the secularization of the West and holds that it remains one of the greatest challenges that the church faces today. Chapter 4 showed that Ratzinger sought a dialectical process inspired by charity to be the way in which the church encounters the prevailing culture. Ratzinger saw the limitations of the neo-scholastic extrinsicist approach to the question of nature and grace, along with the rationalistic approach to theology, and thought that such an approach is ultimately ineffective in addressing the problem of secular culture, as it does not engage successfully with contemporary issues nor address the foundational notions that buttress secularism. Ratzinger prefers a Christocentric personalist approach to theology, and attempts to hold, in paradoxical union, the two polarities of the Incarnation and the Cross. Ratzinger also eschews any possibility of correlationist approaches to theology, maintaining the value of Christian culture and the transcendentals of truth, goodness, and beauty. He also applies a Przywaraian reading of Augustine and is rooted in a Catholic humanism that is, in turn, anchored in the Incarnation. Ratzinger is by no means a neo-Manichean who hates the world. He has written much on the importance of the role of art, music, and culture, and specifically how these can be theophanic. The experience of beauty, he thinks, can open man to reality, and ultimately, to Christ. It is the Incarnation that has meant that all human existence can be henceforth characterized Christologically. Ratzinger qualifies this position, however, by pointing out that a theology of the Incarnation that is too much on the level of essence runs the risk of being too self-contented, struggling to pass beyond the ontological phenomenon of God's becoming man. Ratzinger insists on the paradoxical union of the Incarnation and the Cross as a necessary corrective to the temptation to the self-contentment of Incarnationalism. Christ's own kenosis holds before man the template of what it means to be fully human. In the union of wills between man and God, man finds his true foundation, the ultimate goal of his own being. It follows, therefore, that one finds in Ratzinger an emphasis on dialectics over dialogue, on Revelation over personal experience, and on content over method.

We saw also that Ratzinger cautions against the extremes of either naturalism or supernaturalism, but insists instead on holding nature and grace together in paradoxical tension, rather than collapsing one into the other. Adopting Bonaventure's *gratia praesupponit naturam*, Ratzinger demonstrates that the Christian life does not mean eschewing nature at all, but heightening and perfecting it. In this way, one sees Ratzinger's typically paschal mode of relating nature and grace by means of man's kenotic exodus from self-sufficiency to self-donation in Christ. Accordingly, his nature is healed, perfected, and elevated. Ratzinger demonstrates that the axiom *gratia praesupponit naturam* gives voice to the *analogia entis* and expresses the notion of the all-embracing universal yes to the analogy of being, against a supernaturalist tendency that supposes it honors God by crucifying man. The Cross, therefore, for Ratzinger does not mean man's destruction but the foundation of true humanity. The fundamental law of exodus, perfected in Christ's Pasch, is also the fundamental law of Revelation, and of Spirit. This going forth, this exodus, is that which constitutes conversion, and thus, transformation. Ratzinger's holding in tension of the theology of the Incarnation and the theology of the Cross, bound in paradoxical union by means of a paschal logic, is reflected, accordingly, in his conception of nature and grace.

Chapter 5 compared Ratzinger and Milbank's respective approaches to the question of nature and grace, and accordingly to that of secular culture. As will now be apparent, the phenomenon of secularization is judged to be a challenge in the minds of both authors. For Milbank, relying on the Platonic notion of participation, which grounds his entire theological system, the possibility of a purely secular realm (completely cut off from God) is rejected. Milbank points to Scotus as the initiator of the lamentable modern-day rejection of the *analogia entis*. Ratzinger, relying on Przywara, looks to the *analogia entis* as a central notion in his theology, and relies on the same to ground his notion of *gratia praesupponit naturam*. Unlike Milbank, however, Ratzinger attempts to tie the notion of *analogia entis* with the *analogia fidei*, and notes that it is precisely the Cross that provides the principle of coincidence of these two notions. Ratzinger also seeks a revival of Christian realism, while Milbank does not, based upon the notion that the culture of the West is founded upon the *Logos*, which passes from the Platonic *eidos* to the Christocentric principle, recognized as *forma Dei*. This Christocentric emphasis in Ratzinger distinguishes him from Milbank. The adherence to, and participation in, the person of Jesus Christ is emphasized in Ratzinger, typical of his more personalist, Christological approach. Both authors nevertheless draw from the insights of the *nouvelle théologie*, particularly de Lubac, eschewing the manualistic and formulaic approach to theology typical of neo-scholasticism. Milbank radicalizes de Lubac's position and is inclined to view nature and grace as phases within one single extension rather than as clearly defined realities. In this way, Milbank, irrespective of his own caveats relating to the same, tends towards a certain supernaturalism in the way he conceives of nature and grace. Ratzinger, however, better maintains the integrity of each realm, even while acknowledging the paradoxical interplay and interaction between them. Ratzinger is much more successful in maintaining nature and grace in balanced tension, thanks in part to his adherence to the axiom *gratia praesupponit naturam*. As de Lubac himself saw, the Christian theologian must strive to maintain the unified integrity of a mystery of faith rather than to seek at all costs to alleviate whatever tension may arise from the juxtaposition of various aspects of a given mystery. The ever present problem of how to conceive of the relationship between nature and grace is to resist the temptation of collapsing one into the other, but to allow them to exist in tension. This is part of the brilliance of de Lubac's notion of the paradox. It is an ever present temptation for man to resolve paradoxes (into Hegelian dialectics, for example), rather than to permit them to exist, mysterious as they are.

As already stated, Milbank equates the notion of "participation" with "grace" and in this way aims for a "theo-ontology" in which everything is "engraced." Ratzinger, however, would resist such a position as it collapses the order of nature into grace, as well as the notions of creation into redemption, putting at risk the entire Christian narrative. The notion of sanctification, for Ratzinger, means transformation in Christ by the working of the Holy Spirit, whereas for Milbank it implies a form of "re-humanization," and a restoration of what was lost at the time of the

Fall. Here again, Ratzinger more successfully preserves the de Lubacian paradox, whereas Milbank pushes it beyond breaking point. These varying conceptions of nature and grace have a direct consequence on how each author, accordingly, understands and approaches secular culture.

Both Milbank and Ratzinger concur with de Lubac that the phenomenon of secularism has been aided by positions adopted by the church's own scholars, specifically extrinsicist modes of considering nature and grace. Secular culture is not a merely "neutral" reality, devoid of theological presuppositions. This is emphasized in Milbank, and is one of his key insights. Consistent with his more balanced paradoxical integrity-in-unity approach to nature and grace (wherein both realms are preserved, not collapsed into each other), Ratzinger is prepared to admit of a certain "positive secularism" in which the church is seen as a valuable contributor to the public life of the state and as a protagonist of culture. He does, nevertheless, oppose hostile secularity in which the church is banished from public life, purportedly in the name of the maintenance of neutrality. Milbank, on the other hand, does not admit of the possibility of secularism at all, viewing it as a phenomenon deriving from Christian heresy, and as one that carries an "ontology of violence" (as opposed to an "ontology of peace," as in Christianity) at its core. Milbank would view Ratzinger's position as conceding far too much to secular culture, and urge the project of distinguishing between so-called "positive" and "negative" forms of secularism be eschewed entirely, particularly because secularism in and of itself is inimical to Christianity. Accordingly, Milbank posits a political theology that views the church as a political norm for political activity, a position that does not admit of the possibility of the secular. Ratzinger completely rejects this position, however, and allows for "correctly understood" autonomy of the secular realm and of the church. For Milbank, the faith is meant not merely to transform the political by means of preaching and moral action but specifically to form a site of ecclesial socialism. Ratzinger is adamant, however, that clear boundaries need to be maintained between politics and the doctrinal truths of the faith. Milbank, on the other hand, is creating a lonely and heavy burden indeed for the theologian if one is seeking the "ecclesialization" of everything. Furthermore, Ratzinger emphasizes that the faith cannot be reduced to any political system, nor is any one system exhaustively expressive of it. The truths of the faith are beneficial to politics and allow the church to be an open space for a wide political spectrum. As we have seen, what matters most to Ratzinger, and what, in the final analysis, is most effective for social change, is personal conversion in Christ Jesus.

At the beginning of this project, the fundamental research question was: Can a theological comparison of John Milbank and Joseph Ratzinger on the question of nature and grace assist the church in understanding and evangelizing secular culture?

It is hoped that this book will assist in elucidating the issues facing the church in the present culture even as it presents a comparative analysis of two possible responses to those challenges. By understanding the specific *theological* presuppositions behind secular culture, the church, by means of the application of a balanced, intrinsicist view of nature and grace, and an appropriate theology of politics (not a political theology) may be able to challenge the roots of the secularist cutting religion off from public life. It is beyond the scope of this book, however, to attempt to enumerate specific strategies for local churches to pursue this goal, primarily because these pastoral objectives would vary from place to place, depending on unique local conditions and challenges. What is fundamental, however, is that the church not accept as merely inevitable the fact of an aggressive secularism passing itself off as purportedly "neutral." After all, the absence of religious belief is itself a "belief system." Instead, sure of her own firm roots in the person of Christ, she should work to be an agent of cultural change, which is her proper vocation, seeking to rebuff attempts to silence her, and bringing about a correct understanding of her rightful place in public life, even as she preaches the gospel. As *Gaudium et Spes* §53 sets out, "Catholics should feel free to mount the full range of their arguments in public and should reject the notion that they are bound by rules of engagement set by their intellectual opponents." Too often, the church feels herself on the back foot, intimidated by those cultural forces that would seek to silence her. She must be reminded that she has a right to speak in public, to be truly who she is. This is secularism "correctly understood." It is the only way that true dialogue can take place and it is the direct opposite of the tendency to exclude or privatize faith as an individual matter of personal belief. It is ultimately also the only way to overcome the temptations to sectarianism and fundamentalism, whether of religion or of political creeds; and it is the foundation of authentic pluralism. As Austen Ivereigh points out, the challenge remains, however, to encourage Catholic intellectuals to present integrated arguments for their positions, drawing on both nature and grace. Until the full set of reasons for Christian belief is articulated, those listening can rightly claim to be puzzled and perhaps dismissive of Christians who argue in a way that so lacks passion and conviction that they are not even willing to tell their whole story.[1] In this same vein, Pope Francis has asked us to "seek new ways" to proclaim the gospel, and in so doing to invoke "Mary, Mother of Evangelization," so that "the Virgin Mother may help us to say our own 'yes', conscious of the urgent need to make the Good News of Jesus resound in our time."[2] Despite the cultural challenges facing the church, may we, with confidence, hope, love, and above all, faith, seek from God the "holy audacity needed to discover new ways to bring the gift of salvation to every man and woman."[3]

---

1. Ivereigh, "Catholic Humanism."
2. Francis, *Message for World Mission Day 2017*.
3. Francis, *Message for World Mission Day 2017*.

Bibliography

Adsett, Daniel. "Milbank and Heidegger on the Possibility of a Secular Analogy of Being." *International Philosophical Quarterly* 59.2 (2019) 155–73.
Albacete, Lorenzo. "The Pope against Moralism and Legalism." *Anthropotes* 1 (1994) 81–86.
Aquinas, Thomas. *On Evil*. Translated by Jean Oesterle. Notre Dame, IN: University of Notre Dame Press, 1995.
———. *Questiones Disputatae de Veritate*. Translated by Robert W. Mulligan. Chicago: Henry Regnery, 1952.
———. *Summa contra Gentiles*. Translated by Anton Charles Pegis. Notre Dame, IN: University of Notre Dame Press, 1991.
———. *Summa Theologica*. Translated by Fathers of the English Dominican Province. New York: Benziger Bros, 1948.
———. *Super Boethium De Trinitate*. Questions 1–4. Translated by Rose E. Brennan. Herder, 1946. https://isidore.co/aquinas/english/BoethiusDeTr.htm#64.
———. *Super Boethium De Trinitate*. Questions 5–6. Translated by Armand Mauer. Toronto, 1953. https://isidore.co/aquinas/english/BoethiusDeTr.htm#64.
Augustine. *Confessions*. Translated by R. S. Pine-Coffin. Harmondsworth, UK: Penguin, 1982.
———. *Of True Religion*. Translated by John H. S. Burleigh. Washington, DC: Regnery, 1991.
———. *The Trinity: De Trinitate*. Translated by Edmund Hill. Edited by John E. Rotelle. Hyde Park, NY: New City, 1991.
Balthasar, Hans Urs von. *The Theology of Henri de Lubac: An Overview*. San Francisco: Ignatius, 1991.
———. *The Theology of Karl Barth*. Translated by John Drury. New York: Holt, Rinehart and Winston, 1971.
Bardazzi, Marco. *In the Vineyard of the Lord: The Life, Faith, and Teachings of Joseph Ratzinger, Pope Benedict XVI*. New York: Rizzoli International, 2005.
Barth, Karl. *Die Kirchliche Dogmatik*. Vol. 1. Zürich: Theologischer, 1986.
Benedict XVI. *Address of His Holiness Benedict XVI to Participants in the Plenary Assembly of the Pontifical Council for Culture*. Clementine Hall, Vatican City, March 8, 2008. https://www.vatican.va/content/benedict-xvi/en/speeches/2008/march/documents/hf_ben-xvi_spe_20080308_pc-cultura.html.

BIBLIOGRAPHY

———. *Audience with H.M. the Queen and State Reception.* Palace of Holyroodhouse, Edinburgh, September 16, 2010. http://www.vatican.va/content/benedict-xvi/en/speeches/2010/september/documents/hf_ben-xvi_spe_20100916_incontro-autorita.html.

———. *Caritas in Veritate.* Encyclical Letter. June 29, 2009. https://www.vatican.va/content/benedict-xvi/en/encyclicals/documents/hf_ben-xvi_enc_20090629_caritas-in-veritate.html.

———. *Church Fathers: From Clement of Rome to Augustine.* San Francisco: Ignatius, 2017.

———. *Deus Caritas Est.* Encyclical Letter. December 25, 2005. https://www.vatican.va/content/benedict-xvi/en/encyclicals/documents/hf_ben-xvi_enc_20051225_deus-caritas-est.html.

———. *From the Baptism in the Jordan to the Transfiguration.* Vol. 1 of *Jesus of Nazareth.* New York: Doubleday, 2007.

———. *From the Entrance into Jerusalem to the Resurrection.* Vol. 2 of *Jesus of Nazareth.* San Francisco: Ignatius, 2011.

———. *Fundamental Speeches from Five Decades.* Edited by Florian Schuller. San Francisco: Ignatius, 2012.

———. *General Audience, 21 November 2012.* Paul VI Audience Hall. http://www.vatican.va/content/benedict-xvi/en/audiences/2012/documents/hf_ben-xvi_aud_20121121.html.

———. *General Audience, 25 June 2008.* [Paul VI Audience Hall.] http://www.vatican.va/content/benedict-xvi/en/audiences/2008/documents/hf_ben-xvi_aud_20080625.html.

———. *General Audience, 27 April 2005.* [Paul VI Audience Hall.] http://www.vatican.va/content/benedict-xvi/en/audiences/2005/documents/hf_ben-xvi_aud_20050427.html.

———. *Meeting with the Representatives of British Society, including the Diplomatic Corps, Politicians, Academics and Business Leaders.* Westminster Hall, City of Westminster, September 17, 2010. http://www.vatican.va/content/benedict-xvi/en/speeches/2010/september/documents/hf_ben-xvi_spe_20100917_societa-civile.html.

———. *Meeting with the Representatives of Science: Apostolic Journey of His Holiness Benedict XVI to München, Altötting and Regensburg.* Aula Magna of the University of Regensburg, September 12, 2006. http://www.vatican.va/content/benedict-xvi/en/speeches/2006/september/documents/hf_ben-xvi_spe_20060912_university-regensburg.html.

———. *Spe Salvi.* Encyclical letter. November 30, 2007. https://www.vatican.va/content/benedict-xvi/en/encyclicals/documents/hf_ben-xvi_enc_20071130_spe-salvi.html.

———. *Vigil on the Occasion of the International Meeting of Priests.* St. Peter's Square, Vatican City, June 10, 2010. http://www.vatican.va/content/benedict-xvi/en/speeches/2010/june/documents/hf_ben-xvi_spe_20100610_concl-anno-sac.html.

———. *Visit to the Bundestag: Address of His Holiness Benedict XVI.* Reichstag Building, Berlin, September 22, 2011. http://www.vatican.va/content/benedict-xvi/en/speeches/2011/september/documents/hf_ben-xvi_spe_20110922_reichstag-berlin.html.

———. *Welcome Ceremony and Meeting with Authorities of State: Address of His Holiness Benedict XVI*. Elysée Palace, Paris, September 12, 2008. http://www.vatican.va/content/benedict-xvi/en/speeches/2008/september/documents/hf_ben-xvi_spe_20080912_parigi-elysee.html.

Benedict XVI, and Peter Seewald. *Light of the World: The Pope, the Church, and the Signs of the Times*. San Francisco: Ignatius, 2010.

Benedikt XVI, and Peter Seewald. *Benedikt XVI: Ein Leben*. München: Droemer, 2020.

Betz, John R. "The *Analogia Entis* as a Standard of Catholic Engagement: Erich Przywara's Critique of Phenomenology and Dialectical Theology." *Modern Theology* 35.1 (Jan 2019) 81–102.

Beumer, Johannes. "Gratia supponit naturam: Zur Geschichte eines theologischen Prinzips." *Gregorianum* 20.4 (1939) 535–52.

Bielik-Robson, Agata. "The Post-Secular Turn: Enlightenment, Tradition, Revolution." *Eidos* 3.9 (2019) 57–82.

Billeci, Simone. *Gratia supponit naturam*. Trapani: Il Pozzo di Giacobbe, 2020.

Blond, Phillip, ed. *Post-Secular Philosophy: Between Philosophy and Theology*. London: Routledge, 1998.

Boersma, Hans. "Sacramental Ontology: Nature and the Supernatural in the Ecclesiology of Henri de Lubac." *New Blackfriars* 88.1015 (May 2007) 242–73.

Boeve, Lieven. *Theology at the Crossroads of University, Church and Society: Dialogue, Difference and Catholic Identity*. London: Bloomsbury, 2016.

Breyfogle, Troy. "Is There Room for Political Philosophy in Postmodern Critical Augustinianism?" In *Deconstructing Radical Orthodoxy*, edited by Wayne J. Hankey and Douglas Hedley, 31–48. London: Routledge, 2016.

Burrell, David. "Radical Orthodoxy: An Appreciation." *Philosophy and Theology* 16.1 (2004) 73–76.

Bushlack, Thomas J. "The Return of Neo-Scholasticism? Recent Criticisms of Henri de Lubac on Nature and Grace and Their Significance for Moral Theology, Politics, and Law." *Journal of the Society of Christian Ethics* 35.2 (2015) 83–100.

Butler, Christopher. "The Value of History." *Downside Review* 68.213 (Summer 1950) 290–306.

Carola, Joseph. "The Academics, the Artist, and the Architect: Retrieving the Tradition in Nineteenth-Century Catholicism." *Logos: A Journal of Catholic Thought and Culture* 23.1 (Winter 2020) 65–93.

Casarella, Joseph. "Culture and Conscience in the Thought of Joseph Ratzinger / Pope Benedict XVI." In *Explorations in the Theology of Benedict XVI*, edited by John C. Cavadini, 63–86. Notre Dame, IN: University of Notre Dame Press, 2012.

Chesterton, G. K. *St. Francis of Assisi*. Orleans, MA: Paraclete, 2013.

Chryssavgis, John. *Primacy in the Church: The Office of Primate and the Authority of Councils*. Vol. 2. Yonkers, NY: St Vladimir's Seminary Press, 2016.

Cirelli, Anthony. "The Christian Realism of Benedict XVI." *Gregorianum* 92.4 (2011) 709–36.

Collins, Christopher S. *The Word Made Love: The Dialogical Theology of Joseph Ratzinger / Benedict XVI*. Collegeville, MN: Liturgical, 2013.

Colosi, Peter. "Ratzinger, Habermas, and Pera on Public Reason and Religion." *Logos: A Journal of Catholic Thought and Culture* 19.3 (Summer 2016) 148–69.

Congregation for the Doctrine of the Faith. *Instruction on Certain Aspects of the "Theology of Liberation."* August 6, 1984. https://www.vatican.va/roman_curia/

congregations/cfaith/documents/rc_con_cfaith_doc_19840806_theology-liberation_en.html.

———. *Instruction on Christian Freedom and Liberation*. March 22, 1986. https://www.vatican.va/roman_curia/congregations/cfaith/documents/rc_con_cfaith_doc_19860322_freedom-liberation_en.html.

Conway, Michael A. "Maurice Blondel and *Ressourcement*." In *Ressourcement*, edited by Gabriel Flynn and Paul D. Murray, 65–82. New York: Oxford University Press, 2012.

Corkery, James. *Joseph Ratzinger's Theological Ideas: Wise Cautions and Legitimate Hopes*. New York: Paulist, 2009.

———. "Reflection on the Theology of Joseph Ratzinger (Pope Benedict XVI)." *Acta Theologica* 32.2 (2012) 17–34.

Cross, Richard. "Duns Scotus and Suárez at the Origins of Modernity." In *Deconstructing Radical Orthodoxy*, edited by Wayne J. Hankey and Douglas Hedley, 64–80. London: Routledge, 2016.

Cush, John. "Radical Orthodoxy: An Overview." *Homiletic and Pastoral Review*, Jul 12, 2018. https://www.hprweb.com/2018/07/radical-orthodoxy-an-overview/.

Daniélou, Jean. "Les orientations présentes de la pensée religieuse." *Études* 249 (1946) 5–21.

———. *Prayer as a Political Problem*. London: Burns and Oates, 1967.

D'Costa, Gavin. "Seeking After Theological Vision." *Reviews in Religion and Theology* 6.4 (Nov 1999) 358.

DeHart, Paul J. *Aquinas and Radical Orthodoxy: A Critical Inquiry*. London: Routledge, 2014.

Denzinger, Heinrich, and Peter Hünermann, eds. *Enchiridion Symbolorum*. 43rd ed. San Francisco: Ignatius, 2012.

Depoortere, Frederiek, Lieven Boeve, and Stephan van Erp, eds. *Edward Schillebeeckx and Contemporary Theology*. London: T. & T. Clark, 2010.

De Ravinel, Sophie. "Une 'haine de soi' au sein de l'Europe." *Le Figaro*, Aug 13, 2004.

Dulles, Avery. *The Reshaping of Catholicism: Current Challenges in the Theology of Church*. San Francisco: Harper and Row, 1988.

Dupré, Louis. "On the Natural Desire of Seeing God." *Radical Orthodoxy: Theology, Philosophy, Politics* 1.1 (Aug 2012) 81–94.

———. *Passage to Modernity: An Essay in the Hermeneutics of Nature and Culture*. New Haven, CT: Yale University Press, 1993.

Eller, Matthias. *Veritas creatrix incarnata: Über das Wahrheitsverständnis im theologischen Werk Joseph Ratzingers*. Pontes, Band 53. Münster: LIT, 2011.

Fahey, Michael. "Joseph Ratzinger as Ecclesiologist and Pastor." In *Neo-Conservatism: Social and Religious Phenomenon*, edited by Gregory Baum, 76–83. New York: Seabury, 1981.

Fédou, Michel. "*Sources Chrétiennes*: Patristique et renaissance de la théologie." *Gregorianum* 92.4 (2011) 781–96.

Feingold, Lawrence. *The Natural Desire to See God according to St. Thomas and His Interpreters*. Ave Maria, FL: Sapientia, 2010.

Fields, Stephen M. "On Nature and Grace in *Deus Caritas Est*." *Nova et Vetera* 15.3 (Summer 2017) 817–33.

———. Review of *The Suspended Middle: Henri de Lubac and the Renewed Split in Modern Catholic Theology*, by John Milbank. *Journal of Jesuit Studies* 3.4 (2016) 747–49.

Fiorenza, Francis Schüssler. "From Theologian to Pope." *Harvard Divinity Bulletin* 33.2 (Autumn 2005). https://bulletin.hds.harvard.edu/from-theologian-to-pope/.

Flynn, Gabriel, and Paul D. Murray, eds. *Ressourcement: A Movement for Renewal in Twentieth-Century Catholic Theology*. Oxford: Oxford University Press, 2013.

Fortin, Ernest L. *Classical Christianity and the Political Order: Reflections on the Theologico-Political Problem*. Vol. 2 of *Ernest Fortin: Collected Essays*. Edited by Brian J. Benestad. Lanham, MD: Rowman and Littlefield, 1996.

Fourest, Caroline. "Le piège de la 'laïcité positive.'" *Après-Demain* 4.8 (2008) 32–36.

Francis. *Address of His Holiness Pope Francis to the Members of the Delegation of the Conference of European Rabbis*. April 20, 2015. http://www.vatican.va/content/francesco/en/speeches/2015/april/documents/papa-francesco_20150420_conference-of-european-rabbis.html.

———. *Evangelii Gaudium*. Apostolic Constitution. November 24, 2013. https://www.vatican.va/content/francesco/en/apost_exhortations/documents/papa-francesco_esortazione-ap_20131124_evangelii-gaudium.html.

———. *Lumen Fidei*. Encyclical Letter. June 29, 2013. https://www.vatican.va/content/francesco/en/encyclicals/documents/papa-francesco_20130629_enciclica-lumen-fidei.html.

———. *Message of Pope Francis for World Mission Day 2017*. June 4, 2017. http://www.vatican.va/content/francesco/en/messages/missions/documents/papa-francesco_20170604_giornata-missionaria2017.html.

———. *Message of Pope Francis for World Mission Day 2019*. June 9, 2019. http://www.vatican.va/content/francesco/en/messages/missions/documents/papa-francesco_20190609_giornata-missionaria2019.html.

Francis, and Dominique Wolton. *The Path to Change: Thoughts on Politics and Society*. London: Pan Macmillan, 2018.

Gaál, Emery de. *The Theology of Pope Benedict XVI: The Christocentric Shift*. New York: Palgrave Macmillan, 2010.

Galvão, Henrique. "The Mystery of the Church in the Theology of Joseph Ratzinger." *Communio: International Catholic Review* 37.4 (Winter 2010) 708–16.

Gardner, Lucy. "Listening at the Threshold: Christology and the 'Suspension of the Material.'" In *Radical Orthodoxy? A Catholic Enquiry*, edited by Laurence Paul Hemming, 127–46. London: Routledge, 2000.

Garrigou-Lagrange, Réginald. "La nouvelle théologie où va-t-elle?" *Angelicum* 23 (1946) 126–45.

Gauchet, Marcel. *The Disenchantment of the World: A Political History of Religion*. New French Thought. Princeton, NJ: Princeton University Press, 1997.

Gertz, Bernhard. "Kreuz-Struktur: Zur theologischen Methode Erich Przywaras." *Theologie und Philosophie* 45.4 (1970) 555–61.

Gonzales, Philip John Paul. *Reimagining the Analogia Entis: The Future of Erich Przywara's Christian Vision*. Interventions. Grand Rapids, MI: Eerdmans, 2019.

Gourlay, Thomas V. "Nature, Grace and Catholic Engagement in Contemporary Cultural Dialogue." *New Blackfriars* 100.1085 (Jul 12, 2016) 104–17.

Graulich, Markus. *Unterwegs zu einer Theologie des Kirchenrechts: Die Grundlegung des Rechts bei Gottlieb Söhngen (1892–1971) und die Konzepte der neueren*

Kirchenrechtswissenschaft. Kirchen und Staatskirchenrecht 6. Paderborn: Schöningh, 2006.

Grégoire de Nysse. *La vie de Moïse ou traité de la perfection en matière de vertu.* Edited by Jean Daniélou. Réimpression de la 3. éd. rev. et corr. Sources Chrétiennes 1bis. Paris: Cerf, 2007.

Gregory, Eric, and Joseph Clair. "Augustinianisms and Thomisms." In *The Cambridge Companion to Christian Political Theology,* edited by Craig Hovey and Elizabeth Phillips, 176–95. Cambridge: Cambridge University Press, 2015.

Grumett, David. *De Lubac: A Guide for the Perplexed.* London: T. & T. Clark, 2007.

———. "Radical Orthodoxy." *Expository Times* 122.6 (Feb 15, 2011) 261–70.

Guardini, Romano. *The Lord.* Washington, DC: Regnery, 1996.

———. *Welt und Person: Versuche zur christlichen Lehre vom Menschen.* 6. Aufl. Mainz: Matthias-Grünewald, 1988.

Guerra, Marc D., ed. *Pope Benedict XVI and the Politics of Modernity.* London: Routledge, 2014.

Habermas, Jürgen, and Joseph Ratzinger. *The Dialectics of Secularization: On Reason and Religion.* San Francisco: Ignatius, 2006.

Hanby, Michael. *Augustine and Modernity.* Radical Orthodoxy. London: Routledge, 2003.

Hankey, Wayne J. "Philosophical Religion and the Neoplatonic Turn to the Subject." In *Deconstructing Radical Orthodoxy,* edited by Wayne J. Hankey and Douglas Hedley, 17–30. London: Routledge, 2016.

———. "*Theoria* versus *Poesis*: Neoplatonism and Trinitarian Difference in Aquinas, John Milbank, Jean-Luc Marion and John Zizioulas." *Modern Theology* 15.4 (1999) 387–415.

Hauerwas, Stanley. *The Peaceable Kingdom: A Primer in Christian Ethics.* Notre Dame, IN: University of Notre Dame Press, 1983.

Healy, Nicholas J. "Henri de Lubac on Nature and Grace: A Note on Some Recent Contributions to the Debate." *Communio: International Catholic Review* 35.4 (Winter 2008) 535–64.

Healy, Nicholas J., and D. C. Schindler, eds. *Being Holy in the World: Theology and Culture in the Thought of David L. Schindler.* Grand Rapids, MI: Eerdmans, 2011.

Hedley, Douglas. "Radical Orthodoxy and Apocalyptic Difference: Cambridge Platonism and Milbank's Romantic Christian Cabbala." In *Deconstructing Radical Orthodoxy,* edited by Wayne J. Hankey and Douglas Hedley, 99–116. London: Routledge, 2016.

Hemming, Laurence P. *Benedict XVI: Fellow Worker for the Truth: An Introduction to His Life and Thought.* London: Burns and Oates, 2005.

———. "*Quod Impossibile Est!* Aquinas and Radical Orthodoxy." In *Radical Orthodoxy? A Catholic Enquiry,* edited by Laurence Paul Hemming, 76–96. London: Routledge, 2000.

———. "Radical Orthodoxy's Appeal to Catholic Scholarship." In *Radical Orthodoxy? A Catholic Enquiry,* edited by Laurence Paul Hemming, 3–19. London: Routledge, 2000.

Hovdelien, Olav. "In Favour of Secularism, Correctly Understood." *Australian eJournal of Theology* 21.3 (Dec 2014) 234–47.

Imbelli, Robert. "The Christocentric Mystagogy of Joseph Ratzinger." *Communio: International Catholic Review* 42.1 (Spring 2015) 119–43.

International Theological Commission. *Faith and Inculturation.* http://www.vatican.va/roman_curia/congregations/cfaith/cti_documents/rc_cti_1988_fede-inculturazione_en.html.

Irenaeus. *Against Heresies.* In *The Writings of the Fathers Down to A.D. 325.* Vol. 1 of *The Ante-Nicene Fathers.* Translated by Alexander Roberts and William Hautenville Rambaut. Edited by Alexander Roberts and James Donaldson. Rev. ed. Ex Fontibus, 2020.

Ivereigh, Austen. "Catholic Humanism Is Superior to Today's Exhausted Secularism." *ABC Religion and Ethics*, Oct 21, 2011. https://www.abc.net.au/religion/catholic-humanism-is-superior-to-todays-exhausted-secularism/10101072.

Janz, Paul D. "Radical Orthodoxy and the New Culture of Obscurantism." *Modern Theology* 20.3 (2004) 363–405.

John Paul II. *Redemptor Hominis.* Encyclical Letter. March 4, 1979. https://www.vatican.va/content/john-paul-ii/en/encyclicals/documents/hf_jp-ii_enc_04031979_redemptor-hominis.html.

———. *Veritatis Splendor.* Encyclical Letter. August 6, 1993. https://www.vatican.va/content/john-paul-ii/en/encyclicals/documents/hf_jp-ii_enc_06081993_veritatis-splendor.html.

Jones, E. Michael. *Living Machines: Bauhaus Architecture as Sexual Ideology.* San Francisco: Ignatius, 1995.

Juros, Helmut. "Problems in Catechesis Today: An Interview with Joseph Cardinal Ratzinger." *Communio: International Catholic Review* 11.2 (Summer 1984) 145–56.

Justin Martyr. *First Apology.* https://www.newadvent.org/fathers/0126.htm.

Kasper, Walter. "Nature, Grace, and Culture: On the Meaning of Secularization." In *Catholicism and Secularization in America: Essays on Nature, Grace, and Culture*, edited by David L. Schindler, 31–51. Huntington, IN: Our Sunday Visitor, 1990.

———. "The Theological Anthropology of *Gaudium et Spes*." *Communio: International Catholic Review* 23.1 (Spring 1996) 129–40.

———. *Theology and Church.* London: SCM, 1989.

———. "Das Wesen des Christlichen." *Theologische Revue* 65.3 (1969) 182–88.

Katholische Akademie in Bayern, ed. *Akademische Feier zum 80 Geburtstag von Romano Guardini Katholische Akademie.* Würzburg: Echter, 1965.

Keating, James F. Review of *Aquinas and Radical Orthodoxy: A Critical Inquiry*, by Paul DeHart. *The Thomist: A Speculative Quarterly Review* 79.1 (Jan 2015) 155–60.

Kenny, Anthony. *A Path from Rome: An Autobiography.* Oxford: Oxford University Press, 1986.

Kerr, Fergus. *After Aquinas: Versions of Thomism.* Malden, MA: Blackwell, 2002.

———. "A Catholic Response to the Programme of Radical Orthodoxy." In *Radical Orthodoxy? A Catholic Enquiry*, edited by Laurence Paul Hemming, 46–62. London: Routledge, 2000.

———. *Twentieth-Century Catholic Theologians: From Neoscholasticism to Nuptial Mysticism.* Malden, MA: Blackwell, 2007.

Kirwan, Jon. *An Avant-Garde Theological Generation: The Nouvelle Théologie and the French Crisis of Modernity.* Oxford Theology and Religion Monographs. Oxford: Oxford University Press, 2018.

Kissler, Alexander. *Der deutsche Papst: Benedikt XVI und seine schwierige Heimat.* Freiburg im Breisgau: Herder, 2005.

BIBLIOGRAPHY

Kizewski, Justin James. "God-Talk: The Patristic Patrimony of Medieval Analogy in Theology." STD thesis, Gregorian University, Rome, 2016.
Komonchak, Joseph. "Augustine, Aquinas or the Gospel *Sine Glossa*? Divisions over *Gaudium et Spes*." In *Unfinished Journey: The Church 40 Years after Vatican II*, edited by Austen Ivereigh, 102–18. London: Continuum, 2003.
———. "The Church in Crisis: Pope Benedict's Theological Vision." *Commonweal* 132 (Jun 3, 2005) 11–14.
———. "A Postmodern Augustinian Thomism?" In *Augustine and Postmodern Thought: A New Alliance against Modernity?*, edited by L. Boeve, M. Lamberigts, and M. Wisse, 123–46. Leuven: Peeters, 2009.
———. Review of *The Suspended Middle: Henri de Lubac and the Debate Concerning the Supernatural*, by John Milbank. *Pro Ecclesia* 17.4 (2008) 464–69.
———. "Theology and Culture at Mid-Century: The Example of Henri de Lubac." *Theological Studies* 51 (1990) 579–90.
———. "Vatican II and the Encounter between Catholicism and Liberalism." In *Catholicism and Liberalism*, edited by R. Bruce Douglass and David Hollenbach, 76–99. Cambridge: Cambridge University Press, 1994.
Körner, Bernhard. "Henri de Lubac and Fundamental Theology." *Communio: International Catholic Review* 23.4 (Winter 1996) 710–23.
Krieg, Robert A. *Romano Guardini: A Precursor of Vatican II*. Notre Dame, IN: University of Notre Dame Press, 2017.
Kucer, Peter Samuel. *Truth and Politics: A Theological Comparison of Joseph Ratzinger and John Milbank*. Emerging Scholars. Minneapolis: Fortress, 2014.
Läpple, Alfred. Interview by Gianni Valente and Pierluca Azzaro. *30 Days* 1/2 (2006). http://www.30giorni.it/articoli_id_10125_l3.htm.
Lee, James. "Pope Benedict XVI and Modernity: A Patristic Theologian's Perspective." *Nova et Vetera* 15.1 (Winter 2017) 89–110.
Leo XIII. *Aeterni Patris*. Encyclical Letter. August 4, 1879. https://www.vatican.va/content/leo-xiii/en/encyclicals/documents/hf_l-xiii_enc_04081879_aeterni-patris.html.
Levering, Matthew. "A Note on John Milbank and Thomas Aquinas." *New Blackfriars* 95.1059 (Sep 2014) 525–34.
Lewis, C. S. *Miracles: A Preliminary Study*. San Francisco: HarperSanFrancisco, 2001.
Lim, Hyeongkwon. "John Milbank and the Mystery of the Supernatural: His Postmodern Engagement with Henri de Lubac." DTh thesis, University of Strasbourg, 2013. https://tel.archives-ouvertes.fr/tel-01249536/document.
Long, Steven A. *Natura Pura: On the Recovery of Nature in the Doctrine of Grace*. Moral Philosophy and Moral Theology. New York: Fordham University Press, 2010.
Lubac, Henri de. *At the Service of the Church: Henri de Lubac Reflects on the Circumstances That Occasioned His Writings*. San Francisco: Communio, 1993.
———. *Augustinianism and Modern Theology*. New York: Crossroad, 2000.
———. *A Brief Catechesis on Nature and Grace*. San Francisco: Ignatius, 1984.
———. *Carnets du Concile*. Tomes 1 et 2. Paris: Cerf, 2007.
———. *Catholicism: Christ and the Common Destiny of Man*. San Francisco: Ignatius, 1988.
———. "Duplex Hominis Beatitudo." *Communio: International Catholic Review* 35.4 (Winter 2008) 599–612.

———. *Entretien autour de Vatican II: souvenirs et réflexions*. Théologies. Paris: Cerf, 1985.
———. *The Mystery of the Supernatural*. Milestones in Catholic Theology. New York: Crossroad, 1998.
———. *Surnaturel*. Paris: Lethielleux, 2010.
———. *Theological Fragments*. San Francisco: Ignatius, 1989.
———. *Theology in History*. San Francisco: Ignatius, 1996.
MacIntyre, Alasdair C. *Three Rival Versions of Moral Enquiry: Encyclopaedia, Genealogy, and Tradition; Being Gifford Lectures Delivered in the University of Edinburgh in 1988*. Notre Dame, IN: University of Notre Dame Press, 2006.
Malevez, Léopold. "Deux théologies catholiques de l'histoire." *Bijdragen* 10 (1949) 225–40.
Malloy, Christopher J. "De Lubac on Natural Desire: Difficulties and Antitheses." *Nova et Vetera* 9.3 (2011) 567–624.
Marenbon, John. "Aquinas, Radical Orthodoxy, and the Importance of Truth." In *Deconstructing Radical Orthodoxy*, edited by Wayne J. Hankey and Douglas Hedley, 49–63. London: Routledge, 2016.
Marion, Jean-Luc. *The Crossing of the Visible*. Cultural Memory in the Present. Stanford, CA: Stanford University Press, 2004.
Martinez, Gaspar. "Political and Liberation Theologies." In *The Cambridge Companion to Karl Rahner*, edited by Declan Marmion and Mary E. Hines, 249–63. Cambridge: Cambridge University Press, 2005.
Mawson, Michael. "Understandings of Nature and Grace in John Milbank and Thomas Aquinas." *Scottish Journal of Theology* 62.3 (Aug 2009) 347–61.
McDonald, Thomas. "Imagining a People of Peace: Fundamental Theology and the Problem of Private Christianity." Diss., Gregorian University, Rome, 2019.
McGregor, Peter John. *Heart to Heart: The Spiritual Christology of Joseph Ratzinger*. Eugene, OR: Pickwick, 2016.
Mettepenningen, Jürgen. "*Nouvelle Théologie*: Four Historical Stages of Theological Reform towards *Ressourcement* (1935–1965)." In *Ressourcement*, edited by Gabriel Flynn and Paul D. Murray, 172–84. Oxford: Oxford University Press, 2013.
Milbank, John. *Being Reconciled: Ontology and Pardon*. Radical Orthodoxy. London: Routledge, 2003.
———. "Enclaves, or Where Is the Church?" *New Blackfriars* 73.861 (Jun 1992) 341–52.
———. "The End of Dialogue." In *Christian Uniqueness Reconsidered: The Myth of a Pluralistic Theology of Religions*, edited by Gavin D'Costa, 174–91. Maryknoll, NY: Orbis, 1990.
———. *The Future of Love: Essays in Political Theology*. Eugene, OR: Cascade, 2009.
———. "How Democracy Devolves into Tyranny." *ABC Religion and Ethics*, Nov 18, 2011. https://www.abc.net.au/religion/how-democracy-devolves-into-tyranny/10101002.
———. "Intensities." *Modern Theology* 15.4 (Oct 1999) 445–97.
———. "Materialism and Transcendence." In *The Radical Orthodoxy Reader*, edited by Simon Oliver and John Milbank, 380–412. London: Routledge, 2009.
———. "Only Theology Overcomes Metaphysics." *New Blackfriars* 76.895 (Aug 1995) 325–43.
———. "Postmodern Critical Augustinianism: A Short *Summa* in Forty-Two Responses to Unasked Questions." *Modern Theology* 7.3 (Nov 2008) 225–37.

———. "The Programme of Radical Orthodoxy." In *Radical Orthodoxy? A Catholic Enquiry*, edited by Laurence Paul Hemming, 33–45. London: Routledge, 2000.

———. *The Suspended Middle: Henri de Lubac and the Renewed Split in Modern Catholic Theology*. 2nd ed. Grand Rapids, MI: Eerdmans, 2014.

———. *Theology and Social Theory: Beyond Secular Reason*. 2nd ed. Oxford: Blackwell, 2006.

———. *The Word Made Strange: Theology, Language, Culture*. Cambridge, MA: Blackwell, 1997.

Milbank, John, and Catherine Pickstock. *Truth in Aquinas*. Radical Orthodoxy. London: Routledge, 2002.

Milbank, John, Catherine Pickstock, and Graham Ward. "Introduction: Suspending the Material: The Turn of Radical Orthodoxy." In *Radical Orthodoxy: A New Theology*, edited by John Milbank, Catherine Pickstock, and Graham Ward, 1–20. London: Routledge, 1999.

———, eds. *Radical Orthodoxy: A New Theology*. London: Routledge, 1999.

Montag, John. "Radical Orthodoxy and Christian Philosophy." *Philosophy and Theology* 16.1 (2004) 89–100.

Mulcahy, Bernard. *Aquinas's Notion of Pure Nature and the Christian Integralism of Henri de Lubac: Not Everything Is Grace*. American University Studies. Series 7. Theology and Religion 314. New York: Peter Lang, 2011.

Murphy, Joseph. *Christ, Our Joy: The Theological Vision of Pope Benedict XVI*. San Francisco: Ignatius, 2008.

Neufeld, Karl Heinz, and Michel Sales. *Bibliographie Henri de Lubac SJ, 1925–1974*. Einsiedeln: Johannes, 1974.

Neuner, Josef, and Jacques Dupuis. *The Christian Faith: In the Doctrinal Documents of the Catholic Church*. 7th ed. Edited by Jacques Dupuis. New York: Alba House, 2001.

Nguyen, Thuy-Linh. "The Legacy of Henri de Lubac and the Challenge of Radical Orthodoxy." STD thesis, Gregorian University, Rome, 2007.

Nichols, Aidan. "Joseph Ratzinger's Theology of Political Ethics." *New Blackfriars* 68.808 (Sep 1987) 380–92.

———. *Say It Is Pentecost: A Guide through Balthasar's Logic*. Washington, DC: Catholic University of America Press, 2001.

———. "St Thomas and the Sacramental Liturgy." *The Thomist: A Speculative Quarterly Review* 72 (2008) 569–95.

Oakes, Edward T. "The Paradox of Nature and Grace: On John Milbank's *The Suspended Middle: Henri de Lubac and the Debate Concerning the Supernatural*." *Nova et Vetera* 4.3 (2006) 667–96.

———. "The *Surnaturel* Controversy: A Survey and a Response." *Nova et Vetera* 9.3 (2011) 625–56.

Oliver, Simon. "Henri de Lubac and Radical Orthodoxy." In *T&T Clark Companion to Henri de Lubac*, edited by Jordan Hillebert, 393–418. London: Bloomsbury, 2017.

O'Meara, Thomas F. *Church and Culture: German Catholic Theology, 1860–1914*. Notre Dame, IN: University of Notre Dame Press, 1991.

O'Shea, Gerard. "Nature or Grace and the Appearance of Insincerity: Silencing the Catholic Voice in Public Life." *Solidarity: The Journal of Catholic Social Thought and Secular Ethics* 2.1 (2012) article 6.

Ossewaarde-Lowtoo, Roshnee. "Resurrecting Democracies: Secularity Recast in Charles Taylor, Paul Valadier, and Joseph Ratzinger." *Radical Orthodoxy: Theology, Philosophy, Politics* 3.2 (Jun 2017) 224–49.

Paul VI. *Evangelii Nuntiandi*. Apostolic Exhortation. December 8, 1975. https://www.vatican.va/content/paul-vi/en/apost_exhortations/documents/hf_p-vi_exh_19751208_evangelii-nuntiandi.html.

Peddle, David. "Theology, Social Theory and Dialectic: A Consideration of Milbank's Hegel." In *Deconstructing Radical Orthodoxy*, edited by Wayne J. Hankey and Douglas Hedley, 117–32. London: Routledge, 2016.

Pelikan, Jaroslav. *Reformation of Church and Dogma (1300–1700)*. Vol. 4 of *The Christian Tradition: A History of the Development of Doctrine*. Chicago: University of Chicago Press, 1985.

Peterson, Brandon. "Critical Voices: The Reactions of Rahner and Ratzinger to 'Schema XIII' (*Gaudium et Spes*)." *Modern Theology* 31.1 (2015) 1–26.

Pickstock, Catherine. "Radical Orthodoxy and the Mediations of Time." In *Radical Orthodoxy? A Catholic Enquiry*, edited by Laurence Paul Hemming, 63–75. London: Routledge, 2000.

———. "Reply to David Ford and Guy Collins." *Scottish Journal of Theology* 54.3 (2009) 405–22.

Pius XII. *Humani Generis*. Encyclical Letter. August 12, 1950. https://www.vatican.va/content/pius-xii/en/encyclicals/documents/hf_p-xii_enc_12081950_humani-generis.html.

Politi, Marco. "Il laicismo nuova ideologia l'Europa non emargini Dio." *La Repubblica*, Nov 19, 2004. https://ricerca.repubblica.it/repubblica/archivio/repubblica/2004/11/19/il-laicismo-nuova-ideologia-europa-non-emargini.html.

Pontifical Council for Justice and Peace. *Compendium of the Social Doctrine of the Church*. [May 26, 2006.] https://www.vatican.va/roman_curia/pontifical_councils/justpeace/documents/rc_pc_justpeace_doc_20060526_compendio-dott-soc_en.html.

Portier, William L. "What Kind of a World of Grace? Henri Cardinal de Lubac and the Council's Christological Center." *Communio: International Catholic Review* 39.1 (Spring 2012) 136–51.

Price, R. M. "'Hellenization' and *Logos* Doctrine in Justin Martyr." *Vigiliae Christianae* 42.1 (Mar 1988) 18–23.

Proniewski, Andrzej. "Joseph Ratzinger's Philosophical Theology of the Person." *Rocznik Teologii Katolickiej* 17.3 (2018) 219–36.

Przywara, Erich. *Analogia Entis: Metaphysics: Original Structure and Universal Rhythm*. Grand Rapids, MI: Eerdmans, 2014.

———. *Augustinisch: Ur-Haltung des Geistes*. Einsiedeln: Johannes, 1970.

———. *Logos: Logos, Abendland, Reich, Commercium*. Düsseldorf: Patmos, 1969.

———. *Ringen der Gegenwart: Gesammelte Aufsätze, 1922–1927*. Augsburg: Benno Filser, 1929.

Rahner, Karl. *More Recent Writings*. Vol. 4 of *Theological Investigations*. Translated by Kevin Smyth. Baltimore: Helicon, 1966.

Ratzinger, Joseph. *Behold the Pierced One: An Approach to a Spiritual Christology*. San Francisco: Ignatius, 1986.

———. *Called to Communion: Understanding the Church Today*. San Francisco: Ignatius, 1996.

———. "Cardinal Frings' Speeches during the Second Vatican Council." *Communio: International Catholic Review* 15.1 (Spring 1988) 131–47.

———. *Christ, Faith, and the Challenge of Cultures.* Address at the Meeting with the Doctrinal Commissions in Asia, Hong Kong, March 3, 1993. https://www.vatican.va/roman_curia/congregations/cfaith/incontri/rc_con_cfaith_19930303_hong-kong-ratzinger_en.html.

———. *Christianity and the Crisis of Cultures.* San Francisco: Ignatius, 2006.

———. "Church and Economy: Responsibility for the Future of the World Economy." *Communio: International Catholic Review* 13.3 (Fall 1986) 199–204.

———. *Church, Ecumenism, and Politics: New Endeavors in Ecclesiology.* San Francisco: Ignatius, 2008.

———. "*Communio*: A Program," *Communio* 19.3 (Fall 1992) 436–49.

———. "Concerning the Notion of Person in Theology." *Communio: International Catholic Review* 17.3 (Fall 1990) 439–54.

———. *Co-Workers of the Truth: Meditations for Every Day of the Year.* San Francisco: Ignatius, 1992.

———. *The Current Situation of Faith and Theology.* Address at the Meeting with the Doctrinal Commissions of Latin America, Guadalajara, Mexico, May 7, 1996. https://www.vatican.va/roman_curia/congregations/cfaith/incontri/rc_con_cfaith_19960507_guadalajara-ratzinger_en.html.

———. "The Dignity of the Human Person." In *Commentary on the Documents of Vatican II*, edited by Herbert Vorgrimler, 5:115–63. New York: Herder and Herder, 1969.

———. *Dogma and Preaching: Applying Christian Doctrine to Daily Life.* Edited by Michael J. Miller. San Francisco: Ignatius, 2011.

———. "Eschatology and Utopia." *Communio: International Catholic Review* 5.3 (Fall 1978) 211–27.

———. *Eschatology: Death, and Eternal Life.* Washington, DC: Catholic University of America Press, 2007.

———. *Europe Today and Tomorrow: Addressing the Fundamental Issues.* San Francisco: Ignatius, 2007.

———. *Faith and the Future.* San Francisco: Ignatius, 2009.

———. *Faith and Politics: Selected Writings.* Edited by Michael J. Miller. San Francisco: Ignatius, 2018.

———. *The Feast of Faith: Approaches to a Theology of the Liturgy.* San Francisco: Ignatius, 1986.

———. "Foreword." In *Die Lust an Gott und seiner Sache: Oder Lassen sich Gnade und Freiheit, Glaube und Vernunft, Erlösung und Befreiung vereinbaren?* by Ludwig Weimer, 5–6. 2. Aufl. Freiburg im Breisgau: Herder, 1982.

———. "Funeral Homily for Msgr. Luigi Giussani." *Communio: International Catholic Review* 31.4 (Winter 2004) 685–87.

———. *Der Gott des Glaubens und der Gott der Philosophen: Ein Beitrag zum Problem der theologia naturalis.* 3. Aufl. Trier: Paulinus, 2006.

———. "Homily at the Funeral Liturgy for Hans Urs von Balthasar." *Communio: International Catholic Review* 15.4 (Winter 1988) 512–16.

———. *In the Beginning: A Catholic Understanding of the Story of Creation and the Fall.* Ressourcement. Grand Rapids, MI: Eerdmans, 1995.

———. "Interpretation, Contemplation, Action: Considerations on the Task of a Catholic Academy." *Communio: International Catholic Review* 13.2 (Summer 1986) 139–55.
———. *Introduction to Christianity*. San Francisco: Communio, 2004.
———. "Der Katholizismus nach dem Konzil." In *Das Neue Volk Gottes: Entwürfe zur Ekklesiologie*, 302–21. Düsseldorf: Patmos, 1969.
———. "Liturgy and Sacred Music." *Communio: International Catholic Review* 13.4 (Winter 1986) 377–91.
———. Mass *"Pro Eligendo Romano Pontifice"*: *Homily of His Eminence Card. Joseph Ratzinger Dean of the College of Cardinals*. Vatican Basilica, April 18, 2005. http://www.vatican.va/gpII/documents/homily-pro-eligendo-pontifice_20050418_en.html.
———. *Message of His Eminence Card. Joseph Ratzinger to the Communion and Liberation (CL) Meeting at Rimini (24–30 August 2002)*. https://www.vatican.va/roman_curia/congregations/cfaith/documents/rc_con_cfaith_doc_20020824_ratzinger-cl-rimini_en.html.
———. *Milestones: Memoirs, 1927–1977*. San Francisco: Ignatius, 1998.
———. *The Nature and Mission of Theology: Essays to Orient Theology in Today's Debates*. San Francisco: Ignatius, 1995.
———. *Das neue Volk Gottes: Entwürfe zur Ekklesiologie*. Düsseldorf: Patmos, 1969.
———. *A New Song for the Lord: Faith in Christ and Liturgy Today*. New York: Crossroad, 1996.
———. *Offenbarungsverständnis und Geschichtstheologie Bonaventuras: Habilitationsschrift und Bonaventura-Studien*. Gesammelte Schriften. Freiburg im Breisgau: Herder, 2009.
———. *On the Way to Jesus Christ*. San Francisco: Ignatius, 2004.
———. *Politik und Erlösung zum Verhältnis von Glaube, Rationalität und Irrationalem in der sogenannten Theologie der Befreiung*. Geisteswissenschaften/Rheinisch-Westfälische Akademie der Wissenschaften, Vorträge, G 279. Opladen: Westdeutscher, 1986.
———. *Principles of Catholic Theology: Building Stones for a Fundamental Theology*. San Francisco: Ignatius, 1987.
———. *The Ratzinger Reader: Mapping a Theological Journey*. Edited by Gerard Mannion. London: T. & T. Clark, 2010.
———. *The Ratzinger Report: An Exclusive Interview on the State of the Church*. Edited by Vittorio Messori. San Francisco: Ignatius, 1985.
———. "The Renewal of Moral Theology: Perspectives on Vatican II and *Veritatis Splendor*." *Communio: International Catholic Review* 32.2 (Summer 2005) 357–69.
———. *The Spirit of the Liturgy*. San Francisco: Ignatius, 2000.
———. *Theological Highlights of Vatican II*. New York: Paulist, 2009.
———. *The Theology of History in St. Bonaventure*. Chicago: Franciscan Herald, 1989.
———. *A Turning Point for Europe? The Church in the Modern World: Assessment and Forecast*. San Francisco: Ignatius, 1994.
———. *The Unity of the Nations: A Vision of the Church Fathers*. Washington, DC: Catholic University of America Press, 2015.
———. *Values in a Time of Upheaval*. New York: Crossroad, 2006.
———. *Volk und Haus Gottes in Augustins von der Kirche: die Dissertation und weitere Studien zu Augustinus und zur Theologie der Kirchenväter*. Gesammelte Schriften. Freiburg im Breisgau: Herder, 2011.
———. *What It Means to Be a Christian: Three Sermons*. San Francisco: Ignatius, 2006.

———. "Der Wortgebrauch von natura und die beginnende Verselbständigung der Metaphysik bei Bonaventura." In *Die Metaphysik im Mittelalter: Ihr Ursprung und ihre Bedeutung (Miscellanea Mediaevalia)*, bearbeitet von Paul Wilpert und Willehad P. Eckert, 483–98. Berlin: De Gruyter, 1963.

———. *The Yes of Jesus Christ: Exercises in Faith, Hope, and Love*. New York: Crossroad, 2005.

Ratzinger, Joseph, and Marcello Pera. *Without Roots: The West, Relativism, Christianity, Islam*. New York: Basic Books, 2007.

Ratzinger, Joseph, and Michael Seybold. "An Interview with Joseph Ratzinger: Eichstätt College and the Catholic University." Translated by Brian Benestad. *Agora* 4.1 (Jun 1988) 9–14.

Ratzinger, Joseph, and Peter Seewald. *God and the World: Believing and Living in Our Time*. San Francisco: Ignatius, 2002.

———. *Salt of the Earth: Christianity and the Catholic Church at the End of the Millennium*. San Francisco: Ignatius, 1997.

Ratzinger, Joseph, et al. *Handing on the Faith in an Age of Disbelief: Lectures Given at the Church of Notre-Dame de Fourvière in Lyons, France, and at Notre-Dame Cathedral in Paris*. San Francisco: Ignatius, 2006.

Renczes, Philipp. "Grace Reloaded: *Caritas in Veritate*'s Theological Anthropology." *Theological Studies* 71 (2010) 273–90.

Reno, R. R. "The Radical Orthodoxy Project." *First Things*, Feb 2000. https://www.firstthings.com/article/2000/02/the-radical-orthodoxy-project.

La Repubblica. "Secolarismo, Integralismo, Guerra i Punti di Vista di Benedetto XVI." April 19, 2005. https://www.repubblica.it/2005/d/sezioni/esteri/nuovopapa/puntidifede/puntidifede.html.

Riches, Aaron. "Christology and Duplex Hominis Beatitudo: Re-sketching the Supernatural Again." *International Journal of Systematic Theology* 14.1 (Jan 2012) 44–69.

Rondet, Henri. *The Grace of Christ: A Brief History of the Theology of Grace*. Westminster, MD: Newman, 1967.

Rossi, Attilio. "From Neo-Scholastic to Vatican II: The Debate on Nature-Grace and Church-World." *Lumen* 5.2 (Jul 2, 2017) 1–22.

Rowland, Tracey. "Benedict's Intellectual Mentors and Students." *Crisis Magazine*, Feb 19, 2013. https://www.crisismagazine.com/2013/benedicts-intellectual-mentors-and-students.

———. *Benedict XVI: A Guide for the Perplexed*. Guides for the Perplexed. London: T. & T. Clark, 2010.

———. *Beyond Kant and Nietzsche: The Munich Defence of Christian Humanism*. London: Bloomsbury, 2021.

———. *Catholic Theology*. Doing Theology 3. New York: Bloomsbury, 2017.

———. *The Culture of the Incarnation: Essays in Catholic Theology*. Renewal within Tradition. Steubenville, OH: Emmaus Academic, 2017.

———. "Joseph Ratzinger as Doctor of Incarnate Beauty." *Church, Communication and Culture* 5.2 (Jul 6, 2020) 235–47.

———. "Neo-Scholasticism of the Strict Observance." In *T&T Clark Companion to Henri de Lubac*, edited by Jordan Hillebert, 29–55. London: Bloomsbury, 2017.

———. "Pope Benedict's Theological Legacy: An Augustinian at Heart Who Influenced the Course of Vatican II and Beyond." *America*, Dec 31, 2022. https://www.

americamagazine.org/politics-society/2022/12/31/pope-benedict-theology-obituary-225604.

———. "Ratzinger on the Timelessness of Truth." *Communio: International Catholic Review* 44.2 (Summer 2017) 242–64.

———. *Ratzinger's Faith: The Theology of Pope Benedict XVI*. Oxford: Oxford University Press, 2009.

———. "The World in the Theology of Joseph Ratzinger / Benedict XVI." *Journal of Moral Theology* 2.2 (2013) 109–32.

Ruddy, Christopher. "*Ressourcement* and the Enduring Legacy of Post-Tridentine Theology." In *Ressourcement*, edited by Gabriel Flynn and Paul D. Murray, 185–201. Oxford: Oxford University Press, 2013.

Sánchez, Santiago S., and John Watson. "The Revival of the Notion of Pure Nature in Recent Debates in English-Speaking Theology." *Annales Theologici* 31.1 (2017) 171–250.

Schindler, David L., ed. *Hans Urs von Balthasar: His Life and Work*. San Francisco: Ignatius, 1991.

Schindler, D. C. *Love and the Postmodern Predicament: Rediscovering the Real in Beauty, Goodness, and Truth*. Veritas 28. Eugene, OR: Cascade, 2018.

Schmutz, Jacob. "La Doctrine médiévale des causes et la théologie de la nature pure (XIIIe–XVIIe siècles)." *Revue Thomiste* 101.1 (2001) 217–64.

Seckler, Max. *Instinkt und Glaubenswille nach Thomas von Aquin*. Mainz: Matthias-Grünewald, 1961.

Seewald, Peter. *Benedict XVI: An Intimate Portrait*. San Francisco: Ignatius, 2008.

———. *Benedict XVI: A Life*. London: Bloomsbury Continuum, 2020.

Sévillia, Jean. "Exclure la religion, c'est mutiler l'être humain: un entretien avec le Cardinal Ratzinger." *Le Figaro Magazine*, Nov 17, 2001.

Shakespeare, Steven. "The New Romantics: A Critique of Radical Orthodoxy." *Theology* 103.813 (May 1, 2000) 163–77.

———. *Radical Orthodoxy: A Critical Introduction*. London: SPCK, 2007.

Smith, James K. A. *Introducing Radical Orthodoxy: Mapping a Post-Secular Theology*. Grand Rapids, MI: Baker Academic, 2004.

Ssennyondo, Charles. *Christianity and the Culture of Relativism in the Anthropologies of Joseph Ratzinger and Stanley Hauerwas*. Xlibris, 2012.

Staudt, Jared. "Reality and Sign: Thomas Aquinas and the Christological Exegesis of Pope Benedict XVI." *Nova et Vetera* 12.1 (2014) 331–63.

Strand, Vincent. "On Method, Nature, and Grace in *Caritas in Veritate*." *Nova et Vetera* 15.3 (Summer 2017) 835–52.

Swafford, Andrew Dean, and Edward T. Oakes. *Nature and Grace: A New Approach to Thomistic Ressourcement*. Eugene, OR: Pickwick, 2014.

Sweeney, Conor. *Sacramental Presence after Heidegger: Onto-Theology, Sacraments, and the Mother's Smile*. Cambridge: James Clarke, 2015.

Taylor, Charles. *Sources of the Self: The Making of the Modern Identity*. Cambridge, MA: Harvard University Press, 1989.

Thils, Gustave. *Histoire doctrinale du mouvement oecuménique*. Paris: Desclée de Brouwer, 1962.

Tilliette, Xavier. "Henri de Lubac: The Legacy of a Theologian." *Communio: International Catholic Review* 19.3 (Fall 1992) 332–41.

Triffett, Brendan P. "*Processio* and the Place of Ontic Being: John Milbank and James K. A. Smith on Participation." *Heythrop Journal* 57 (2016) 900–916.
Twomey, D. Vincent. *Pope Benedict XVI: The Conscience of Our Age: A Theological Portrait*. San Francisco: Ignatius, 2007.
Valente, Gianni. "The Difficult Years." *30 Days* 5 (2006).
Vatican II Council. *Gaudium et Spes*. Pastoral Constitution. December 7, 1965. https://www.vatican.va/archive/hist_councils/ii_vatican_council/documents/vat-ii_const_19651207_gaudium-et-spes_en.html.
Voderholzer, Rudolf. *Meet Henri de Lubac*. Translated by Michael J. Miller. San Francisco: Ignatius, 2008.
Vorgrimler, Herbert, ed. *Commentary on the Documents of Vatican II*. Vol. 5. New York: Herder and Herder, 1969.
Vorster, Nico. "A Critical Assessment of John Milbank's Christology." *Acta Theologica* 32.2 (2012) 277–98.
Wallbrecher, Traudl, Ludwig Weimer, and Arnold Stötzl, eds. *30 Jahre Wegbegleitung: Joseph Ratzinger, Papst Benedikt XVI und die Katholische Integrierte Gemeinde*. Bad Tölz: Urfeld, 2006.
Ward, Graham. *Cities of God*. Radical Orthodoxy. London: Routledge, 2000.
———. "Questioning God." In *Questioning God*, edited by John D. Caputo, Michael Scanlon, and Mark Dooley, 274–90. Bloomington: Indiana University Press, 2001.
———. "Radical Orthodoxy and/as Cultural Politics." In *Radical Orthodoxy? A Catholic Enquiry*, edited by Laurence Paul Hemming, 97–111. London: Routledge, 2000.
———. *Theology and Contemporary Critical Theory*. London: Palgrave Macmillan, 2000.
Weimer, Ludwig. *Die Lust an Gott und seiner Sache: Oder Lassen sich Gnade und Freiheit, Glaube und Vernunft, Erlösung und Befreiung vereinbaren?* 2. Aufl. Freiburg im Breisgau: Herder, 1982.
Wilken, Robert Louis. *The Spirit of Early Christian Thought: Seeking the Face of God*. New Haven, CT: Yale University Press, 2008. https://www.degruyter.com/doi/book/10.12987/9780300127560.
Wood, Jacob W. "Henri de Lubac, *Humani Generis*, and the Natural Desire for a Supernatural End." *Nova et Vetera* 15.14 (2017) 1209–41.
———. *To Stir a Restless Heart: Thomas Aquinas and Henri de Lubac on Nature, Grace, and the Desire for God*. Thomistic Ressourcement. Washington, DC: Catholic University of America Press, 2019.
Wood, Susan. "The Nature-Grace Problematic within Henri de Lubac's Christological Paradox." *Communio: International Catholic Review* 19.3 (Fall 1992) 389–403.
Zatwardnicki, Sławomir. "Radical Orthodoxy as Suspended Middle." *Wrocław Theological Review* 27.2 (2019) 121–47.
Ziegler, Aloysius K. "Pope Gelasius I and His Teaching on the Relation of Church and State." *Catholic Historical Review* 27.4 (Jan 1942) 412–37.
Žižek, Slavoj, and John Milbank. *The Monstrosity of Christ: Paradox or Dialectic?* Edited by Creston Davis. Cambridge, MA: MIT Press, 2011.

Author Index

Adorno, Theodor 13, 183
Albacete, Lorenzo, 174
Aquinas, Thomas, xi, xxiii, 14, 39, 40–42 47–51, 53–55, 57, 57–60, 63–64, 69–70, 74–76, 79–80, 85, 88–90, 92, 96, 99, 100–101, 103, 107–8, 110–12, 114–15, 122–23, 125, 130–31, 136–44, 147, 152, 159–64, 169, 189, 204, 213, 214, 216–17, 219–20, 225, 263–66, 295, 312
Aristotle, 50, 58, 76, 80, 81, 91, 92, 100, 116, 294, 312
Assmann, Hugo, 151
Augustine, xx, xxii, 2, 7, 11, 12–14, 16, 19–20, 24, 31, 35–36, 39–40, 46, 52–53, 64, 71, 106–7, 110, 112, 147, 152, 163, 164, 169, 179, 181, 204, 210, 211, 212–17, 220, 222, 253, 258, 263–64, 266–67, 284, 295, 296, 297, 302, 315

Baius, 49–50, 64, 71–77, 97
Balthasar, Hans Urs von, xxiii, 2, 11–12, 15, 44, 58, 65, 73, 103, 116, 125–26, 145–49, 160, 166–67, 173–75, 179, 181, 185, 188, 210, 220, 228, 243, 262
Bardazzi, Michael, 164
Betz, John, 215–16
Beumer, Johannes, 191
Blond, Philip, 109

Blondel, Maurice, 44, 60, 87, 101, 114, 150, 226, 299–300, 313
Boersma, Hans, 129
Boeve, Lieven, 13, 21, 165
Bonaventure, 2, 7–8, 19–20, 58, 162–64, 170–71, 181, 189, 194–97, 199, 204–5, 290, 316
Bouillard, Henri, 60
Bouyer, Louis, 44
Boyer, Charles, 51
Brunner, Emil, 14
Buchez, Philippe-Joseph-Benjamin, 301
Burrell, David, 39, 41–42, 127, 138, 153
Butler, Christopher, 208–9

Cabasilas, Nicholas, 181
Cajetan, Thomas, 50–51, 57, 63, 70, 81, 91–92, 147, 277
Charlier, Louis, 61
Chenu, Marie-Dominique, 61–62, 151, 177
Chesterton, Gilbert Keith, 27, 52, 53
Chryssavgis, John, 253
Cirelli, Anthony, 182, 229–31
Collins, Christopher, 40, 172, 209, 290
Colosi, Peter, 247
Congar, Yves, 11, 60–61, 151
Corkery, James, 13–16, 19, 171, 201–7, 216
Curci, Carlo Maria, 57
Cush, John, xxi, 22, 24–25, 27, 35, 37, 41–42, 44–47

AUTHOR INDEX

D'Costa, Gavin, 23
Daniélou, Jean, 60–63, 168, 208
De Ravinel, Sophie, 251
DeHart, Paul, 42, 130, 137–38, 140
Depoortere, Federiek, 165
Descartes, René, 59, 106–8, 159, 188, 211
Draguet, René, 61
Drury, John, 147
Du Chesne, Jean-Baptiste, 49
Dulles, Avery, 206
Dupré, Louis, 55, 64, 81
Dupuis, Jacques, 75

Fahey, Michael, 13–14
Fédou, Michel, 62
Feingold, Lawrence, 67, 71, 93, 136
Féret, Henri-Marie, 61
Fessard, Gaston, 60
Fields, Stephen, 115, 146, 217–21, 265–66, 268
Fiorenza, Francis, 163–65, 282–83
Fourest, Caroline, 260
Francis, Pope, xviii, xix, 5–6, 320

Gaál, Emery de, 7–12, 161–64, 168, 170–73, 187–90, 203–4, 263, 265–67, 284, 287, 292–96, 306–7
Galvão, Henrique, 172
Gardeil, Ambroise, 59
Gardner, Lucy, 105
Garrigou-Lagrange, Réginald, 51, 59, 61, 64, 70, 265
Gauchet, Marcel, 289
Gilson, Étienne, 26, 59, 108
Giussani, Luigi, 169, 249
Gonzales, Philip John Paul, 226–29
Gourlay, Thomas, 85
Grumett, David, 22, 63
Guardini, Romano, 9–10, 164, 167, 170, 179, 187, 210, 294
Guerra, Marc, xxi

Habermas, Jürgen, 35, 157, 247,
Hamann, Johann Georg, 27
Hanby, Michael, 107
Hankey, Wayne, 104, 111

Harnack, Adolf von, 246
Hayek, Friedrich, 304
Healy, Nicholas, 93, 96, 290
Hemming, Laurence Paul, 11, 12, 44, 137
Hobbes, Thomas, 28, 56
Hofmann, Fritz, 210
Hovdelien, Olav, 254
Hume, David, 56

Imbelli, Robert, 11, 172
Irenaeus, Saint, 52, 84–85, 192
Ivereigh, Austen, 319–20

Jacobi, Friedrich, 35
Janz, Paul, 130, 138, 281–82
John Paul II, Pope, xiv, 3–4, 20, 42, 63, 68, 84, 168, 178, 207, 275–76
John XXIII, Pope, 63, 149
Jones, Michael, 261

Kasper, Walter, xix, 160, 202–3, 207–24, 263–64
Keating, James, 137–38
Kerr, Fergus, 11, 23, 61, 64, 140, 159–61, 277
Kierkegaard, Søren, 27, 211
Kirwan, Jon, 61
Kissler, Alexander, 292
Kizewski, Justin, 42
Kleutgen, Joseph, 57, 59–60
Komonchak, Joseph, 61, 86, 127–28, 151, 162, 263–64, 283–84
Körner, Bernhard, 85
Kucer, Peter Samuel, 7, 234–35, 285–86, 290–291, 297–302, 304, 307–8
Küng, Hans, 3, 12, 151, 203

Leo XIII, Pope 54, 56–59, 63, 101, 159, 312
Lepidi, Alberto, 57
Levering, Matthew, 114, 116, 120–21, 141–45, 237
Lewis, Clive Staples, 69
Liberatore, Matteo, 57
Lim, Hyeongkwon, 103, 105, 116, 126
Long, Stephen, 67

338

AUTHOR INDEX

Lubac, Henri de, xix, xx, xxii–xxiii, 2, 8, 10–12, 19, 44, 48–52, 60–67, 70, 77–78, 81–82, 85–101, 103–4m 109, 113–36, 144–55, 163, 166–67, 172, 179, 199–200, 204, 207, 210, 218, 221, 224–26, 228, 234–39, 257, 260, 262, 265, 277, 285, 292, 298, 300–302, 309–10, 312–14, 317–18

MacIntyre, Alasdair, 44, 59
Malevez, Léopold, 207–8
Malloy, Christopher, 93
Marcuse, Herbert, 13, 35, 265
Marenbon, John, 130
Marion, Jean-Luc, 33, 103, 108, 326
Martinez, Gaspar, 151
Maurras, Charles, 299
Mawson, Michael, 130–31
McDonald, Thomas, xviii-xix
MacIntyre, Alasdair, 44, 59
Mettepenningen, Jürgen, 58, 61–62
Molina, Luis de, 51, 147
Montag, John, 27
Montcheuil, Yves de, 60
Mulcahy, Bernard, 64, 124–26, 130, 137–38, 150, 152

Neuner, Josef, 75
Newman, John Henry, 7, 160, 169, 181, 185, 210–211
Nguyen, Thuy-Linh, 131–36
Nichols, Aidan, 180, 184, 242–43, 287, 291, 295, 299

O'Shea, Gerard, 52–53, 55–57, 59, 65, 241
Oakes, Edward, xx, 48, 66–70, 72, 74–76, 78–80, 82–86, 88–89,91–93, 95, 97–99, 113–16, 122–23, 128–29, 145–49
Oliver, Simon, 44, 109, 113, 115–25, 256–57
Ossewaarde-Lowtoo, Roshnee, 250

Paul VI, Pope, xvii-xviii, 3, 59, 63, 187
Péguy, Charles, 44, 276
Pelikan, Jaroslav, 73–74

Pera, Marcello, 157, 246–47, 307, 323
Pickstock, Catherine, xxi, 23–27, 31–32, 40–41, 44–46, 102, 104, 110–12, 114, 130, 137–40, 225, 235–36, 256, 269–71
Pius X, Pope, 58
Pius XII, Pope, 61, 65, 81–82, 128, 145
Plato, xxii, 6, 13, 14, 15–16, 31, 40, 42, 47, 60, 94, 102, 106, 107, 110–12, 137, 153, 181–83, 208, 217, 226, 229–30, 232, 244, 277, 309, 313–14, 316–17
Politi, Marco, 249, 255
Price, Robert, 230
Proniewski, Andrzej, 168, 232, 282
Przywara, Erich, 116, 176, 210–217, 222, 226–29, 309, 315–16

Rahner, Karl, xxiii, 3, 12, 88, 103, 114, 149–52, 177, 179, 206–7, 210, 263, 298–300, 302, 306–7
Renczes, Philipp, 173, 207
Reno, R.R., 23–24, 36
Riches, Aaron, 51, 72, 73, 100, 113
Rondet, Henri, 71, 74, 76
Rossi, Attillo, 58–60, 89
Rousselot, Pierre, 63
Rowland, Tracey, xiv, 7, 12, 57–60, 150–51, 157–60, 165–66, 168–29, 174–77, 179–80, 183, 185–87, 208–13, 241, 243–47, 261–65, 282–84, 288–90

Schillebeeckx, Edward, 12, 165, 177
Schmaus, Michael, 8–9, 11, 163
Scotus, Duns, xxii, 39, 42, 45–56, 58, 104, 107–10, 122, 138–40, 152, 154, 225–26, 228, 257, 260, 309, 316
Seckler, Max, 146, 203
Seewald, Peter, 1, 8, 10, 13, 157, 169, 203, 242
Shakespeare, Steven, xiii, 25, 37–43, 45–46, 137, 258–59, 269, 272–81
Smith, James, 24, 27–32, 34–36, 38, 40–41, 47, 104–13, 131, 137, 139–41, 259–60, 269, 271–72

AUTHOR INDEX

Söhngen, Gottlieb, 2, 6–9, 11, 167, 189, 210, 216, 229
Spaemann, Robert, 248
Ssennyondo, Charles, 189, 191
Suárez, Francisco, 8, 51–52, 55, 57, 59, 63, 70–71, 81, 91–92, 101, 147, 170, 299, 312
Swafford, Andrew, xx, 48, 66–70, 72, 74–76, 78–80, 82–86, 88–89, 91–93, 95, 97–99

Tapper, Ruard, 51
Taylor, Charles, 44, 107
Thils, Gustave, 208
Tilliette, Xavier, 60, 97
Triffett, Brendan, 105
Twomey, D. Vincent, 157

Vénard, Olivier-Thomas, 41
Vico, Giambattista, 22
Voderholzer, Rudolf, 62
Vorster, Nico, 104

Wallbrecher, Traudl, 163, 305
Ward, Graham, 22–23, 25–27, 31–36, 44–45, 50, 102, 104, 111, 139, 225, 256, 269–70.
Weimer, Ludwig, 163, 305
Wilken, Robert, 84, 85
Wolton, Dominique, xix
Wood, Jacob, 50
Wood, Susan, 93, 94, 95, 100,

Zatwardnicki, Sławomir: 254
Ziegler, Aloysius, 267
Zigliara, Tommaso, 57

www.ingramcontent.com/pod-product-compliance
Lightning Source LLC
Chambersburg PA
CBHW071150300426
44113CB00009B/1150